CRIMINAL JUSTICE

in

AMERICA

second edition

Developed by

Marshall Croddy

Todd Clark

Teri Engler

Bill Hayes

The development of these materials was financially assisted through the United States Office of Juvenile Justice and Delinquency Prevention, Grant #85-JS-CX-0007.
ISBN# 1-886253-00-5
© Los Angeles, 1983, 1991, 1993. Second Edition. All Rights Reserved.

CONTENTS

No matter who you are, crime affects your life. As a student, your school might be vandalized or your wallet stolen. Statistically, chances are very good that sometime in your life you will be a victim of some crime. As a future taxpayer, you will be forced to contribute money in the fight against crime or to repair the damage it does. As a voter, you will be asked to choose candidates based in part, at least, on their view about solutions to crime. Everyone agrees that crime is a serious problem. Few agree about its causes or solutions.

Although the debate over the causes and solutions to crime will probably never end, society has evolved a criminal justice system for dealing with crime. Essential to an understanding of this system are two areas of jurisprudence. These are called **criminal law** and **criminal procedure.**

Criminal Law

Criminal law focuses on defining crime itself. That is, for what conduct or behavior does our society punish people? After all, if society had no standards for human behavior, we would not have any crime, let alone a crime problem.

Today, our criminal law is contained in a wide array of statutes and ordinances enacted by federal, state, county, and municipal government. Each law spells out the ingredients of the crime in question and the punishment for those who break it.

The process of defining and applying criminal law never stops. Legislatures repeal out-of- date laws, modify existing laws, and enact new ones. Criminal trial courts interpret the meaning of various laws and apply them to particular cases. Criminal appeal courts check the decisions of trial courts and set precedents for other trial courts to follow. Thus the body of criminal law keeps changing.

Criminal Procedure

Criminal procedure comes into play when the police start investigating a particular crime. It focuses on the steps taken and decisions made in the investigation, accusation, trial, verdict, and sentencing of a criminal defendant. It is the process by which we decide the what, when, where, how, and who questions of criminal justice.

Criminal procedures are also designed to protect a defendant from being falsely accused or convicted of a crime. The Constitution of the United Sates requires "due process of law," safety from "unreasonable searches and seizures," and forbids "cruel and unusual punishment." These, and many other constitutional provisions, have done much to shape our criminal procedure.

Criminal procedure has other functions also. Rules of court attempt to assure an orderly and consistent decision - making process. Rules of evidence are designed to ensure that the facts of the case are relevant, accurate, and not overly prejudicial. There are also rules of conduct for judges, lawyers, and juries.

Like criminal law, criminal procedure is ever - changing. Legislators enact new laws, judges and courts adopt new rules, and the Supreme Court interprets and applies the Constitution.

Criminal Justice

This book will have a lot to do with criminal law and procedure. They are important parts of criminal justice. Yet, there is much, much more to consider. Criminal justice also involves people, institutions, and important societal issues. Perhaps even more importantly, it raises vital questions in each of us about fairness, security, and rights in a free society.

As you explore the selections in this book, you will meet the people who investigate crime and enforce our laws. You will learn about judges and courts and their struggle to protect individual rights while determining guilt or innocence. You will see the darker side of the criminal justice system and find out how society deals with people after they have been found guilty beyond a reasonable doubt. You will visit prisons and prisoners, guards, and parole officers, and in doing so you will discover the problems they face on a daily basis.

The Problem of Crime

Beyond criminal law and procedure and the system which investigates, apprehends, and punishes lawbreakers, you will study crime itself. Social scientists who take this role are called **criminologists**. They try to find answers to some very difficult questions. Why do people become criminals? How serious is our crime problem? How can crime be reduced? Although you won't be a professional criminologist after studying this book, you will have a much better understanding about some of the important issues of criminal justice.

C R I M E

Friday evening, 9:30 p.m. . . . .

In an underground parking garage downtown, a young man staggers to a pay phone on the wall and leans against it to hold himself up. Finally he gets the strength to call 9-1-1. A few seconds later, a voice comes on the line.

"Emergency services."

"My name is Sam Peterson," the man stammers. "I've just been robbed."

Meanwhile, in a middle-income residential area, a young husband and wife arrive home from a movie. The wife is the first to notice that the glass in the back door has been smashed in. Inside they find a horrible mess, with furniture tipped over and china broken on the floor. The television and stereo are gone. They both start to tremble. They don't even know why. A place that they believed was private and safe had been torn open and violated.

A major crime happens somewhere in America every two seconds. But this isn't just a number on a chart. Behind each crime are people: victims who are hurt, criminals who often live a violent and unhappy life in their own way, and those who must deal with the aftermath—the police, social workers, attorneys, judges, and legislators.

In this chapter, we will examine crime in terms of victims, criminals, and society. What is it like to have your life changed in an instant by someone else's wrongdoing? Who are the criminals and why do they do it? What acts does our society, through its laws, define as crimes? What must be proved before a person is convicted of a crime? By considering these questions, you will learn a lot about crime and its consequences. And you will be able to take an intelligent part in a great debate going on in our society: What should we do about crime?

CRIME AND ITS VICTIMS

Who Are the Victims?

S uzanne Rossetti, 26, was driving home from the theater at Arizona State University in Phoenix. On the way, she stopped at the market, where she accidentally locked her keys inside her car. Two young men got the door open for her with a coat hanger and then asked her for a lift. She agreed, but once in the car, they turned vicious almost immediately.

The young men forced Suzanne to drive them to her apartment. There they beat and raped her for several hours. Then they drove her into the desert and threw her off a cliff. When they heard her moans down below, they climbed down after her. She pleaded with them to leave her alone.

"I'm dying anyway," she begged.

"Damn right you are," one of them growled. He picked up a rock and crushed her skull.

In Detroit, Keisha Jackson, 13, was walking home with friends after a day at a Detroit roller rink. Suddenly a 16-year-old boy walking past pulled a gun and fired into the group. Keisha was hit in the head, and she died a few days later. Her killer could give no reason for what he did.

No one seems safe. Shocking stories like these have frightened most of us. *The streets just aren't safe at night. I've had my third car stereo stolen. I hate putting bars on my windows, but what choice do I have?* The American public has become more and more concerned about the crime rate and the effectiveness of the criminal justice system.

Down through the years this concern has sparked many studies of the causes of crime and many proposals for possible solutions. But recently attention has shifted to the *victims* of crime. Who are they? How can we help them through the tangle of the legal system? What can be done to protect them? And what can be done to help them recover from the effects of the crime?

First, who are the victims? They come from all walks of life and all age groups. But studies show that the most common victim of violent crime is a black male teen-ager from a low-income family. And the most common victim of theft is a white male teen-ager from a low-income family. Most studies show that criminals tend to victimize members of their own race.

Being a victim can be deeply disturbing. It can take years to recover, and some victims

A bank swindle can take away a home that an elderly couple worked all their lives to pay for.

Crimes against property like fraud, burglary, and theft are the most common crimes in the United States. Violent crimes such as murder, rape, and robbery are less common. But they probably cause more anxiety and fear. Violent crime can leave a victim crippled, physically or emotionally. It's hard to imagine the effect if it hasn't happened to you. Some victims never want to leave the safety of their homes again.

In the following sections, we will examine some victims of violent and property crimes. First we will find out what **victimology**—the study of victims—tells us about victims of these crimes. Then we'll listen to some victims describe the effect crime had on their lives.

Victims of Violent Crimes

Violent crimes, such as murder, rape, robbery, and assault, are also known as **crimes against the person.** In these crimes, the criminal either uses force or threatens to use force against the victim. Below, we will take a closer look at victims of two kinds of violent crime—rape and robbery.

The Rape Victim

FBI statistics have shown staggering increases in reports of forcible rape over the last 30 years. Experts estimate that one in four women will be raped in her life. In America, a rape is reported every six minutes. But these statistics mislead, because many rapes go unreported—perhaps as many as 90 percent.

Studies of victims can tell us a few facts. Rapes happen most often in places where women are isolated —a lonely street, a home, or a car. At least 75 percent of the rape victims belong to the same race and economic class as their attackers. Also, the rape victim is likely to be approximately the same age as her attacker. In nearly three -fourths of all rape cases, the victim knows the rapist. Some are friends; others are neighbors or even relatives. The most likely rape victim is a black female teen -ager from a low -income family in a large city. Victims under age 18 are the least likely to report the crime.

What is it like to be a rape victim? And why do rape victims often fail to report the attacks to the police? The following is excerpted from a statement made by a rape victim.

Nicole's Story

"The summer before my junior year in high school, I was dating a guy who I thought was my dream. I thought he was a popular, caring, wonderful football player, and he seemed crazy about me. My dream was quickly shattered. A month after our first date, we went on a summer outing one Saturday. On that day, he changed my life forever by brutally raping me.

"How do I even begin to explain what I went through? It is not the gory details that you need to hear to understand. It is the suffering, the loss of feeling any control, the incredible self-blame, and the disruption of a survivor's life that can't often be heard.

**A s k
a n**

Expert

There are many rape crisis centers around the country today. And many police departments have specially trained officers to deal with rape victims. Invite a representative from a local rape crisis center or a rape counseling officer from your local police department to visit your class. Have the guest speaker explain how rape victims are treated and what special services are available in your community.

NEWSBREAK

In this activity, you should bring news articles from home on crime, create victim profiles, and discuss the articles with the class.

1. Find a story in a newspaper or newsmagazine about a crime.

2. From the story, create a profile of the crime victim. This should include the name of the crime, a description of what happened, where it happened, the age of the victim, and any other information about the victim.

3. Figure out how much of the story is devoted to the victim. (You can count the number of lines in the story and count the number of lines devoted to the victim.)

4. In class, write the crimes on the board and discuss the following:

- *Which of the crimes listed on the board are property crimes and which are violent crimes? Which are neither? (If you need a crime defined, look in the glossary at the back of the book.)*
- *In the crime stories you found, which victims got the most coverage? Which got the least? What factors could account for the difference? Explain.*
- *The readings discuss several findings from victim studies, e.g. that the most common victim of violent crime is a black male teen-ager from a low-income family. Review the findings of victim studies in the readings and compare them with the articles you found in the newspaper. Did the newspaper articles you found reflect the findings of the victim studies? If not, how do you account for*

"There was no support system for me. I was a 15-year-old girl, frightened to tell anyone—*silenced*. I was silenced because it just wasn't safe for me to come forward. Who would understand? Who would believe that 'Mr. All-American' could do anything like that to me? I certainly never would have believed I would be raped, and certainly not by someone I trusted.

"So I pretended that it *didn't* happen. I wore long sleeves and high necks for two weeks in the summer to cover the bruises. I cleaned away the blood and I stored the whole experience deep in my subconscious and denied that it had happened. I continued my life robotically, striving socially, academically, and athletically—but inside there was a crying young girl.

"But memories started invading my everyday life. Brutal flashbacks kept me from concentrating. And as nightmares interrupted my every night of sleep, I began to realize how desperately I needed support. It took me three and a half years until I got the courage to seek therapy. I learned that I was not alone, that hundreds of thousands of other women are raped by people

they know and trust. And most importantly, I learned that it was not my fault."

The Robbery Victim

In a robbery, the criminal takes property by force or by threat of force. In this scary crime, victims can lose their property, suffer injuries, and even die. Statistically, the chances of being killed are small: Almost 99.8 percent of all robbery victims survive. About one-third of all victims suffer injuries, mostly minor. Only two percent receive wounds serious enough to stay overnight in a hospital. Strangely, victims are most likely to be hurt by unarmed robbers, probably because these robbers often attack their victims to establish control in the robbery. Victims are most likely to be killed, however, by robbers armed with guns. Victims who resist are more likely to be injured or killed than those who do not resist.

The most likely victim is a male between the ages of 12 and 24. As a person's age increases, the likelihood of being robbed declines. People over 65 make up the age group least likely to be robbed.

Even the president of the United States can be a victim of crime. Police and Secret Service agents help two shooting victims wounded in an attempt on President Reagan's life in 1981. In the background, they surround the assailant. (UPI/Bettmann.)

What is it liked to be robbed? The following is excerpted from a robbery victim's statement.

Harry's Story

"My dad and I were walking to meet my brother at a cafe where we went to lunch a lot. As we walked up, we saw the owner down the street waving and jumping up and down. We waved back. Later, we found out he was trying to warn us not to go in. He had been in the bathroom when the robbery started and had climbed out a window and run down the street.

"When my dad opened the cafe's door, a guy grabbed him and pulled him in. I turned and started to walk away, but a guy came out, pointed a sawed-off shotgun at me, and ordered me into the cafe. I did what he said. Inside, he threw me on the ground and pressed the shotgun against my head. Everyone in the cafe—about 25 people—was lying on the ground. There were seven robbers, all with guns. They went around from person to person grabbing wallets and jewelry. One man didn't like how they had talked to his wife. When he objected, a guy hit him with his gun. I lay there thinking, 'I hope the cops don't come until these guys get outside.' I was afraid of being taken hostage.

"They took my wallet, refused my old watch, and tried and failed to get my ring off. It stuck on my finger. They didn't want to spend any more time in the cafe, so they left. We had come in near the end of the robbery.

"The next day I had a large knot on my head. I don't understand why. The guy had just pressed his gun against my head. He didn't hit me. My dad had lost a ring he had owned his whole life. My brother to this day has never gone back to the cafe. The robbery shook up the owner so much that he sold the cafe to someone else."

For Discussion

1. Why do you think so many women do not report rapes? Would you if you were raped? Why or why not?

2. What do you think would help victims of violent crimes recover from the crimes? Explain.

3. Victims of violent crimes sometimes report that witnesses do not call the police or try to help them. Why do you think people might not respond when they hear screams or see crimes?

Victims of Property Crimes

Property crimes, such as theft, burglary, and fraud, involve stealing property. They differ from violent crimes because the criminal does *not* use force and does *not* threaten to use force. If the criminal uses force, the crime is a violent crime—a crime against the person—not a property crime.

According to FBI statistics, losses from property crime add up to more than $16 billion a year. Every family in the country suffers—some from direct loss, some from high insurance rates, and some just from fear and insecurity. In the following sections, we will take a closer look at victims of two kinds of property crime—burglary and fraud.

The Burglary Victim

Burglary is the unlawful entry into a building with the intent to commit a crime, normally theft. Over $4 billion in losses are reported each year. Crime surveys reveal that victims report about half of all household burglaries to the police. Although not a violent crime, burglaries often greatly upset the victims, because the criminal has intruded into the privacy of the home. The following story is excerpted from a statement given by a burglary victim.

Helen's Story

"I was coming home from work on a Monday. My front door was unlocked. I walked in, and the first thing I noticed was the television and VCR were missing. I thought, 'How dare she (my younger sister) take them out of this apartment without asking me!' Then I noticed clothes scattered in the hallway and thought, 'She must be doing the laundry, but why does she have to dump it in the hallway?' It wasn't until I walked into the bedroom that it dawned on me that we had been burglarized. The stuff in our nightstands was scattered on the bedroom floor. I ran into the living room to look for my camera equipment. It was gone. I ran around the apartment—anything and everything of great value they took. I was in shock and felt so helpless. When I called the police, I had to repeat everything twice because I was crying and talking at the same time.

"The burglars had picked the lock to enter the apartment. So I replaced my deadbolt lock with a new one, which, according to the police, was 'practically unpickable.' I replaced the TV, VCR, stereo, and camera equipment. A month later on another Monday, I came home to find my apartment burglarized again. They had not picked my unpickable lock. They had broken down the door with a crowbar. They took everything I had replaced and looked through places they missed the first time. The police took fingerprints both times and came up with a suspect. But they haven't caught him yet.

"After the second burglary, I no longer felt safe. The thought of being invaded a third time was too much. So within a month, my sister and I moved to a new apartment in a different neighborhood."

The Fraud Victim

Fraud is a form of stealing. The criminal does not, however, simply grab something and run off. The criminal relies on deception and lies to induce the victim to turn over property to the thief. The criminal, for example, may offer goods in exchange for money. The victim turns over the money, but the goods will never be delivered. So fraud depends on the victim at some point cooperating with the thief.

Why do fraud victims fall for the criminals' lies? Sometimes the thieves are very clever. Sometimes the victims' greed blinds them. Sometimes the victims are elderly and vulnerable. The following is excerpted from a statement made by a fraud victim.

Rose's Story

"My husband and I were in a terrible car accident. My husband was killed and I was in the hospital with broken ribs and a broken clavicle bone. When I got out of the hospital, I was in pretty bad shape and very uncomfortable. My friends and family had to help me with everything.

"I received an advertisement in the mail for an adjustable bed. I thought this might make me more comfortable since I had spent the last three months in a hospital bed that I had to rent. I wrote to their company in Colorado. They sent a salesman out to the house to talk to me. He took measurements for the bed and then told me that I had to pay the money in advance in order for the manufacturer to make the bed for me. I gave him a check for $2,200. He said that they would either call me or send me a card when the bed was ready.

"After a couple of months, I had not heard anything so I contacted them and was told not to worry, that they were still working on it and would deliver it when it was ready.

"After a few more months, I received a notice [that the people were being criminally prosecuted for fraud]. I was told that after the hearing I might get part of my money back, but I never did.

"I live on a fixed income like most seniors and receive only Social Security. I paid for this bed with what was left of my husband's insurance money because I didn't want any outstanding bills to pay. I ended up having to buy another bed.

"I think that something should be done to keep companies like this from ripping off not only seniors, but anyone. The public should be aware of these types of businesses and know how to check them out before giving them any money. I still wish that someday I would get my money back. I sure could use it."

For Discussion

1. Many victims speak of not being the same person after being victimized. Why do you think this is so? What has changed for them?

2. Many victims of burglary describe the crime as an invasion of their privacy. What do you think they mean by this?

3. Have you ever had anything stolen? If so, how did it affect you? Do you worry that it may happen again?

4. States make receiving stolen property a crime. Do you think it should be? Why or why not?

5. What sorts of crimes do you think people are most likely to report to the police? Least likely? Why do you think some people don't report crimes to the police?

(AP/Wide World Photos.)

Helping Victims of Crime

Some ancient legal codes called for compensating crime victims. The Code of Hammurabi (c. 1750 B.C.), for example, forced the criminal to pay as much as five times the value of the damage caused. If the criminal couldn't be caught, the state would compensate the victim.

Early English and American law forced criminals to make direct payments, called **restitution**, to victims. Gradually, however, criminal law shifted away from helping victims and focused exclusively on punishing lawbreakers. The only way for a victim to get restitution was to sue under civil law. Unfortunately, this was usually impossible. Either the criminal had escaped or the criminal was poor and couldn't pay the victim.

It was only in the 1960s that we again began looking for ways society could help crime victims directly. In an influential 1964 *New York University Law Review* article, former Supreme Court Justice Arthur J. Goldberg wrote that:

Government compensation of victims of crime . . . is long overdue here. The victim of a robbery or an assault has been denied the 'protection' of the laws in a very real sense, and society should assume some responsibility for making him whole.

The first victim-compensation legislation was developed in New Zealand in 1963. This pioneering act set up a board to pay cash awards to crime victims. The idea spread quickly to England in 1964 and then to California in 1965. Most other states soon followed.

One State's Model

- During a street mugging, a man is assaulted and hit several times in the face. The mugger takes the man's wallet with $35 in it and flees. Bruised, scared, and with broken glasses, the man is taken to a nearby emergency room for treatment. The New York State Crime Victims Board would pay for the replacement of the eyeglasses, the lost cash, and the emergency room bill if the man did not have insurance.

- A young woman, age 16, sitting in the park becomes the victim of a random shooting. Rushed to the hospital, she dies after several days. The New York State Crime Victims Board would pay for any unreimbursed medical expenses, funeral costs up to $2,000, and counseling for her parents and brothers and sisters.

The state of New York offers monetary aid to families who have suffered financially from violent crime. This plan is run by the Crime Victims Board, a five member panel.

Crime victims, their dependents, or immediate family members can apply for compensation. The board will pay for medical expenses, mental health counseling, job retraining, funeral or burial expenses, lost earnings, and loss of support. It will also compensate for losses of cash or essential personal property if the victim has suffered a personal injury. The limits on the amounts of the awards are as follows:

Medical expenses......................................unlimited

Counseling...unlimited

Vocational rehabilitation.........................unlimited

Funeral or burial..$2,000

Lost earnings......................$20,000 ($400/week)

Loss of support....................$20,000 ($400/week)

Loss of cash or essential
personal property...$100

The New York plan only compensates for losses caused by crimes of violence, such as assault, rape, murder, and hit-and-run. And the board will not pay for losses that have already been covered by insurance. Serious financial hardship must be shown on claims over $5,000.

The New York plan also requires the victim to cooperate with the police and prosecution. And the board checks to make sure that the victim did not contribute to the incident in some significant way. This is particularly important in cases involving drugs or substance abuse.

These are the main standards that the New York Crime Victims Board checks before making an award:

(1) a violent crime occurred, resulting in an injury;

(2) the victim suffered a serious financial hardship;

(3) the victim cooperated with authorities; and

(4) the victim did not contribute to the crime.

The main problem with the New York plan and other victim compensation programs is money. Many state compensation boards are behind in the settlement of claims because of lack of funds and inadequate staffing. In fact, many programs would be overwhelmed if every eligible person applied for benefits. With increased public awareness of the programs, more funds will be needed in order for them to meet their goals.

Other Victim Programs

Cash awards aren't the only victim assistance programs. Government agencies and private organizations offer many other services: shelters for battered women, rape counseling, crisis intervention programs, child-abuse intervention, and medical counseling.

In many cities, the prosecutor's office or a private help organization has a unit to aid victims when they first come into contact with the criminal justice system. This service is aimed at comforting the victim, notifying the victim of court dates, and even helping the victim find transportation to court.

Many communities have programs that offer crime victims free or low-cost legal advice, psychological counseling, or employment assistance. And some agencies offer help in replacing items stolen or destroyed in crimes. It can be a great comfort to a crime victim to have someone's help in as simple a task as replacing a stolen ID or a broken door lock. The primary goal of most victim assistance programs is to help the victim get through the crisis with dignity and get back to as normal a life as possible.

Class Activity: Crime Victims Board

Imagine that you are a member of a Crime Victims Board similar to the New York model. It is your responsibility to review applications for crime victim compensation and decide which, if any, should be approved.

1. Form small groups of four students each.

2. Review the standards used for making awards in New York on page 8.

3. Read each of the cases which follow and decide, based on the standards, whether compensation should be awarded. For each case, write down the following:

(1) the case number;

(2) whether you approve or deny an award of compensation;

Activity: Community Awareness Project

1. Break into teams of four students each. Check in the Yellow Pages, at your local police department and courthouse, and around your neighborhood for special programs and services that are available to crime victims. Each member of the team should find at least one. Find out as much information as you can about the program.

2. Report on the purposes and operation of these programs to your class and list all of them on the chalkboard. When everyone has described at least one, select the five most important services that other students and people in your area should know about.

3. Assign one service to each team. Work in the teams to develop a poster or brochure to make people aware of that service.

4. Develop a plan for displaying or distributing copies of the brochure or poster to the community.

---

(3) your reasons for your decision;

(4) the total amount of your award; and

(5) the amount of award money allocated to medical expenses, vocational rehabilitation, funeral or burial, lost earnings, loss of support, and loss of cash or essential personal property.

Be prepared to discuss and support your recommendations.

Case No. 1

William Hall was at the Shady Oak Bar playing a game of pool with the suspect, Ken Ross. William had a $50 bet on the game. He lost the pool game, and the two men began arguing over the bet. According to witnesses interviewed by the police, William threw a punch at Ken and missed. Ken picked up the pool cue and struck

William in the mouth, causing him to lose several teeth.

William claims that he did not try to strike Ken and that they had no argument.

The District Attorney's office refused to prosecute Ken because of insufficient evidence.

William is claiming $1,000 in medical damages and $400 in lost wages.

Case No. 2

Robert Samuelson, owner of the Valley Drug Store, was shot during a robbery of the store. He died as a result of gunshot wounds to his chest. His widow, Ruth, is claiming a wage loss of $30,000 per year for five years due to her husband's death. Funeral expenses totaled $5,000.

Ruth will receive her husband's estate, which is valued at $80,000. In addition, she receives Social Security benefits of $400 per month.

Case No. 3

Rocky Pineda was playing with his two children at Allstone Park, when he was approached by two young men. One of them had a gun and demanded money. Rocky attempted to explain that he could not speak much English. He tried to take his children and run when one of the young men shot him in the back. He died a few moments later from the gunshot wound. The suspects were never found.

The funeral expenses were $3,000, to be paid by Maria Pineda, his widow. She is eight months pregnant and has no health insurance to cover her medical expenses. She is claiming a $20,000 wage loss due to her husband's death.

Case No. 4

Susan Jones was sitting in the Whaling Ship Bar with two of her girlfriends. They were listening to music and having a drink. Three men sat down at their table and began to talk. After a while, they all started dancing and continued drinking.

One of the men, Mike, offered Susan a ride home. She accepted. When they arrived at her apartment, she invited him in for coffee. He followed her into the kitchen, grabbed a knife, and then forcibly raped her and cut her several times with the knife.

Her medical insurance covered her hospital bills. She stayed away from work for three weeks because of the psychological trauma. She is claiming $2,000 for seeing a psychiatrist and $1,200 in lost wages.

Debriefing Questions

1. Which claims did groups deny? Why?

2. Are the standards for awarding compensation fair? Why or why not? How would you change the standards?

3. If you could write your state's law regarding compensating victims, what would your laws provide?

4. New York is one of a handful of states that requires serious financial hardship for compensation awards. Most states have done away with this requirement. Do you think the requirement makes sense? Why or why not?

5. What is the difference between state victim compensation and restitution for victims? Which do you think is better? Why?

6. What are the benefits of victim compensation laws? What are their drawbacks? Do you think states should have such laws? Why or why not?

DUE TO VIOLENT CONTENT, VIEWER DISCRETION IS ADVISED.

This cartoon implies that everyday life in America can be as violent as any television program. (Bennett Clay. Reprinted with permission of the St. Petersburg Times.)

The Push for Victims' Rights

As the crime rate has grown since the 1960s, so has concern about how the criminal justice system treats crime victims. Citizens have banded together to form groups to represent crime victims and their families.

These groups have often complained that crime victims are injured twice—first by the criminal and then by an insensitive criminal justice system. They claim that too often victims have been ignored or even subtly blamed for the crime. Many victims have found themselves caught up in police investigations and judicial proceedings that they don't really understand. They have been moved from hearing to hearing at the convenience of attorneys or judges or the police. In the early 1980s, the President's Task Force on Crime said, "Somewhere along the way, the system began to serve lawyers and judges and defendants, treating the victim with institutionalized disinterest."

Advocates of crime victims have pressed for reforms in the criminal justice system. They have been joined by many groups, including women's groups interested in helping victims of rape and wife-beating. They have met with remarkable success.

New Federal Programs

In the 1980s, two federal acts were passed to begin addressing the needs of crime victims. The Victim and Witness Protection Act of 1982 had three main goals:

(1) to protect crime victims and witnesses in the criminal justice system;

(2) to ensure that in federal cases the government does all it can to help victims and witnesses without infringing on the defendants' constitutional rights; and

(3) to serve as a model for legislation for state and local governments.

The following are some specific features of the act:
- The crime's impact on the victim should be considered in deciding penalties.
- Anyone threatening or harming a witness should be punished severely.
- Court orders should be used to restrain anyone from harassing a witness.
- A victim is entitled to restitution from the criminal.

The second federal act is the Victims of Crime Act of 1984. This act set up a Crime Victims Fund, which provides grants to local victim compensation programs. Today it supplies almost 40 percent of the funds in these programs. The money comes from fines and forfeitures paid by federal criminals.

Government payments to individual crime victims now range from $100 to $50,000 or more. The majority of the grant money goes to victims of rape and family violence.

Responses from States

Many states have passed what are called **victims' bills of rights** into law. These laws focus on procedures within the criminal justice system. They attempt to make the victim an important part of the process. Michigan, for example, in 1988 passed a constitutional amendment that reads as follows:

> Crime victims . . . shall have the following rights, as provided by law:

> The right to be treated with fairness and respect for their dignity and privacy throughout the criminal justice process.

A s k
a n

Expert

Does your state have a victims' bill of rights? A victims' compensation board? What does your state do for crime victims? Invite a prosecutor to your classroom to discuss these questions.

The right to timely disposition of the case following arrest of the accused.

The right to be reasonably protected from the accused throughout the criminal justice process.

The right to notification of court proceedings.

The right to attend trial and all other court proceedings the accused has the right to attend.

The right to confer with the prosecution.

The right to make a statement to the court at sentencing.

The right to restitution.

The right to information about the conviction, sentence, imprisonment, and release of the accused.

Other Proposals

A number of other recommendations have been offered to assist victims. Some of the following have been discussed in state legislatures or at the federal level:

- States should pay the costs of all medical examinations for sexual assaults.
- School officials should be criminally liable for failing to report to the police any violent crimes, possession of weapons, or narcotics offenses on school grounds.
- Programs should be developed to help crime victims employed by the government to readjust to their jobs.
- Victims should not have to testify at preliminary hearings. Investigating officers should be allowed to read victims' statements from police reports.

While almost everyone favors helping crime victims, some proposals have drawn fire when they intrude on the rights of criminal defendants. Some critics question, for example, the wisdom of the last recommendation in the list above. They argue that denying criminal suspects the right to see and contradict their accusers may well result in unjust prosecutions. They say that the idea of using secret accusers goes against the grain of the entire Anglo-American judicial system. The right to a public trial is guaranteed by the Sixth Amendment. These critics worry about secrecy creeping into any portion of the judicial process. And they are alarmed by any proposals that may weaken constitutional rights.

For Discussion

1. At preliminary hearings, judges determine whether defendants should stand trial. Since California voters passed a Victims' Bill of Rights in 1982, crime victims no longer have to testify at preliminary hearings in California. Investigating police officers may read what the victims said in the police report. This means defendants no longer have the opportunity to cross-examine their accusers. Do you agree with this policy? Why or why not?

2. Some victims' rights group propose that statements made by victims during post-crime counseling sessions should not be used in court or made available to the defense. Do you agree with this policy? Why or why not?

3. The Supreme Court now allows victim-impact statements to be used at penalty hearings. So judges and juries may hear accounts of victims' suffering when penalties are being considered. Can you see any dangers in doing this? Would you support stronger penalties for killing a nun as opposed to killing a prostitute? Why or why not?

4. Make a list of the problems that crime victims face. How can society address these problems?

Hooded members of the Ku Klux Klan gather at a rally. (The Bettmann Archive.)

A Look Back . . .

When I was young, I could play in the park at night. Now it's all drug dealers. You could leave all your doors unlocked. Now you can't walk down your own street without getting robbed.

Many older people look back on their past as a time when streets were safe and crime happened somewhere far away. There is some evidence in statistics that the decades from the 1930s through the 1950s were less crime -ridden than today. Yet those decades may be exceptions in American history. If you take a careful look back into our history, you will find that violent crime has always played a part in American life.

During the 1700s, robbery and other violent crimes were already troubling the English Colonies of America. Land was becoming scarce. The English were fighting a series of wars and demanding high taxes from the colonists to pay for them. In turn, the Colonies suffered high rates of unemployment and poverty. Crime flourished in this environment.

Adding to the crime problem, criminals from England's jails, both men and women, were deported to America as indentured servants. Before the Revolution, over 50,000 of these law-breakers were sent to the American Colonies. Some ran away once they arrived and became part of the growing criminal population.

Philadelphia, one of America's first important cities, was known as the "crime capital of the Colonies" during the early 1700s. Robbery, rape, murder, and arson occurred with frightening regularity.

By the mid-1700s, New York City was challenging Philadelphia for the dubious title of "crime capital." Its population was exploding. New immigrants were arriving by the boatload. Along with the increasing population, came a rise in violent crime. A New York newspaper editorial complained: "It seems to have now become dangerous for the good People of this City to be out late at night without being sufficiently strong or well armed."

In the countryside and on the frontier, gangs of thieves and robbers preyed on farmers. Gangs in the North Carolina backwoods provoked citizens to take the law into their own hands. In 1767, the citizens formed the first American vigilante group, which attacked and punished gang members.

Crime in the 1800s

During the 1800s, many American cities grew rapidly. Workshops and new industries attracted immigrants from England and Northern Europe. By 1800, New York had passed Philadelphia and Boston to become the biggest city in the country, with 60,000 people. Further waves of immigrants came to escape famines and wars in Europe. With the rise of heavy industry and mining in New England and the industrial Midwest, many corporations actively recruited in Europe for laborers.

Many of the new immigrants had to squeeze into crowded tenements in urban areas. Cities like New York gained a reputation for overcrowding and criminal violence. In the decade before the Civil War, over 3,000 homeless children roamed the streets of New York. Many of them became pickpockets and street robbers. One civic leader wrote in 1842: "Thronged as our city is, men are robbed in the streets . . . . The defenseless and the beautiful are ravished in the daytime and no trace of the criminals is found."

Before the Civil War, few cities in America had anything like a police department to keep order. Boston had a night watch, but it was mainly a fire lookout. Watchmen were afraid to enter many neighborhoods at all. In some places, vigilantes were the only organized resistance to criminals.

There were more murders in New York than London, a far bigger city. One English traveler wrote: "Probably in no city in the civilized world is life so fearfully insecure." The same fear plagued other cities. In Philadelphia during the mid-1800s, bands of robbers began to prey on wealthy citizens, stripping them of their cash.

Out in the West, it became commonplace for men to wear guns wherever they went. Horse and cattle theft became a major problem. Los Angeles was only a sleepy village of about 8,000, but in one 15-month period in the 1850s, there were 40 murders. In much larger San Francisco to the north, there were entire neighborhoods where no one dared go after dark.

Ethnic Urban Gangs

In many cities, jobless immigrants formed violent gangs in ethnic slum neighborhoods. In Philadelphia, lower-class Irish and black groups formed gangs. With names like the Bleeders, Garroters, Rangers, Tormentors, and Killers, the gangs sometimes fought bloody battles on a spot known as the Battle Ground. Gang members as young as 10 carried clubs, knives, brass knuckles, and pistols. They attacked lone pedestrians, younger children, or members of other ethnic groups.

In New York, well-organized adult street gangs controlled the immigrant areas of Five Points and the Bowery. Made up mostly of young Irish immigrants, gangs called the Dead Rabbits, Plug Uglies, and Shirt Tails became famous for mugging people. In the nearby Fourth Ward, the Daybreak Boys were responsible for 20 murders between 1850 and 1852. Political parties recruited squads of toughs from these gangs to intimidate voters.

Probably the most violent New York street gang at this time was called the "Whyos." The Whyos came from Mulberry Bend, another slum neighborhood. They robbed people and burglarized homes and stores throughout the city. At one time the Whyos had over 500 members, all of whom supposedly had killed at least one person. The gang even advertised their services. A handbill found on a gang member set their rates:

Punching	**$ 2**
Both eyes blacked	**$ 4**
Nose and jaw broke	**$ 10**
Jacked out (blacked jacked)	**$ 15**
Ear chewed off	**$ 15**
Leg or arm broke	**$ 19**
Shot in leg	**$ 25**
Stab	**$ 25**
Doing the big job (murder)	**$100**

Dandy Johnny Dolan, their leader, invented a copper device for gouging an eye out and kept an eye as a trophy.

In the cities of the Northeast, the 1830s through the 1850s were a period of sustained urban rioting. The pressures on the urban slums boiled over. There were ethnic riots, labor riots, election-day riots, anti-black riots, and anti-Catholic riots. In that period Baltimore alone had 12 major riots, Philadelphia had 11, and New York had eight. It was this burst of lawlessness that spurred the development of police forces in most cities.

Post Civil War Violence

The Civil War killed over 600,000 people, more than any other war in our history. It also left behind enduring habits of hatred and violent revenge. The famous Hatfield and McCoy families had supported different sides in the Civil War. Their feud along the Kentucky-West Virginia border killed or wounded dozens of people between 1873 and 1888.

The most vicious and widespread postwar violence was directed against blacks. During the period of Reconstruction, freed slaves served in state legislatures in the South. Former slaves educated themselves, voted, and many started businesses or began farming their own small fields.

In response to these developments, some Southern whites created the Ku Klux Klan and other groups to terrorize blacks and help end the social changes of Reconstruction. In a reign of terror in Louisiana in the 1870s, a group called the White League killed over 3,500 blacks, many by **lynching**—a form of mob violence that punishes an accused person without a legal trial. Most lynchings are hangings.

The Klan executed lynchings against poor blacks and their supporters for decades. In incidents all over the country, almost 2,000 African-Americans were lynched from 1882 to 1903.

Outlaws in the Countryside

After the Civil War, violence in the West took a new turn. The Reno brothers of Indiana invented train robbery, and dozens of small gangs followed their example. The most famous robbers were the James brothers—Jesse and Frank. They had been Confederate guerrillas and after the war they turned to robbing trains and banks, terrorizing Union states from Missouri to Minnesota. They killed 16 people.

In the 1870s, Billy the Kid, who was born in a New York slum tenement, roamed the West, gambling, killing, and hiring out as a cattle rustler. Sheriff Pat Garret finally tracked him down and shot him. According to legend, Billy the Kid had killed 21 men, one for each year of his life. The actual number was probably smaller.

John Wesley Hardin from Texas killed his first victim at age 15. The victim was a black teen who had beaten him at wrestling. He went on to kill more than a dozen more men, including one because he had badmouthed Texas. Hardin was shot and killed in 1895 and became another outlaw legend, though today we would probably think of him as a psychotic serial murderer.

Even more violent were the range wars. Throughout the Western states, cattle and land barons hired armies of gunmen to guard or expand their private empires. In some cases, the cattlemen had the law squarely on their side. But often their gunmen settled scores and fought battles. Texas had the Sutton-Taylor feud, the Horrell-Higgins feud, the Jaybird-Woodpecker feud, and several others. Montana had the Johnson County War which pitted European immigrant homesteaders against a cattle baron. Arizona had the worst range war of all. In the Pleasant Valley War, the cattle-raising Grahams fought the sheep-raising Tewkesburys with hired armies. The conflict raged for six years and was fought literally "to the last man."

Racial Violence

The end of the century marked the beginning of a long era of race riots. As early as 1871, a white mob in Los Angeles went on a rampage and hanged 20 Chinese workers from street lamps. Near the turn of the century, mobs in Eastern cities began descending on black neighborhoods to lynch any black man unlucky enough to be caught. There were major race riots against blacks in Atlanta in 1906, Springfield, Illinois, in 1908, and in many other cities.

Prohibition and Organized Crime

The 20th century saw the rise of what we know as organized crime. In 1920, the 18th Amendment to the Constitution made the manufacture, transport, or sale of alcoholic beverages illegal. The era of Prohibition, one of this country's most violent crime periods, extended from 1920 until the 18th Amendment was repealed in 1933. Prohibition created the conditions for thriving illegal businesses.

In Chicago, gangsters set up illegal beer-brewing and distribution businesses, plus a network of bribed police and politicians to protect them. The business was so lucrative that rival gangs fought for control. Between 1923 and 1926, the Chicago beer wars killed over 200 people. By 1927, the mobster Al Capone had come out on top. His beer business took in over $60 million a year—which would be well over $1 billion in today's dollars.

During the early 1930s, various crime organizations sought to form alliances to control gambling, prostitution, narcotics, and other illegal money-making activities. Gangster rivalry and greed, however, led to the murder of numerous underworld figures.

Depression and World War II

As the Great Depression began in the early 1930s, violent crimes reached a peak. In 1933, the murder rate was 9.7 murders for every 100,000 Americans. The murder rate would not be this high again until the late 1970s.

A curious thing happened as the Depression worsened and unemployment skyrocketed: The crime rate went down. Despite widespread news coverage of Depression-era bank robbers like John Dillinger, "Pretty Boy" Floyd, and Bonnie and Clyde, violent crime actually declined. The murder rate, for example, dropped 50 percent

Dutch Schultz, a notorious bootlegger and gangster, walks out of federal court in New York in 1935. (The Bettmann Archive.)

between 1933 and the early 1940s. Other serious crimes fell by a third.

Why did crime decrease during a time of great hardship for almost all Americans? According to some historians, the Depression brought Americans closer together, because almost everyone was in the same boat. World War II unified Americans even more. In addition, the birthrate had dropped in the 1920s, which meant that the youth population—14 to 24 year olds—declined in size. Young people commit most crimes, especially violent crimes.

The Postwar Years

Following World War II, the 1950s were a period of relative calm, but the turbulent 1960s saw an increase in many kinds of violence. A dozen civil-rights activists were murdered in the South, and many tens of thousands of anti-war activists took to the streets in demonstrations that sometimes turned violent. The major urban riots of the later 1960s exploded in African-American communities in Los Angeles, Newark, Detroit, and other cities where jobs had been disappearing and urban problems growing.

Street crime, too, began to increase again. At this time the 14-24 age group grew rapidly. Many crime experts believe that this surge of young people in the population contributed significantly to the increase of crime in the 1960s and 1970s.

In the early 1980s the sudden appearance of crack cocaine caused a tremendous rise in drug addiction and associated crimes. Many Hispanic and African-American communities became plagued by drug-dealing gangs. And with the rise in unemployment and homelessness, reports of street crime skyrocketed. Crime became so much of a concern to ordinary citizens that it spawned whole communities barricaded with walls, barred windows, and burglar alarms.

To older Americans, the increase in violent crime may signal a frightening new trend. But violent crime has almost always existed at a high level throughout American history.

For Discussion

1. Why do you think that violent crime has existed at such a high level throughout American history?

2. Why do you think American outlaws like Jesse James and Billy the Kid have so often been portrayed as heroes? Is there anyone like them today who is portrayed as a hero?

3. How do you account for so much mob violence directed against African-Americans throughout our history?

4. Why did the crime rate go down in the 1930s? Why did it go up again in the 1960s?

5. List on the board as many causes of crime in American history as possible. Discuss the list and select the five most important. Explain your reasons.

6. Are there countries that you think have a more violent history, or a less violent history? Why do you think this is true?

7. What do you think caused the urban riots in the 1960s, or the Los Angeles riot of 1992?

How Much Crime Is There?

How do we know how many murders, rapes, robberies, burglaries, and other crimes there are each year? Where do crime statistics come from? There are two main sources: (1) the Uniform Crime Reports (UCR) and (2) the National Crime Victimization Survey (NCVS).

Since 1930, police departments from across the country have sent crime data to the Federal Bureau of Investigation for inclusion in its Uniform Crime Reports. The UCR lists eight so-called index crimes—four violent crimes and four property crimes. They are murder and non-negligent manslaughter, forcible rape, robbery, aggravated assault, burglary, larceny-theft, motor vehicle theft, and arson. Almost every police department in the United States reports its crimes for inclusion in the UCR.

Even so, the UCR has at least two built-in weaknesses. First, it does not attempt to account for all crime—only for crime reported to the police. If someone does not report a crime, it cannot possibly get included in the UCR. Second, it relies on police departments to relay the information accurately. This may not always happen.

To get a fuller picture of crime, the Department of Justice instituted an annual National Crime Victimization Survey in 1973. (Until 1991, it was called the National Crime Survey.) The survey polls 49,000 households, representing about 100,000 persons over age 12. Following a detailed questionnaire, poll takers ask individuals if they have been victims of rape, robbery, assault, larceny, burglary, or car theft. Unlike the UCR, the NCVS reflects both reported and unreported crimes.

But the NCVS has problems also. It cannot count homicides because the victims are not alive to be interviewed. It doesn't include crimes against businesses, such as robberies and burglaries, because it only interviews households. Of the crimes it does count, the survey could be flawed by either the interviewer or interviewee. Many interviews are conducted over the telephone. Others are held with everyone in the household

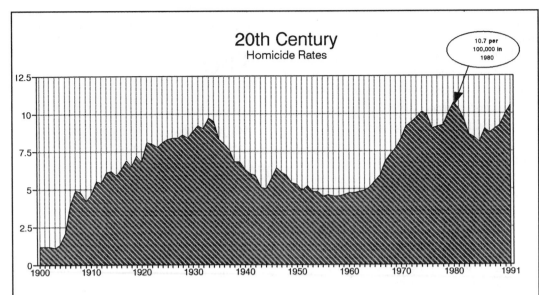

20th Century
Homicide Rates

10.7 per 100,000 in 1980

The U.S. homicide rate dropped in the 1930s, but started rising in the 1960s. (Vital Statistics of U.S., adapted from a Bureau of Justice Statistics chart.)

together. If there is no rapport, the interviewee may not want to confide in the interviewer. Even with rapport, an interviewee may not want to talk about certain crimes in front of other members of the household—either because the crime is too embarrassing or because the perpetrator is sitting right there. Thus many cases of rape and domestic assault probably go unreported.

The Trend of Crime

Since the UCR and NCVS measure different data, they come up with different numbers for most crimes. As would be expected, the NCVS consistently reports far higher numbers than UCR, except for auto theft. NCVS reports only slightly higher numbers of auto thefts than the UCR.

What do the UCR and NCVS say about the trend of crime? Is it increasing, decreasing, or staying the same? Is it worse than in previous years or better? In 1973, the NCVS reported 1,107,800 robberies. By 1990, the number had grown to 1,149,710. So does this mean crime got worse during this period? Not necessarily. The population in 1990 was greater than in 1973. To make comparisons between two different time periods, you need to know the **crime rates**—the amount of crime per person. The NCVS usually

calculates these rates as the number of crimes for every 1,000 persons age 12 or older. The UCR calculates them for every 100,000 persons.

According to the NCVS, the robbery rate dropped during the period 1973 to 1990. In 1973, the rate was 6.7 for every 1,000 persons age 12 or older. By 1990, it had fallen to 5.7. In fact, the NCVS shows that the rate of all violent crime had declined slightly over this period. In 1973, the rate of violent crime was 32.6 per 1,000. It reached a peak of 35.3 per 1,000 in 1981, declined to a low of 28.1 in 1986, and then rose slightly to 31.7 in 1990.

The UCR paints a slightly different picture. It shows a rapid rise in crime from 1973 to 1980. From 1981 to 1984, the UCR's rate of violent crime dropped. So far the UCR trend coincides with the NCVS. But from 1985 to 1990, the UCR shows a large increase in violent crime—from 556 to 731.8 violent crimes per 100,000 persons.

Most experts tend to trust crime trends from the NCVS over the UCR. But experts also believe the UCR statistics for murder and non-negligent homicide are highly accurate. The NCVS does not cover homicide. The UCR homicide statistics follow the same pattern as its other violent crime statistics. They rise from 7.9 homicides per 100,000 in 1985 to 9.4 in 1990. Other homicide studies back up these figures.

For Discussion

1. What are the differences between the Uniform Crime Reports and the National Crime Victim Survey? Which do you think most accurately paints a picture of crime in America? Why?

2. Why do you think the UCR and NCVS report similar numbers of car thefts each year? Why do you think the other crimes are not similar in number?

3. Why do you think experts believe UCR homicide statistics are so accurate?

4. What do you think could account for the difference in the UCR's and NCVS's trends in violent crime since 1985? Which do you think is more accurate? Why?

Class Activity: Crime Victim Survey

How has crime affected you and the people who live in your community? The following survey can help you find out what experiences your class and members of your community have had with crime.

Directions:

1. Break up into small teams. Each team should prepare several copies of a Crime Victim Survey following the suggested questions below. Leave room for brief explanations to each answer.

2. Within the team, each student should target a person with a different occupation in the community, e.g. a small storekeeper, homemaker, religious leader, business supervisor, fast-food employee. Survey the targeted person.

3. Summarize and compare the responses within your team. Try to account for any differences, based on different occupations. Then have the teams compare their surveys and list results on the board. Do you find similarities among the answers given by people with similar occupations? Why or why not? Do you find similarities based on other factors?

Crime Victim Survey

1. Have you ever been a victim of a crime such as bike theft, burglary, assault, etc.?

2. Have any members of your family been victims of crime?

3. Have any nearby neighbors ever been victims of crime?

4. Do you feel unsafe alone at night in your own neighborhood?

5. Do you believe a crime problem exists at the local schools?

6. Have the people in your family been forced to change any part of their lives because of crime?

7. Do you think the police in your community are doing an adequate job of protecting you and other citizens from crime?

8. Compared to one year ago, do you think the crime problem in your community has gotten worse, stayed the same, or improved?

Debriefing Questions

1. Were there any surprises in the results? How do you explain the surprises?

2. Make a list on the board of the kinds of crimes reported in the survey. Do you think other areas in your town or other towns would have a different list? Why or why not?

3. Discuss ways your family and neighbors attempt to protect themselves from crime. For example, you might consider special locks, bars on the windows, watchdogs, guns in the home, neighborhood patrols, etc.

4. What crimes occur most frequently at school? What could be done to prevent them?

5. What are the police in your area doing to prevent crime? What should they be doing?

WHO ARE THE CRIMINALS?

Youth, Gangs, and Violence

About 60 percent of all violent crimes are committed by young males under the age of 25. In fact, males commit most crimes. They account for 84 percent of all arrests and 90 percent of violent crime arrests.

One of the most common types of violent criminal today is the street robber. In his book *Criminal Violence, Criminal Justice*, Charles Silberman described the typical street robber as a male minority teen-ager or young adult from a poor family. This type of robber takes money from people impulsively if the opportunity arises. Rarely does he plan a holdup.

Sometimes street robbers steal because they want money for drugs, food, or goods. Sometimes they just need to impress someone. At other times, the street robber acts out of boredom. The victims of street robbers are often weak or vulnerable. They could be an old person walking alone or a drunk who has passed out on a park bench.

Silberman interviewed many young street robbers and gained some insight into why they apparently enjoyed stealing from people and

threatening them with violence. "I get a kick out of it," said one. Another explained, "If I had a .38 right now, I can make you do just about anything I wanted to do." Others told Silberman that robbing people with a gun makes them feel important, like a judge or a king or a god.

Not all criminals who commit acts of violence think this way, but those who do are especially dangerous. For a few dollars some would maim or kill their victims with little hesitation or feeling.

A disturbing characteristic of many young violent offenders is their apparent lack of feelings. For example, three young Miami boys covered a tramp with lighter fluid and set him on fire. They told police that it was just a prank.

Some criminologists believe that many young violent criminals have been so brutalized by their own families and surroundings that they cannot feel anything when they maim or kill. With no parental supervision, no education, no skills, no hope of a job, they find that it is all too easy to lash out. James Galipeau, a veteran probation officer in Los Angeles says, "There are a million kids out there who have no skills other than fighting. They are not afraid of the police or jail or of dying."

Youth Gang Violence

Youth gangs are not new to our cities. Throughout American history, gangs of young men have come together in immigrant and poverty areas of cities. In the late-19th and early-20th century, Eastern cities such as Boston, New York, and Philadelphia saw the rise of numerous gangs. They were often made up of newly arrived or first-generation groups—Irish, Jewish, and Italian. In the early 1900s, the sociologist Frederick M. Thrasher studied the youth gangs of Chicago and found over 1,000 of them. These early gangs mainly took part in street crime. Later some developed ties to political machines and formed the basis of organized crime in America.

The Latino street gangs of Los Angeles arose in the 1920s during a huge wave of Mexican immigration from poor rural farms. In the 1930s and 1940s, these early gangs solidified into the *pachuco* lifestyle. They wore special clothes, called zoot suits, had nicknames, and spoke their own slang, called *Calo*. Feeling shut out of American society, they became heavily territorial, each defending a small neighborhood or *barrio*. They acquired names like Los 39s and Clarence Street Locos. Many of these groups have survived in the same area for over 60 years. Puerto Rican youths in New York formed similar gangs, as portrayed by the Sharks in the popular 1961 film *West Side Story*.

To some degree these gangs were social clubs, but they also took part in street crime, drugs, and long-running turf warfare. In fact, by the 1970s, this turf warfare had given rise to the characteristic gang crime—the drive-by shooting. Gang kids as young as 13 would lean out the windows of cars to avenge some wrong by shooting at an enemy gang member. Often the shots hit the wrong target, a guest at a wedding party or a tiny child playing on a lawn.

Some poor white communities in the 1950s gave rise to outlaw motorcycle gangs. As shown in the 1950 film *The Wild One*, these bikers were less interested in defending turf than in appearing like a marauding band of pirates. Later, motorcycle gangs became associated with drug trafficking and other crimes.

Outlaw motorcycle gangs were often marked by a vicious anti-black, anti-Latino racism. In the 1970s and 1980s, some impoverished white communities saw the development of similar groups who called themselves skinheads. They modeled themselves on British punk gangs who shaved their heads. Often identifying with punk music and avowing overt racism, the skinhead groups produced an embittered subculture of hatred and violence.

Mike Thompson cartoon reprinted with permission.

African-American youth gangs had a different history. They arose in the 1950s to protect local turf, much like the Latino gangs. In the period of political protest of the 1960s, some of these gangs turned to radical politics. The Blackstone Rangers in Chicago became Black P. Stone (the "P" stood for power). After the Watts riots of 1965, the Slausons became the nucleus for the Los Angeles Black Panthers. These politicized groups did not survive long into the 1970s. Black P. Stone, for example, changed again and eventually became a drug-dealing gang called El Rukn.

In the early 1970s, Los Angeles saw the beginning of a new federation of gangs called the Crips. Unlike other gangs, the Crips spun off subgroups called "sets" in many areas around Southern California. An archrival group called the Bloods also developed, spinning off its own sets, until many Los Angeles neighborhoods became a patchwork of gang territories. The two super-gangs sported official colors—blue for the Crips, red for the Bloods—and each set had a hand sign, like a letter of the deaf alphabet, to identify itself. Gang members, known as gang-bangers, also used pro football and basketball jackets to announce their identities.

The black gangs might have settled into the pattern of earlier gangs—street crime, turf wars, and petty vendettas. But in the early 1980s, crack cocaine hit the streets. The normal powdered form of cocaine cost about $100 a gram. Crack, however, could be bought as cheaply as $5. This cheap and highly addicting drug instantly transformed cocaine use into a widespread and deadly problem. With millions of dollars to be made overnight, many sets of the Bloods and Crips turned themselves into drug-dealing networks to rake in the profits.

This flood of cash plus ties to Latin American drug suppliers brought along a huge increase in violence. Gang members now used automatic weapons like the Uzi or AK-47. Some sets of the Crips and Bloods started sending out exploration parties to set up business in cities across the country. The drug network spread.

On the Eastern seaboard, Jamaican immigrants formed similar crack-dealing gangs called

Gang graffiti in Los Angeles. (AP/Wide World Photos.)

posses, and they too started to spread outward from Boston, New York, and Washington, D.C. The Untouchables from Miami and El Rukn from Chicago did the same. By the late 1980s, gangs of second-generation Vietnamese, Cambodian, and Chinese immigrant youth were also jumping into the crack trade.

The number of drug- and gang-related murders soared to over 400 a year in Los Angeles county. Even tiny Martinsburg, West Virginia, which had been colonized by a Jamaican posse, went from an average of one murder a year to 20 drug killings in 18 months.

Crack addiction created many social problems. With more addicts searching for small amounts of ready cash to buy crack, reports of street crime and theft continued to rise. Crack addiction also increased prostitution rates and the use of injected drugs like heroin. These were major factors in the spread of AIDS.

Following the Los Angeles riots of 1992, there was some hope that a gang truce between many sets of the Bloods and Crips could help lower the murder rate. It is hard to foresee a permanent end to the youth gang problem, however, as long as the same conditions continue. Joblessness, child abuse, and family breakdown still plague impoverished communities. And for many youth, the gang provides a substitute for a functioning, supportive family. Here are two brief biographies that illustrate the problem.

Wizard

Wizard is the nickname or *placa* of a Chicano youth who grew up in the Maravilla area of East Los Angeles. His parents divorced when he was young and he rarely saw his father, who was in and out of jail. Rebellious, he helped found a *clica*—a youth sub-gang—called the Maravilla Pee-Wees when he was 10.

In junior high, he and his *clica* spent time breaking windows, shoplifting, smoking marijuana, and fighting with rival *clicas*. He became a *vato loco*, which means a crazy guy, gaining a reputation for getting away with many crimes. Eventually he joined a full-fledged gang.

"The respect was there," he says. "They would brag about me, like, 'You know what Wizard did, man?' I got a good feeling of respect, status, and excitement out of it."

B-Dog

B-dog is an African-American who grew up in South Central Los Angeles. Both his parents worked long hours at low-wage jobs, and he rarely saw them. He joined a set of the Bloods, and by his mid-20s, he qualified as an O.G., which means original gangster or oldtimer. In eight years with his set, he was shot nine times. He is now a paraplegic and confined to a wheelchair.

"Just like when I was coming up. All I knew was my set and the jungle. I don't feel like I done nothing wrong in my life. . . To me, the street gangs're better than school. . . You gotta learn how to survive."

For Discussion

1. List some of the factors that might push a young male toward violence. Do these factors also affect young females? As a group, why are young males more violent than young females?

2. Does gang activity exist in your community? How has it changed in the last 10 years? In the last 20 years?

3. What can we do for young people like Wizard and B-dog?

Class Activity: Take Back the Park

Read the following scenario:

Once a haven for young children, Cowan Park has slowly changed into a hangout for rival gangs. Several gang-related shootings have taken place there in the last three months. Two weeks ago, a stray bullet killed four-year-old Monica Hines, who had been playing on the swings. Since that time, mothers have kept their young children away from the park.

Several community members have banded together to form a group called "Take Back the Park" (TBP). They want to rid the park of gang members and make it safe again for ordinary citizens. They have proposed the city adopt the following ordinance:

No person who is a member of a criminal street gang may enter any city park. A criminal street gang is any organization whose members have committed two or more of any the following crimes: murder, voluntary manslaughter, assault with a deadly weapon, robbery, or selling narcotics. Any person found guilty of this ordinance shall be subject to a $250 fine.

While this proposal has garnered support, it has also drawn criticism from a citizens group called "Keep It Constitutional." KIC is concerned that the ordinance violates the First Amendment to the U.S. Constitution. This amendment protects everyone's right to assemble in peace. KIC says this even includes gang members, because being in a gang is not against the law. If gang members break any laws, says KIC, they should be arrested. Otherwise, KIC believes, they should enjoy the same rights as everyone else. KIC also fears the police will use the law to pick up anyone who looks like a gang member. KIC believes the park problem can be solved by stationing police officers there.

TBP does not believe the ordinance violates the Constitution. According to TBP, gang members do not meet in the park to assemble in peace. They commit acts that keep others from the park. As things stand, law-abiding people are currently banned from the park. Police will have no trouble telling who are and who are not gang members. Gang members practically advertise who they are—with tattoos and gang colors. They flaunt their membership to intimidate others.

* * *

In this role-play, you will take the roles of members of TBP, KIC, and the city council. Each member of TBP and KIC will meet with a city council member and debate the ordinance. Then the city council as a whole will discuss and vote on the ordinance.

1. Divide the class into triads. Assign each student in the triads a role of KIC member, TBP member, or city council member.

2. Regroup the class to consult with one another while preparing for the role-play. KIC members should sit on one side of the room, TBP members on other side, and city council members in front. KIC and TBP members should think up their best arguments and city council members should think of questions to ask each side.

3. Redivide into triads and begin the role-play. TBP members will present their case first. Each side will have two minutes to make its presentation. The city council member can interrupt to ask questions. After both sides present, each council member should return to his or her seat at the front of the room.

4. The city council should discuss and vote on the ordinance.

Debriefing Questions

1. What were the strongest arguments for the ordinance? Against the ordinance? Why?

2. Do you think the ordinance violates the First Amendment? Why or why not?

3. Do you think it might sometimes be necessary to violate the Constitution to control crime? Why or why not?

4. What do you think could be done to reduce gang violence in parks? Explain.

Swindlers and Con Artists

The average loss from a street crime—a burglary or mugging or theft from a car—is less than $500. White-collar criminals, however, take far more from their victims. White-collar crime refers to acts like bank fraud, selling worthless stocks and bonds, even taking people's homes through illegal mortgage schemes.

Swindlers don't rely on violence or breaking and entering—they rely on the victims' trust. And in the process, they steal not only money and property, but often they destroy the victims' self-respect. They leave people fearful and less willing to trust others in the future.

The fast-money era of the 1970s and 1980s saw two notable swindles that cost many people *hundreds of millions* of dollars. These two swindlers were just examples of many other financial manipulators who nearly bankrupted the country. The saving-and-loan collapse brought on by junk bonds, corporate wheeling and dealing, and shaky investments has left America with a bill estimated at over $1 trillion. It will take generations to pay off this debt.

C. Arnholt Smith

C. Arnholt Smith started out as a teller for the Bank of America in Southern California. From this modest beginning, he built an empire of businesses, investment companies, and banks. His own bank in San Diego had nearly $1 billion in deposits, and he controlled $200 million more in tuna-packing, produce, transportation, and real estate. From this maze of holdings, Smith devised an operation that funneled millions into his own pockets.

Simply put, Smith made loans from his bank to his own companies, much of the money ending up in his private accounts. When the loans became due, Smith opened secret accounts in his bank to funnel money to his companies so that they could meet their loan payments. In effect, his bank was paying off the loans to Smith's companies. As head of the bank, Smith could deceive the bank depositors and stockholders he was stealing from.

From 1963 to 1973, the illegal loans increased from $17 million to $345 million. Even federal bank examiners did nothing. Smith had either fooled or pressured them into not reporting his illegal loan operation. But in 1972, a bank examiner finally blew the whistle. Smith's bank folded in 1973, and he was charged in federal court with conspiracy and fraud.

In 1975, Smith, age 76, was fined $30,000 and put on five years probation.

Charles Keating

One swindle that developed in the 1980s was even larger than Smith's. In 1984, an Arizona home builder named Charles H. Keating Jr. bought Lincoln Savings and Loan in Irvine, California. Keating immediately began funneling bank loans into gigantic high-risk ventures, land deals, luxury resorts, and junk bonds. He also set up a plan that moved profits and loans around from Lincoln to his own American Continental Corporation and to 55 subsidiaries, using land swaps and phony loans.

As the scheme got shaky, he needed more and more cash to hold his empire together. Keating directed his high-pressure sales force to begin selling another $200 million in nearly worthless investments to small investors, including many retired people. These people often wanted safe, government-insured investments. The sales force was instructed to tell the investors that the new junk bonds were "just as good" as insured deposits.

Former Lincoln Savings and Loan chief Charles Keating Jr. listens during one of his multi-million-dollar fraud trials. Keating was convicted in both state and federal courts. (Reuters/Bettmann.)

This scheme, too, began to come apart, and federal regulators started investigating. Keating appealed to friends in Washington, including five U.S. senators to whom he had contributed large sums. He managed to stall the investigation another two years.

The government finally seized Lincoln Savings and Loan in 1989, but it was too late for thousands of small investors. Paying off the insured loans will eventually cost the taxpayers over $2 billion, and there are many thousands of small investors who will get nothing.

Many of the victims were elderly, trying to stretch out their incomes during retirement. Some had to return to work. Others were forced on welfare. Several became so despondent from their financial loss that they committed suicide.

Keating, age 69, was convicted in California on 17 counts of state securities fraud and received the maximum sentence of 10 years in state prison as well as $250,000 in fines. In federal court, he was convicted on 73 counts of racketeering, conspiracy, and fraud. He was sentenced to 12 years and 7 months in federal prison and ordered to pay restitution of $122.4 million. He will serve his state and federal prison terms concurrently—at the same time—rather than consecutively—one after the other.

A s k
a n

Expert

Invite a police officer from the bunco squad to discuss with your class different con games and swindles.

Smaller Swindles and Con Games

Not all swindles involve banks and huge sums of money. Smaller swindles—called con games, scams, or buncos—cost Americans billions of dollars each year. Con games can vary from small schemes that take a few dollars from schoolchildren up to elaborate plots to steal large sums from the rich.

P.T. Barnum, the great showman, said, "There's a sucker born every minute." In fact, almost any of us could be suckered at one time or another. Con artists tend to be bright, articulate people. They are clever actors and very patient at waiting for the right moment to strike. In addition, they often work in groups to help bamboozle their victims. Often someone called a "shill," who seems to be an innocent bystander, begins the process of drawing in the victim. Complex con games can involve several other people called "cappers" who also pretend to be innocent. In fact, they are all part of the swindle team.

In the end, most con games rely on the victim's desire to get something for nothing. The swindler offers huge rewards at some later date in exchange for some of your money right now. Dallas police investigator W.E. Orzechowski says, "Con men basically are using the same old schemes, time after time, and they still work." The best bet to avoid a con game is to remember: If it seems too good to be true, it almost certainly is. Everyone should say no to schemes suggested by strangers.

The following section describes several classic swindles, and a few new ones developed for the telephone and computer age. To help you keep the bad guys straight, in each case we will call the swindler "Bunco" and the accomplice "Capper."

Pigeon Drop

Mr. Bunco approaches a well-dressed elderly woman named Ms. Green at a bus stop. While chatting in a friendly way, Mr. Bunco spots an envelope on the sidewalk. He peeks into the envelope and says it contains $6,000. Now Ms. Capper arrives and joins the conversation.

Mr. Bunco asks both women what they should do with the money. Soon they all agree to share the money, but Ms. Capper recommends that Mr. Bunco go to a nearby lawyer for advice.

Mr. Bunco returns and says the lawyer told him the three should share the $6,000. But Mr. Bunco reports that the law requires a neutral party to hold the money for six months. He says the lawyer has agreed to hold the $6,000 if they will each put up $1,000 to show good faith.

The minute poor Ms. Green adds her $1,000 to the envelope, the swindlers find a way to go off with it. They may even leave her with the original envelope—full of worthless paper.

Bank Examiner Swindle

Mr. Bunco visits Maria, a young housewife, and identifies himself as a bank examiner. He picked her out as a victim by watching her fill out a deposit slip at the bank. Mr. Bunco tells

---

Some Con Game Slang

Big Store—An elaborate confidence game involving a fake office and many people. The film *The Sting* shows a good example.

Blowoff—The last move in a con game.

Capper—An apparent bystander who is actually an accomplice of the swindler. Also, a steerer.

Fish—The victim. Also the mark, the pigeon, the customer.

Green—A very naive victim.

Hang paper—To write a fraudulent check.

Hurrah—The point in a con game where the victim is totally committed.

Red inking—The threat to eliminate the victim from some elaborate scheme just as he or she gets greedy.

Salt a mine—Placing a few real gems in a worthless mine, or something similar.

Squeeze—A crooked wheel game such as roulette.

Stall—The point in a swindle where the victim is momentarily delayed in order to increase his or her greed.

Touch—The money taken from a victim.

Maria that he believes one of the tellers at the bank is embezzling money. He asks Maria to help him trap the teller and offers her a reward of $500. After she agrees, Mr. Bunco asks Maria to withdraw a large sum of money from her account. "Bring the money home," he says. "One of our security people will come by and pick up the bills to examine the serial numbers." Maria withdraws the money, but of course it is picked up by Ms. Capper, who disappears with it.

Widow Scheme

Velma has just lost her husband. Mr. Bunco, acting as a Bible salesman, knocks at her door and asks for her husband. When she tells him of her husband's death, he expresses his deepest sympathy. He explains that her husband had ordered a beautiful, leather-bound family Bible as a surprise for her. "He paid $10 down, but the balance is $60." He is very apologetic, but he says he is only a poor man trying to make a living. Already emotionally vulnerable, the widow hands over the $60 for a Bible that is worth only $10. Mr. Bunco is off to the obituary columns to find another victim. (The film *Paper Moon* shows an example of this con.)

Badger Game

Ms. Bunco meets Fernando, a well-dressed traveling salesman, at a bar. They hit it off and Fernando tells her all about himself and his wife. Ms. Bunco invites Fernando to her apartment. As soon as they snuggle down on the sofa, Mr. Capper bursts in, pretending to be Ms. Bunco's husband. Mr. Capper shouts and raves on about how he, the honest husband, has been double-crossed. Mr. Capper then starts talking about going to Fernando's wife with the sordid details of his liaison with Ms. Bunco. At this point, Fernando almost begs Mr. Capper to take a large sum of money to keep quiet. After Fernando leaves, Ms. Bunco and Mr. Capper split the night's profits.

The Luxury Tax Scam

This is one of the most common telephone frauds. Mr. Bunco telephones Henry and tells him he has won a $2,500 cruise to the Bahamas and two diamond-studded Omega wristwatches, worth $500 each. Mr. Bunco promises to send the watches by express mail, but Henry has to pay the tax of $220. Henry mails off his check and either receives two imitation watches worth a few dollars or nothing at all. The cruise tickets never show up.

Telephone Boiler Rooms

Telephone swindles like the luxury tax scam have become big business, stealing as much as $10 billion a year. They are called "boiler room" scams because there are often whole banks of callers located in a room or office somewhere. When authorities begin to investigate, the whole operation can move on easily.

Here are some common boiler room schemes that either steal money directly or offer a service at hugely inflated prices:

- Phony prize offers, often vitamins and water purifiers
- Magazine subscriptions that are overpriced or never appear
- Schemes to fix bad credit for a fee
- Schemes to sell rare coins or gems
- Work-at-home offers that promise huge incomes

If you are approached by a caller like this, you should try to get an address or telephone number and then call the police or a local consumer affairs agency.

For Discussion

1. Do you think the penalty that C. Arnholt Smith received was appropriate? Was Charles Keating's sentence appropriate? Explain your answers.

2. Should the criminal justice system treat white-collar criminals like Charles Keating less harshly than violent criminals? Why or why not?

3. Why do victims fall for swindles? How can they avoid them?

CRIME AND DEFENSES

The Basics of Crime

Criminal cases differ from civil cases. In most civil cases, individuals sue one another seeking compensation for injuries done to them. But in criminal cases, the state prosecutes individuals for injuring *society*. Instead of seeking compensation from defendants, the state seeks to punish them. A criminal case focuses on whether a defendant has committed a crime against society and what sentence is appropriate to punish the defendant for the crime.

But what conduct should society outlaw? In many instances, this question is easy to answer. Almost everyone would agree that murder, rape, and arson should be prohibited. Debates arise, however, over other acts. Should prostitution or the use of drugs be made criminal? What about gambling or private sexual activity? What conduct should society prohibit? These debates raise questions about where criminal laws come from in the first place.

The Sources of Criminal Law

Our criminal laws spring from two major sources, laws passed by legislatures and what is called **common law**. Common law is judge -made. Instead of being created by a legis-

lature, it is based on legal precedents—court decisions—set by judges in earlier cases. English common law is an important root of our current legal system. Originally, the criminal laws in England were mostly unwritten. If a judge heard a case and believed that certain conduct was anti-social, he made it a crime and punished the offender accordingly.

The definitions of crimes and defenses that developed in the decisions of the English courts later became part of the common law adopted in early America. In turn, American courts began contributing to the common law. Over the years, a rather unwieldy body of law developed.

Common law has one serious problem. If it isn't written down in some simple way, how do people know if they are breaking the law? These excerpts from the trial of William Penn in 1670 show this problem:

> **Penn**: *I desire you would let me know by what law it is you prosecute me.*
>
> **Court**: *Upon the common law.*
>
> **Penn**: *Where is that common law?*
>
> **Court**: *You must not think that I am able to run up so many years, and over so many adjudged cases, which we call common law, to answer your curiosity. . . .*
>
> **Penn**: *It is too general and imperfect an answer, to say it is the common law, unless we knew both where and what it is. For where there is no law, there is no transgression . . . .*

Criminal Justice and the Branches of Government

The legislative, executive, and judicial branches of government play an important role in criminal justice. The following is a thumbnail sketch of the role of each at the local, state, and federal levels.

Legislative Branch. This branch **enacts** criminal laws. City councils and county supervisors pass ordinances. State legislatures enact the provisions of state penal codes. Congress passes federal criminal laws.

Executive Branch. This branch **enforces** the criminal laws passed by the legislative branch. Enforcement requires investigating crime, arresting suspects, prosecuting the case against them in court, and supervising convicted criminals. City police, county sheriffs, state police, and federal agencies, such as the FBI, catch suspected criminals. Government attorneys, known as prosecutors, then take charge and prosecute the cases under their jurisdiction. Prosecutors may represent a city attorney's office, district or county attorney's office, state attorney general's office, or U.S. attorney's office.

The executive branch also manages corrections—the housing and supervising of defendants convicted of crimes. Corrections officials manage city or county jails, state prisons, or federal prisons. Other corrections officials, such as probation and parole officers, supervise convicted criminals in the community.

Judicial Branch. This branch **applies** the criminal law. Applying the law entails interpreting it and deciding guilt or innocence in criminal cases. Each state has its own court system for trying people suspected of breaking state laws or local ordinances. The federal government has a separate federal court system for those suspected of breaking federal laws. But both systems, state and federal, have basically the same structure. Both have trial courts, appeals courts, and a final court of appeals.

• **Trial courts** hold criminal trials. In these courts, prosecutors and defense attorneys present evidence. Trial court judges and juries weigh the evidence, decide the facts of the case, and apply the law. If the defendant is found guilty, the judge pronounces a sentence. Normally this is the end of the criminal case. Sometimes, however, a defendant appeals to a higher court—an appeals court, also known as an appellate court.

> • **Appeals courts** do not decide the facts. They do not hear evidence. They hear arguments from attorneys about the law in the case. Appellate court judges review whether a trial court applied the law correctly. If the trial court did, then the appeals court **affirms** the trial court's decision. If it did not, then the **appeals court** reverses it. The losing side may appeal to the highest appeals court—the final court of appeals.

> • The **final court of appeals**, often called the supreme court, makes the final decision on the law of the jurisdiction. If it is the final court for a state, it decides the meaning of state laws and the state constitution. The U.S. Supreme Court, as the final court of appeals in the federal system, decides the meaning of federal laws and the U.S. Constitution. Because it decides the meaning of the U.S. Constitution, the Supreme Court may also hear appeals from state supreme courts on issues of U.S. constitutional law. The U.S. Supreme Court does not, however, decide the meaning of state laws or state constitutions.

For Discussion

1. What are the roles of the three branches of government? What agencies perform each of these roles? What are the names of these agencies in your state?

2. What is the difference between appeals courts and trial courts? Why do you think there is this difference?

3. What role does the U.S. Supreme Court play in criminal law? How is it different from the role of state supreme courts?

Court: It is . . . that which many have studied 30 or 40 years to know, and would you have me tell you in a moment?

Penn: Certainly, if the common law be so hard to understand it is far from being common.

American states are divided on the issue of whether criminal courts can declare an act criminal if there is no specific statute against that act. Some states still recognize the power of the courts to create common law crimes, although this power is very seldom exercised. In most states and in the federal courts, however, common law crimes have been abolished altogether. In these jurisdictions, only conduct that is expressly forbidden by a criminal statute is a crime.

Thus the primary source of criminal law today is legislative enactment. By the second half of the 19th century, legislatures had seen the problems of relying on common law and had begun to enact comprehensive criminal codes. Many of these codes embodied all of the elements of the old common law.

Classification of Offenses

The common law divided crimes into two categories—felonies and misdemeanors. Common law felonies were murder, manslaughter, rape, sodomy, mayhem, robbery, arson, burglary, and larceny. All other crimes were misdemeanors.

Under modern criminal law, the distinction between felonies and misdemeanors is spelled out by statute. Most states make any crime punishable by death or by imprisonment in a state prison a felony. A crime punishable by time in a local jail is a misdemeanor. Other states distinguish by length of imprisonment, not place of imprisonment. For example, a felony is often defined as a crime punishable by one year or more in prison.

For Discussion

1. What characteristics distinguish criminal from civil cases?

2. What are the two sources of criminal law? How are they different?

3. Today, many states have done away with common law crimes. Only acts specifically defined as illegal can be punished. What would happen if some criminal managed to find a loophole? What if an individual did something

A s k
a n

Expert

Invite a criminal attorney to come to your class and discuss the legislative, executive, and judicial agencies involved in criminal law in your state.

obviously harmful to others that was not specifically outlawed by statute? Should the courts be allowed to recognize a new crime to fill the gap? Explain your answer.

Class Activity: Felony or Misdemeanor?

Break into pairs. Read and discuss with your partner the acts listed below. Then fill out a chart answering the following questions:

- Should the act described be a crime? Why or why not?
- If so, should it be a felony or misdemeanor? Why?

Then reconvene as a class and share group answers.

a. Margaret tells the police that an officer who stopped her on the street was verbally abusive to her. She is lying.

b. Sam sees a young boy struggling in a pond and calling for help. Sam does nothing and the boy drowns.

c. Dick and Suzanne are living together. They have no intention of getting married in the near future.

d. Robert holds a toy pistol to Ashley's head and demands all of her cash and jewelry. She believes it's a real gun and hands over the goods.

e. Pedro calls a local pizza parlor and orders five pizzas to be delivered to a phony address.

f. Jane's country is at war. She shoots and kills an enemy soldier.

g. John lets his dog run wild around the neighborhood, even though he knows that the dog scares young children and constantly knocks over garbage cans looking for food.

CRIME BEAT

Imagine you are a crime beat reporter for a local news outlet. This job often requires that you find information for fast-breaking stories, long feature articles, and even for editorials on crime-related issues. To get this information, you will need to use different sources depending on what your editor assigns you. These sources include:

- **Criminal lawyers**, such as prosecutors, public defenders, and private defense attorneys. Call or visit your local prosecutor's or public defender's office. Or you may even call your state attorney general's office.

- **Court personnel**, such as judges, commissioners, bailiffs, and clerks.

- **Police officers**. Visit your local police station.

- **Criminal justice professionals**, such as probation officers, parole officers, and corrections officials at jails and prisons.

- **News reporters**, especially those who work for legal newspapers distributed to lawyers.

- **Library**, especially a law library, often located at a courthouse or law school. A law library will have your state's penal, or criminal code, appeals court decisions, legal dictionaries, and numerous other books. The reference librarians can be a particularly helpful source.

Today your editor has assigned you to get background information for a series of feature stories and editorials on how crimes are classified in your state. You need to find out if the crimes listed below are felonies or misdemeanors in your state and what their penalties are. Since the series includes some editorials, you have been asked to give your opinion on some issues. Decide for each crime:

(1) Do you agree with the classifications and punishments for these offenses? Explain.

(2) Should any of them be treated as more or less serious crimes than they are currently classified? Explain.

Submit a one-page summary of your findings.

- **Murder**
- **Battery**
- **Shoplifting**
- **Marijuana Possession**
- **Prostitution**
- **Robbery**
- **Automobile theft**
- **Vandalism**
- **Arson**
- **Bigamy**

Ingredients of a Crime

The criminal justice system has become very careful to define exactly what a crime is. The system is also careful to define what must be proven to show who committed a crime. This is only fair if an individual is to be punished.

Almost every crime has four basic ingredients:

1. A prohibited act. At common law, this was called the *actus reus*. The act is almost always defined by a statute. The law does not punish people for having criminal thoughts alone. There must be an act. In murder, for example, the act is killing someone. In a few rare cases, *failing to act* is a crime when a person has a legal duty to act. For example, if a parent lets a child die of a long illness without seeking medical help, it can be a crime.

2. Criminal intent. At common law, this was called *mens rea*, or a guilty mind. This can be the most difficult ingredient to prove. It will be discussed in more detail below.

3. Concurrence of the act and the intent. The person has to intend the act at the same time he or she commits it. For example, Sluggo wants to kill Nancy. Then he changes his mind and forgets all about it. A month later he hits her by accident with a car and kills her. This is not legally murder because the intent to kill and the act did not occur at the same time.

4. Causation. The act has to cause the harmful result.

Criminal Intent

Criminal laws generally punish only those who have criminal intent, a guilty mind. But what constitutes a guilty mind, the so called mens rea, depends on the crime. The criminal intent required for most crimes usually falls into one of four categories:

1. Specific intent. This is the easiest type to define. It means the person intended just the result that happened. The person did it on purpose. Certain crimes, such as theft, require specific intent. To convict John of theft, for example, the prosecution must prove not only that John took Mary's car, but also that he did not intend to return it.

2. General intent. This means that the person either knew the result would happen or consciously disregarded the extreme likelihood that it would happen. For example, John picks up a gun on New Year's Eve and shoots it toward a crowd of people. A bullet hits Mary and kills her. He didn't kill Mary on purpose, but he must have known he would kill, or was likely to kill,

a CRIME *is made up of*

CRIMINAL ACT	+	CRIMINAL INTENT	+	CONCURRENCE of ACT and INTENT	+	CAUSATION
Conduct prohibited by law		**Kinds** (1) General (2) Specific (3) Criminal Negligence (4) Strict Liability		Act and intent must occur at the same time.		Result must be caused by the act.

= *crime*

someone. This would meet the general intent requirement of second-degree murder.

3. Criminal negligence. This means that a person does some act unintentionally but with an extreme lack of care. For example, John is drag racing down a city street when Mary, a pedestrian, steps in front of his car. Mary is killed.

4. Strict liability. This means no mental state is required at all. Anyone doing the act is guilty regardless of intent. Almost all common law crimes required some mental state. But bigamy is an example of a common law crime that requires no intent. For example, if John mistakenly believes he has divorced his first wife and he marries Mary, he can be convicted of bigamy. Other examples of strict liability crimes include most health, safety, and traffic offenses.

Class Activity: Did They Commit Crimes?

1. Break into groups of four. Read and discuss the five cases that follow. Refer to the explanations above of the four basic elements of a crime—(1) act, (2) intent, (3) concurrence of act and intent, and (4) causation. Assign one element of a crime to each person in the group. Have that person say whether that element is present in each case, then discuss whether or not it is. Refer to the glossary if you need a crime defined.

2. When the discussion is completed, assign one case to each student for reporting back to the whole class.

3. Reconvene as a class and share your answers. Be prepared to explain and discuss them.

Case 1: Tim

Marcos and his friends, Tim and Jill, were having a beer together at their local bar. When Tim went to the jukebox to play more music, Marcos asked Jill to dance. Tim became jealous and punched Marcos in the face. Tim has been charged with battery.

Case 2: Karen

Karen told everyone that she hated Emily for stealing her boyfriend. Karen said she wanted to hurt Emily. Two months pass and Karen nudges a flowerpot off her second-floor patio. The flowerpot hits Emily and gives her a concussion. Karen swears that she forgot all about her threats and didn't mean any harm. Karen is charged with battery.

Case 3: Ray

Mr. Ray Anderson sat on his front porch cleaning his rifle. Many children were playing on the sidewalk in front of his home. When Mr. Anderson turned the gun over it went off, killing one of the children in the crowd. He has been charged with involuntary manslaughter.

Case 4: Gina

Gina was shopping in her favorite department store. She saw a sweater that she liked, stuffed it into her book bag, and ran out of the store. A security guard caught her. Gina has been charged with shoplifting.

Case 5: Gayle

Gayle shoots Mary in the big toe. Mary goes to the hospital to have her toe examined and treated. One week later, Mary dies of blood poisoning that she got from an unsterilized medical instrument. Gayle is charged with murder.

Murder Most Foul and Other Crimes

Murder most foul. . .most foul, strange and unnatural.
> —Shakespeare, *Hamlet*, Act I, Sc. 5

No crime seems to fascinate people more than murder. Most religions teach the basic tenet, "Thou shalt not kill." Yet, throughout the ages, storytellers have told and retold tales of murder: Cain and Abel, many Greek tragedies, Shakespeare's *Macbeth*, thousands of mystery novels, crime TV shows. In our country, the most severe penalty our society can inflict—death—is reserved for those who commit murder under certain conditions.

Like all crimes, murder is made up of particular elements. These must be proved before a person can be convicted. Let's examine some of the specific elements of murder and those of some other important crimes.

Murder at common law and under many modern statutes is the unlawful killing of a human being with *malice aforethought*. Malice aforethought is the intent, or *mens rea*, element of this crime. It doesn't mean what you might expect it to. Malice aforethought is sometimes defined as an *actual or implied intention* to kill with no provocation by the victim.

Actual intent is found when the defendant consciously meant to cause another's death.

CRIME BEAT

Imagine you are a crime beat reporter for a local news outlet. Your editor has assigned you to do background research for a feature on murder and theft crimes. You need to find out:

• *What are the homicide offenses under your state's criminal laws? What are their penalties?*

• *How are the crimes of larceny, burglary, and robbery defined in your state? What are the penalties for each?*

Submit a one-page summary of your findings.

For ideas on sources for this information, see "Crime Beat" on page 31.

Implied intention exists when the defendant either

(1) intended to cause great bodily harm *or*

(2) should have known that the act would result in death or great bodily harm.

Consider some examples:

• If Barbara hates Michael, decides to kill him, and picks up a knife and does so, malice aforethought is present. In this case, Barbara's malice aforethought was an *actual* intent to kill Michael and she could be charged with murder.

• If Barbara decides to hurt Michael badly, stabs him in the chest and kills him, malice aforethought is also present. This time the intent to kill is *implied*, because she did not specifically intend to kill, but only cause great bodily harm.

• If Barbara hates Michael, decides to scare him, pushes him in front of oncoming traffic at a street corner, and Michael dies as a result, malice aforethought is also established. In this case, though Barbara didn't intend to kill or even seriously injure Michael, she should have known her actions would cause him to die or suffer great bodily harm. Under the law, Barbara had *implied* intent to kill Michael.

Degrees of Homicide

Over the years, law has developed several degrees of criminal homicide. The punishment a convicted person may receive depends on the degree of the homicide. The worst degrees of homicide are commonly called murder and the lesser degrees manslaughter.

First-degree murder is a deliberate and premeditated killing done with malice aforethought. This is a cold-blooded murder. "Deliberate" means it was done with a cool mind, capable of reflection. "Premeditated" means the person actually reflected on the murder before committing it. And "malice aforethought," of course, means that the killer had the intent to kill. It takes all three elements—deliberation, premed-

Mass murderer Charles Manson has spent most of his life in prison. (UPI/Bettmann.)

itation, and malice aforethought—to establish the *specific intent* for first-degree murder.

Second-degree murder is a killing done with malice aforethought, but without deliberation and premeditation. This covers all murders that are not in the first degree.

Felony murder is any killing done while a person is committing a felony. If the killing is done while committing certain felonies, such as robbery, rape, arson, or burglary, it is classified as first-degree murder. Killings done while committing other felonies are considered second-degree murder.

Voluntary manslaughter is an intentional killing committed without malice aforethought. The killer must:

• be seriously provoked by the victim;

• act in the heat of the anger; and

• not have had an opportunity to cool off.

The provoking act does not excuse the killing, but it makes the crime a lesser degree than second-degree murder.

Involuntary manslaughter is an unintended killing that takes place during a crime that is not a felony. It can also be a killing caused by criminal negligence.

Vehicular homicide is a crime recognized by many states. It covers killings from automobile accidents when the driver is criminally negligent.

Different Kinds of Stealing

The law recognizes many forms of stealing. The differences depend on where and how the theft occurred.

Larceny is the usual legal word for theft. It means illegally taking someone else's property with no intention of giving it back. For example, if someone walks by your desk and takes your wallet, that person has committed larceny.

In some states, larceny also includes embezzlement, tricking others into handing over their property, or even writing a bad check. There are usually two categories of larceny or theft:

1. **Grand theft** means stealing property worth over a certain amount. The amount varies from state to state, but it is usually around $400. Grand theft is a felony. If your wallet contained $1,000, stealing it would be grand theft.

2. **Petty theft** means stealing property worth less than the grand theft amount. Petty theft is a misdemeanor.

Burglary is the unlawful entry into any building with the intent to steal or commit a felony. At one time, in common law, burglary meant breaking into a home at night to steal. That definition has been expanded to include illegally entering any building at any time of day to steal or commit any felony. Some states have expanded it to include breaking into cars. If a thief broke into your office to steal your wallet, the crime would be burglary.

Robbery, unlike burglary, is a crime against the person. It is forcible stealing—the taking of a person's property by violence or by threatening violence. If someone grabs you and demands your wallet, then takes it and runs away, that person has committed robbery.

Armed robbery means using a dangerous weapon to take something from a person. Even pretending to have a weapon is considered armed robbery. If someone pulls a knife on you and steals your wallet, that person has committed armed robbery. Armed robbery is a more serious offense than simple robbery, and it carries a stiffer penalty.

For Discussion

1. The penalties for these forms of stealing in every state are increasingly harsh:

> Theft—Burglary—Robbery—Armed Robbery

If a wallet containing only $20 is stolen in each of these cases, why do you think the punishments get harsher? Is this fair?

2. The penalties for these forms of homicide in every state are increasingly harsh:

> Involuntary Manslaughter—Voluntary Manslaughter—Second-Degree Murder—First-Degree Murder

If one person is killed in each of these cases, why do you think the punishments get harsher? Is this fair?

3. Howard attempts a first-degree murder but fails and harms no one. Fred is guilty of involuntary manslaughter when he accidentally kills a person. Which person should be punished more harshly—Howard or Fred? Why? (If you do the "Crime Beat" activity on page 34, find out what punishment your state gives for attempted murder and involuntary manslaughter.)

Class Activity: Death in the School Halls

1. Break up into groups of four, and read the following case:

> One day in gym class, Adam made fun of the way Rick was shooting a basketball. Rick told Adam to shut up or else he would take care of him. Adam couldn't help making another comment on the way Rick was shooting. Rick grabbed Adam and beat him up.
>
> Adam ended up with a broken nose and a black eye, and he decided to get even. He dug his

NEWSBREAK

1. As a whole class, brainstorm and list as many crimes as you can think of, including any mentioned in this book, such as murder, rape, etc. List them on the board, or on a large sheet of paper so the list can be saved.

2. All students should watch their daily newspapers for a week or two, looking for articles which mention these crimes. Bring the articles to class.

3. Select one article for each of the different crimes on your list. Break into small groups and assign one article or more to each small group.

Your group should discuss the article and try to identify the elements of the crime from the facts given in the newspaper stories. For example, explain:

- *What type of criminal intent is required for the crime? Is there any evidence of intent in the newspaper story?*

- *What prohibited act did the suspect commit? How?*

- *What was the result of the suspect's act?*

father's pistol out of the attic, loaded it, and headed off to school to find Rick. He waited at Rick's locker for almost an hour, but Rick never showed up. Adam became impatient. Nervously he checked the gun again to make sure that all the chambers were loaded. Just then the school bell rang out, startling Adam into firing the gun by accident. The bullet ricocheted off a locker and hit a student who was walking out of class. She was killed instantly.

2. In each group, assign one person to each of the following crimes: murder, felony murder, voluntary manslaughter, and involuntary manslaughter. Each person should decide whether the crime described in "Death in the School Halls" fits the crime assigned to him or her. Be prepared to explain why or why not.

3. Discuss the case in your group. Go through the crimes, one by one, and the person responsible for that crime should explain whether the case fits that crime or not. Discuss why or why not.

4. Reconvene the class and compare your findings.

Legal Defenses to Crime

In our criminal justice system, persons accused of a crime are innocent until proven guilty. In our system, defendants do *not* have to prove they are innocent. The prosecution must prove that defendants are guilty.

During a trial, the criminal defendant and the defense lawyer do everything they can to prevent the prosecutor from proving guilt. They introduce their own evidence, they examine and cross-examine witnesses, and they make arguments. If they keep the prosecution from establishing every element of the crime beyond a reasonable doubt, the defense wins.

Defendants in our society have even a further protection. Our criminal law recognizes some special legal defenses, known as **affirmative defenses**. The three most common affirmative defenses involve issues of **insanity**, **self-defense**, and **entrapment**. If the defendant successfully establishes one of these defenses, it does not matter whether the prosecution can prove the elements of the crime or not. The defendant is not guilty. These affirmative defenses have raised many controversies.

The Insanity Defense

Defendants will be acquitted if they can prove that, at the time their crime was committed, they were legally insane. This defense has always been controversial. But public debate intensified after President Ronald Reagan was shot in 1981 and his attacker was found not guilty by reason of insanity. The defendant in that case, John Hinckley Jr., purchased a gun and stalked the president for some time. He wrote a letter to a famous actress telling her what he planned to do. Millions of Americans watched in horror as videotapes of Hinckley shooting straight at the president played over and over again on national television. "How could this person be found not guilty?" they demanded.

For criminal law, "insanity" has a special meaning. Even in this context, legal scholars and lawmakers have disagreed about what constitutes insanity for a defense to a criminal charge. Over the years, several different legal tests for determining insanity have been developed, but none has been universally accepted as valid. These different standards are currently used at the federal and state levels:

1. The *M'Naghten* Rule. Under this traditional approach, defendants must show that because of their mental illness, they either did not know what they were doing or they did not know it was wrong. (*M'Naghten Case*, 1843.)

Critics of the *M'Naghten* rule point out that it does not protect defendants who cannot control themselves. Thus defendants can be convicted under the *M'Naghten* rule even if they cannot avoid committing the crime because of mental illness.

2. The Irresistible Impulse Rule. In some states, defendants will be acquitted if they can prove that the crime was committed because of an insane impulse which controlled their will. This test of insanity often supplements the *M'Naghten* approach. (*Parsons v. State*, 1887.)

3. The *Durham* Rule. To prove insanity under this rule, defendants must show that the crime was "the product of mental disease or mental defect" of some sort. Because of the vagueness of this rule, it has a limited following today. (*Durham v. U.S.*, 1954.)

4. *Model Penal Code* Test, also known as the substantial capacity test. A much stricter rule than *Durham*, this test has grown popular in recent years. Many states have abandoned the *M'Naghten* rule in favor of it. Under this approach, defendants are insane if, because of a mental disease or defect, they:
   • Lacked substantial capacity to appreciate the criminality of their conduct; *or*
   • Lacked substantial capacity to conform their conduct to the requirements of the law. (*Model Penal Code* Sec. 4.01 [1].)
   Some jurisdictions omit this part of the test.

Under any of these tests, defendants who prove their case will be found not guilty by reason of insanity. Often this means the defendants will be committed to mental hospitals. They will not be released in many jurisdictions until they can prove beyond a reasonable doubt that they are sane or that they no longer pose any threat to society.

Some jurisdictions have developed a new verdict—**guilty but mentally ill**. The meaning of this verdict varies from jurisdiction to jurisdiction. In some jurisdictions, it *replaces* the verdict of not guilty by reason of insanity. In these jurisdictions, a jury must return one of three verdicts—guilty, not guilty, or guilty but mentally ill. The latter verdict means that the defendant was legally insane when committing the crime.

In other jurisdictions, "guilty but mentally ill" means the defendant was *not* legally insane, but was mentally ill when committing the crime. It means that the defendant's defense of insanity has fallen short, but the jury recognizes that the defendant has mental problems. These jurisdictions have not replaced the insanity defense. They have added this new verdict—guilty, but mentally ill—to the other verdicts juries may return—guilty, not guilty, and not guilty by reason of insanity.

The effect of the verdict is the same in most jurisdictions. The defendant will receive a standard prison sentence, but may serve it in a mental hospital.

Self-Defense

You're alone in your apartment, asleep at 3 a.m. You wake up all of a sudden with your heart pounding. Then you realize your bedroom window is sliding open inch by inch. Your legs begin to tremble. A tall shadowy figure steps into the room. In terror, you pick up a lamp by your bed and hurl it. The lamp shatters against the man's head and he slumps to the floor.

Can you be charged with battery? Yes, it's possible, but it's not very likely. Even if you were prosecuted for battery, you would have a strong claim of self-defense.

John Hinckley Jr., who attempted to kill President Reagan, returns with agents after completing extensive psychiatric tests at federal prison. A jury ultimately found Hinckley not guilty by reason of insanity. (UPI/Bettmann.)

Generally, you have a right to use whatever force is necessary to defend yourself if you feel you face a threat of immediate violence. For a proper claim of self-defense, you must establish that:

- you reasonably believed that the force was required for your own or someone else's protection—even it that belief turns out to be mistaken;
- the threatened harm was about to happen and the attacker was willing and able to injure you; *and*
- the force used in self-defense was reasonable—that is, no more than was necessary to prevent the victim from inflicting harm.

The law is much stricter about using *deadly* force in self-defense. Deadly force may only be used when you reasonably believe, based on the circumstances, that

- the attacker was about to kill you or inflict great bodily harm; and
- the deadly force was the only way of preventing the harm.

Entrapment

Several famous trials have featured the issue of entrapment. Entrapment occurs when a police officer, or any agent of the government, lures a defendant into committing a crime. Most people would agree that it is unfair to entice someone into committing an act and then punish the person for it.

But the issue is not always that simple. Under the law, if the defendant would not have committed the crime, except for the government's enticement, then the defendant is not guilty. But if the defendant already had the idea of the crime in mind and an officer only made it possible to commit the crime, then an entrapment defense would fail.

The federal government's **Abscam** operation in the early 1980s is an example of an entrapment defense that failed. The FBI invented a phony Arab sheik, Kambir Abdul Rahmen, to try to bribe one U.S. senator and seven representatives. The FBI filmed the sting operation and used the films as evidence in the trials for accepting bribes. The defendants argued that the FBI had entrapped them, but this defense failed. Why?

The FBI had received reliable information that these particular congressmen were corrupt. "Sheik Rahmen" did not approach just any congressmen. He chose ones who were reported to show criminal intent already. The FBI, said the courts, had merely given them an opportunity to do something they already had the intent to do.

On the other hand, the **John DeLorean** case at about the same time, demonstrates an entrapment defense that succeeded. DeLorean was an auto company executive who left Ford in the late 1970s to set up his own sports car company in Northern Ireland. His new gull-wing DeLorean sports car, named after himself, came out in the midst of a gasoline crisis and did not sell very well. It was well known that his company was in deep trouble.

FBI agents claimed that an informant told them DeLorean was searching for illegal ways to keep the company afloat. In an elaborate sting operation, similar to Abscam, undercover operators approached him with a scheme to import

$24 million in cocaine. They videotaped him accepting the deal and brought him to trial in 1983.

DeLorean's lawyers argued that he had a clean record, that the government's witnesses were unreliable, and that the FBI had lured and entrapped him into the crime. Despite the video-tape, the jury found him not guilty. One juror said, "The way the government acted in this case was not appropriate." After the result, many legal experts suggested that the government would probably be much more wary of setting up elaborate sting operations.

In a similar development in 1992, the Supreme Court threw out the conviction of a man they felt had been entrapped. Postal inspec-tors thought that a Nebraska man named **Keith Jacobson** was predisposed to buying child pornography. They sent him an offer in the mail and he turned it down. For the next 26 months, they repeatedly sent him offers to buy child pornography. Finally, he bought two magazines and they arrested him. He was convicted, but the Supreme Court on a 5-4 vote overturned the con-viction. The court said that the government had "overstepped the line between setting a trap for the 'unwary innocent' and the 'unwary criminal' . . . and . . . failed to establish that [Jacobson] was independently predisposed to commit the crime." (*Jacobson v. U.S.*)

For Discussion

1. What special protection do affirmative defenses offer defendants?

2. What are the differences among the various insanity defenses?

3. What must you prove for a claim of self-defense?

4. In recent years, several victims of long-term child and spousal abuse have claimed self-defense as a justification for killing their abusers. Do you believe this defense is valid if they kill their abusers when they are not being threatened? Why or why not?

5. Do you think the defense of entrapment makes sense? Why or why not?

Class Activity: The Insanity Defense

1. Break up into groups of four. Assign each person in the group one of the insanity tests described in the preceding section.

2. Read "Mark's Statement" below. Have each person apply his or her assigned insanity test to Mark to see if it fits. Have the whole group discuss whether each test fits.

3. Reconvene and compare the findings from each group.

Mark's Statement

During his trial for murdering a friend, defendant Mark Khasabian made the following statement:

> I knew that it was wrong, but I couldn't help myself. During the night of April 30, Beelzebub, grand duke of Hell, came to me with biddings from the master. He told me to kill my friend. I resisted, but his will was too strong and finally I had to do what I was told.

Debriefing Questions

1. Which insanity tests fit Mark's case? Which do not?

2. If Mark's statement is true, do you think he should be found not guilty by reason of insanity? Why or why not?

3. Which insanity test, if any, do you think is best? Why?

Class Activity: What Defense is Valid?

1. Break up into groups of three. Assign each person in the group one of the following legal defenses: insanity, self-defense, entrapment.

2. Read each of the hypotheticals below. Have each person apply his or her assigned legal defense to each hypothetical to see if it fits.

3. Have the whole group discuss why that legal defense might or might not work.

4. Reconvene and compare the findings from each group.

CRIME BEAT

Imagine you are a crime beat reporter for a local news outlet. Your editor has assigned you to do background research for a feature article on the insanity defense and some other affirmative defenses. Find out:

1. What test for insanity is applied by criminal courts in your state? What happens in your state to someone found not guilty by reason of insanity? Does your state allow a verdict of guilty but mentally ill?

2. Define and give an example of the following defenses to crimes: infancy, intoxication, necessity, and duress. Are these defenses included in your state's criminal code?

Submit a one-page summary of your findings.

For ideas on sources for this information, see "Crime Beat" on page 31.

Peter Hope

Peter Hope is charged with assault with a deadly weapon. He was walking down the street. Without warning, a man began hitting him with a rolled-up newspaper. Peter Hope pulled out a gun and shot him.

Martha Heart

Officer Martin, in plain clothes, approached Martha Heart on the street and offered to sell her a "hot" radio for a cheap price. Martha at first refused, but the officer convinced her to buy it. He then arrested Martha for receiving stolen property.

Karen Sanchez

Karen Sanchez had her home burglarized twice in the last month. One evening, she heard a noise on her front porch. She grabbed her son's baseball bat and flung open the door to discover a man bending forward with his hand on the doorknob. He jumped upright and reached into his pocket. Afraid that he had a weapon, Karen struck him across the face, partially blinding him. As it turned out, the man had come to ask for a charitable donation and had been reaching for his identification card. Karen has been charged with assault with a deadly weapon.

Class Activity: Debate on Insanity

Choose a pro or con position on the following statement:

The insanity defense should be abolished.

Research the question at your school or community library. Magazines should be a good source, so check the computer index to periodicals or the *Reader's Guide to Periodical Literature*. Write a two-or three-page essay supporting your opinion. These can be used for a class discussion or debate.

THE
POLICE

Police officers do not have an easy job. When enforcing the law, they deal with society's problems—quarreling spouses, drug and alcohol addiction, serious traffic accidents, and senseless violence. Sometimes they must face danger and make lightning-quick decisions.

To be effective, the police need public support. Many of their contacts with the public help build this support—the police find a child, solve a crime, return stolen property to its owner. But other contacts may erode public support. Some of us have received traffic tickets or had other minor unpleasant encounters with the police. We grumble and go on our way. Others of us report serious problems with the police including harassment, beatings, and other abuses of authority.

When abuses do occur—whether through error, indifference, or overzealous enforcement—the criminal justice system must act to correct them. In a democracy, part of enforcing the law is upholding the constitutional rights of all citizens. Police authority cannot go unchecked. What that authority should be and whether it is properly used in particular situations are issues that can make police work difficult and sometimes controversial.

In this chapter, we go behind the badge to explore law enforcement in our society. In doing so, you will encounter some interesting questions: What might it be like to be a police officer responding in the line of duty? What are people's attitudes about the police and how might that affect police work? How do our laws affect police investigations and arrests? What are the proper limits of police authority? This chapter will give you a better picture of police in our society.

POLICE AND SOCIETY

Question of Attitude

In 1829, when Sir Robert Peel organized the first police force in England, he said: "The police should maintain a relationship with the public that gives reality to the historic tradition that the police are the public and the public are the police." Has this ideal of police -community relations been borne out over time? Does the public believe that the police serve its interests? Do the police think of themselves as public servants? Consider the following viewpoints.

"Thank God, They Got There Fast"

"I live in an apartment house with a swimming pool. For a long time, they didn't let people with small children live there. Last year they changed the rules so they could fill all of the apartments. Several families with little kids moved in.

"Two weeks ago, I was walking down the outside stairs when I saw him—a little kid floating face down in the pool with all his clothes on. My mother had worried about somebody drowning ever since the little kids got there. I ran over fast to get him out of the water. He was in the shallow end. I reached right down and grabbed his arm and pulled him out. He really looked weird. I guess I started

yelling because people started coming over fast. Somebody yelled to call the cops. Somebody else grabbed the kid and started giving artificial respiration, you know, the old kind where you push on the back.

"Well, it couldn't have been more than 60 seconds before I heard a siren. By that time, the little kid's mother was there, yelling and just about out of her mind. A minute later, two cops came running in. One of them grabbed the kid and started doing mouth-to-mouth resuscitation. That one kept working on the kid. The other asked for the mother, and then, almost as fast as they came they were gone with the kid and the mother.

"That kid was really lucky. They got him to the hospital and saved his life. I couldn't believe it. I thought he was dead for sure. Thank God, the cops got there fast."

"I Was Just Driving Home From the Movies"

"I was taking out a new girl in my brother's car. I wanted to make a good impression. After the show, we stopped off for pizza, and I suppose it was about 12:30 or 1 a.m. when we really started for home. I was driving slow because I wasn't in any hurry to get there. I can't remember doing anything unusual at all.

"The car behind me turned out to be a cop. All of a sudden, on goes the red light. Well, I couldn't figure out what was happening, but I sure stopped as fast as I could. As the officer approached the car, I got out my driver's license. I've always been scared of cops for some reason, and so my hand was shaking. I hoped the girl wouldn't notice because it would be embarrassing to show that I was scared.

"When the cop got to the car, I rolled down the window. He said, 'Out of the car, boy!' I got out, and he made me lean up against the car. Then he kicked one of my legs out so far I thought I was going to fall down. He searched me and patted me down or whatever they call it. He didn't find anything, so I thought he would let me stand up straight, but he made me stay where I was.

"Then he asked my date to get out of the car. He asked her to open her purse, and he looked inside with his flashlight. Then he had her put the purse back in the car and told her to stand in front of the car in the light.

"After that, he searched the whole car—the glove compartment, the ash trays, under the seats. He even pulled the back seat loose and just left it that way. Then he took my keys from the ignition, opened the trunk, took out every-

thing, and laid it on the ground. When he still didn't find anything, he said, 'Don't let me catch you out this late again, boy!' Then he went back to his patrol car and just drove off.

"I don't think it's fair to treat people like that. He just left me there with my car all torn up without any explanation or anything. At least he could have told us what he was looking for or something."

"If I Live To Be a Hundred, I'll Never Understand!"

"The guys I feel sorry for are the new ones, the guys straight out of the Police Academy. How they'll ever adjust to this city, I'll never know. About the time they get used to working in one area, they'll be moved to another. Then by the time they're used to that, they'll go out west. When I started, things were much easier—you knew who your friends and enemies were. Now, you never can tell. Just last week, two officers were killed answering a medical emergency call. Imagine, going to help somebody and getting killed. It wasn't a

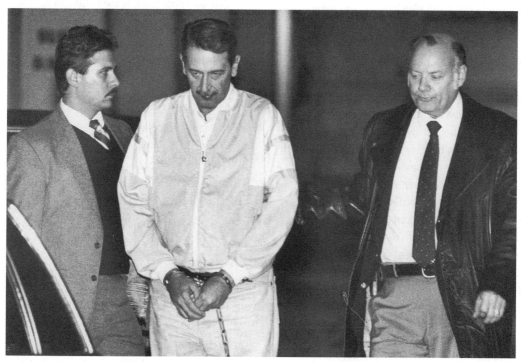

U.S. marshals escort a defendant to federal court. (UPI/Bettmann.)

robbery or a silent alarm or anything—just a medical emergency.

"As if things weren't bad enough, now we have to worry about people complaining about excessive force and police brutality. Let me tell you, you don't understand the pressure of police work. Even the most innocent encounter can turn violent. You have to be on guard all the time. When something happens, you better be ready. You don't know how difficult it is to make a split-second decision that may affect not only your life but the lives of many other people. If we make a mistake, we have to worry about possible legal proceedings and losing our jobs. Everyone is worried about the criminal and his legal rights, but what about dead cops? Isn't anyone worried about us?

"It's getting so hard to arrest a man correctly that we really need a lawyer in the car. You arrest a guy, give him his rights, and ask him questions, but why should he answer your questions? You've just told him he doesn't have to. If you are lucky enough to make an arrest that the D.A. will file on, the court will probably throw it out on a technicality, or else the judge and the lawyers will plea bargain, and some guy who deserved 10 years will get probation.

"What I'd like to know is, why are we stuck with all this crap? I mean, who gave us the problems that we deal with every day? Why do the kids take drugs? Why do we have to worry about the lives of criminals more than our own? It's not our fault they choose to attack and threaten us, but everybody thinks we have perfect, planned responses to every possible incident that could occur. All we can do is play it by ear and hope we've done the right thing. Doing the wrong thing can mean the end of our lives, and—even if we live—a possible police brutality charge or suspension.

"No, I'll tell you, if I live to be a hundred, I'll never understand."

* * *

Many people today, including police officers, wonder about the role of the police. According to research, young children think police give orders and punish people. They don't envision the police as helping people and enforcing laws. Research also indicates that the police's **power**, not their service to the public, captures the imagination of young people. Similarly, adults often believe that police officers perform their jobs not out of any sense of dedication to the community, but for the pleasure that comes from exercising power over others.

How accurate are these perceptions of the police? One study suggests that the police themselves have a much different view of their motivations. Five hundred officers, from new recruits to veterans, were asked to respond to a form entitled, "I am a policeman because . . ." Given a list of 40 possible responses, they were asked to choose the 10 most important to them. The top five vote-getters were:

- I want to improve the community.
- I want to improve police work.
- I am part of a team effort.
- I feel a civic responsibility.
- My imagination is stimulated.

On the other hand, at the bottom of the list, only about 10 percent of the officers said:

- I can find excitement regularly.
- I can wear a uniform.
- I can order other people around.
- I can carry a gun.
- I can use force legally.

For Discussion

1. Would you ever consider becoming a law-enforcement officer? Why or why not?

2. Do you think it's important for the police to have good relations with the community? Explain your answer.

3. Why might people develop negative views of the police? Brainstorm and list reasons. How can the public develop more positive views?

4. Why might the police develop negative views of the public? Brainstorm and list reasons. How can they develop more positive views?

Class Activity: Sampling Class Opinion

This activity will help you get an idea about your class's attitudes toward police.

1. Each member of the class should answer the questionnaire below on a sheet of notebook paper. Write the letters "a" through "j" down the left-hand column of the paper.

2. Next to each letter, write the number that indicates the degree of your agreement or disagreement with the statements below.

5—strongly agree **4**—agree **3**—uncertain

2—disagree **1**—strongly disagree

3. After you have marked your responses, average the answers across the whole class. (Add all the numbers for each statement and then divide by the number of students providing answers.)

4. Discuss the statements that show the strongest agreement and the strongest disagreement. Why do you think the class responded most strongly to these statements?

Questionnaire

a. Police in my community treat most teen-agers fairly.

b. The police in my community are doing a good job.

c. Police officers in my community would refuse bribes offered to them.

Activity: Sampling Police Attitudes

To find out about police attitudes, conduct your own survey of **police** in your community. Use a form like the one from the study described on page 46. How do your results compare with the officers' responses in that study? What might be some reasons for any differences?

Activity: Sampling Public Opinion

To find out about your community's attitudes toward police, construct an attitude survey for your community. You may wish to conduct one survey for the general population, or several surveys directed at specific groups (e.g. homeowners, college students, women and men, racial groups, religious groups, business persons, etc.). Here are some additional statements you might consider using in your surveys.

- The community would be better off with fewer police.
- Police in the United States are often criticized unfairly.
- Police in the community enforce drug laws too strongly.
- I would call the police if I saw someone break into a store.
- I would call the police if I saw a friend stealing a car.
- In the past four or five years, my attitude about the police has become more favorable.

---

d. Police officers in my community generally avoid using physical force against people.

e. Police officers in my community generally treat wealthy people the same as poor people.

f. Police officers in my community generally treat males the same way as females.

g. Police officers in my community generally treat all racial groups in the same way.

h. Police should have the right to use whatever means are necessary to capture criminals.

i. The police often abuse their authority.

j. Police officers, undercover if necessary, should be assigned to school campuses.

From Citizen Volunteers to Professional Police

Law enforcement in some form has been part of nearly every civilization. Anthropologists have discovered written records of laws and law enforcement over 5,000 years old.

An 1882 woodcut of a policeman by Thomas Nast. By 1870, most large American cities had full-time police departments. (The Bettmann Archive.)

Citizen Volunteers in England

In early English history, it was considered each citizen's duty to defend king and country from foreign invaders and local lawbreakers. In some cases, citizens received rewards for capturing criminals. Individuals or even entire villages could be fined for not assisting the king in enforcing the laws of the land.

As English towns grew in size, the need arose for regular law-enforcement officers. So able-bodied men began to take turns looking out for the safety of their neighbors. These volunteers, called constables, depended heavily on other citizens to help them.

Over the years, towns were grouped into counties, or shires. Each shire had a shire-reeve, or sheriff, responsible for getting the citizens of the shire to enforce the law properly.

During the 1300s, large towns and cities organized citizen-volunteer groups to protect the streets at night. This form of policing, called the nightwatch, was eventually adopted in the American colonies.

City Police Forces in the U.S.

From colonial times until the late 1800s, citizen volunteers enforced the law in most American cities. Often, volunteer night-watchmen carried rattles or noisemakers to warn off criminals. According to jokes at the time, the rattling noise was caused by the night-watchmen themselves who shivered and shook with fear.

In 1829, Sir Robert Peel organized a force of paid law-enforcement officers, called Peelers or bobbies, to patrol London. About 10 years later, Boston established the first round-

the-clock police force in the United States. In 1844, New York City formed a 24-hour professional police department. By 1870, most American cities had police forces patterned after those organized in Boston and New York.

While U.S. cities organized police departments, rural areas were also developing law-enforcement agencies. Rural police forces followed the form of the old English shire-reeve system. In many parts of the country, they evolved into agencies headed by county sheriffs.

The need for law enforcement on the frontier led to the establishment of the first *state* police force, the Texas Rangers. Later, other states established their own statewide police forces. Today, state law enforcement agencies include highway patrols, bureaus of narcotics, fish and game departments and civil defense bureaus. Each of these agencies responds to different law-enforcement needs.

The *federal* government has developed various agencies to handle its law-enforcement responsibilities. The Secret Service, among its other duties, investigates counterfeiting and protects the life of the president. The Internal Revenue Service investigates tax evasion. The Bureau of Alcohol, Tobacco, and Firearms monitors these products. These agencies fall under the control of the Treasury Department. The Department of Justice, headed by the attorney general of the United States, directs such agencies as the Immigration and Naturalization Service, and the Federal Bureau of Investigation (FBI).

The FBI operates throughout the nation. But it may only investigate *federal* law violations. For example, the FBI investigates kidnappings, bank robberies, civil-rights violations, and crimes committed on federal territory and property. Most criminal acts in the United States, however, are handled by state and local police.

Policing Today

Unlike most countries in the world today, the United States does not have a national police agency that enforces the laws throughout the country. Rather, more than 40,000 independent law-enforcement agencies exist at the local, state, and federal levels of government. Each agency has its own special function and enforces specific laws in a well-defined geographical area. For example, fire inspectors enforce local fire codes, and health department inspectors enforce a city or town's health and sanitation ordinances. Sheriff deputies patrol counties to enforce county ordinances and state law. Local police enforce a state's and city's criminal laws.

Today, the public often views the police primarily as crime fighters. In reality, while the police do fight crime, they also spend substantial time on many other tasks within the community. They settle disputes, handle many forms of social work, monitor public protests, control traffic, and respond to medical emergencies.

To understand the police, it helps to consider the pressures and fears officers work under. Their duties have become more dangerous and more complex in recent times. Many factors have contributed to this: the rise in the crime rate, the increase in numbers of dangerous weapons, a more critical news media, a more critical general public, and budgetary problems, including a lack of funds to hire enough officers. Also, the police must cope with the realities of law enforcement in a democratic society. Under law, they must protect the constitutional rights of the public. The tension between fighting crime and the restraints on police power can make the job of a police officer very difficult.

For Discussion

1. How does the organization of police forces in the United States differ from most other countries? Why do you think these differences exist?

2. Read the "Police Officer's Oath" on page 50. It describes the ideals of law enforcement. Do you agree with these ideals? If not, what would you change? Why?

3. Today, some people argue that the crime problem could be better handled if there were one large police agency to enforce all criminal laws throughout the United States. What would be the advantages of having such a force? What would be the disadvantages? Do you think the United States should have this kind of police force? Why or why not?

Class Activity: Police Call

What is it like to be a police officer responding to a call for assistance? What is police work like? The following activity will help answer these questions.

Prearrangements: Contact your police department and arrange for an officer to visit your class on the day of the activity. The officer's role will be to observe and help debrief the role-plays. You may wish to conduct the activity over a two-day period and have the officer only present on the second day. Also, you may want to hold the activity in a large multipurpose room or auditorium, if one is available.

When conducting the activity:

1. Form the class into four groups of equal size.

2. In each small group, select two members to play police officers and one or two members to act as observers and group spokespersons. The remaining members will role-play citizens.

3. Send the police officers to a circle in the center of the room.

4. *Police Group Assignment:* The visiting police officer should take part in the group's preparations. At the center circle, the students taking the role of police officers should:

    a. Select a patrol partner; and

    b. Read and discuss the following "Police Officer's Oath" and "Departmental Regulations" to determine how they will conduct themselves on a police call.

The Police Officer's Oath

"As a law-enforcement officer, my fundamental duty is to serve humankind; to safeguard lives and property; to protect the innocent against deception, the weak against oppression or intimidation, and the peaceful against violence and disorder; and to respect everyone's constitutional rights to liberty, equality and justice."

Departmental Regulations

On patrol, the police must try to enforce society's laws fairly, be polite and courteous to all citizens, follow procedures established by the courts and their superiors, solve many problems not connected with fighting crime, and respond to each call quickly and efficiently.

Cautions:

- Always be on guard to protect yourself, your partner, and other citizens from attack and injury.
- Handcuff anyone you take into custody.
- Be prepared for unusual public reactions when you are present.
- Treat all people firmly and fairly.
- Treat all people equally: The law is blind to race, sex and religion, and status.

5. *Citizen Group Assignment* (including Observers): Assign one of the following Police Calls to each group. Each should then take about 10 minutes to decide how it will role-play the situation. (Be sure to act as realistically as possible. For example, how would youngsters caught shoplifting react to the store owner and police? Passively and quietly, or loud and defensively?) Also, one member of the group should prepare to call the police for help by

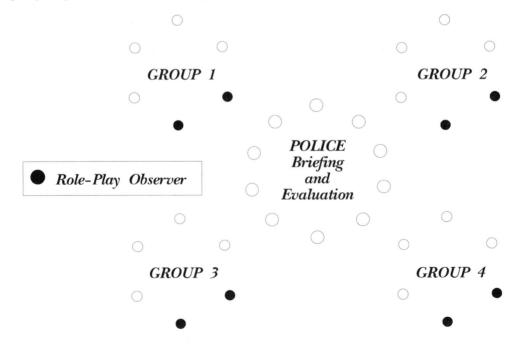

GROUP 1   GROUP 2

● Role-Play Observer

POLICE Briefing and Evaluation

GROUP 3   GROUP 4

Observer Evaluation Form

So that you can remain objective, please do not participate in the discussion of your group's incident prior to the role-play.

During the role-play, observe the contact between your group and the police. After the role-play, use the checklist to evaluate it. Then present and discuss your impressions with the group.

1. How many of the incident role-players were (mark the number in front of each item):
   - realistic
   - too positive and friendly to the police
   - too negative, hostile, and violent to the police
   - totally unrealistic—overplayed their roles

2. The police role-players were:
   - realistic
   - too polite and willing to please the others
   - too negative, hostile, and violent with the others
   - unrealistic—overplayed their roles

3. From the standpoint of fairness, I believe the:
   police should have . . .
   others should have . . .

4. In real life, I believe the following would have happened:

giving a minimum amount of information about the assigned Police Call. For example, "Come quick . . . there is a robbery in progress at Green's Drugstore."

Observers should read and discuss the information contained in Observer Reports and the Observer Evaluation Form. They should make a copy of the Observer Evaluation Form on a sheet of notebook paper. After their group's role-play, they should fill out the copy of the form to evaluate their group.

6. *Role-playing*: When all the groups are ready, a member from each should approach the Police Group and call for help based on the assigned Police Call. A team of police officers responds to each call. The role-play may begin or be in progress as the police arrive. Role-plays can be conducted simultaneously, but if noise or space are a problem, conduct them one at a time in front of the class. In either case, the visiting police officer should comment on the role-plays after observing them individually or by

listening to the observer reports of what happened.

7. *Observer Reports*: After the role-plays, each observer team should complete their forms and analyze what happened for the rest of the class. If the role-play is conducted in front of the entire class, all students may wish to act as observers or compare their views with the official observers. Be objective. Try to describe the problems that arose and explain them in terms of citizen and police behavior. The visiting law-enforcement officer should also comment on each role-play.

8. *Debriefing*: After the activity, conduct a class discussion including the visiting police officer. Use the following questions as a guide:

   a. What have you learned about the kinds of jobs police officers are called upon to do?

   b. How did you feel when you played the police officer's role? The suspect's role?

The role of a citizen in need of help? The observer?

c. What different kinds of incidents have you been involved in or heard about that were not included in the simulation? How many involved violent crimes?

d. What part do you believe fear plays in the interactions between police and community members? When do you think police officers are most afraid? What might cause police to be afraid? What causes others to fear the police? What could be done to reduce fear?

e. What effect might police officers' fear have on their attitudes toward civil liberties? Politics? Suspects? Explain.

f. Does fear of the police keep people from breaking the law? Why or why not?

g. Try to describe the ideal police officer. Use examples from the game, from your own experiences, from stories you have heard.

h. Do you believe society might expect too much from the police? Why or why not?

9. As a follow-up activity, you might create additional "police calls" based on similar or typical incidents and have groups role-play them for the class.

Police Call: Group One

The police will be called to investigate a shoplifting incident.

Design an incident in which a shopkeeper has reported catching a youth shoplifting, and the police are called to the scene. Keep in mind the following questions:

1. How do you think a young person feels to be caught shoplifting?

2. Should the police arrest the youth, or do something less drastic, such as taking the youth home and talking to the parents, etc.? Explain.

3. Should people report all crimes that they know about? Why or why not?

4. What else could the shopkeeper have done instead of calling the police?

Police Call: Group Two

The police will stop a car with a broken tail light. The car, full of young people, is cruising suspiciously in a shopping district late at night.

Design an incident in which the police stop a car cruising suspiciously. Keep in mind the following questions:

1. What would give the police the right to stop the car?

2. Should the police treat the people in the car differently depending on their age, gender, or ethnic group?

3. How do you think innocent people will feel and act when they are stopped by the police?

Police Call: Group Three

The police will be called to calm a domestic quarrel between a husband and wife.

Design an incident in which a husband and wife fight violently enough for the neighbors to call the police. Keep in mind the following questions:

1. Considering that most murders happen in the home between people who know each other well, what special precautions should the police take?

2. How should police draw the line between private family matters and legitimate law-enforcement concerns?

3. Since many homes have at least one gun, how might the police protect themselves?

Police Call: Group Four

The police will be called to a bar on a drunk-and-disorderly call.

Design an incident involving a drunk, disorderly man in a bar who has threatened another person with violence. Keep in mind the following questions:

1. Does it make a difference to the police what neighborhood the bar is in?

2. Since much violent crime involves people who have been drinking, what precautions should police take?

3. If the drunk resists arrest, what should the police do?

4. If the call had said that the drunk was armed with a gun, how differently do you think the police would have reacted to the situation?

Activity: Visiting the Police

To help you further understand day-to-day police work, arrange a visit to your police department. Many departments have community-relations or school-liaison officers who can help make the arrangements for classes or small groups of interested students.

The purpose of your visit should be to make a brief, but fairly comprehensive, study of your local police. Listed below are some questions you might want to ask at the police station. Make up any additional questions you feel are necessary to complete your study.

- What is the population and racial composition of the area served by your police department?
- How many officers work for the department?
- How many officers are on patrol during each shift? Are they evenly distributed? If not, why not?
- What special units does your department have? (Detective, narcotics, traffic, vice, etc.)
- What is the salary range for officers at each level? (Officer, sergeant, lieutenant, captain, inspector, chief, etc.)
- Do the officers have a union? What does it do?
- How closely does the racial composition of the department mirror that of the service area?
- About what percentage of the department is made up of women officers? Has this percentage changed in recent years? If so, how?
- Does the department have special educational programs in the schools or community? What do these programs do?
- How much special training do members of the department have in community relations and what does it consist of?
- Does the department welcome visitors, maintain a ride-along program for adults or teen-agers, or otherwise educate citizens about the police? Describe.
- What are the most common problems that officers must handle?
- What police calls tend to be the most dangerous?
- What is the procedure for filing a citizen complaint about a police officer's conduct?
- What is the department's policy about the use of guns?
- Does the department have any special policies for supervising areas where youth hang out (e.g. arcades, shopping centers, etc.)?

POLICE AND THE LAW

Criminal Procedure

There are two areas of law that police officers must study. One is **criminal law**, which you learned about in Chapter One. It defines which acts are illegal. Because police enforce the criminal law, they must know it. The second area of law that police must study is criminal procedure.

Criminal procedure deals with procedures for arrests, trials, and appeals. It sets out the rules for processing someone through the criminal justice system. Because illegal arrest or investigation procedures may jeopardize a criminal case, the police must pay close attention to criminal procedure.

Criminal procedure comes from a variety of sources, including federal and state statutes. Most importantly, it comes from the U.S. and state constitutions. Appellate courts interpret these statutes and constitutions when criminal defendants appeal their convictions claiming that their constitutional rights have been violated. Deciding these cases, appellate courts

RIGHTS INCORPORATED BY THE 14TH AMENDMENT			
Rights	Amendment	Supreme Court Decision	Date
Freedom of Speech & Press	First	Gitlow v. New York	(1925)
Defense Counsel in Capital Cases	Sixth	Powell v. Alabama	(1932)
Free Exercise of Religion	First	Hamilton v. Regents of U.C.	(1934)
Freedom of Assembly & Petition	First	DeJonge v. Oregon	(1937)
Freedom from Establishment of Religion	First	Everson v. Board of Education	(1947)
Public Trial	Sixth	In re Oliver	(1948)
Protection Against Unreasonable Searches and Seizures	Fourth	Mapp v. Ohio	(1961)
Protection from Cruel & Unusual Punishments	Eighth	Robinson v. California	(1962)
Defense Counsel	Sixth	Gideon v. Wainwright	(1963)
Privilege Against Self-Incrimination	Fifth	Malloy v. Hogan	(1964)
Confrontation of Witnesses	Sixth	Pointer v. Texas	(1965)
Impartial Jury Trial	Sixth	Parker v. Gladden	(1966)
Speedy Trial	Sixth	Klopfer v. North Carolina	(1967)
Compulsory Process in Obtaining Witness	Sixth	Washington v. Texas	(1967)
Trial by Jury	Sixth	Duncan v. Lousiana	(1968)
No Double Jeopardy	Fifth	Benton v. Maryland	(1969)

produce rules that police and criminal trial courts must follow. As the highest appellate court in the land, the U.S. Supreme Court often decides whether particular criminal procedures meet the federal constitutional standards of the Bill of Rights, particularly the Fourth, Fifth, and Sixth amendments.

Originally, the Bill of Rights only applied to the federal government. But after the Civil War, the 14th Amendment was added to the Constitution. Its so-called "due process clause" declares that no state shall "deprive any person of life, liberty, or property, without due process of law. . . ." This means that states cannot deprive people of certain rights. But what rights does the 14th Amendment's due process clause include?

In the 1930s, the Supreme Court ruled that the clause **incorporates** those guarantees in the Bill of Rights that are "rooted in the tradition and conscience of our people." (*Palko v. Connecticut*, 1937.) Since that time, the Supreme Court has decided on a case-by-case basis which rights in the Bill of Rights were fundamental and were therefore rights that every state had to grant to individuals.

In a series of landmark cases beginning in the 1960s, the Supreme Court applied almost all the rights found in the Fourth, Fifth, and Sixth amendments to the states. Not only did the court apply these rights to the states, it also strengthened them. When speaking of the court, it should be noted that not every justice on the court agreed with all of these decisions. Some justices complained that strengthening the constitutional rights of individuals made law enforcement too difficult. But the majority stressed the need for the police to respect rights. The court made so many profound changes that the era marked a revolution in criminal procedure.

Following this period of rapid expansion of the rights of criminal suspects and defendants, the court changed. New justices were appointed to the court forming a new majority. Although these justices did not directly overturn the decisions of the 1960s, they often did restrict them.

So while the court minority complained that the court was eroding basic rights, the new majority stressed the need for crime control.

This tension on the court reflects the tension between the two, often conflicting, goals of the criminal justice system: protecting society from criminals and protecting the constitutional rights of those being processed through the system. Criminal procedure attempts to achieve both.

For Discussion

1. What is the difference between criminal law and criminal procedure?

2. How do appellate courts create rules of criminal procedure?

3. What are the two, often conflicting, goals of the criminal procedure? How might they conflict? Which do you think is more important? Why?

The Law of Search and Seizure

One of the most important and complex areas of criminal procedure comes from the Fourth Amendment. This amendment affects how police officers investigate crimes and gather evidence, because the Supreme Court has ruled that illegally seized evidence may not be used at trial. The Fourth Amendment provides:

> *The right of the people to be secure in their persons, houses, papers, and effects, against unreasonable searches and seizures shall not be violated, and no Warrants shall issue, but upon probable cause, supported by Oath or affirmation, and particularly describing the place to be searched, and the persons or things to be seized.*

All police searches, seizures of evidence, and arrests must comply with this amendment. Courts have interpreted the amendment's meaning in hundreds of search-and-seizure cases. These interpretations have grown into a full body of law, known as the law of search and seizure. Although the law is complicated, determining whether a search or seizure is legal comes down to two basic questions:

- Has a governmental search or seizure taken place?
- If so, was the search or seizure reasonable?

In the sections that follow, you will learn how to answer these questions for most searches or seizures.

Has a Search and Seizure Taken Place?

Did a government employee or agent conduct the search or seizure?

The first step in analyzing search-and-seizure problems is to determine who conducted the search or seizure. The Fourth Amendment protects citizens from actions by government officials. The Fourth Amendment does not usually cover actions by private individuals. If, for example, your neighbor breaks into your house, finds evidence of a crime, and turns it in to the police, your rights under the Fourth Amendment would not have been violated. If you were prosecuted, this evidence could be used against you at trial. Of course, the police could also arrest the person who broke into your house for burglary and you could sue the person in civil court.

Note, however, that if the police had requested your neighbor to break into your house, then Fourth Amendment protections would come into play. The neighbor would be considered an agent of the government.

Was it a search or seizure as defined by the courts?

The Fourth Amendment protects people from unreasonable searches and seizures of their "persons, houses, papers, and effects." But what is a "search"? What is a "seizure"? The next consideration is to decide whether a government official's conduct amounted to a search or seizure.

In the landmark case of *Katz v. U.S.* in 1967, the Supreme Court defined a search as any governmental intrusion into something in which a person has **a reasonable expectation of privacy**. This privacy interest covers places and things such as houses, yards, garages, apartments, diaries, briefcases, and mail.

The court has held, however, that there is no reasonable expectation of privacy in places or things that are in **plain view**. For example, a person growing a four-foot-high marijuana plant in a front bay window cannot claim that a search was conducted if a police officer spots it from the street. But officers who detect things in plain view must do so from places they have a legal right to be in. For instance, if an officer climbs over a six-foot fence surrounding a yard and spots marijuana growing in some back corner, a search has taken place. Persons normally have a reasonable expectation of privacy in their private property which cannot be seen except by trespassing.

But the court has held there is no reasonable expectation of privacy for **open fields** away from a residence. Even though they are private property, they usually are readily accessible to the public. Thus police walking through open fields are not conducting a search.

A similar rule applies to **abandoned property**. For example, if a person placed letters containing incriminating statements into the trash, the police could retrieve them from the garbage dump without having conducted a search. There is no reasonable expectation of privacy in such items.

The idea of "seizure" is somewhat easier to understand. A seizure is any taking into possession, custody, or control. Property may be seized, but so may people. An arrest is one form of seizure, because in making an arrest, the police take someone into custody. Thus arrests fall under the requirements imposed by the Fourth Amendment.

For Discussion

1. What is the difference between a search and a seizure?

2. The Supreme Court has ruled that the police have **not** conducted a search if the object is in plain view, in an open field, or has been abandoned. Why does the court say this in each instance? Do you agree? Why or why not?

3. Why do you think the Fourth Amendment protects only against intrusions by the government? Are these intrusions more dangerous than intrusions by individuals? Why or why not?

4. For each of the following, decide whether a search or seizure has taken place and explain why or why not. Don't be concerned whether it was legal.

    a. Mark Weylon, an off-duty police officer, arrests Mary Clark for shoplifting.

    b. Lois Kindel, a custodian at the Shadyville Police Department, believes her neighbor deals drugs. She tells police but they have no evidence. She agrees to keep a close watch on her neighbor. One day she spots a marijuana plant, which has grown taller than her neighbor's fence.

    c. Officer Sanchez climbs a hill in a public park and spots three stolen cars in a nearby backyard surrounded by a 10-foot-high fence.

    d. On surprising George Meyers, a known narcotics dealer, police observe him swallow several capsules. They take him to the hospital and have his stomach pumped.

    e. The police stop Anna and question her for a few minutes about where she's been and what she has been doing the past few days. (Anna has been arrested twice in the last year for prostitution but has never been convicted.)

Class Activity: Is It a Search?

Divide the class into groups of six. Working in your groups, decide if a search or seizure has taken place in the following situations and explain why. Then assign each member of the group one of the cases cited to look up at a law library. Law libraries can be found at law schools and at county and municipal courts. (The librarian can help you find the cases you are looking for.) After researching at the library, meet in one of six groups according to the case you looked up. In your "expert" group, discuss the case and prepare to report on it to the class. Assign one person to report on the facts of the case, another to report on what the court majority decided and why, another on what the court dissenters believed and why, and finally each member should state how he or she would have decided the case and why.

a. Unable to see over Mike's 10-foot-high fence, police hire a plane and fly over the house at 1,000 feet and see marijuana plants growing in the backyard.

    • See *California v. Ciraolo* (1986) and *Florida v. Riley* (1989).

b. Police install a device at the phone company office that keeps track of the numbers that Gilbert dials from his home phone.

    • See *Smith v. Maryland* (1979).

c. Suspecting drug dealing, police have the trash collector turn over Bill's trash to them instead of throwing it in the trash truck.

    • See *California v. Greenwood* (1988).

d. The FBI listens to Joe's conversation by attaching an electronic eavesdropping device to the outside of the public telephone booth he uses at 11 a.m. every day.

    • See *Katz v. U.S.* (1967).

e. Investigating a shooting, police legally enter an apartment looking for weapons and the shooter. While inside, an officer spots a high-priced stereo which seems out of place in the rundown apartment. The officer picks it up, jots down the serial number, puts it down, calls headquarters, and finds out the stereo is stolen.

• See *Arizona v. Hicks* (1987).

f. Oliver posts "no trespassing" signs around his land and locks the gate to his property. Police go onto a highly secluded part of his land about a mile from his house and find marijuana plants growing.

• See *Oliver v. U.S.* (1984).

Debriefing Questions

1. What is the test used by the Supreme Court to determine whether a search has taken place?

2. Do you think this is a good test? Explain.

3. Has the Supreme Court applied this test satisfactorily in these cases? Why or why not?

Is the Search and Seizure Reasonable?

After a court determines that a search or seizure has taken place, then it must determine whether it was reasonable. This section will help you analyze whether searches or seizures are reasonable.

Was the search or seizure conducted pursuant to a warrant?

In general, the courts have held that a search or seizure is unreasonable without a **warrant**. A warrant is a court order issued by a judge authorizing a search, an arrest, or a seizure of evidence. Warrants must specifically describe the place to be searched or the person to be seized.

Before issuing a warrant, a judge must receive evidence presented under oath—usually supplied by a police officer. The evidence must show that there is probable cause to believe that:

> (1) a crime has been or is about to be committed, *and*

> (2) the person, place, or thing to be searched or seized is related to that crime.

Probable cause means that the evidence must be strong enough that an independent, cautious person would have good reason to believe it.

Once the police get a search warrant, they must carry out the search promptly—usually within 72 or 96 hours, depending on the state. Many states allow police to execute warrants only during daytime hours except in special cases. Police must normally announce that they have a warrant. But they can forgo this formality if they have reason to believe that a fugitive is hiding out or that evidence is being destroyed. In most jurisdictions, the police may forcibly enter a place when no one will let them in.

If police do not obtain a warrant, does one of the court-recognized exceptions to the warrant requirement apply?

The courts do not require the police to obtain a warrant before every search and seizure (though probable cause is still required in almost all cases). Over the years, courts have created exceptions to the warrant requirement. They have made these exceptions for several reasons:

• to protect the safety of officers and the public;

• to ensure that evidence will be seized before it can be hidden or destroyed; or

• to help apprehend suspects or prevent their escape.

In determining whether a warrantless search or seizure is reasonable, the courts weigh the need for immediate police action against the invasion of individual privacy involved. Here is one such case.

U.S. v. Ross (1982)

Late one evening, a reliable informant telephoned Detective Marcum and told him that an individual known as "Bandit" was selling drugs. The informant had just seen Bandit complete a narcotics sale and Bandit had told him that he had more drugs in the trunk of his car. The informant gave the detective a detailed description of Bandit, described his car as a maroon Chevrolet Malibu, and told Marcum the address where it was parked.

Detective Marcum, along with two other police officers, immediately drove to the address and found a parked maroon Malibu. A license check disclosed that the car was registered to Albert Ross. A computer check on Ross revealed that he fit the informant's description and was known to use the alias "Bandit." The officers cruised through the neighborhood but did not see anyone matching Ross' description.

When they returned to the address, they saw the maroon Malibu going down the street. They pulled alongside the Malibu, saw that the driver matched the informant's description, and stopped the car. They ordered Ross out of the car. While the officers were searching him, Detective Marcum noticed a bullet on the car's front seat. Marcum took Ross' keys and opened the trunk, where he found a closed brown paper bag. He opened the bag and discovered many cellophane envelopes containing white powder.

Later at the police station, the officers thoroughly searched the car again. They discovered a red leather pouch in the trunk. Unzipping the pouch, they found $3,200 in cash.

The police laboratory later determined that the powder in the cellophane envelopes was heroin. Ross was charged with possession of heroin with intent to distribute.

The police had not obtained a search warrant at any time, and Ross claimed the searches were unreasonable. He made a motion to suppress the heroin and the cash from evidence at his trial.

Police search vehicles for a suspected murderer. In making automobile searches, police do not need warrants, but they must have either probable cause or the consent of the owner. (UPI/Bettmann.)

For Discussion

1. What do police officers have to prove before they can get a warrant from a judge?

2. Why do you think courts require police officers to obtain warrants?

3. Did Detective Marcum's opening of Bandit's car trunk constitute a search? What about the brown paper bag? The cellophane envelopes? Explain your answers.

4. Assume that opening the trunk, brown bag, and cellophane envelopes were searches. Do you think they were reasonable under the circumstances or should the officers have secured a warrant first? Why?

5. Was unzipping the red leather pouch at the police station a search? If so, was it reasonable under the circumstances or should the officers have obtained a warrant first? Why?

The Court's Decision

In a 6-3 decision, the U.S. Supreme Court ruled that the searches and seizures were reasonable and did not violate Ross' Fourth Amendment rights. Police officers who have legitimately stopped an automobile (as they did in this case) and who have probable cause to believe that contraband is concealed somewhere within it (as they did in this case) may conduct a warrantless search of the vehicle.

In addition, when the police have probable cause to search a vehicle, they may conduct a warrantless search of every part of the vehicle and its contents. This includes all containers and packages that may conceal whatever the police are searching for. But it excludes containers that could not hold what they are looking for. For example, probable cause to believe that undocumented aliens are being transported in a van will not justify a warrantless search of a suitcase in the van.

Justice White argued in dissent:

> The majority . . . not only repeals all realistic limits on warrantless automobile searches, it repeals the Fourth Amendment warrant requirement itself. By equating a police officer's estimation of probable cause with a magistrate's, the Court utterly disregards the value of a neutral and detached magistrate . . . .

> The court simply ignores the critical function that a magistrate serves. And although the Court purports to rely on the mobility of an automobile and impracticability of obtaining a warrant, it never explains why these concerns permit the warrantless search of a container, which can easily be seized and immobilized while the police are obtaining a warrant.

Justice Marshall disagreed with the decision as well. In his dissenting opinion, he warned that the majority ruling would have

Ask an Expert

1. As you can see, the law of search and seizure is quite complex. How do police officers learn about the Fourth Amendment limits on their actions? Invite police officers to your class to explain their training in this area of the law, or make arrangements to visit a police training academy and sit in on a class about search and seizure.

2. Find out about officers' views on search-and-seizure law. Ask whether they think the courts have properly balanced the interests of individuals and law enforcement in search-and-seizure cases.

"profound implications for the privacy of citizens traveling in automobiles."

The *Ross* case removed the warrant requirement for **motor vehicle searches**. The court made this exception because, if the police had to wait to get a warrant, motor vehicles could easily be moved and any evidence in them concealed or destroyed. (Of course, before searching any vehicle, police must still have probable cause to believe it was used in the commission of a crime or it contains evidence of a crime.)

Other Recognized Exceptions

There are other situations in which searches and seizures may be conducted without a warrant:

- In *Chimel v. California* (1969), the U.S. Supreme Court held that searches and seizures incident to lawful arrests may be done without a warrant. The court said: "When an arrest is made, it is reasonable for the arresting officer to search the person arrested in order to remove any weapons that the latter might seek to use in order to resist arrest or effect his escape [and to] seize any evidence on the arrestee's person in order to prevent its concealment or destruction." These so-called "Chimel searches" may extend to everything within the area of the arrestee's immediate control. Questions sometimes arise as to whether the arrest itself was lawful. If it was not, any search conducted along with it would not be valid.

Examples:

Reasonable Search: Didi is arrested outside of Elliot's Department Store for shoplifting. Without a warrant, the police search the book bag she is carrying.

Unreasonable Search: Didi is arrested outside of Elliot's Department Store for shoplifting. The police go to her home, a block away, and search her bedroom. (The search is not *incident* to the arrest. The police could have obtained a warrant if they had probable cause to believe there was evidence of a crime in the house.)

- In certain cases, the police may **stop and frisk**, or pat down, the outer layers of a person's clothing without making an arrest. "[W]here a police officer observes unusual conduct which leads him reasonably to conclude in light of his experience that criminal activity may be afoot and that the persons with whom he is dealing may be *armed* and *presently dangerous* . . . he is entitled for the protection of himself and others in the area to conduct a carefully limited search of the outer clothing of such persons in an attempt to discover weapons which might be used to assault him." *Terry v. Ohio* (1968). (Emphasis added.) Thus a brief stop and frisk does

not require **probable cause**—evidence strong enough to give a careful person good reason to believe it. A stop or frisk requires **reasonable suspicion**—evidence that would make an experienced police officer suspicious. Most searches and seizures require probable cause.

Examples:

Reasonable Search: The police see Fritz run out of a dark alley at 3 a.m. They stop him, ask him who he is and what he has been doing, and frisk his outer clothing. In doing so, the officers detect what feels like a large metal object in his coat pocket. They reach inside and pull out a gun.

Unreasonable Search: The police see Fritz run out of a dark alley at 3 a.m. They stop and frisk him. In doing so, the officers detect what feels like a plastic bag in his coat pocket. They reach inside and pull out a small bag of marijuana. (Because of the nature of the object, it could not possibly have been a dangerous weapon.)

- The police may search without a warrant if the person "knowingly and voluntarily" **consents**. (But these searches are not reasonable if the police use deception or fraud to get the person's consent.) Sometimes an individual may consent to a search of

Ask an Expert

Invite a criminal attorney to visit your classroom and briefly discuss search-and-seizure law with you. Then have the attorney take part in the class activity "Applying the Checklist." The attorney can help pairs of students and discuss each case when the activity ends.

someone else's property if the consenting party owns or shares the property with the one being searched.

Examples:

Reasonable Search: The police stop Luis on the highway for driving with a broken brake light. They ask him to open his glove compartment. Luis opens it and the officers look inside.

Reasonable Search: Without a warrant, the police go to Meg's house and ask her parents if they can search her room for illegal drugs that they believe she has been selling at school. Meg's parents let the officers in to search.

Unreasonable Search: Mike and Murray are roommates in a two-bedroom apartment. The police go to their apartment and ask Mike to let them search Murray's bedroom and file cabinet. Mike consents to the search. (Though they share the common areas of the apartment, Mike has no right to consent to a search of Murray's private space.)

• Police in **hot pursuit** of a criminal do not need a warrant to enter a place where they saw the suspect go.

Examples:

Reasonable Search: The police see Josie knock down an old lady, hit her with a lead pipe, and take her purse. They chase Josie into a building about a mile away and see her run into apartment #10B. When she refuses to answer, the officers kick down the door.

Unreasonable Search: Mrs. Thackaberry reports that someone broke into her mailbox and stole her Social Security check. The police suspect Josie, a known robber of the elderly. They trail her for a few days and finally follow her into an apartment building where she often goes. The police knock on the door to #10B, but Josie won't let them in. The police kick down the door. (There is no "hot pursuit" in this case. The police were only following a lead and could have gotten a warrant.)

• In **emergency situations**, the police do not need a warrant to conduct a search or seizure.

Examples:

Reasonable Search: An officer on the beat hears a woman's loud screams and the sound of shattering glass coming from a trailer home. He radios for help and then opens the front door to see what is happening.

Unreasonable Search: The police are concerned about gang violence at Jackson High School. Three students have been killed already. The police hear that a fight between two rival gangs is supposed to take place on Friday. The day before, they ask the principal of Jackson High to assemble all students in the gym. Without a warrant, the officers then open all the lockers with a passkey and search for dangerous weapons. (The police are not reacting to an immediate emergency.)

A number of other kinds of searches have been held to be reasonable by the courts. They include:

• **Airline searches** of passengers and carry-on baggage by means of metal detectors, physical pat-downs, or drug-sniffing dogs.

• **Border searches** by immigration control officers within areas reasonably close to U.S. international boundaries.

• **Customs searches** at borders, ports, and international airports by U.S. customs agents.

For Discussion

1. What reasons does the court consider in making exceptions to the warrant requirement? What are the dangers in making exceptions?

2. Why did the court carve out an exception to the warrant requirement in automobile searches? What reasons did the dissenters give in opposing it? Do you agree with the decision in *Ross*? Why or why not?

3. The court has carved out several other exceptions: searches incident to a lawful arrest, stop and frisks, consent searches, searches done in hot pursuit, searches in emergency circumstances, border searches, and airline security searches. Do you disagree with any of these exceptions? Why or why not?

A Search and Seizure Checklist

This checklist provides a summary analysis of whether the Fourth Amendment has been violated. Use the checklist to help you determine the legality of searches and seizures.

Major Questions

Considerations Checklist

I. Has a search or seizure taken place?

• Did a government employee or agent conduct the search or seizure?

[If NO, then no violation]

• Was it a search or seizure as defined by the courts?

• Did the person have a reasonable expectation of privacy?

[If NO, then no violation]

• Was the item

• in plain view?

• in an open field?

• abandoned?

[If YES, then no violation]

II. Was the search or seizure reasonable?

• Was the search or seizure conducted with a valid warrant?

[If YES, no violation]

• If not, does one of the court recognized exceptions to the warrant requirement apply?

___ Motor Vehicles

___ Incident to a Lawful Arrest

___ Stop and Frisk

___ Consent

___ Hot Pursuit

___ Emergency Circumstances

___ Border Searches

___ Airline/Security Searches

[If YES, no violation]

Class Activity: Applying the Checklist

Work in pairs. Using the checklist on page 63 and what you have learned about search-and-seizure law, analyze the following cases and decide if any Fourth Amendment violations have occurred. Be prepared to explain your answers and discuss any differences of opinion that may arise.

- Smith and Houston, special investigators from the district attorney's office, had been following Hans Metcalf, a suspected bookie. They saw him enter a telephone booth with a briefcase in his hand and make a short call. He then left the phone booth, but without his briefcase. Smith and Houston rushed to the phone booth, opened the briefcase, and found several bundles of betting slips. Just then, Metcalf returned to retrieve his briefcase and he was arrested.

- Mary Krensy was angry with her roommate, Vivian Madison. She went to the police and offered to show them where Vivian was hiding 50 stolen holiday turkeys. The police accompanied her to the garage both women shared and discovered 50 turkeys reported stolen from the Henderson Poultry Company. The police confiscated the poultry and placed Vivian under arrest.

- Officer Hanano was on patrol late at night. Suddenly, she spotted a house trailer behind, but not attached to, a car with no license plates. On closer inspection, she noticed a thin wisp of smoke escaping from one of the trailer windows. She walked to the door and knocked a few times. A voice called back, "Go away!" The officer forced opened the door and found a young man preparing a liquid substance in a makeshift laboratory. Officer Hanano arrested the man for the manufacture of illegal drugs.

- Acting on an informant's tip that Betty Kim was receiving stolen property, Detective Drebs went to her apartment to talk to her. She invited him in, but when he started to poke around the living room she screamed, "I said you could talk, not search the place. Get out!" He grabbed her, put handcuffs on her, then frisked her. He found a scout knife in her pants pocket and arrested her for disturbing the peace and carrying a concealed weapon. He then searched the living room and found a stolen stereo receiver.

Interrogation and Confessions

Another important area of criminal procedure comes from the Fifth Amendment to the U.S. Constitution. Part of this amendment says "(no) person . . . shall be compelled in any criminal case to be a witness against himself. . . ." This means that unless you agree to talk to the police, they cannot force you to answer questions about a crime they think you committed. Unlike the Fourth Amendment, which balances your right to privacy against the police's need to act, your Fifth Amendment right not to talk to police is absolute. If you invoke it, the police may not legally make you talk.

The Supreme Court did not apply the Fifth Amendment to the states until 1964. But even before this, it struck down cases where confessions were not made voluntarily. The court determined that these cases violated the due process clause of the 14th Amendment. This clause declares that no "State shall deprive any person of life, liberty, or property, without due process of law. . . ." Due process of law guarantees fair procedures and basic liberties. Among the cases that the court struck down as violating due process were:

- *Brown v. Mississippi* (1936). Trying to get a confession, deputies hung the defendant from a tree twice. Then they whipped him.

Ernesto Miranda, right, shown with his attorney. His 1966 case led to a landmark Supreme Court decision on police interrogation. (UPI/Bettmann.)

Whipping him a second time, they told him they would not stop until he confessed, which he finally did. Then they took him to jail.

- *Ward v. Texas* (1942). So that no friend or attorney could contact the defendant, the police took him out of the county to three different jails in three days. Questioned continuously, the defendant at one point said he would make whatever statement the police wanted even though he claimed not to have committed the crime. Finally he confessed.

- *Ashcraft v. Tennessee* (1944). Police put the defendant in an interrogation room on Saturday night at 7 p.m. and questioned him in relays so they would not get tired. On Monday at 9:30 a.m., the defendant confessed. During the 36-hour interrogation, police had given the defendant only one five-minute break.

- *Malinski v. New York* (1945). Instead of taking the defendant to jail, police took him to a hotel room. They told him to remove his clothes. They questioned him for three hours while he was naked. Then allowing him to put on his underwear, they questioned him for seven more hours until he confessed. Then after letting him dress, they took him to jail.

- *Leyra v. Denno* (1954). After questioning the defendant for days and allowing him little sleep, police brought in a doctor trained in hypnosis. The police had wired the room so they could listen in. During his one-and-one-half hour visit, the doctor repeatedly suggested that the defendant confess. Eventually the defendant did. The doctor then brought officers into the room and had the defendant repeat the confession.

- *Spano v. New York* (1959). Although the defendant refused to talk and asked for his lawyer, police continued to question him for eight straight hours. Police sent in a childhood friend, a policeman with four children, who falsely told the defendant he would be fired unless the defendant confessed, which he ultimately did.

- *Lynum v. Illinois* (1963). Police told the defendant that if she confessed, nothing would happen to her, but if she did not, her children would be taken away from her. She confessed.

Finally in 1964 in *Malloy v. Hogan*, the Supreme Court ruled that the Fifth Amendment protection against self-incrimination applied to the states. But courts still faced the difficult task of determining on a case-by-case basis whether confessions were coerced or voluntary. So in 1966 in the landmark case of *Miranda v. Arizona*, the Supreme Court laid down clearer guidelines for police and courts to follow.

Miranda v. Arizona (1966)

In this case, Ernesto Miranda was arrested at his home and taken to a police station. A witness identified him, then two detectives took him into a special room. After two hours of interrogation, the officers got Miranda to sign a written confession.

At his trial, Miranda was convicted of kidnapping and rape and was sentenced to 20 to 30 years in prison. But he had never been told of his right not to talk to the police. He had never been told of his right to a lawyer. These rights are guaranteed by the Fifth and Sixth amendments. When the Supreme Court heard this case, it decided that any interrogation of suspects in custody is unconstitutional unless the police clearly tell suspects before any questioning begins that:

- they have the right to remain silent;
- anything they say may be used against them in court;
- they have a right to a lawyer; and
- if they want a lawyer but can't afford one, the court will appoint one before any questioning.

Also, after giving a suspect these warnings, the police cannot go on interrogating unless the suspect "knowingly and intelligently" waives his or her rights. That is, suspects must completely understand their rights before they can give them up.

This important decision meant that if police did not give suspects in custody these warnings before questioning them, nothing that they said could be introduced as evidence against them at their trials.

The Supreme Court believed that police questioning of suspects in the station house was inherently coercive. In other words, the court believed that the station house surroundings and police interrogation put tremendous pressure on suspects to say what the police wanted them to say. It felt that the only way to prevent coerced confessions was to make sure suspects knew their rights. Thus police need to tell suspects that they do not have to say anything and that they can have a lawyer with them during questioning. The court concluded that if police do not give a suspect this information, they violate the suspect's Fifth Amendment rights.

Miranda's Aftermath

Miranda requires the police to read suspects **in custody** their rights before any **interrogation**. Police do not need to get people to waive their rights if they are not in custody or not being interrogated. Since *Miranda*, the court has clarified its decision by focusing on what "in custody" and "interrogation" mean.

To be in custody, a person's freedom must be significantly restrained. The court has held that most people stopped briefly by police are not in custody, because they will soon be on their way. Thus routine traffic stops and even stop and frisks do not normally require *Miranda* warnings. (*Berkemer v. McCarty*, 1984.)

In *Rhode Island v. Innis* (1980), the high court defined interrogation as "words or actions on the part of police officers that they should have known were reasonably likely to elicit an incriminating response." In that case, police officers talked to each other as they drove the defendant to the police station. One mentioned that it would be too bad if children attending a nearby school for the handicapped found the abandoned shotgun that Innis had supposedly used to rob one taxi driver and kill another. Innis, who had previously requested a lawyer after hearing his *Miranda* rights, spoke up and directed the officers to the gun (a major piece of evidence in his later conviction for robbery and murder). The court ruled that the officers' remarks did not constitute interrogation so his rights were not violated.

In 1984 in *New York v. Quarles*, the Supreme Court carved out a major exception to *Miranda*. In that case, police chased a rape suspect through a supermarket. Finally catching and handcuffing him, they found he had an empty shoulder holster. An officer asked him where the gun was. Nodding toward some empty boxes, the suspect said, "The gun is over there." The police retrieved a loaded .38 caliber handgun from a box. Since the suspect had not been given any *Miranda* warnings, his incriminating statement and perhaps the gun should have been excluded from evidence. But the court created a **public safety exception** to *Miranda*. It ruled that the police do not have to give *Miranda* warnings when their questions are "reasonably prompted by a concern for the public safety." Since the loaded gun in the store caused reasonable concern for public safety, the court ruled that the evidence was admissible.

For Discussion

1. Supreme Court Justice Arthur J. Goldberg once wrote: "We have learned the lesson of history, ancient and modern, that a system of criminal law enforcement which comes to depend on 'confession' will, in the long run, be less reliable than a system which depends on extrinsic evidence independently secured through skillful investigation." What did he mean by this? Do you agree? Why or why not?

2. According to the *Miranda* decision, why should the incriminating statement in the *Quarles* case be excluded from evidence?

3. The court majority in *Quarles* said that the public safety exception did not give the police the right to coerce confessions from suspects. According to the *Miranda* decision, was Quarles' incriminating statement made in a coercive situation? Why or why not?

4. Both the majority and dissenting opinions in *Quarles* stated that the decision would "lessen the desirable clarity" of the *Miranda* rule. Why is it desirable that the rule be clear?

5. When *Miranda* was decided, its critics claimed that suspects would stop making confessions. This claim has proved false. Suspects confess today as often as before *Miranda*. In fact, one commentator has stated that "next to the warning label on cigarette packs, *Miranda* is the most widely ignored piece of official advice in our society." Do you think *Miranda* sufficiently protects suspects' Fifth Amendment rights? Do you think it goes too far?

Class Activity: Taking the Fifth

In this activity, you will use your knowledge of the Fifth Amendment to argue actual cases that have come before the Supreme Court.

1. Divide the class into triads. Assign students in each triad a number—one, two, or three. All ones will role-play a justice of the Supreme Court. All twos will role-play defense attorneys. All threes will role-play attorneys for the government. Assign each triad one of the cases below—a, b, c, d, e, or f.

2. Regroup the class so they can consult with one another while preparing for the role-play. Students arguing for the government should sit

on one side of the room, students arguing for the defendants on the other side, and the student justices in front. Follow your group's instructions:

Attorneys' Instructions

As attorneys, you are responsible for presenting the court with sound arguments supporting your side.

If you represent the government, you will argue that the incriminating statements should be allowed in evidence at the trial.

If you represent the defendant, you will argue that the incriminating statements should be excluded at trial.

Carefully read your case. Then review the section above on *Miranda* and the cases following it. How do these cases apply to your case?

To prepare your argument, write a clear, brief statement of your position. Include:

- At least one fact from the case that supports your position.
- An explanation of how that fact supports your position.
- One previous court decision that supports your position.
- An explanation of how that decision supports your position.
- One reason why your position is fair to the government or defendant.
- One reason why a court decision in your favor will benefit society.

Make an outline ordering this information so that you can include all of it in a two-minute presentation.

Justices' Instructions

When preparing to hear arguments, Supreme Court justices review the cases and the law with their clerks and develop questions they want to ask the attorneys. Working with other justices, read each case. Take notes while you discuss the following:

- How do *Miranda* and the cases following it apply to your case?

- What questions would you like to ask the attorneys about your case?

Remember: When you decide your case, you must consider the previous Supreme Court cases interpreting the Fifth Amendment, but you are not bound by them.

3. Regroup into triads and begin the role-play. The defense will present its case first. Each side will have two minutes to make its presentation. The justice can interrupt to ask questions. After both sides present, each justice should stand and prepare to present a decision on the case.

4. When every justice is ready, go around the room and have each justice read the facts of the case and present his or her decision and reasons for it.

Cases

The issue in each case is the same: **Can the defendant's confession or incriminating statements be introduced in evidence at the trial?**

a. *Illinois v. Perkins* (1990). Police suspect that Perkins, an inmate in jail on another charge, has committed a murder. They put an undercover agent in Perkins' cell. After gaining Perkins' trust, the agent asks him if he has ever killed anyone. Perkins confesses to the murder.

b. *Duckworth v. Eagan* (1989). Duckworth confessed to a crime after receiving *Miranda* warnings from police. Police had deviated from the standard warnings in one way. They had told Duckworth: "You have a right to talk to a lawyer for advice before we ask you any questions, and to have him with you during questioning. You have this right to the advice and presence of a lawyer even if you cannot afford to hire one. *We have no way of giving you a lawyer, but one will be appointed for you, if you wish, if and when you go to court.* If you wish to answer questions now without a lawyer present, you have the right to stop answering questions at any time. You also have the right to stop answering at any time until you've talked to a lawyer." (Emphasis added.)

c. *Arizona v. Mauro* (1987). Arrested for killing his son, Mauro declined to answer any questions without a lawyer. The police let his wife in to talk with him, but they conspicuously placed a tape recorder on the table between them, which recorded incriminating statements.

d. *Fare v. Michael C.* (1979). Police gave *Miranda* warnings to Michael, a 16-year-old boy accused of murder. When asked if he wanted a lawyer during the interrogation, Michael asked if instead he could call his probation officer. When the police told him they would not call the probation officer right away, Michael somewhat reluctantly agreed to talk and eventually incriminated himself.

e. *Oregon v. Mathiason* (1977). Weeks after a burglary, police sent Mathiason a note asking him to call. He called and made an appointment at his convenience to come into the station. On his arrival, an officer informed him he was not under arrest, but led him into a conference room. The officer falsely told Mathiason that police had found his fingerprints at the burglary scene. Mathiason confessed to the crime. The officer then let Mathiason leave without arresting him that day.

f. *Beckwith v. U.S.* (1976). Arriving at Beckwith's house at 8 a.m., IRS agents asked Beckwith if they could ask him some questions. He invited them in and they interviewed him for three hours. During the interview, he made incriminating statements. He was later arrested for tax fraud.

Debriefing Questions

1. Which of the justices' decisions expand the *Miranda* decision? Which restrict it? Why?

2. What were some strong arguments presented by the attorneys for the government for each case? What arguments would have improved their cases?

3. What were some strong arguments presented by the attorneys for the defendants? What arguments would have improved their cases?

Many people complain that legal technicalities get in the way of prosecuting criminal defendants. (Asay cartoon reprinted by permission)

4. What were some key questions asked by the justices? What other questions should they have asked?

5. Which decisions do you agree with? Why?

The Exclusionary Rule

"Criminals always get off on technicalities." You have probably heard this before or even thought it yourself. But do you know what these "technicalities" are? Generally, they refer to the individual rights protected by the Constitution, particularly provisions of the Fourth and Fifth amendments. When these rights have been violated by an illegal search, seizure, or interrogation, an accused person may invoke the exclusionary rule. This is done by making, in court, a motion to suppress any illegally obtained evidence.

The **exclusionary rule** is a special remedy created by the courts to compel police to respect the constitutional rights of suspects. Under the rule, no illegally obtained evidence—whether papers, objects, or testimony—may be presented in court to convict a defendant whose

Police mugshot of Dollree Mapp. (AP/Wide World Photos.)

constitutional rights have been violated. This does not mean that the accused will automatically be set free. But in some cases, this evidence makes up the bulk of the government's case. In such cases, the charges may have to be reduced or dropped altogether.

The exclusionary rule is based upon two theories:

- **Judicial integrity.** Courts are supposed to uphold the law. If they allow illegally obtained evidence to be used at trial, they fail to uphold the law. They condone, even encourage, illegality. How can citizens respect our judicial system if the system accepts illegal practices?

- **Deterrence.** Excluding tainted evidence is the only effective way to prevent police abuse of constitutional rights. If illegally obtained evidence may not be introduced in court, police will not resort to illegal searches and seizures.

The rule has applied to *federal* criminal cases since 1914. The Supreme Court did not at first apply the rule to the states. Instead, the court let states decide how to uphold constitutional rights—whether by the exclusionary rule or by other methods. But in 1961, the Supreme Court decided that the exclusionary rule was required to assure that police would obey the Constitution. In *Mapp v. Ohio*, it applied the exclusionary rule to state criminal trials.

Mapp v. Ohio (1961)

The petitioner, Dollree Mapp, lived with her young daughter in a two-story house in Cleveland. On May 23, 1957, police arrived at Ms. Mapp's house and demanded entry. Although they gave Mapp no explanation, they later said they were responding to a tip about a recent bombing. After phoning her attorney, Mapp refused to let the officers in without a warrant. They left. Three hours later, they returned, still without a warrant, but with reinforcements. They pounded on the door. When Mapp did not come to the door immediately, the police broke into the house.

When they entered, Mapp was coming down the stairs. She demanded to see a warrant. An officer waved a piece of paper at her, but it was not a warrant. She grabbed it and stuffed it down her blouse. The officers forcibly retrieved it and handcuffed her. Then they dragged her upstairs to her bedroom and searched through her belongings and personal papers.

Meanwhile, Mapp's attorney arrived, but the officers would not let him in the house. They continued searching through the rest of the house. After searching everywhere, officers found some obscene materials tucked away in a basement trunk. Mapp was arrested, tried, and convicted of possessing these materials.

During Mapp's trial and the subsequent appeals, the state never denied that the search was illegal. Instead, the state argued that the illegal search was irrelevant. Mapp had obscene materials in her basement. She had broken the law and was guilty as charged. Her conviction should not be overturned because of an illegal search.

The Supreme Court disagreed. Ruling that "nothing can destroy a government more quickly than its failure to obey its own laws," the court threw out Mapp's conviction and

Fruit of the Poisonous Tree

If police find evidence during an illegal search, the exclusionary rule bars prosecutors from using this evidence at trial. But what if the illegally obtained evidence leads police to other evidence? For example, police conduct an illegal search of an office building and find cocaine in Dan's office. When Dan comes to work, they read him his *Miranda* rights and question him. He confesses to possessing and selling cocaine. The cocaine cannot be used as evidence at Dan's trial because of the illegal search. But can the confession be used? Police have complied with *Miranda*. But if Dan can show that police never would have had reason to question him except for their illegal search, then the confession would be excluded from the trial under the "fruit of the poisonous tree doctrine." This doctrine holds that if illegally obtained evidence (the poisonous tree), leads police to new evidence (the fruit), this new evidence may not be used in court against the person whose rights have been violated.

Courts have recognized several exceptions to this doctrine, and in recent years the Supreme Court has liberally interpreted these exceptions:

- **Independent source**. If police did not have to rely on the illegal evidence to find the new evidence, then the new evidence could be used at trial. For example, if a witness had told police that Dan dealt drugs, then they would have had reason to question him and the confession would be admitted. (*Silverthorne Lumber Co. v. U.S., 1920, Segura v. U.S., 1984, and Murray v. U.S., 1988.*)

- **Inevitable discovery**. If police would have found the evidence eventually, then the evidence can be admitted in court. In *Nix v. Williams* (1984), police were searching for a body. They illegally obtained a confession that indicated where the body was. The body could be used as evidence at the trial because the court ruled the police would have found it eventually.

- **Cleansed taint**. If the connection between the illegal action and the new evidence is weak, then the new evidence will be allowed at trial. For example, if Dan's confession had not taken place the day of the search but had been volunteered by him a week later, a court might allow the confession as evidence. (*Wong Sun v. U.S., 1963.*)

For Discussion

1. What is the fruit of the poisonous tree doctrine? Do you agree with this doctrine? Why or why not?

2. What are the exceptions to the doctrine? Do they make sense? Why or why not?

---

returned the case to a lower court for further proceedings. In doing so, the court extended the exclusionary rule to all criminal trials in the country—both state and federal.

The court stated that the constitutional right against invasions of privacy by police should not be an empty promise. The court said it could no longer permit this right

to be revocable at the whim of any police officer who, in the name of law enforce-ment itself, chooses to suspend its enjoy-ment. Our decision, founded on reason and truth, gives to the individual no more than that which the Constitution guaran-tees him, to the police officer no less than that to which honest law enforcement is entitled, and, to the courts, that judicial integrity so necessary in the true adminis-tration of justice.

The Exclusionary Rule Since Mapp

The *Mapp* decision affected police behavior immediately. Police, who had rarely bothered to get warrants, started applying for them. In New York City, for example, police had requested no search warrants in 1960, the year before the *Mapp* decision. The year after *Mapp*, the police requested more than 800 search warrants. The exclusionary rule, with its threat of suppressing illegal evidence, pushed police into seeking warrants.

But the *Mapp* decision did not end legal debate over the exclusionary rule. The Supreme Court has considered the issue many times. In recent years, the court has carved out several exceptions to the rule:

- If criminal defendants testify in their own defense, evidence illegally seized can be used to challenge the defendants' testimony. (*Harris v. New York*, 1971, *Michigan v. Harvey*, 1990, and *James v. Illinois*, 1990.)

- Evidence gathered by police acting in good faith can be admitted if the police have reasonably relied on a search warrant issued by a judge which turns out to be technically defective or, through a judge's error, turns out not to be based on probable cause. (*U.S. v. Leon*, 1984.)

Critics of the exclusionary rule believe it hampers the fight against crime. Some argue that too many criminals escape conviction because the rule excludes evidence at trial. Others simply say the rule makes no sense. Justice Benjamin Cardozo reflected this opinion in 1926 when he asked: "Is it right the criminal is to go free because the constable has blundered?"

Supporters of the rule say that it affects few criminal prosecutions, partly because police today do a good job of following proper procedure. In response to critics who claim the procedures themselves hinder law enforcement, supporters point out that these procedures are required by the Constitution. The exclusionary rule simply helps ensure the police follow the Constitution.

For Discussion

1. What is the exclusionary rule? Why was it established? What two justifications are given for it?

2. Do you think it is necessary? Why or why not?

3. Why do you think the court created the good-faith exception to the rule? What problems could arise from this exception? Why?

4. Critics of the exclusionary rule have set forth a variety of proposals to change the rule. These proposals include:

- Abolishing the exclusionary rule and allowing all relevant evidence to be used in court;

- Abolishing the exclusionary rule but establishing other civil and criminal remedies for citizens when the police violate their rights (e.g. a person could bring a civil suit against the officer for invasion of privacy in cases of unreasonable searches and seizures);

- Extending the good-faith exception to all situations where the police act in good faith and in the reasonable—although mistaken—belief that their actions were legal.

What are the advantages and disadvantages of these proposals?

5. Critics of the exclusionary rule claim it needs to be changed to prevent criminals from avoiding punishment when police make technical violations of the law. Its supporters argue that any change would encourage police lawlessness.

a. Which of these positions do you agree with? Explain your answer.

b. Are there other alternatives that would respect people's Fourth and Fifth Amendment rights but not place too heavy a burden on law enforcement? Explain.

THE LIMITS OF POLICE AUTHORITY

Use of Force

O ne of the most controversial aspects of police work is the use of force. Controversy does not arise over whether police should be allowed to use force. Police are authorized to use force to enforce the law and make arrests. Questions arise when an officer uses a gun, a baton, or even restraining holds in particular situations. Did the officer need to use force? Was the force the officer used excessive? Did the force amount to brutality?

As a general rule, police may use whatever level of force is reasonable and necessary to make an arrest. For instance, shooting an unarmed person who has stolen an apple from a fruit stand would not be reasonable. Clubbing a suspect with a nightstick when a simple arm hold would suffice is not necessary.

In training programs, police officers learn how much force may be used in specific cases. They practice adjusting the level of force to the circumstances. For each situation—whether it is an arrest, crowd control, or citizen confrontation—they are taught to begin with the lowest level of force possible. They should only escalate the level of force if the situation requires it. For example, if a suspect quietly submits to an arrest, a simple pat -down search

and handcuffing is all that is necessary. But if the suspect suddenly throws a punch, a higher level of force is probably required, such as using a physical-restraint technique. All of this works well in theory. On the street, other factors—including fear, anger, darkness, and split -second changes—can make deciding what force is reasonable and necessary much more difficult.

When Is It Wrong for the Police to Use Force?

Police may use whatever force is reasonable *and* necessary to make an arrest. Often it is not reasonable or necessary for police to use force. Professor Albert Reiss has listed six examples when an assault by an arresting police officer would be wrong:

- When the officer does not attempt to arrest the person after using force to subdue the person.
- When the person does not resist arrest.
- When the person resisting arrest can be easily restrained by other methods.
- When many other officers are on the scene and can easily control the person.
- When the person is handcuffed and does not try to escape or resist violently.
- When the use of force goes on after the person stops resisting.

The Tempe, Arizona, SWAT team surrounds a house where an armed robbery suspect holds an 8-year-old boy hostage. (UPI/Bettmann.)

Police use of deadly force, especially firearms, is often highly publicized and controversial. Deadly force is commonly defined as "force that poses a high risk of death or serious injury to its human target, whether or not death or serious injury actually result." Laws governing the use of deadly force are found in state criminal codes. Some police agencies and departments have even stricter standards for their officers. The following factors, among others, are used in determining whether the use of deadly force is justified in a particular situation:

• The officer is making an arrest for a felony violation. (In general, deadly force is not justified in apprehending a person suspected of committing a misdemeanor or lesser offense.)

• The officer has made the reason for the arrest known to the suspect.

• The officer believes that deadly force is necessary to prevent death or great bodily injury to the officer or another person.

• The officer believes that the deadly force does not create a substantial risk to innocent persons.

• The criminal used deadly force or probably will use it if arrest is delayed.

NEWSBREAK

Citizen complaints about police use of force or abuse of authority commonly concern:

• *Unnecessary use of firearms or other weapons (e.g. batons, tear gas, stun guns, etc.)*

• *Use of dangerous restraint techniques (e.g. choke holds)*

• *Strip searches*

• *Ill-treatment of suspects in custody*

• *Harassment of citizens on the street*

Watch television-news broadcasts or search through magazines or newspapers or to find an example of an alleged instance of police misconduct. Write a brief report of the incident for the class giving both the citizen and police view of the incident.

In *Tennessee v. Garner* (1985), the Supreme Court ruled the Fourth Amendment puts a constitutional limit on the police's use of deadly force. In that case, police investigating a burglary saw an unarmed teen-age boy run out of a house. Giving chase and calling for him to halt, they saw the boy start to climb a chain-link fence. Realizing that the boy would escape if he made it over the fence, an officer shot and killed him. The officer had acted in accordance with Tennessee law. The law gave police authority to use *any means necessary* to arrest a fleeing felon.

The Supreme Court ruled the law did not meet the constitutional standards of the Fourth Amendment. The court held it was not reasonable to use deadly force to arrest someone unless that person posed a threat to another person.

For Discussion

1. Why might deciding what force is reasonable and necessary be difficult for a police officer in the field?

2. Do you agree with the Supreme Court's decision in *Tennessee v. Garner*? Why or why not?

3. In *People v. Gilmore* (1988), Gilmore, a private citizen, found a man trying to burglarize his house. The man ran, but Gilmore yelled three times for him to halt and then fired his gun and killed the man. Gilmore was convicted of manslaughter, but a California Court of Appeals reversed his conviction. It stated that *Tennessee v. Garner* only limits what police officers may do, not private citizens, because the Fourth Amendment only applies to government officials. Under California law, any killing "necessarily committed in attempting, by lawful ways and means, to apprehend any person for any felony committed" is justifiable. So the court found the killing justifiable. Do you think private citizens should be able to shoot non-violent fleeing felons? Do you think police should be able to? Who should have more right to use force—police or private citizens? Why?

Class Activity: Split Second

If you were a police officer in a dangerous situation, how do you think you should respond? To find out, complete the following activity.

Step I: Break into teams of two students each and read the following cases. Decide how you would handle each case and how much force, if any, is reasonable and necessary. Be prepared to discuss your answers.

Case #1: Eulia

Eulia, a 39-year-old black woman, had a dispute with a gas company serviceman. The serviceman appeared at Eulia's home to turn off the gas because of an unpaid bill. She attacked the serviceman and struck him several times with a shovel. The serviceman left and called the police.

When two police officers arrived at Eulia's home to arrest her for the aggravated assault, Eulia screamed at them and threw some dishes on the floor. The noise attracted several curious neighbors to her front porch to see what was going on. While the officers talked to Eulia from a corner of the kitchen, she suddenly picked up an 11-inch knife from the counter and prepared to throw it at them.

Case #2: Tony

Tony, a tall, thin, 17-year-old boy, was speeding and swerving his car back and forth between the lanes on the highway late one night. Two police officers stopped him and asked to see his driver's license. Tony, who had obviously been drinking, became enraged and verbally abusive.

One of the officers, a 20-year veteran of the police force, attempted to handcuff him, but Tony pushed him away, grabbed a crowbar from his back seat, and waved it at the other officer. "I'll kill you if you come near me again," he screamed.

Step II: Review the following list of factors that police officers might take into account when deciding how much force to use. Which, if any, went into your decision in the previous cases? Did any additional factors go into your decision? Be prepared to explain your answers to the class.

1. Suspect's sex
2. Suspect's age
3. Suspect's race
4. Suspect's demeanor
5. Suspect's height
6. Suspect's weight
7. Suspect's mental condition
8. Your weapon
9. Suspect's weapon

10. Time of day
11. Visibility
12. Location
13. Distance between suspect and you
14. Cover for you
15. Cover for suspect
16. Possibility of suspect's escape if deadly force is not used.
17. Presence of bystanders.
18. Availability of backup
19. Number of suspects
20. Number of officers

Step III: The teacher will call on teams to report and discuss their findings.

Debriefing Questions

1. What was the minimum use of force suggested for each case? What was the maximum?

2. After hearing all the team reports, would you modify the approach you suggested? Why or why not?

3. What factors from the list were most commonly used in making a decision? (List them on the board.) Which factors were least commonly used?

4. What factors should affect an officer's decision to use force in a particular situation? Why?

Note: In a study, 50 police officers were asked to respond to hypothetical cases just as you did here. A majority of the officers considered the following factors important:

1. Suspect's weapon
2. Location
3. Number of suspects
4. Cover for officers
5. Presence of bystanders
6. Availability of backup

7. Distance between suspect and officer

From this study, it appeared that most officers focused on location and the suspects' actions, not the suspects themselves. Other factors, such as suspects' race, sex, height, and weight, did not have as much bearing on the officers' decisions.

(AP/Wide World Photos.)

The Police Board—Policing the Police

But who will guard the guardians?

—The Roman writer Juvenal
(A.D. 50-130)

Who polices the police? This question has repeatedly come up, especially in minority communities, after incidents of alleged police brutality. Perhaps the most famous incident involved an African-American named Rodney King. Several Los Angeles police officers were videotaped beating King in 1991. The Los Angeles County district attorney filed charges against four officers. But in April 1992, a jury acquitted them of all charges. This provoked rioting and outrage in Los Angeles and other cities. It also provoked the federal government to bring criminal charges against the four officers for violating King's civil rights. At the federal trial, two of the officers were convicted. In August 1993, they were sentenced to 30 months in prison.

A CBS/New York Times poll, conducted shortly after the King beating, revealed that 65 percent of white Americans felt most charges of police brutality were probably justified. Over 80 percent of black Americans agreed. Many members of minority groups have long complained about police brutality and harassment on the street.

What can be done about police officers who behave improperly?

In cases of severe misbehavior, officers can be charged with crimes, such as in the King case. If officers use excessive force, they can face, depending on the circumstances, charges of assault under color of authority, assault with a deadly weapon, or even manslaughter or murder. Except in the most blatant cases, however, it can be very difficult to convict a police officer for using excessive force. Police reform experts point to the following as likely reasons for this difficulty:

- **Prosecutors may resist bringing charges against police**. Prosecutors work with police on a daily basis. They depend on officers to investigate crimes and testify at trials. When an officer is accused of using excessive force, other police officers tend to rally around the accused officer. Because prosecutors have working relationships with police, many avoid prosecuting police except in obvious cases of excessive force.

- **Proving excessive force can be difficult.** Since police are authorized to use force, the prosecutor does not merely have to prove that the officer assaulted the victim. The prosecutor must show that the officer used excessive force. Many of these incidents happen at night with few witnesses other than the victim and the police. And as with all criminal trials, the prosecution must convince all 12 jurors that no reasonable doubt exists that the officer used excessive force.

- **Many jurors tend to identify with the police**. Like most Americans, jurors worry about crime. They see the police as the thin blue line between them and the criminal element. Knowing how hazardous police work is, they are thankful for the protection police offer them. Since police work is so important and so dangerous, most jurors tend to give the police the benefit of the doubt at trial.

Advocates for the police see the matter in quite a different light. They believe that criminal prosecutions for excessive force are normally inappropriate. They argue that police work is highly regulated and that incidents of abuse are extremely rare. In addition, they claim that criminal laws and departmental rules regulating excessive force are difficult to apply in the field, where officers sometimes work under life-and-death circumstances. Finally, they argue that police are expected to protect citizens, be tough on criminals, and deal with the most dangerous elements in society, often with inadequate resources and little public support.

What about civil lawsuits? Are they more effective at policing the police? The number of lawsuits against police officers has risen steadily over the last 20 years. Some cities pay out millions of dollars annually to plaintiffs alleging police brutality. Because of their high cost, these suits must have some effect on encouraging cities to root out problem officers.

But for an individual with a complaint against the police, filing a lawsuit is seldom an option. Since few people can afford to pay lawyer fees, those choosing to sue must find a lawyer who will take the case on a contingency fee. This means the lawyer will not charge the client unless the client wins. Since lawyers want to get paid, they will only take cases that they have a reasonable expectation of winning. Lawyers know these cases must be very strong. For although civil suits do not share all the obstacles of a criminal trial, they do share one—jurors, most of whom are concerned about crime, may tend to see the case from the police's point of view. This means that civil suits, like criminal cases, are likely to succeed in dealing with only the most outrageous misbehavior by the police.

So what can individuals with complaints against the police do? One option is to file complaints against the officers. Most police departments have a set procedure for taking citizen complaints. But methods for handling these complaints vary.

In some cities, the police department itself handles complaints against police officers. Other police officers or the chief of police investigate the charges. In larger police departments, an "internal affairs" section staffed by special officers investigates citizen complaints and disciplines police officers who violate the law or police department regulations. These are the ways the police "police" themselves.

In recent years, the number of citizen complaints against the police has increased. Complaints range from relatively minor matters, such as failing to investigate a crime properly, to more serious cases involving police corruption or police brutality. Some complaints charge the police with mistreating people in custody.

Many people have seen a need to give citizens more control over police behavior. Some cities have used **citizen review boards** for this purpose. Composed of community members, these boards investigate reports of police misconduct and recommend what action should be taken. Citizen review boards may or may not have the power to carry out their recommendations.

Controversy, however, surrounds these boards. On the one hand, the police often

Dallas police use batons to stop a demonstration that turned violent. (UPI/Bettmann Archive.)

oppose creating these boards. They feel that their job is dangerous and not easily understood by the public. The police admit that misconduct sometimes occurs and citizen complaints must be treated seriously. But they usually insist that justice is more likely to be obtained if an accused officer is investigated by other officers who know what police work is really like. Furthermore, many police officers believe citizen controls may hamper police work and that outsiders may be hostile to the police.

On the other hand, many citizens argue that in our society civilians must exercise direct control over police behavior. Without effective civilian control, the police may apply their own standards and abuse may be more acceptable. If this occurs, citizens will lose respect for the police and for the law that the police are expected to enforce.

For Discussion

1. There are several ways of disciplining problem officers—criminal prosecutions, civil lawsuits, departmental action, and citizen review boards. What are the strengths and weaknesses of each?

2. Who should police the police? How should it be done? Explain your answer.

Class Activity: A Board of Rights

Break into groups of four members each. Each group will function as a Police Board of Rights whose purpose is to decide about possible disciplinary action against officers receiving complaints from citizens.

Each board will deal with the same two cases. In each case, the board must

(1) determine the guilt or innocence of the officers, and

(2) if guilty, decide the punishment the officer should receive.

These cases have been thoroughly investigated by the police department's Internal Affairs Division and the accused officers are fully aware of the charges against them. You and the other Board of Rights members are all high-ranking police officers. You have already heard the evidence for and against the accused officers and you have discussed the contents of each officer's personnel file. (A summary of the events of each case and the evidence before you is given below.)

Your job is to evaluate the evidence and decide on the guilt or innocence of the officers accused in the two cases. You should review each case thoroughly with the other members of your group and make a decision by majority vote. Use the following procedures to complete the activity:

1. In each group, select a chairperson. Read the materials on the two cases to be presented to the board on pages 80-82.

2. Using the questions listed under "Recommendations," discuss each case, vote on the guilt or innocence of the accused officer, and decide on an appropriate penalty, if necessary. The chairperson should record the answers to the questions and the recommendations of the group. Minority opinions should also be noted by the chairperson.

If you determine that an accused officer is innocent, you should recommend that the complaint be dropped. If you find an officer guilty, you should decide on one of the following penalties:

>   a. Reprimand (warning to be placed in the officer's file);

>   b. Suspension up to six months with loss of pay;

>   c. Removal from the force.

3. After deciding, prepare a brief report discussing the reasons for your decision and be prepared to discuss them with the class.

Case #1: Officers Mark Thomas and Stephen Campbell

Description of Events:

Mark Thomas has been on the force for six years and Stephen Campbell for five years. They are good friends. Recently, they met in a cocktail lounge at about 1 a.m. Both were just off duty and still in uniform. They had five or six beers, and Officer Campbell bought several drinks for one of the off-duty waitresses.

The two officers had a running joke about Officer Thomas wanting to buy Officer Campbell's gun. Campbell had brought the gun that evening to sell it to Thomas. Thomas kept offering more money than Campbell was willing to accept and the matter became a joke between them as they passed the gun back and forth under the table.

Meanwhile, Officer Thomas and the waitress had some disagreeable words because the waitress felt Thomas had insulted her. Thomas contends he did not mean to insult her and was only joking.

Later, when Officer Thomas left the lounge, he pretended he was going to steal a decorative keg of beer from the cocktail lounge. Thomas claims he was only joking and had no intention of stealing the keg. But the waitress grabbed the keg and took it back to the bar. The waitress was upset and Officer Campbell was unable to calm her down.

The next day, the waitress complained to the police department that the two officers had been at the bar waving guns around. She stated it was "a regular O.K. Corral without the shots fired." She also accused Officer Thomas of trying to steal the beer keg. In her written complaint, she said both Thomas and Campbell were drunk.

The waitress and her girlfriend were later interviewed together by Internal Affairs Division investigators, and so they could not be used to corroborate one another's stories. The parking lot attendant was not interviewed, nor were other witnesses found who could verify whether the officers were drunk. The bartender claimed the two officers were not drunk, but by law he must not serve intoxicated persons, so he would most likely claim they were sober. The waitress has a record of being under psychiatric care. All evidence indicates, however, that she is completely sincere and truthful.

Three charges currently exist against the two officers. They are listed below. The recommendation of the captain in charge of these officers was 15 days suspension without pay for Thomas, and 10 days for Campbell. Both officers have appealed their case to the Board of Rights contending that the punishment is unjust and the investigation was improperly handled.

Personnel Records:

Officer Mark Thomas has received only one previous complaint. This was from a motorist who objected to the traffic ticket he received and said that Officer Thomas was rude and did not call him "sir" when he spoke to him. Officer Thomas' evaluation from his superiors describes him as energetic, high spirited, and a good marksman.

Officer Campbell has received no previous complaints and has been found an excellent officer by his superiors.

Recommendations:

Based on your review of this information, do you feel that Officer Mark Thomas should be found guilty of any of the following:

>   (1) exposing a firearm unnecessarily in public;

(2) misappropriation of property (beer keg);

(3) disturbing the peace?

Should any penalty be applied? If so, what? Do you feel that Officer Stephen Campbell should be found guilty of any of the charges listed above? If so, what penalty should be applied in this case?

Case #2: Officers Sam Allen and Mary McCrea

Description of Events:

Officers Allen and McCrea were summoned about 2 a.m. to a wealthy area of town by a resident. The resident complained of a disturbance from a loud party going on next door. The resident also stated that three people wearing black leather motorcycle jackets who apparently were attending the party had come to his door, obviously drunk. One of the three reportedly carried a kitchen knife and asked to borrow a "cup of sugar and maybe some blood."

As the officers approached the caller's house, they saw a young man, about 21, standing by three motorcycles. When the man saw the officers, he joined a young woman and began walking toward the front door of the house. The officers followed them and ordered them to stop.

Officers could hear a stereo playing music seemingly at full volume inside the house. But the two people in front said that nearly everyone had gone home except maybe for "two or three people in the back yard." It was clear to the officers that the two were under the influence of alcohol or narcotics or both.

When asked what had been going on, the two people replied that some people had "just been listening to music" and "having a good time." The officers explained that a neighbor had called about a disturbance and someone using a knife in a threatening manner. The officers overheard the girl say, "I wonder if Dusty was at it again."

Officers Allen and McCrea asked to speak to the owner of the house but were told that he was not at home. Then the officers asked to speak to the host or hostess and were informed that it was an open party and there was no host or hostess. The two did not know who lived at the house. They went inside leaving the officers on the front lawn.

Just then, three people wearing black leather motorcycle jackets appeared from the side of the house. Officer Allen ordered the group to halt. He and Officer McCrea approached them. The trio was somewhat belligerent and, when questioned about the neighbor's call, said they knew nothing.

Officer Allen asked for their names. One of the group identified himself as Dusty Adams. The officer asked the group to remain until they could be identified by the complaining neighbor. They refused and said they were going to leave. At this point, Officer Allen ordered the three to stand spread-eagle with their hands on the stone wall next to the driveway. All of them began to curse.

While Officer McCrea held her gun, Officer Allen began to frisk the group. He found a kitchen knife in the boot of one. As he searched the second man, Dusty Adams turned saying, "Hey, man, listen, you don't want any trouble do you?"

"Keep your hands on the wall or we'll shoot," said Officer Allen. Adams took a step away from the wall. Officer McCrea fired, wounding Adams in the shoulder. No weapon was found on his person.

Subsequently, a complaint was filed against Officer McCrea charging that she overreacted and used unreasonable force. Internal Affairs investigated the complaint and referred it to the Board of Rights.

Officers Allen and McCrea contended that under the circumstances they had probable cause to act as they did and probable cause to believe that Dusty Adams was reaching for another weapon when he moved suddenly and removed his hands from the stone wall. Furthermore, the officers stated that the suspects had been warned, and that under the circumstances the officers had not acted unreasonably. The captain has recommended that no disciplinary action be taken against officers Allen and McCrea.

Personnel Records:

Officers Allen and McCrea have been on the force for three and two years respectively. Both are highly regarded by their superiors. Neither has received any previous complaints.

Recommendations:

In your opinion should Officer Sam Allen or Officer Mary McCrea be found guilty of using unreasonable force? If so, what should the penalty be?

Debriefing Questions

1. What was the most difficult part of deciding these cases? Why?

2. What factors might make the job of a police rights board difficult and controversial? Why?

3. What if your group had been made up only of citizens concerned about police behavior? Would you have decided any of these cases differently?

Community Policing

The 1980s saw several experiments in developing a new relationship between the police and their communities. These programs involved major changes in the way the police were trained and organized. The new type of policing—called **community-oriented policing**, or **problem-solving policing**—was strongly backed by some police departments, but opposed just as strongly by determined voices within many departments. The new movement went against reforms that police departments across the country had instituted from the 1930s through the 1960s.

During that period, most police departments in America went through a reform process that left them more disciplined and more professional. Also, by the 1950s, the police had come to rely heavily on squad cars, radio, and other technology. Their primary activity was responding to emergency calls. Some of this change was driven by corruption scandals. Reformers felt that beat cops were too close to local criminals and too easy to corrupt. But economics accounted for much of the change. Through mobility and technology, reformers believed effective policing could be maintained with fewer officers.

The system that developed did away with foot patrols in favor of squad cars. Often called **proactive policing** or **motorized rapid response**, this approach relied on radio to direct cruising police cars to emergency calls. This meant that most officers had little contact with their communities, except when they were arresting suspects or investigating crimes. And what officers did see of a community was often from the window of a car.

By the 1980s many people were criticizing the shortcomings of rapid motorized response. They felt this system left the police too divorced from the community, and created a bitter "us and them" feeling on both sides. Cities such as Houston, Texas, Newark, New Jersey, and Flint, Michigan, began to experiment with different systems. They sent many officers back on beat patrols on foot, or horseback, or even bicycle. They also tried to develop **neighborhood watch** programs of local residents who would watch over their communities and tell the police of any problems they could see developing.

The point of most of these new programs was to get the patrol officers to think in terms of patterns of criminal activity, not single radio calls for help. Officers would be visible continuously in an area, not just sent periodically into a community. And most of all, the officers would work actively to win local cooperation and look for causes of crime.

Experiments in community policing have now spread to the nation's two largest cities, New York and Los Angeles. Police Comissioner Raymond Kelly in New York is now restoring foot patrols throughout New York City. Chief

Members of Seattle's bike squad make their rounds on special heavy-duty, 18-speed mountain bikes. (UPI/Bettmann.)

Willie Williams in Los Angeles had instituted community policing in Philadelphia. He began strengthening community support groups and changing policies when he took over the Los Angeles police after that city's 1992 riots.

At root, community policing tries to go beyond seeing the police officer as someone who simply prevents crime or catches criminals. Officers are expected to be visible in their communities, to work with neighborhood organizations to identify social problems, and even to suggest solutions to some of the problems. Officers are not really expected to be social workers.

But since they are often the only representatives of the city or county who are widely visible in the community, they are expected to establish a working relationship that will help neighborhoods help themselves.

In Flint, Michigan, statistics suggest that after the introduction of community policing, crime rates went down, as did the number of emergency calls. Residents say they feel safer, and the police, too, say they are happier with their jobs. They no longer feel the community is made up entirely of hostile faces peering at them—the old "us and them" relationship.

On the other hand, community policing is expensive. It takes much more personnel to patrol an area continuously than to respond once in a while to 911 calls. Also many police command structures resist it. Senior officers have become used to the old rapid response style, and many of them dismiss community policing as a misguided experiment that just wastes personnel. One further problem is that promotions often take officers off the street. This means that the most capable officers wind up in investigation or administration and not on street patrol.

It remains to be seen how well community policing will catch on. It will probably take a noticeable success in reducing the crime rate in one of our major cities before the new approach can win widespread support. At the moment, police efficiency is still widely judged by arrest rates and response times. Community policing is not geared to these statistics, but instead tries to identify and alleviate long-term problems.

Many police departments have committed themselves in principle to community policing. But they don't have the money to hire enough officers or to train officers in community-policing techniques. Most cities will probably not commit the necessary money and energy to community policing until there is some clear evidence of success.

For Discussion

1. What are the advantages and disadvantages of community policing?

2. What are the advantages and disadvantages of motorized rapid response?

3. Why might some police officers prefer working in a department that uses community-oriented policing? Why might others prefer a department that uses motorized rapid response?

4. Which type of policing would you prefer in your community? Why?

You and the Police

At some time, you may have a difficult contact with the police. They may want to question you. You may be subject to arrest. It might be because of your conduct or just because you happen to be in the wrong place at the wrong time.

It is important to remember that the police work for you as a citizen of your community, whatever your age, race, or job. The police are required to respect your rights. You, in turn, should respect their authority and understand the difficulties of their job. Mutual respect can go a long way toward easing tension in a difficult situation.

The following is some general advice on what to do if the police stop you. In any particular situation, you should always rely on your best judgment and, when possible, the advice of a lawyer.

If You Are Stopped by a Police Officer

1. Be courteous and cooperative. Avoid hostility, profanity, or aggressive movements. Do nothing to cause an officer to believe you are a threat.

2. Give your name and address, or show an I.D. if requested.

3. The police can search you for concealed weapons by patting your clothing. Do not physically resist, but you have the right to tell the officer that you do not agree to any search of yourself, your car, or your surroundings. By making it clear that you do not consent to any search, you can protect your right against unlawful searches. The police may search you or your surroundings anyway. Do not try to stop them physically. You can question the legality of the search in court. If the police say that they have a warrant, ask to see it.

4. If you believe the police have violated your rights, you have the right to file a complaint.

If You Are Arrested or Held

1. Never run away, strike an officer, or physically resist, whether you are innocent or guilty. If you resist or try to escape, the police can use whatever force is reasonable and necessary to stop you.

2. You are entitled to your *Miranda* rights, which include the right to remain silent. You are required to tell the police nothing except your name and address. Giving explanations or stories or trying to excuse your conduct will rarely benefit you unless your lawyer advises you to do so.

3. Ask to see a lawyer immediately. If you cannot pay for a lawyer, you have the right to request the police to get you a lawyer before you talk to officials.

4. After arrest, use your right to make a telephone call to a relative, trusted friend, or lawyer for assistance. If you are under age 18, you may not be permitted to make telephone calls. Ask to see a lawyer. You generally have the right to go into court the next court day after your arrest and you can ask to be released on bail, although the law may differ for minors.

5. Do not make any decisions in your case until you have talked to a lawyer and understand what your choices are.

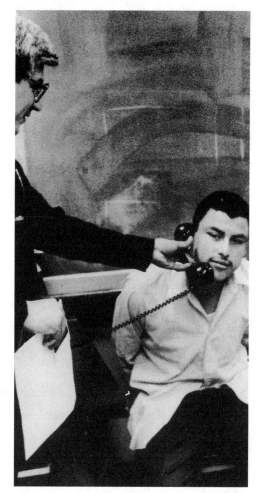

Suspect in custody and restrained is given phone call. (AP/Wide World Photos.)

For Discussion

1. How can you best assure mutual respect between you and the police?

2. Do you think mutual respect between you and the police is important? Why or why not?

3. Why is it important not to resist police?

chapter three:

THE
CRIMINAL
CASE

On July 6, shots ring out in a quiet residential community. A human life is taken and a suspect arrested. . .

So begins the criminal case of People v. Carter. Although fictional, it is like real-life events that take place each day in cities and towns throughout the United States. There is only one important difference.

This time, you and your class will be on the scene from beginning to end—and not just as observers. You will step into the roles of lawyers, judges, and jurors in a criminal case. You will study the police report, meet the defendant and hear his side of the story, help the prosecutors prepare their case, rule on motions, and select a jury. Eventually, you will see the trial itself unfold and participate in finding the truth about the events on that hot July evening. Ultimately, your actions and decisions will take the case to a final verdict. When you are finished, you will have taken a behind-the-scenes look at how the criminal justice system handles a criminal case and the philosophies and procedures that shape the system.

CRIMINAL CASE, INVESTIGATION, AND ARREST

The Criminal Case Process

Every year, state and federal criminal justice systems handle thousands of criminal cases. Most cases are routine: A crime occurs, a suspect is identified, arrested, and charged. If the defendant pleads guilty, which most do, a trial does not take place. Aside from realizing that police departments are overworked, courts are overburdened, and prisons are overcrowded, the general public is barely aware of the daily routine of criminal justice activity.

What does capture public attention is the big case. A sensational murder or a multi-million dollar fraud case can make headlines in our daily newspapers for months. Reporters clamor for interviews with the prosecution and defense teams, TV-news programs detail the day's courtroom events, and the defendant's name becomes a household word.

Although these big cases are not typical, they do give us a dramatic glimpse of the criminal justice process. These cases introduce us to a mind-boggling array of courthouse characters, legal termi-

nology, procedural steps, and legal issues. At any point along the way, we might throw up our hands and mutter, "What's the point of all this? Did he do it or didn't he do it?" Since no one can read a suspect's mind and no one can peer back into the past to find out exactly what happened, we need some system to find the truth.

The Adversary System

Central to truth-finding in our criminal case process is the so-called adversarial process. In it, opposing attorneys introduce evidence to neutral fact finders—the judge or jury. Ultimately, the fact finder must decide the facts of a particular case and come to a verdict.

In this process, the attorneys are advocates and adversaries. They try to present facts in a light most favorable to their side and point out weaknesses in their opponents' case. Through well-planned strategies and legal arguments, they try to convince the court to see "truth" as they do. In a criminal case, the opposing sides are the prosecution and the defense.

The basic goal of the prosecution is to protect society from crime by making sure the guilty are tried, convicted, and punished. By filing charges against a particular defendant, the prosecutor is claiming that the individual has committed a crime.

At trial, the prosecutor must prove the claim beyond a reasonable doubt.

The basic goal of the defense is to challenge the prosecutor's case by raising all reasonable doubts about the defendant's guilt. Defense attorneys must also make sure that the defendant gets every right and benefit guaranteed under the law and Constitution.

By pitting these two sides against one another, it is believed that the truth will come out. For example, if the prosecution's case depends on an eyewitness's identifying the defendant as the robber, the defense might go to great lengths to question the memory or eyesight of the witness. The defense can be assured of a similar strict examination of any evidence it produces. Under the adversary system, the judge or jury must decide which version is true.

The fact finder must go through this process with all the evidence produced at trial. Before determining a defendant's guilt or innocence, the fact finder must weigh a lot of evidence and establish facts. Are the witnesses believable? Are the lab tests accurate? Are the connections between the various pieces of evidence logical and supportable? What other explanations for the alleged events are possible? Indeed, the quest for truth pervades a criminal trial.

Because the adversarial process involves humans, it is not foolproof. Memories fail, witnesses see the same event in different ways, reasonable people differ about what is true. Sometimes, biases and prejudices arise, lies are told. In extreme cases, truth can get lost when an advocate goes too far in trying to win. An emotional argument can sway a jury in spite of the facts. Important evidence can be concealed.

To protect against these problems, our criminal case process has developed sophisticated checks and balances. Some protect the process itself, while others protect the defendant. Judges and jurors can be removed for bias or prejudice. Witnesses are sworn to tell the truth and can be punished if they lie. Criminal defendants in serious cases can count on representation by an attorney, a trial by jury, the right to confront accusers, a speedy and public trial, and the right

to appeal. They are also protected against having to post an excessive amount for bail or having to testify against themselves. These protections come from the Constitution of the United States and the constitutions and laws of the various states.

Facts, Facts, Facts

Basic to every criminal case are facts. When used to prove a point before a court, they are called **evidence**. Evidence comes from the testimony of witnesses or from physical items related to the crime. Woven together, the evidence can tell a story of guilt or innocence.

As you will discover, facts are important at every stage and to every person in the criminal-case process. Consider just a few examples. A police officer must have sufficient facts to show probable cause to arrest a suspect or conduct a search. A judge examines these facts before issuing a warrant. A criminal trial judge may be called upon to decide whether facts offered in evidence are relevant to the case.

The facts in the case of *People v. Carter* will be important throughout this chapter. They are found, among other places, in the Police Investigation Report, in the defendant's story, and in the witnesses' statements. Sometimes you will be using facts as attorneys do. For example, in one activity you will take the role of prosecutors and, based on the facts, decide whether to bring a particular charge. In another, you will cross-examine witnesses to establish or refute facts contained in their testimony.

Other times you will take a more impartial attitude toward the facts. For example, as jurors you will decide what the facts are and whether taken together they amount to the defendant's guilt beyond a reasonable doubt.

For Discussion

1. What is the main purpose of the criminal-case process?

2. What is the adversary system? How does it aid truth-finding in a criminal case? What might be some weaknesses in the system?

3. What are some checks and balances found in the criminal-case process?

4. Imagine that a defendant (D) is being tried for assault with a deadly weapon.

The following chart summarizes the facts as introduced at trial:

A. Prosecutor's Facts

a. D owns a .38 caliber Smith & Wesson handgun registered in his name.

b. D's pistol was found by the investigating officers at the scene of the shooting.

c. A fingerprint expert testified that D's fingerprints were all over the handgun found at the scene. The gun had no other fingerprints on it.

d. One witness testified that two hours before the assault he heard D threaten to shoot the victim.

e. The victim's neighbor, who reported the crime, testified that he heard shots fired at 7:35 p.m. on August 1.

B. Defendant's Facts

a. D testified that his pistol was stolen from his house about July 29. No police report was made because D did not discover it missing until August 2.

b. D's business partner testified that D was having dinner with her between 6:45 and 8:30 p.m. on August 1.

In your own words, summarize the sequence of events as the prosecutor might see them. Do the same thing from the defense's point of view. Then answer the following questions:

- To prove a case beyond a reasonable doubt, which facts must the prosecutor cast doubt upon? Why?
- If the facts described in B-b are proved false, could the defense still win? Why or why not?
- Why would the examination of witnesses under oath be very important to this case?

A sheriff's investigator examines the spot where a body of a murder victim was found. (AP/Wide World Photos.)

Using This Chapter

This chapter has four major features:

The Criminal Justice Case Guide

This chart on pages 92-93 will show you each important step in a criminal case. It starts when a crime is committed and continues until a court imposes sentence. Because procedures vary in different jurisdictions, your state's procedures may vary slightly from this guide.

Key Steps

These special sections are found throughout the unit and provide more detailed information about the various steps outlined in the Criminal Justice Case Guide. A typical key step will give a particular procedure's purpose and describe what happens during that procedure.

Case Notes

These reading selections tell you about the Carter murder case. In them, you will meet all the main characters, discover facts, and learn law about the case.

Activities

Each activity focuses on the criminal case—an issue or event—and *you* will be on the firing line. Sometimes you will be asked to take the role of an attorney, sometimes a judge or juror. By the time the unit is over, you will have argued constitutional questions, evaluated evidence, examined witnesses, made judicial rulings, and come to a verdict in the case of *People v. Carter*.

Case Notes: Cast of Characters I

A criminal case depends on people. Many of them are professionals who devote long hours to investigating, preparing, trying, and administering criminal cases. Other people, as witnesses or jurors, are drawn into one particular case by chance or civic duty. The process needs them all.

As you go through the case of *People v. Carter*, you will learn about many of these people. Since at times you will be asked to take on their roles, you must find out as much about them as you can. The following descriptions will give you an idea about some of the participants you will meet first.

1. *Police Officers*

Police officers investigate crimes and arrest suspects. Many criminal cases begin when police uncover enough facts to establish probable cause to make an arrest. During a criminal case, judges, prosecutors, and defense attorneys test these facts many times.

2. *Prosecutor*

The prosecutor—sometimes called the district attorney or state's attorney—represents the public. The prosecutor presents the government's case against the defendant. At trial, the prosecutor must prove the defendant's guilt beyond a reasonable doubt.

3. *Defense Attorney*

The defense attorney prepares and presents the defendant's case. To present the defendant's version of the facts, the defense attorney tries to find supportive witnesses and calls them to testify. The defense attorney raises reasonable doubts about the defendant's guilt and may present affirmative defenses.

4. *Judge*

Judges preside over all court hearings. In some criminal cases, several different judges participate. For example, a lower-court judge will often preside at the defendant's first pretrial appearance. These judges are sometimes **magistrates** or **municipal-court judges**. A judge from the court handling felonies will preside at the **arraignment** (a pretrial hearing where formal charges are made) and at the trial itself. If the defendant appeals, appellate court judges will rule on the appeal. Appeals court judges are often called **justices**.

For Discussion

1. Briefly review the different jobs that judges must do. Which would you say is the most important job? Why?

2. What is the main function of a prosecutor in a criminal trial? What is the main function of a defense attorney?

3. During a criminal case, why is it important to test the facts uncovered by investigating police officers?

NEWSBREAK

1. All students should watch their daily newspapers for a week or two. They should cut out articles on the following nine steps in a criminal case: (1) arrest, (2) first appearance before a judge, (3) bail, (4) preliminary hearing or indictment, (5) arraignment, (6) pretrial motions, (7) trial, (8) sentencing, and (9) post-trial motions.

2. Bring the articles to class.

3. Select one article for each of the 10 steps and make a bulletin board display.

The Criminal Justice

INVESTIGATION AND ARREST 1

- Incident
- Warrant
- Arrest

PRETRIAL 2

- First Court Appearance
- Probable Cause Hearing—
  Indictment or Information
- Arraignment
- Pretrial Motions

CASE GUIDE

POST TRIAL 4

- Post-trial Motions
- Appeals to Higher Court

TRIAL 3

- Jury Selection
- Trial
- Sentencing

Class Activity: Criminal Case Characters

On a sheet of paper, number from one to seven. Place the appropriate letter next to the number that matches the individual's duty in a criminal case. (Letters will be used more than once.)

A. Police Officer
B. Prosecutor
C. Defense Attorney
D. Lower-Court Judge
E. Trial Level Judge

1. Raises reasonable doubts about the prosecutor's case.
2. Presides at defendant's first court appearance.
3. Presents the government's case.
4. Presides at the arraignment.
5. Must have probable cause to arrest.
6. Establishes affirmative defenses.
7. Sometimes called a district attorney or state's attorney.

Key Step: Arrest

What It Is:
An arrest is the taking of a criminal suspect into custody to charge the suspect with a crime.

What Is Required:
An arrest must be based on probable cause; and:
- must be made with a valid warrant;
or
- must be made without a warrant under one of the judicially recognized exceptions to the Fourth Amendment warrant requirement.

Who May Arrest:
Depending on the jurisdiction, arrests may be carried out by:
- Law enforcement officials.
- Private citizens. (Many jurisdictions, however, restrict your right as a private citizen to make an arrest. In some jurisdictions, you may only arrest people for certain offenses, for example, felonies and misdemeanors, but not for violating ordinances. In other jurisdictions you may not make a citizen's arrest for a misdemeanor unless the misdemeanor is committed in your presence. In a few jurisdictions, you cannot make a mistake: If it turns out that the suspect did not actually commit the offense, then the arrest is not valid and you can be sued for false arrest. *It is important to find out the law in your own state.*)

Police Crime Investigation Report

Date of Investigation
July 6-7

Investigating Officer
Lt. Tony Jackson

Crime Description
At approximately 7 p.m. on Tuesday, July 6, Joyce Ann Miller, age 4, was hit in the head and chest by a shotgun blast at a range of about 10 yards. The victim died instantly.

Arrest
At 11:45 p.m. on July 7, I arrested Thomas Wade Carter and booked him for murder in the first degree.

Report of Investigation
1. On Monday evening, July 5, the arrestee, Thomas Wade Carter, age 18, went to a party at the home of his girlfriend, Gail Duran. Witnesses at the party report that almost everyone there, including the suspect, consumed a lot of beer. A fight broke out at about 3 a.m. Witnesses could not identify everyone who was involved in the fight, but told me that suspect Carter was clubbed over the head with a beer bottle by another guest named Oscar Hanks. Friends took

Carter to the hospital for treatment. Five stitches were required to close the wound.

2. On Tuesday, July 6, at about 5 p.m., Carter visited the apartment of a friend, Joel Robertson. Robertson stated that Carter was still angry about being hit during the fight the night before. Robertson also said that Carter remarked, "I'm going to get that guy once and for all. That man is going to pay in a big way." Carter also asked Robertson how to work one of his shotguns. Robertson is a hunter who owns several guns.

3. At about 6:30 p.m. on July 6, Carter visited the home of Gail Duran. Ms. Duran told me that Carter was still angry about what had happened the night before. She also said that Carter told her he knew who had hit him. Carter invited Duran to go for a ride with him and she agreed. He asked Duran to drive his car while he sat in the back seat giving her directions. Duran stated that Carter directed her to Fourth Street. When he spotted a red Toyota truck parked in front of one of the houses, he told her to slow down. At this point, according to Duran, she noticed for the first time that Carter was handling a shotgun. She said she became very nervous. Suddenly, according to Duran, there was a loud explosion inside the car. Startled, Duran stepped on the gas pedal and quickly drove away. She stopped on a quiet street nearby. Carter then got into the driver's seat and took her home. Duran stated that Carter told her on the drive back to her home that all of a sudden the shotgun had gone off by itself. He also stated that he did not think he had hit anything.

4. The only eyewitness to the shooting of Joyce Ann Miller was her mother, Ms. Karen Miller. At about 7 p.m. on July 6, Ms. Miller told her daughter to close the front gate to the yard. Ms. Miller watched as her daughter went to close the gate. Ms. Miller then noticed a black car driving slowly on the street in front of her house. She also saw a long gun barrel pointing out of its rear window right at her daughter. Before she could say or do anything, Ms. Miller stated, there was a loud blast and Joyce Ann collapsed. Ms. Miller and her neighbors rushed to help Joyce Ann. Paramedics were called, but Joyce Ann was pro-

nounced dead on arrival at Central Receiving Hospital. Ms. Miller stated that she had no idea who killed her daughter and could offer no description of the occupants of the black car except that she thought the driver was a young woman.

5. The Miller residence is located three doors to the east of Oscar Hanks' residence on Fourth Street.

6. That evening at 10:05 p.m., I received an anonymous phone call at the police station. The caller said, "If you want to know who murdered that little girl, you better check out what happened at Gail Duran's party last night." After interviewing a number of witnesses at the party, including Joel Robertson and Gail Duran, I arrested Thomas Wade Carter at 11:45 p.m. on July 7. I read the suspect his *Miranda* rights and booked him for the first-degree murder of Joyce Ann Miller.

For Discussion

1. To arrest Carter, Lt. Jackson must have had **probable cause**. Probable cause means that the officer has enough evidence to cause a reasonable person to believe that a crime was committed and that the suspect committed it. Murder is often defined as the unlawful killing of a human being with **malice aforethought**. "Malice aforethought" refers to the state of mind of the person doing the killing. Malice aforethought can mean that the killer with no serious provocation from the victim

- intended to kill; or
- intended to inflict great bodily harm; or
- intended to do any act where there was an obvious risk that death or great bodily injury might result.

What evidence did Lt. Jackson have that might give him probable cause to arrest Carter on a charge of murder? *Explain your answer.*

2. According to the information gathered by Lt. Jackson, do we know for sure what happened inside the Pontiac at the moment the shotgun was

fired. What else *could* have happened? What are some other ways the shooting could have taken place?

Case Notes: State Criminal Code Sections

In the state where Joyce Ann Miller was killed, the following criminal laws define the various forms of criminal homicide.

Section 274: Degrees of Murder

(a) *Murder in the First Degree*: All killings committed with malice aforethought and which are premeditated.

(b) *Murder in the Second Degree*: All other killings with malice aforethought.

Section 298: Manslaughter

Any killing committed without malice aforethought.

(a) *Voluntary Manslaughter*: All *intentional* killings committed as a result of serious *provocation* or *extreme anger*.

(b) *Involuntary Manslaughter*: All *unintentional* killings which are the direct result of committing:

> 1. any *dangerous* and *unlawful* act; or
>
> 2. any *lawful act* in an extremely *careless* or negligent manner.

For Discussion

1. Under the laws of Joyce Ann Miller's state, what is the major difference between the crimes of murder and manslaughter?

2. What is malice aforethought? What is premeditation? (If necessary, review materials in Chapter 1.)

3. Reread section 274 of the state code. What is the major difference between first and second-degree murder?

4. Reread section 298 of the state code. What is the major difference between voluntary and involuntary manslaughter?

Class Activity: Is It Murder?

In pairs, read the following descriptions of other killings in Joyce Ann Miller's state. For each one, decide which form of criminal homicide should be charged, based on the elements from the state criminal code.

a. Mr. Jones poisoned his wife's coffee over a period of several weeks, resulting in her death.

CRIME BEAT

Imagine you are a crime beat reporter for a local news outlet. Your editor has assigned you to do background research for a story about the upcoming Carter trial. You will need to find answers to the following questions:

• *How does your state classify homicide?*

• *What elements must the state prove in each?*

• *What would the state have to prove to convict Carter of the various homicide offenses in your state?*

The editor advises you to ask a criminal attorney or police officer to read the Police Crime Investigation Report on page 31 and then answer the questions.

Submit a one-page summary of your findings.

---

b. David, not aiming at anyone, fired his rifle into a passing bus, killing the driver.

c. Mary, furious because Joan hit her with an umbrella, stabbed and killed Joan.

d. Jim threw apples onto the highway from an overpass, causing a car to swerve off the road and crash. The driver died from his injuries. (A state law makes throwing anything off an overpass a misdemeanor.)

e. Donna, a scuba diver, pulled her friend's mouthpiece regulator out when they were 50 feet underwater as a joke. Her friend drowned.

When everyone finishes, discuss each situation with the whole class.

Case Notes: In the Defense of Thomas Carter

A police officer conducts a stop-and-frisk search of suspected gang members. (AP/Wide World Photos.)

After his arrest, Thomas Carter exercised his *Miranda* rights and remained silent. He called his parents, who hired a private attorney, Susan Jaffee, to represent him. Many defendants cannot afford an attorney and must wait for the court to appoint a public defender or free private attorney to represent them. To qualify for such an appointment, defendants must show that they cannot afford to pay an attorney.

The first thing Carter's attorney did was to go to the police station to interview her client. Jaffee asked Carter to explain what happened. Carter told his side of the story, and she took notes.

Carter's Story

"Last Monday night I went to a party at my girlfriend Gail's house. We drank some beer and had a good time. Then sometime around 3 a.m. a bunch of guys started to fight. I don't even know why it started. All I know is that I got hit on the head with a beer bottle. It split my scalp, and I was all bloody. I had to go to the hospital. It took five stitches to stop the bleeding.

"While we were driving to the hospital I was mad, and I wanted to know who hit me. When one of the guys mentioned that Oscar Hanks could have done it, I knew he was right. Oscar and I got into a fight about a month ago, and he knifed me in the leg.

"The day after Gail's party, I decided to get back at Oscar. I know it was dumb, but I decided to take my Dad's shotgun and blast a bunch of holes in Oscar's truck. He really loves that truck, you know. Well, this is when I got into trouble. I got the shotgun, and even asked Joel Robertson how to work it. He's a hunter and has a couple of his own. Then I went over to Gail's to get her to drive me around Oscar's neighborhood. I spotted his truck and was going to blast it. Before I had a chance, the car swerved or something, and the gun went off. I didn't even think I hit anything. I didn't see anybody. Still, it was real scary! I told Gail to get us out of there fast.

"Look, I know I'm in big trouble. But believe me, I didn't mean to fire the gun or shoot that little girl. I didn't even know she was there! I swear, it was an accident."

How It Looks to Carter's Attorney

Susan Jaffee finished jotting down her notes and then gave Carter an overview of her thoughts on the case.

"Tom, I hope you are telling me the truth. But, even if you are, it's still going to be a tough case to defend. For one thing, the shooting death of a 4-year-old girl is going to stir up a lot of emotion in this community. The newspapers have been running stories for weeks on youth violence and gangs, and your case will get a lot of coverage. At this point, the police are talking about first-degree murder, and with all this publicity the prosecutor could stick to those charges. We'll just have to wait until they review the evidence and decide what charges to file. They might decide to charge you with something less serious. Meanwhile, I'll start checking out the witnesses. A lot can happen between now and the trial.

"First, we have to get through your first court appearance. I'll need to ask you some questions. This information might help get you out of here on bail. It will be difficult, but if your parents can raise the money, I'll try.

"Next, we have to face a probable cause hearing where the judge will decide whether you have to stand trial on whatever the prosecution charges you with. In the meantime, we have the right to discovery. This means we will find out exactly what evidence the prosecution is relying on. The probable cause hearing will give us a chance to test some of their witnesses.

"If there is a finding of probable cause, you will have to make an appearance at an arraignment. There, depending on what happens, you'll have to plead to the charges and a trial will be scheduled. At that stage, I might be able to do something about the publicity problem. At the very least, we'll do our best to make sure the jurors are not influenced too much by media reports.

"While we are waiting to hear from the prosecutors, I want you to think about some things. I want you to think over everything you have told me today. If you have forgotten anything, I want to know. If you did not give me the whole story, I want to know. Right now, I'm the best friend you've got. No surprises, OK?"

Back in her office, Jaffee reviewed the information Carter had given her about his background. She knew that another court agency would be compiling a similar report for the judge to consider in deciding on the issue of Carter's pretrial release. A summary of her notes follows.

File: *Thomas Carter/*Background

Prior Arrests/Convictions

No prior convictions. One arrest for disturbing the peace. The charges were subsequently dropped. At the age of 17, Carter was cited for reckless driving and his driver's license was suspended for six months.

Employment

Employed full time as an assistant manager of the parts department of a local auto dealership. He has held his present position for nearly six months after having worked there part time during high school. His current income is $20,000 a year.

School Record

Carter was an average student throughout high school. Because of poor attendance, however, he completed some credits for graduation at a continuation high school. He was suspended twice, once for fighting, once for truancy. Recently, he completed a special three-week course offered by Ford Motor Company in parts management before qualifying for his present job.

Residence

Carter lives at home with his mother, sister, and younger cousin. He makes monthly contributions for rent, utilities, food, and maintenance.

two

PRETRIAL

Key Step: First Appearance Before a Judge

Purpose:

To ensure that criminal suspects know their rights and are not abused by authorities, most jurisdictions require that the police bring an arrested person (arrestee) before a judge. Some states require that this first appearance take place within a specified period—for example, within 24 or 48 hours after arrest. Other jurisdictions simply say that it must take place without unnecessary delay.

Typical Procedures

The judge:

• *Informs the arrestee of the charges.*

• *Informs the arrestee of the right to counsel.* If the arrestee cannot afford to hire an attorney, the judge will appoint one. (These court-appointed lawyers for criminal defendants are often government employees, known as public defenders. In some cases, the judge appoints private attorneys to represent criminal defendants for no fee.)

• *Determines bail.* Generally, state laws or court rules set bail schedules for misdemeanor offenses. Thus, if a person is accused of committing a misdemeanor, the judge simply

refers to the predetermined bail list to set bail. In felony cases, the judge must either:

> 1. fix the amount of bail (often with reference to state-imposed standards);
>
> 2. release the arrestee without bail (on the arrestee's own recognizance); or
>
> 3. in limited instances, deny bail altogether.

Class Activity: The Question of Bail

As outlined in the *Key Step*, there are two ways for criminal defendants to be released from jail pending trial. First, a judge might set bail: The judge will require defendants to deposit a certain amount of money with the court as security that they will come back for trial. Some defendants have enough money to pay for bail themselves. Others rely on private bail bond companies which post the necessary amount for a fee—usually between 10 and 20 percent of the amount. If defendants post bail and show up for trial, they get all their bail money back. Defendants who fail to appear in court lose all their bail money.

The second method of pretrial release is release on one's own recognizance. This means that a judge releases a criminal suspect after the suspect promises to return for trial. No bail is required. This method is usually available only to persons accused of non-violent and relatively minor crimes. As in bail cases, the judge must be convinced that the defendant will not leave town or try to intimidate witnesses before the trial.

In certain cases, a judge may refuse to release a defendant prior to trial. Many state criminal codes define particular crimes as non-bailable offenses. Typically, these are crimes punishable by death or by life imprisonment without possibility of parole. In some states, defendants who have stalked their victims, who are members of criminal organizations, or who pose a high risk of running away may also be denied bail. These cases present a much greater danger to society or a higher risk of the defendant fleeing to avoid prosecution.

Judicial Criteria for Setting Bail

Under the criminal laws of the state where Joyce Ann Miller was killed, the offense in this particular case is bailable. As for being released on his own recognizance, Carter would have almost no chance in this or any other state. Therefore the criminal court judge must determine an appropriate amount of bail for Thomas Wade Carter.

The criteria that a judge must take into consideration in setting bail include among other things:

- the crime;
- the past record of the accused; and
- the likelihood that the defendant will remain in the state and appear in court.

Procedures

Preparation

Invite a criminal lawyer into the class to take part in the activity and debriefing.

1. *Review:*

a. Police Crime Investigation Report on page 94;

b. Thomas Carter's statement on page 97; and

c. Susan Jaffee's file on page 98.

Defendants, dressed in jail garb, wait in a holding cell for their pretrial hearings. (AP/Wide World Photos.)

2. *Divide the class into three groups:* Students in the first group will role-play prosecuting attorneys, those in the second will role-play defense attorneys, and those in the third will role-play judges. Assume that $100,000 is the minimum bail set by law and that the maximum would be $500,000.

3. *Attorney instructions:*

- *Prosecutors:* To make sure Thomas Carter appears for trial, you believe that a high bail is necessary. Work with a partner from within your own group to develop arguments to support your position. List five or more facts you think are the most important to support your position. Keep in mind the criteria (mentioned above) that the judge will apply in deciding. Once you have developed your arguments and have listed the facts to back them up, share your ideas with the other members of the prosecution group. What are the three best arguments in favor of a higher bail for the accused in this case? What facts do you have to support your arguments?

- *Defense attorneys:* Follow the instructions in the paragraph above, except that you will be trying to convince the judge to set as low a bail as possible for your client, Thomas Carter. You believe he will appear for trial and want to minimize his financial burden. Carter's parents have told you that at most they can raise $15,000. Since a bond requires 10 percent up front, this means the maximum bail they can meet is $150,000. Work with a partner from within your group to develop arguments in favor of your position. List five or more facts you think are the most important to support your position. Keep in mind the criteria (mentioned above) that the judge will apply in deciding. Once you have developed your arguments and have listed the facts to back them up, share your ideas with the other members of the defense group. What are the three best arguments in favor of a low bail for the accused in this case? What facts do you have to support your arguments?

3. *Judge Instructions:*

Your job will be to listen to the lawyers' arguments and determine what bail should be set for Thomas Carter. Work with a partner from within your group to develop questions to ask the attorneys. List five or more questions you think are important. Keep in mind the criteria (mentioned above) that you, the judges, will apply in deciding. Once you have developed your

---

CRIME BEAT

Imagine you are a crime beat reporter for a local news outlet. Your editor has assigned you to do background research for an editorial on bail. You need to find out if your state's criminal law has any non-bailable offenses. If so, what are they? Your editor also wants your opinions: Do you believe bail should be denied in the instances allowed by your state? Why or why not?

Submit a one-page summary of your findings.

For ideas on sources for this information, see "Crime Beat" on page 31.

---

questions, share your ideas with the other members of the judge group.

At the bail hearing, let the attorney for the defendant speak first, then the prosecutor. You may interrupt the attorneys to ask questions. After hearing both sides, make your decision on what Thomas Carter's bail should be. Be sure to base your decision on the criteria. Do not announce your decision to the attorneys. Instead write it on a piece of paper. Be prepared to discuss the facts and arguments that influenced your decision.

4. *Role-play:*

After the groups have prepared, form small groups consisting of one prosecutor, one defense attorney, and one judge. The judge in each group should conduct the bail hearing.

5. *Decision:*

After both sides have presented their arguments, the judges should write down their decisions on Thomas Carter's bail and their reasoning. Regroup the class and have each judge announce the bail set for Thomas Carter and discuss the facts and arguments that influenced the decision. If a criminal lawyer has taken part in the activity, he or she should be asked to discuss the likely outcome of the bail hearing if this had been a real case.

6. *Debriefing:*

Hold a class discussion using the following questions:

- Do you agree that bail should sometimes be denied and an accused person held in custody? Explain your answer. If you agree, under what circumstances should judges be allowed to deny bail? Why?

- The American criminal trial system is based on the notion that a person is presumed to be innocent until proved guilty. Do you think that the system of bail runs contrary to this concept? Why or why not?

Case Notes: Prosecutorial Review

After the police make a felony arrest, the prosecutor reviews the case to decide what crimes should be charged and what strategies might be used in handling the case. The prosecutor exercises what is called **prosecutorial discretion** in choosing how to approach the case. Depending on the jurisdiction, the review can be made by an individual prosecutor or by a special team of prosecutors working closely with the police in evaluating cases after arrest. After the review, the case may be assigned to another prosecutor.

During the initial review, prosecutors must first decide if they have enough evidence to file formal charges against the arrestee. To do this, they must go over the possible charges. Then they must review each element of these crimes and decide if they have enough evidence to prove it. For example, the crime of larceny usually has the following four elements:

(1) The taking and carrying away

(2) of personal property

(3) that belongs to another person

(4) with the intent to *permanently deprive the owner* of possession of the property.

In addition, many states distinguish between the crime of grand larceny (a felony) and petty larceny (a misdemeanor) depending on the value of the property taken. (In many states, for example, taking property valued at $400 or more is a felony; taking property of a lesser value is a misdemeanor.)

Analyzing a Case

Imagine that prosecutors have to decide whether to file formal court charges for grand larceny in a state with the theft laws described above. They have the following evidence drawn from the police investigation and report:

John Witness saw Mary Defendant reach into a car, remove a watch from the dashboard, and walk away with it. John summoned the police. They caught Mary several blocks away while she was trying to sell the watch to a passerby. Other evidence includes a statement by the owner identifying the watch as her property.

Should Mary be charged with grand larceny? To find out, it is necessary to match the evidence with each element of the crime.

In this case, John Witness' testimony establishes a taking and carrying away of the watch. The location of the property (on the dashboard) and the owner's statement establish another person's ownership. The law defines a watch as personal property. The testimony of the police officer and passerby establishes the necessary intent element. (By trying to sell the watch to another, Mary has demonstrated an intent to permanently deprive the owner of the property.)

So far it looks as if the prosecutors have enough evidence to prove a case of larceny beyond a reasonable doubt. But should they file a felony or misdemeanor complaint? The answer to this question depends on the value of the watch. The prosecutor can have an investigator find evidence of the watch's value. If it turns out the watch was worth more than $400, a felony charge can be made. If the evidence does not support such a high value, a charge for the lesser crime of petty larceny can be filed.

As you can see, evaluating a case can be quite complex. Many related issues may come into play. Was all the important evidence legally obtained? Are the witnesses reliable and believable? What evidence might the defense produce which counters the prosecutor's case?

Factors in Exercising Discretion

In general, the prosecutors should prosecute if, after a thorough investigation, they find that:

(1) a crime has been committed,

(2) they can identify the person who committed it, and

(3) they have evidence that supports a guilty verdict.

(Andrew Costly/CRF.)

But, as has been mentioned, the prosecutor does have discretion in deciding what charges, if any, to bring. To decide, a prosecutor might consider many factors, for example:

- Is there reasonable doubt that the defendant is guilty?
- Was the harm caused by the offense inconsequential?
- Is the probable punishment out of proportion to the offense or the offender?
- Is the crime itself rarely enforced (to the extent that the community no longer considers it a crime)?
- Is the offender extremely young or old?
- Is the crime not a high priority of the prosecutor's office (e.g. violent crimes tend to have high priority; so-called victimless crimes may not)?
- Is the case too old to find witnesses or physical evidence?

What Should the Charge Be?

In the following scene, three prosecuting attorneys—Martin, Stein, and Kawahara—have been assigned to review the Carter case. They are going over the crimes that they might bring against Carter.

Martin: Let's start with the most serious offense. First-degree murder requires *malice aforethought* and *premeditation* The decision to kill someone had to have been weighed and reflected upon after the intent to kill was formed. Now, in Carter's case we have evidence that he had more than 12 hours to consider killing Oscar Hanks. . .

Stein: Just one problem—he didn't kill Oscar Hanks.

Kawahara: I don't see any big problem there. If we can show that Carter did form the intent to kill Hanks, we might be able to invoke the **transferred intent doctrine**. It holds that the elements of first-degree murder can be satisfied even if the killer gets someone other than his intended victim. Also, Carter may have thought that the little girl was Hanks' sister or maybe a relative. Or maybe he formed a whole new intent to kill the little girl and premeditated before pulling the trigger.

Martin: Maybe, but it doesn't seem likely. What about second-degree murder? Remember malice aforethought can be established by an intent to do any act where there is an obvious risk that death or great bodily harm may result. Here we have a guy who stated a desire to get Hanks. He loaded a shotgun, got into a car, and started blasting away. I don't care if he was trying to hit the little girl, the house, or the truck. There were people on the street. He didn't care about their safety, and he should have known that he was endangering them. Also, just firing at the truck is a felony. Any killings that take place while attempting to commit a felony are murder under the **felony murder rule**.

Stein: Let's not be too hasty. What if Carter didn't "start blasting away," as you put it? What if the gun just went off accidentally?

Martin: You would consider a charge of involuntary manslaughter?

Stein: Sure. Such careless handling of a loaded shotgun in a residential area amounts to criminal negligence in my book.

Kawahara: At the very least.

Martin: I suppose voluntary manslaughter is also a possibility.

Stein: Be serious, Martin. After 12 hours? Even if he was seriously provoked by Hanks, he had plenty of time to cool off.

Martin: Maybe so. Anyway, we've got plenty to think about and we've got to decide. The newspapers are showing a lot of interest in this case. The boss told me that she has a personal interest in this case—top priority and all that. We've got to charge Carter with something. But what?

For Discussion

1. In your own words, what is prosecutorial discretion? What are its advantages and disadvantages?

2. Review the factors in exercising prosecutorial discretion on page 102. Which do you think are valid? Which, if any, don't you think should be used? Why?

3. Review "What Should the Charge Be?" on page 103. Then answer the following questions:

   • What is the doctrine of transferred intent? How does it apply to the Carter case? (Try drawing a diagram on the board using the characters from the case.)

   • Why might Prosecutor Stein think that the facts do not support premeditation or transferred intent?

   • Why did Prosecutor Stein argue against a charge of voluntary manslaughter? Explain your answer.

   • What additional evidence, if any, do the prosecutors need to make a decision?

Class Activity: The Prosecutor Decides

In the following activity, assume that you are a prosecutor working with Martin, Stein, and Kawahara on the Thomas Carter case. Form small groups and exercise your prosecutorial discretion as directed below.

1. Review the following materials:

   a. "Police Crime Investigation Report," pages 94-95.

   b. "State Criminal Code Sections," page 96.

   c. "What Should the Charge Be?" page 103.

   (You may also wish to consult "Murder Most Foul and Other Crimes," page 33, for additional background information.)

2. As a group, answer the following questions about the possible charges. One person should record the group's answers on a sheet of paper. Be prepared to discuss your answers with the class.

CHARGES:

First-Degree Murder

• Is there evidence that Thomas Carter formed an intent to kill Oscar Hanks? Explain.

• Is there evidence of premeditation? Explain.

• Is there evidence which would show that this intent was transferred to the killing of Joyce

A New York City police officer stands guard at a barricade surrounding a murder scene. (AP/Wide World Photos.)

Ann Miller (using the doctrine of transferred intent)? Explain.

OR

• Is there evidence to show that Thomas Carter formed an intent to kill and premeditated the killing of Joyce Ann Miller? Explain.

Second-Degree Murder

• Is there evidence that Thomas Carter formed an intent to kill Joyce Ann Miller? Explain.

OR

• Is there evidence that Thomas Carter had the intent to do an act where there was an obvious risk that death or great bodily harm would result? Explain.

Voluntary Manslaughter

• Is there evidence that Thomas Carter formed an intent to kill Oscar Hanks? Explain.

• Is there evidence that Oscar Hanks seriously provoked the actions of Thomas Carter? Explain.

• Is there evidence that Thomas Carter did not have sufficient time to calm down after being provoked? Explain.

Involuntary Manslaughter

• Is there evidence that Thomas Carter committed an act in a criminally negligent manner? Explain.

3. Considering all relevant factors, what crime would you charge Thomas Carter with? (Be prepared to present and discuss your final recommendation with the class.)

A s k

a n

Expert

Invite a criminal attorney to your class. Ask how prosecutorial review and discretion work in your area. What factors does the prosecutor use to decide which crimes to charge? Invite the attorney to join you in the following activity and lead the debriefing.

Key Step: Probable Cause Hearing

Purpose

Before a felony case can go to trial, a court must find that there is *probable cause* to believe that a crime was committed and the arrestee committed it. The purpose of the probable cause hearing is to keep charges with insufficient evidence from being brought to trial. The hearing thus protects both the accused and the state from spending time and money unnecessarily.

Types of Hearings

• *Preliminary Hearings.* Some states use preliminary hearings or examinations to determine if the arrestee should be brought to trial. Other states use them to determine if the accused should be bound over for a grand jury hearing. At the preliminary hearing, the prosecution presents evidence to a judge to prove that there is probable cause. The defense may cross-examine the prosecutor's witnesses. In many states, however, crime victims do not have to testify in person. Their statements can be read to the court, so the defense cannot cross-examine them.

If the judge finds that there is probable cause, the prosecution is authorized to file a document called an "information" with the court, and preparations for the trial begin.

• *Grand Jury.* In some states and in all federal felony cases, grand juries determine probable cause. A grand jury is made up of citizens—usually 23 people—from the county where the crime occurred. It meets in closed session, and the prosecutor calls witnesses. The defense attorney does not get to cross-examine these witnesses or participate in the hearing. After the prosecution presents its case, the grand jury votes on whether probable cause exists. If a certain number of the 23 grand jurors—often 12 or 14—find probable cause, then an indictment is issued. Like an informa-

tion, an indictment is a document accusing the defendant of committing a crime. Following an indictment, preparation for trial begins.

In most states, the prosecutor has the option of using a grand jury or a preliminary hearing. Since the accused has no right to counsel or to cross-examine the state's witnesses in grand jury hearings, a prosecutor might be more likely to seek a grand jury indictment when cross-examination would be traumatic to a witness (e.g. for sex crimes or for very young or frail witnesses). Most felony cases, however, commence by information.

• *Complaint*—for misdemeanors only. In misdemeanor cases, there is no separate hearing to establish probable cause after the accused has been arrested. A written complaint against the arrestee serves as the formal accusation to get the prosecution of misdemeanor cases underway. (The defendant can ask for a copy of the complaint with copies of the police report attached.)

Defendants with their attorneys prepare to enter pleas at an arraignment. (AP/Wide World Photos.)

Case Notes: Probable Cause Hearing

When Tom Carter heard Susan Jaffee's voice on the phone, he felt nervous. What she said did not calm him down.

"I've got some news for you, Tom. The prosecutor decided to take your case to the grand jury instead of holding a preliminary hearing."

Tom remembered her saying that the next step would be the probable cause hearing. He asked, "Is it worse to have a grand jury instead of a preliminary hearing?"

"It's worse in that I won't get to cross-examine any of the witnesses. But sometimes prosecutors take their weaker cases to grand juries, because the prosecutors are more in control at grand jury hearings than preliminary hearings. So maybe it's not such bad news."

"So what do we do now?" asked Tom.

"We wait. You might be called to testify before the grand jury. If you are, I cannot go in with you. But you will just refuse to testify. You will take the Fifth Amendment."

Tom heard nothing about the grand jury for two weeks. Finally, Susan Jaffee called. "The grand jury returned an indictment today—second-degree murder."

CRIME BEAT

Imagine you are a crime beat reporter for a local news outlet. Your editor has assigned you to do research for stories on the upcoming Carter trial. Your editor wants you to find out as much as you can about how probable cause hearings and arraignments work in your state.

Submit a one-page summary of your findings.

For ideas on sources for this information, see "Crime Beat" on page 31.

The words stunned Tom. "Murder?" he stammered.

"Second degree."

"How did the grand jury decide that?" Tom asked.

"I don't know, Tom. We'll get a copy of the grand jury's transcript. We'll read what the witnesses had to say. Then we'll be ready for our next step—your arraignment."

Key Step: Arraignment

Purpose

After an information, indictment, or complaint has been filed, the defendant is called into court to *plead to the charges.* This court appearance is known as the arraignment. (In most misdemeanor cases, this step takes place at the defendant's first and only pretrial hearing.) Aside from various insanity pleas, the defendant has three basic choices of pleas:

- **Not guilty.**
- **Guilty.**
- **Nolo Contendere. (No contest. This has the same effect as a guilty plea, except it does not serve as an admission of guilt if the defendant is sued in a civil case.)**

Typical Proceedings

The judge

- **Informs the defendant of various constitutional rights.**

- **Reads the information or indictment and usually gives the defendant a copy.**

- **Asks the defendant to plead to the charges.**

- **Asks whether the defendant wants a jury trial or a court trial (decided by the judge without a jury).**

The defendant may make pretrial motions (e.g. to suppress illegally obtained evidence or to transfer the case to a different judge).

Juries are supposed to base their verdicts solely on the evidence presented at trial. In highly publicized cases, issues of outside influence often arise. (Callahan cartoon reprinted with permission.)

Case Notes: An Issue at the Arraignment

Joyce Ann Miller's death shocked the residents of the community. Many citizens and community leaders condemned what they called "this latest example of youth violence." Newspapers covered the case extensively. Neighbors of the Miller family told TV reporters that they wanted the death penalty for Carter. A police officer was quoted in a local newspaper as saying that he thought Joyce Ann's death must have been a "joy killing." A representative of the district attorney's office announced at a press conference that he believed "drugs were involved." One newspaper headline read, "Child Killer Says It Was 'An Accident!'" Thomas Carter's attorney, Susan Jaffee, also received several anonymous phone calls threatening to harm her if she did not drop out of the case.

A Problem for the Defense

All of this deeply concerned Jaffee. She was afraid that the publicity would hurt her client's chances of getting a fair trial. Finding jurors who had not already formed an opinion about the case would be difficult. Even if such jurors were found, they could still be influenced by publicity and public opinion during the trial itself.

After the grand jury found that Carter would have to stand trial, his attorney decided to act. At the arraignment he would plead not guilty and ask for a jury trial. Then she would make a motion for a gag order.

Motion for a Gag Order

Judges may issue **gag orders** to ensure that criminal defendants receive a fair trial. These orders prohibit trial participants and government officials from making statements to the press. By preventing these statements, gag orders make it less likely that pretrial publicity will influence the fact finder—the judge or jury.

It is crucial that the judge or jury be impartial. When judges act as the fact finder, it is assumed they will be able to ignore outside influences and decide the facts solely from the trial evidence. Jurors, who have little or no experience with the law, might be more easily swayed by outside influences, including opinions of friends, statements by public officials, and newspaper or TV accounts of the crime. For example, what might happen if a juror were to read about a piece of evidence which had been legally excluded from consideration at trial, but which pointed to the defendant's guilt? Knowing this fact might influence that juror's opinion and if he or she shared it with other jurors, it could sway the whole jury. Gag orders are designed to prevent such interference. Those who disobey gag orders can be held in contempt of court and punished.

At the close of her argument for her motion, Ms. Jaffee made the following statement:

> Public reaction to the death of Joyce Ann Miller has almost reached hysteria. Public officials, including the police and representatives of the district attorney's office, have made prejudicial and unfounded statements about the case. The news media is behaving irresponsibly by suggesting that Thomas Carter is already guilty. If these incidents continue, it will be impossible to conduct a fair trial, if indeed it is even possible now. Under these circumstances, a gag order is essential, your honor.

In opposition, the prosecutor argued against issuing a gag order. He reminded the judge that public attention to such a case was natural. Under the First Amendment of the U.S. Constitution, the news media has a right to keep the public informed. If denied access to participants in the trial, various reporters might print or broadcast misinformation. Furthermore, he argued that a gag order should only be used in exceptional circumstances and that normal procedures such as cautioning the jury not to discuss or read about the case would probably be sufficient.

The judge thanked the attorneys and said that she would consider the matter and announce her decision the next day.

Class Activity: Ruling on the Motion

Imagine that you are the judge who must rule on the defense's motion for a gag order in this case. To prepare your ruling, complete the following steps:

1. Review "An Issue at the Arraignment," pages 108-109.

2. In coming to a decision, consider these questions:

- What is the purpose of a gag order?
- What are some arguments in favor of issuing a gag order in this case?
- What are some arguments against issuing a gag order? What rights and interests would be affected?
- Are the alternatives to a gag order mentioned by the prosecutor sufficient to preserve a fair trial in this case?
- Should a gag order be issued in the Carter case? Why or why not?

3. Write a one-page decision stating your reasons for it. Be prepared to present it to the rest of the class for discussion.

TRIAL

Key Step: Trial Procedures

Strict rules ensure that each side in a trial will have an equal chance to present its case. A judge must make sure that each side follows these rules closely. The major procedures observed in a criminal court trial are outlined below.

1. *Jury Selection*

In all criminal jury trials, the first step is to impanel, or select, a jury. Prosecution and defense attorneys pose questions to prospective jurors. The judge may also take an active role in the process.

2. *Opening Statements*

After calling the court to order, the judge will ask for the trial to begin with opening statements from the prosecution and defense. The opening statement outlines the evidence each side intends to present during the trial. The prosecution delivers its opening statement first. The defense attorney usually follows immediately with a statement, but may delay it until after the prosecution presents all its evidence.

3. *Presenting Evidence*

The prosecution presents its side of the case first. This is called the prosecution's case-in-chief. It usually consists of introducing material objects called exhibits (e.g. a gun), as well as questioning prosecution witnesses. After the prosecution has finished presenting its side, the defense may introduce its exhibits and witnesses. Both exhibits and witnesses' testimony are trial evidence. Strict rules of evidence must be followed, however, before either is allowed into the trial.

Attorneys conduct *direct examination* when they question their own witnesses. After direct examination, opposing attorneys *cross-examine* the witnesses. Lawyers conduct cross-examination to test and find weaknesses in the testimony of their opponents' witnesses. They may also try to put doubts into the minds of the jurors about the believability of these witnesses.

4. *Closing Arguments*

After each side has presented all its evidence, each side makes a closing statement to the jury. In these closing arguments, attorneys summarize what has been established or not established during the trial. The closing argument presents attorneys with their last chance to persuade the jury. The defense delivers the first closing argument to the jury. The closing argument of the prosecution ends the evidence phase of the trial.

5. *Instructions to the Jurors*

Following the closing arguments, the judge gives instructions to the jury. These instructions state the law that applies to the case. The judge reminds the jurors to base their verdict solely on the evidence admitted during the trial. Since the prosecution has the burden of proof, the judge instructs the jurors to find a verdict of guilty only if the state has proved its case beyond a reasonable doubt.

6. Jury Deliberations

After hearing the judge's instructions, the jury leaves the courtroom and meets in a jury room to decide on a verdict. The jury members first select a foreman who will lead their discussions. The jury then reviews the evidence and votes on a verdict. Although the U.S. Supreme Court has ruled that unanimous verdicts of guilty or not guilty are not mandatory in all criminal cases, most states still require them.

CRIME BEAT

Imagine you are a crime beat reporter for a local news outlet. Your editor has assigned you to do research for stories on the upcoming Carter trial. Your editor wants to find out as much as you can about your local court procedures. The editor fired off some questions you might look into:

• *How are prospective jurors selected to come to the courthouse? What requirements must they meet?*

• *How are jurors selected to serve on a jury?*

• *What procedures are used for bringing witnesses into court?*

• *What procedures are used for admitting physical evidence or exhibits at a criminal trial?*

• *How are jurors protected from outside influences?*

• *What are the ceremonial duties of a clerk and bailiff?*

• *What are the most important duties of a court clerk?*

Submit a one-page summary of your findings.

For ideas on sources for this information, see "Crime Beat" on page 31.

Several votes may be necessary before the jurors arrive at a unanimous verdict. If, after a reasonable time, the jurors cannot reach a unanimous verdict, they become a "hung jury." The foreman will report this fact to the judge. If the judge believes that further jury deliberations are futile, the judge will declare a mistrial. The prosecutor will then have to either request another trial with a new jury or drop the charges against the defendant. If the jury returns a unanimous verdict of not guilty, the defendant goes free. When the jury unanimously finds the defendant guilty, the judge will set a date for a sentencing hearing.

Case Notes: Cast of Characters II

A criminal courtroom in session is filled with people. Some are spectators. Some are friends and family of the victim or accused. Others take an active part in the trial itself. The following descriptions will give you an idea about the major participants. (Some you have already met, but review them again carefully.) As the trial of Thomas Carter progresses, you will be asked at times to take on their roles.

• The **judge** presides over the trial. He or she rules on all motions made by the attorneys, on the admissibility of testimony or items in evidence, and on the procedures to be followed during the trial. At the end of the trial, the judge instructs the jury about the applicable rules of law. In a criminal trial, if the jury reaches a verdict of guilty, the judge then determines the sentence to be given the convicted person. (In almost all states, the jury determines the punishment in death penalty cases.) If the jury reaches a verdict of not guilty, the judge discharges the defendant.

• The **bailiff** is usually a deputy sheriff, marshal, or some other law enforcement officer. The bailiff

  • keeps order in the courtroom;

  • protects the jury from outside influence; and

  • assists the court clerk in ceremonial duties

An ornate courtroom in the 1920s. (The Bettmann Archive.)

such as asking all to rise when the judge enters the court.

- The **court clerk** is the main administrative assistant to the judge. The clerk

  - keeps track of courtroom proceedings;

  - catalogs and takes custody of exhibits and other items of evidence;

  - prepares all written orders of the court (summons and warrants, for example) as directed by the judge;

  - administers oaths to witnesses; and

  - calls the jurors for selection.

- The **court reporter** records by machine or shorthand everything said in the trial. The court reporter prepares a typewritten transcript of these records.

- The **prosecution lawyers** are members of the district attorney's office, city attorney's office, or state and federal attorney general's office. They represent either the people of the state or the U.S. government. They must prove that the accused is guilty of a particular crime beyond a reasonable doubt.

- The **defense lawyers** are private attorneys or members of publicly supported organizations, such as the public defender's office. They must defend the accused by showing that the govern-

ment does not have enough evidence to convict the defendant. All lawyers—both prosecution and defense—are officers of the court. They must therefore observe all rules of law and ethics so that a fair trial will take place.

- The **defendant** is a person accused of a crime. The defendant assists the defense lawyers in presenting the case and accepts or appeals the results of the trial.

- **Witnesses** are persons asked to tell under oath what they know about the case. Most may only testify about what they actually saw and heard. But **expert witnesses** may testify about their knowledge and give opinions. They are persons with special knowledge, such as doctors, psychologists, and scientists.

- The **jury** is a panel of adult citizens (usually 12) from the community. It must decide questions of fact from the evidence presented in the courtroom and reach a verdict based on those facts.

For Discussion

1. Which role is charged with deciding issues of law?

2. Which role is charged with deciding issues about facts?

Activity: In the Halls of Justice

There is perhaps no better way to understand the criminal court process than to observe it in person. To do this, you must visit a courthouse.

As a class or in small groups, make arrangements to visit a criminal courthouse. Many courthouses have tour programs or will accommodate groups. Contact the court's clerk of services or the clerk of the criminal docket for information. The clerk can suggest an appropriate time for the visit and help you plan an itinerary. Try to include a visit to:

(1) a preliminary hearing,

(2) an arraignment,

(3) a jury selection, and

(4) a criminal trial.

When you arrive at the courthouse, observe appropriate decorum. Be especially quiet when entering or leaving courtrooms. Use the following information guide and questions to help arrange your visit and for reporting your experience to the class.

Information You will Need for Courtroom Visit

- Name of Courthouse
- Address
- Telephone
- Reporting Time
- Contact Person (if any)

Questions for Field Experience Report

1. Describe the general environment of the courthouse. Are the court facilities crowded and noisy, or calm and businesslike?

2. Describe the security arrangements in the court building and in the courtrooms.

3. In the arraignment court, *describe what is going on.*

4. In a preliminary hearing, *describe what is going on.*

5. At a criminal jury trial:

- What is the case about?
- Is it a felony or misdemeanor prosecution?
- Who is the prosecutor—a deputy district attorney, deputy city attorney, a federal prosecutor?
- *What do you observe* the prosecutor doing during the trial?
- Who is the defense attorney—a deputy public defender, private attorney?
- *What do you observe* the defense attorney doing during the trial?
- *What do you observe* the judge doing during the trial?

- *Describe* the questioning of one witness in the trial.
- Do the jurors seem to be attentive? Describe them.
- What is your overall impression of the courthouse visit? Were you confused by anything you saw or heard?

6. If the opportunity arises or can be arranged, interview an officer of the court (e.g. court clerk, judge, attorney). Select questions from the following list or make up your own.

- Does the court have a large backlog of cases? If so, why?
- What is plea bargaining? What is your opinion of it?
- What percentage of the cases before the court are disposed of by plea bargaining?
- How long does it take a criminal case to come to trial in this court? A civil case?
- What percentage of defendants at trial are represented by public defenders?
- In what percentage of trials is the defendant found guilty?
- What percentage of those convicted by the court are locked up in a correctional institution? Put on probation?
- What percentage of accused persons remain in jail awaiting their trials?

The Courtroom Setting

As with all dramas, there is a setting for a criminal trial. It is the courtroom. In it the judge presides, the jury is impaneled, witnesses are sworn in and examined, and a verdict is rendered. On this stage, the fates of individuals are debated and decided and the aims of justice are pursued. Some courtrooms are ornately carved in dark woods and rich furnishings. Others are designed with an eye towards efficiency and practicality. Some are old and threadbare. Others are new and starkly modern. All serve the same purpose.

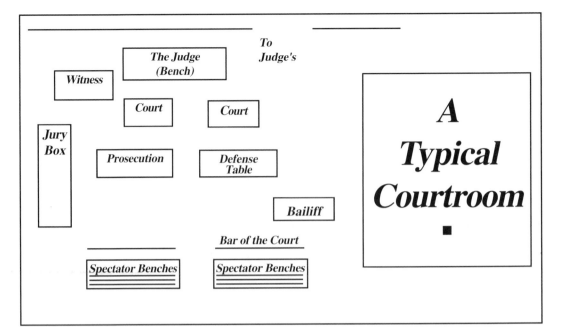

A **Typical Courtroom**

Above is a diagram of a typical courtroom. When conducting the activities in the trial of Thomas Carter, arrange your classroom similarly.

For Discussion

1. In most courtrooms, the judge's bench is on a raised platform. Why do you think this is so?

2. In all courtrooms, the witness stand is on the side of the judge's bench closest to the jury box. Why do you think this is so?

3. The partition between the spectators and the active courtroom participants has traditionally been called the bar. Why do you think it is there? Who may pass the bar?

Activity: A Courtroom of the Future

In the last few years, a number of criticisms have been leveled at the design of typical courtrooms. They include:

- Courtrooms are too formal and inhuman
- Courtrooms do not make adequate provisions for victims and their families
- Courtrooms do not accommodate modern technology, including television, acoustical devices, and computers.

Imagine that you are an architect with the task of designing a courtroom of the future. How would you address these criticisms? Design a courtroom that would best suit the needs of participants and the pursuit of justice. Make diagrams and share them with the class.

Case Notes: The Trial of Thomas Carter

Thomas Carter felt mixed feelings of dread and relief as he climbed the wide steps leading to the massive courthouse door. In the weeks since the shooting, he had thought of little else. His mind played the events over and over again. Often, he hoped for the trial to start—only when it was over could his life begin again. There had been delays. Motions were made and extensions of time granted. Though he had complete trust in his lawyer, he wished she could move things along faster. Now, at last, his trial would begin. Today was the day.

Inside the main lobby of the courthouse, Tom looked at a blur of moving figures. The footsteps of people going about court business echoed off the cold marble walls. The drone of a hundred conversations filled his ears, yet he and his parents barely spoke at all. They were too occupied with trying to find the right courtroom by the appointed hour, 9 a.m.

At last they found it, Department D, Criminal Trials Division. Tom breathed a sigh of relief when he saw Ms. Jaffee leaning against the court rail. She smiled as he approached and directed his parents to seats in the spectator gallery directly behind the defense table.

Although she had already prepared Tom for what would take place at his trial, she briefly explained it all again. He listened carefully, vaguely comforted by the confidence in her voice, until she repeated what the charge would be: "Second-degree murder." No matter how she said it, it sent a chill through his body. Ms. Jaffee reached across and patted his arm. "It's a serious thing, Tom," she smiled, "but they haven't proved anything yet."

Just then the clerk stood up and said in a loud voice: "All rise and come to order. The Superior Court is now open and in session. The Honorable Judge Coghlan presiding."

Tom looked up just in time to see a black-robed figure enter from a door behind the bench and sit down. She softly tapped her gavel several times and said, "The case of *People v. Carter*. Is the state ready?"

The prosecutor said, "The state is ready to proceed, your honor."

Turning to Ms. Jaffee, the judge repeated the question, "Is the defendant ready?"

Ms. Jaffee spoke in a loud firm voice, "Yes, your honor."

The trial of Thomas Carter had begun.

For Discussion

1. What is the charge in the Thomas Carter case? What are its elements?

2. Review the "Key Step: Trial Procedures" on page 110. What will happen next in Thomas Carter's trial?

Key Step: Jury Selection

Selected at random, people on juries come from the defendant's community. Their names may be gathered from voter registration lists or drivers' license lists, depending on the state. These citizens are then called to jury duty. Before a trial starts, a group of up to 40 from the jury pool go to the courtroom where the trial will take place. The court clerk draws the names of 12 of them—called prospective jurors—and asks them to sit in the jury box. Prospective jurors then take an oath promising to answer truthfully the questions put to them by the judge and lawyers.

Next comes voir dire—questioning of the prospective jurors by the judge and attorneys for both sides. The judge starts the voir dire by telling the jurors the charge(s) against the defendant and by asking them their name, age, address, occupation, and previous jury experience. The judge might also inquire if there is any reason why they should not be jurors in this particular case. (For example, a person who had been a victim of a similar crime might not be able to be a truly impartial juror.) The judge will excuse prospective jurors from a case if their answers indicate a bias or prejudice toward one side. Prospective jurors may also be excused if they would suffer economically due to the length of the trial. The excused jurors, however, may have to serve in another case.

If the judge finds no reason to excuse a prospective juror, the attorneys for both sides normally get an opportunity to question them in greater depth. In most states, the attorneys themselves question the jurors. In others, the attorneys submit questions to the judge who conducts the questioning. Based on the answers jurors give, attorneys can raise challenges to jurors and thus have them excused from a case.

There are two types of challenges. A challenge for cause occurs when a lawyer claims the prospective juror does not meet the government's legal requirements or is biased and could probably not reach an impartial verdict. After the attorney explains the reasons for challenging for cause, the judge must decide whether to excuse or accept the prospective juror. Usually there is no limit on challenges for cause.

A peremptory challenge needs no explanation from the attorney. When a lawyer makes a peremptory challenge, the prospec-

tive juror being questioned is automatically excused. Each side, however, has only a limited number of these challenges. According to recent U.S. Supreme Court rulings, neither the prosecution nor defense may make a peremptory challenge on the basis of a juror's race. (*Batson v. Kentucky*, 1986, and *Georgia v. McCollum*, 1992).

The voir dire continues until 12 jurors and alternates have been chosen, usually two or four. (Some jurisdictions allow juries of six, seven, or eight persons.) In some cases, especially those that have been highly publicized, lawyers challenge many prospective jurors before a full jury is selected. This process may take anywhere from a few hours to many days to complete. Once the jury has been chosen, it is impaneled, or made official, by taking another oath. Jurors swear that they will try to reach a fair and impartial verdict based solely on the evidence presented during the trial.

For Discussion

1. Why is there no limit on the number of challenges for cause and a limit on peremptory challenges?

2. Should the Supreme Court ban peremptory challenges based on gender, religion, or disability? Why or why not?

3. The goals of the judge, prosecution, and defense in criminal trials are often quite different. What differences might they have about jury selection?

Class Activity: Choosing a Jury

In this activity, you will simulate the jury selection for the Thomas Wade Carter trial.

1. Invite an attorney to attend your simulation and play the role of the judge.

2. Assign the class members the following roles:

   • 2-4 prosecuting attorneys

   • 2-4 defense attorneys

- 14 prospective jurors
- 1 court clerk
- observers (remainder of class)

3. Students should read their appropriate role descriptions below. In addition, observers and lawyers should read the materials on "How to Ask Effective Questions" and "Sample Questions for Lawyers in a Criminal Case."

4. The court clerk should:

- swear in the prospective jurors before the voir dire begins, and
- call the first prospective juror (by name) to the jury box.

5. The judge should tell all of the prospective jurors the charge against Thomas Carter, then ask the first prospective juror some introductory questions.

6. Prosecutors, then defense attorneys, question the first prospective juror and either accept or challenge the juror. If a challenge for cause is raised, the judge should rule on it. Each side is allowed only one peremptory challenge.

7. Repeat steps 4, 5, and 6 above until all prospective jurors have been questioned. Observers should watch the proceedings carefully and then complete the Observer Evaluation Form.

Role Descriptions

Lawyers for Both Sides

Lawyers will question each prospective juror searching for persons to accept or to challenge for cause. Before the simulation begins, lawyers should prepare a list of questions to ask prospective jurors.

How to Ask Effective Questions

The following list should be used by the attorney role-players in preparing effective questions. In addition, observers should use this list for evaluating the questions asked by the attorney role-players.

1. Plan most of your questions ahead of time. Make sure that they are precisely worded.

2. Begin with basic questions about the juror's background. Then, ask more advanced questions on the juror's feelings about the case.

3. Always keep the question's purpose in mind when you are formulating it.

4. Individualize your questions. Reword any long or complex question if an individual juror does not understand it.

5. Develop questions that call for short responses. Don't include too many things in one question.

6. Avoid questions that require a single "yes" or "no" answer. You do not want to limit jurors' responses. Prepare questions that allow jurors to express their feelings in their own words. For example, the question, "Do you have any prejudices against insurance companies?" might be changed to "What is your opinion of insurance companies?"

7. Explore incomplete answers. If a juror claims not to know an answer, you should ask questions to find out why.

8. Unless it is crucial to your case, try to avoid questions already addressed to a juror by another attorney. You usually do not need to go over the same ground twice.

Sample Questions for Lawyers: Criminal Case

1. Are you married? Do you have any children? If so, what are their ages?

2. What type of work do you do?

3. Do you belong to any union?

4. What is your educational background?

5. Have you ever had any jury experience before?

6. Would any of the criminal cases you heard in previous jury duty limit your ability to sit on future cases?

7. Was there anything about your previous jury experience that would lead you to feel that you may have some prejudices either for or against the prosecution? For or against the defendant?

8. Do you have an opinion on this case?

(AP/Wide World Photos.)

9. Is there anything about what you have seen since you came for jury duty that would lead you to feel that you have an opinion on this case?

10. Was there anything in the news media, television, or radio that leads you to believe the defendant is guilty or not guilty?

11. Do you believe that the defendant is innocent until proven guilty?

12. Would you tend to believe the police officers in their testimony more readily than you would a person who was not a police officer?

13. Were you ever connected with any type of police force?

14. Do you have any relatives who would have any interest in seeing the jury reach a verdict either for or against the defendant in this case?

15. If you are chosen as a juror, will you stand on your own individual analysis of the evidence and not be swayed by the emotions of other jurors?

Court Clerk

Before voir dire begins, the court clerk will ask all the prospective jurors to raise their right hands and state: "I solemnly swear I will answer all questions truthfully and to the best of my ability." The court clerk will call each prospective juror, in turn, to the witness stand for voir-dire questioning.

Prospective Jurors

Each student should assume the role of one of the prospective jurors described in the biographies below and answer the judge's and attorneys' questions accordingly.

Biographies of Prospective Jurors

1. **Michael:** Anglo, 38 years old, junior high school education. He is a third cousin to Tom Carter, but has never met him. He is a mechanic, married with five children and is a non-drinker. He has no prior jury duty.

2. **Ralph**: Latino, 61 years old, married with two children, college education. Ralph is a union leader and an officer in his United Auto Workers local. He has no prior jury duty.

3. **Judy:** Of Greek descent, 22 years old, and single. She attends law school and wants to become a criminal defense lawyer. She lives with her parents, does not work, and has no prior jury duty.

4. **Bob:** Anglo, 69 years old, single. High school graduate. Bob is a retired construction worker and has no prior jury duty.

5. **Richard:** Anglo, 38 years old. He is married with six children and is an attorney-at-law. He has no prior jury duty.

6. **Rosa:** Latina, 62 years old, married with two children and three grandchildren. She finished high school, has been married for 30 years, and is a supervisor at the post office. Her niece was once wounded in a drive-by shooting by a youth gang. She has served on one prior jury, which heard a criminal prosecution for being drunk in a public place. She voted to convict.

7. **Bernice:** African-American, 39 years old, married with one child. College graduate with a B.A. in English. Bernice is a counselor at Freedom High School, where she has worked for the past 13 years. She has no prior jury duty.

8. **Russell:** Anglo, 57 years old, college graduate. He has been a vice president in charge of a large business corporation for 10 years. He is married with two children and is a former alcoholic. No prior jury duty.

9. **Carol:** African-American, 39 years old, divorced three years ago, with one child. Protestant. She is a marketing analyst, but is currently unemployed and is receiving unemployment benefits. Active in the feminist movement and the Black Community Action Council. She has no prior jury duty.

10. **James:** Of Irish descent, 58 years old, high school education. James is a produce manager in a supermarket, is married and has one child. As a young man, he was once convicted for a misdemeanor—disturbing the peace. No prior jury duty.

11. **Mary:** African-American, 54 years old, widow with three children who live with her. Mary has worked as an insurance agent for over 35 years. She has managed to pay off the mortgage on her modest home, and send her oldest child to college. She has no prior jury duty.

12. **Larry:** African-American, 38 years old, married with four children. He is a computer programmer. No prior jury duty.

13. **Priscilla:** Asian, 62 years old, widow, ex-college professor. She derives her income from her pension. She has had two prior jury duties. Both cases involved grand theft auto, and she voted to acquit both times.

14. **Janis:** Anglo, 70 years old, single. She works as a secretary for a small accounting firm. She has no prior jury duty.

Observers

As part of the courtroom audience, you can observe all the role-players. Your job is to evaluate the simulation. The observer evaluation form should help you focus on the key issues. Copy the form onto a sheet of paper leaving enough room for you to answer the questions.

You will present and discuss your impressions with the entire group at the end of the simulation.

Observer Evaluation Form
Copy this form on a sheet of paper.

Observer Evaluation Form

1. Put a (+) next to the most realistic role-players. Put a (-) next to the least realistic groups.
  • *Prospective jurors*
  • *Lawyers*
  • *Judge*

2. The jurors who most realistically portrayed their roles were:

3. Based on the jury that was finally selected, who do you think will win this case? Why?

4. An effective question asked by the defense attorney was:

5. An effective question asked by the prosecuting attorney was:

6. A good question not asked of the prospective jurors is:

Debriefing Questions

1. Have the observers read their evaluations to the class. Discuss the answers.

2. Ask your visiting attorney:

- How did this simulation compare with real voir dire in your local courts?
- How fair and effective is voir dire?

Class Activity: Opening Statements

Once the jury has been impaneled, the attorneys for both sides deliver an **opening statement** about the case to the jury. Opening statements outline the facts that the attorneys expect to prove during the trial. An opening statement should present the jury with an orderly, easy-to-understand, and unemotional version of the case from the attorney's perspective.

In criminal trials, the prosecuting attorney goes first. Usually, the defense gives its opening statement immediately afterwards. The defense may, however, choose to wait until the prosecution has called all its witnesses and the defense is ready to present its case-in-chief.

Writing an Opening Statement

To prepare an opening statement, attorneys must organize and outline the entire case they intend to prove at trial. In this out-of-class activity, you will prepare an opening statement for one side of the Thomas Wade Carter case. Use the following guidelines to help you prepare your opening statement.

A good opening statement should:

- Explain what you plan to prove and how you will do it.
- Present the events of the case in a clear, orderly sequence.
- Suggest a motive or emphasize a lack of motive for the crime.

Attorneys usually begin their statement with a formal introduction:

> "Your honor, ladies and gentlemen of the jury, opposing counsel, my name is [full name], representing the [people of the state of _____ —or—defendant _____] in this action."

The attorneys then turn to the jury and begin their statements.

Opening statements often include such phrases as:

- The evidence will show that . . .
- The facts will prove that . . .
- Witness [name] will be called to testify that . . .
- The defendant will explain . . .

To Complete the Assignment

1. Divide the class in half: one half to take the role of lawyers for the state, the other for the defense.

2. At home, list the most important facts of the Thomas Carter case *from your assigned point of view* (prosecution or defense).

3. Write a one or two page opening statement from your assigned point of view.

4. In class, several students from each point of view should stand and deliver opening statements to the rest of the class.

5. As a class, select the best opening statement given for each side on the basis of: a) use of facts, b) clarity, and c) presentation.

Case Notes: "The Evidence Will Show . . ."

Evidence proves or disproves facts in a trial. The trier of fact—judge or jury—must base its verdict solely on the evidence presented during the trial. Testimony of witnesses, documents, drawings, and physical objects such as weapons, drugs, clothing, and other items—these are all forms of evidence that the fact finder considers and weighs in reaching a verdict.

Direct and Circumstantial Evidence

There are two basic kinds of evidence: direct and circumstantial. In a criminal case, **direct evidence** is evidence of one or more of the elements of a given crime. For example:

- Will sees Maria point a gun at Marsha and pull the trigger. In a trial for murder or manslaughter, Will's testimony about what he saw Maria do would be *direct evidence* against her.
- Miguel hears Warren scream at his neighbor, "I'm going to take this bat and kill you, old man!" In a trial for assault, Miguel's and the old man's testimony would be *direct evidence* against Warren.

Circumstantial evidence in criminal cases *indirectly* supports one or more elements of a crime. Circumstantial evidence requires the fact finder to make an inference that something happened. For example:

- Will sees Maria with a smoking gun in her hand standing over Marsha's dead body. In a trial for murder or manslaughter, this would be *circumstantial evidence* that she shot Marsha.
- Miguel sees Warren running away from the old man's house with a bat in his hand. In a trial for assault, this would be *circumstantial* evidence.

It is possible for the same evidence to be both direct and circumstantial. It all depends on

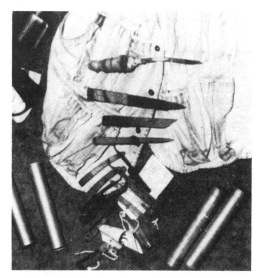

After seizing evidence, police must label and store it for use at trial. (UPI/Bettmann.)

how it is used. Imagine that Brad's fingerprints are found on a murder weapon. The fingerprints are direct evidence that Brad had possession of the weapon. It is circumstantial evidence that Brad had used it in a murder.

The distinction between direct and circumstantial evidence may make little difference. Both are important if the fact finder believes them to be convincing or credible in a particular case. In fact, many criminal suspects are tried and convicted only with compelling circumstantial evidence.

Class Activity: Direct or Circumstantial

Have each student do the following:

1. Down the side of a sheet of paper, write the letters "a" through "e."

2. Read the items below. For each one write on your paper whether the evidence described is *direct* or *circumstantial*. Explain your answers.

> a. Suzanne is charged with resisting arrest. Officer Monroe testifies that the defendant hit him with her briefcase after he had stopped her on the highway for speeding.

b. Charles is on trial for vandalism. An expert testifies that the color and composition of the paint found on the school building is identical to that of a can of paint found in Charles' book bag.

c. Jennifer is on trial for the burglary of a local record shop. Mrs. Ramirez testifies that she saw Jennifer's car parked outside the record shop at the time the burglary is believed to have taken place.

d. Jeff is charged with the sale of marijuana. An undercover narcotics agent testifies that Jeff handed him a large bag of marijuana and took $2,000 in cash from him.

e. Danny is on trial for kidnapping a two-year-old girl. Ms. Joseph, Danny's landlady, testifies that she saw Danny loading an unusually large bundle covered with a sheet into his car just minutes after the crime was reported by the victim's parents.

Case Notes: Rules of Evidence

Many rules dictate when and how evidence may be presented in court. Known as rules of evidence, they help ensure that trials will be fair, orderly, and more likely to discover the truth. They do this, for example, by excluding from court any evidence that is unreliable or unreasonably prejudicial or inflammatory. Also, in some instances, the rules require that attorneys in a trial take certain steps before they can introduce evidence.

Sometimes judges make their own objections to an attorney's questions or a witness's answer. But in most situations, all evidence will be admitted into a trial unless an attorney objects that it violates one of the rules of evidence. So lawyers must know the rules of evidence backwards and forwards. Such knowledge helps them prove their case, because they can present evidence important to their case and keep out an

(UPI/Bettmann.)

opponent's improper evidence, which could hurt their case.

The rules of evidence in state and federal courts are complex and often differ. On the next few pages, you will find an explanation of some basic rules of evidence followed in all American courts.

1. *Relevance*

First and foremost, evidence must be **relevant** to an issue in the case. It must help prove the defendant's guilt or innocence. This rule prevents the fact finder from confusing essential facts of the case with extraneous details.

Suppose that a prosecutor is trying to prove that Bob robbed a bank. Evidence offered to prove that Bob speaks several languages is probably not relevant. The defendant's skills in foreign languages are not at issue.

But what if a witness has testified that the robber spoke French? Evidence offered to prove that Bob speaks French would, in this case, be relevant.

But what is relevant to prove that fact? Evidence that Bob owns a French poodle would not be relevant, because it has no value in proving he speaks French. But evidence that Bob has a master's degree in French would be relevant.

Even relevant evidence may not be admissible if its value in deciding an issue—its **probative value**—is *outweighed* by other considerations. Thus a judge may disallow relevant evidence if it is unfairly prejudicial, confusing to the jury, or a waste of time.

How to Object:

- "Objection, your honor. This evidence is not relevant to the issues of this trial."
- "Objection, your honor. Counsel's question calls for irrelevant testimony."
- If the objection is made *after* the witness answers:

  "Objection, your honor. The testimony is not relevant to the facts of this case. I ask that it be stricken from the record."

If the judge thinks an objection is invalid, the judge will say, "Objection overruled." But if the judge agrees with the objection, the judge will say, "Objection sustained."

2. *Foundation*

To establish the relevance of evidence, attorneys may need to **lay a proper foundation**. Laying a foundation means that, before a witness can testify to certain facts, it must be shown that the witness was in a position to know about these facts. For example, if a prosecutor asks a witness if he saw Bob leave the scene of the bank robbery, the defense attorney may object for a lack of foundation.

After the court sustains—or upholds—this objection, the prosecutor would have to ask the witness if he was near the bank on the day of the robbery. This lays the foundation that the witness is legally competent to testify to the underlying fact.

Sometimes when an attorney is laying a foundation, the opposing attorney may object that the testimony is irrelevant. The questioning attorney then has to explain how the testimony relates to the case.

How to Object:

- "Objection, your honor. There is a lack of foundation."

3. *Personal Knowledge*

Witnesses in a trial must have personal knowledge of what they testify about. Jessica could not, for example, testify that Isaac is a bad driver if she had never seen Isaac drive.

How to Object:

- "Objection, your honor. The witness has no personal knowledge to answer the question."
- If the objection is made *after the witness answers*: "Objection, your honor. I ask that the witness's testimony be stricken from the record because the witness has no personal knowledge of the matter."

4. *Hearsay*

In general, witnesses must have personal knowledge of the facts they testify about. Evidence is more trustworthy if a witness observed something directly ("I saw Bill steal the wallet") rather than heard something secondhand ("Mary told me Bill stole the wallet"). Second-hand statements are normally hearsay evidence.

Consider some examples:

- Sam, a witness in Marty's murder trial, tells the court that he overheard a friend of Marty's say, "Marty killed Joe because he had to."
- The prosecution attempts to introduce a letter written by Marty's sister, which states: "Marty needed the money so he killed him."

Both of these are examples of hearsay evidence. Neither of them is admissible as evidence in a trial. Hearsay evidence is any out-of-court statement—oral or written—offered to prove the truth of that statement. (Think about the word "hearsay." It is something "heard" out of court and "said" in court to prove that what was asserted is true.)

Consider another example from Marty's trial:

• Sam testifies, "I heard Joe yell to Marty, 'Get out of the way.'"

Is this hearsay? It's an out-of-court statement. But it's not offered to prove the truth of the statement. Instead, it is being introduced to show that Joe had warned Marty by shouting. So it is not hearsay, and a court would admit this testimony into evidence. Hearsay is a tricky subject.

It grows even more complicated because there are various exceptions to the rule that hearsay is not admissible. Below are a few of the most common exceptions:

a. *Admissions against interest.* When parties to a case make statements that go against their legal interest, these statements are admissible evidence. If, for example, Sam testified, "Marty told me that he wanted to kill Joe," this statement would be admissible because it was made by Marty (the defendant and thus a party to the case) and it goes against his legal interest (i.e. it hurts his case).

b. *Excited utterance.* Any statement made by a person in an excited state is admissible.

c. *State of mind.* Any statement that shows the speaker's state of mind is admissible. For example, if before the murder Joe told Sam, "I'm really scared." This statement would be admissible in testimony by Sam.

d. *Official records and writings by public employees.*

e. *Records made in the regular course of doing business.*

How to Object:

• "Objection, your honor. Counsel's question calls for hearsay."

• If the objection is raised *after the witness answers:*

"Objection, your honor. This testimony is hearsay. I ask that it be stricken from the record."

5. *Opinion Testimony*

With a few limited exceptions, only experts with special knowledge and qualifications can give their opinions in a trial. An attorney who calls an expert to testify, must first qualify the individual as an expert. In other words, an attorney must lay a foundation that the person qualifies as an expert. The attorney does this by asking a series of questions about the person's professional training and experience in a particular field. The attorney then asks the court to acknowledge the witness's specific expertise.

All witnesses, even non-experts, may give their opinions about things like color, size, weight, drunkenness, speed of a moving object—anything within the realm of a person's ordinary, everyday experience or perception.

How to Object:

• "Objection, your honor. Counsel is asking the witness to give an opinion."

• If the objection is made *after the witness answers:*

"Objection, your honor. This witness was not qualified as an expert. I ask that the witness's opinion be stricken from the record."

6. *Argumentative Questions*

Witnesses may ordinarily only be asked questions to get facts from them. Questions which challenge witnesses to reconcile differing parts of their testimony may be objected to as being argumentative. For example, an attorney asks, "How can you expect the court to believe that you were at Main Street that day when you previously testified you were out of town?" This question may be objected to as argumentative.

How to Object:

• "Objection, your honor. Counsel is being argumentative."

• "Objection, your honor. Counsel is badgering the witness."

7. *Special Rules for Direct Examination of Witnesses*

Direct examination takes place when lawyers call their own witnesses to the stand and ask them questions.

a. *Form of Questions*

Generally, attorneys must ask questions that evoke a short narrative answer from the witness, but not an answer too long or rambling. Attorneys may not ask leading questions. A leading question is one that suggests the desired answer. It usually elicits a "yes" or "no" answer. Often, leading questions are really statements with something like, "Isn't that right?", "Isn't that so?", or "Didn't you?" tacked on the end.

For example, this question would be proper on direct examination (assuming that the fact was in issue): "Mr. Stevens, when did you and your wife adopt Charles?"

This one would be improper: "You and your wife adopted Charles two years ago, didn't you, Mr. Stevens?"

How to Object:

• "Objection, your honor. Counsel is leading the witness."

b. *Character*

Unless a person's character is at issue in a case, witnesses generally cannot testify about a person's character. But a witness's honesty is one aspect of character always at issue. In addition, the defense may introduce evidence of the defendant's good character and, if relevant, show the bad character of an important prosecution witness. Once the defense introduces character evidence, however, the prosecution can try to refute it.

Consider these examples:

• The prosecutor calls the owner of the defendant's apartment to testify. She testifies that the defendant often stumbled in drunk at all hours of the night. This character evidence would not be admissible unless the defendant had already introduced evidence of good character. Even then, a judge might disallow it because its prejudicial nature would probably outweigh its probative value.

• The defendant's minister testifies that the defendant attends church every week and has a reputation in the community as a law-abiding person. This would be admissible.

How to Object:

• "Objection, your honor. The witness's character is not at issue in this case."

• "Objection, your honor. The question calls for inadmissible character evidence."

c. *Refreshing Recollections*

Imagine that you are a witness of a hit-and-run accident. Two years later, the driver of the car comes to trial. The prosecutor calls you to the stand and asks you to describe what you saw. You give as many details as you can, but when the attorney asks you what the license plate number was on the car, you draw a blank. "I know I saw it and I know I told you when you talked to me after the accident," you answer, "but it's been so long—I just can't remember the number."

Since cases often take time before coming to trial, witnesses often may have a hard time recalling specific details of events occurring months or years earlier. In addition, witnesses may be so nervous that their memories fail them. The rules of evidence deal with this problem by allowing attorneys to help their witnesses remember. This is called "refreshing the witness's recollection." In the example above, the attorney could take a typed copy of a statement you made near the time of the accident, mark it as an "exhibit," have you read it, and then take the statement away. She could then ask you the question about the license plate number again. "*Now* I remember," you answer. "The number was XOJ 489." Although the pretrial statement can be used this way, it is not entered into evidence.

8. *Special Rules for Cross-Examination of Witnesses*

After direct examination, the lawyer for the opposing side cross-examines each witness.

Cross-examination has two purposes. It is designed to:

(1) clarify the witness's testimony from the other side's point of view, and

(2) give the opposing side an opportunity to **impeach** the witness—that is, to attack the witness's credibility.

a. *Form of Questions*

While leading questions (e.g. "You drank like a fish that night, didn't you, Mr. Saski?") are usually not permitted during direct examination, they *are* allowed during cross-examination.

b. *Scope of Cross-Examination*

Cross-examination questions are limited to matters that were brought out on direct examination. In other words, cross-examination may not go beyond the scope of the direct examination. Most judges, however, broadly interpret this rule.

How to Object:

• "Objection, your honor. Counsel's question is going beyond the scope of direct examination."

c. *Impeachment*

Impeaching a witness on cross-examination is designed to reduce the importance that the fact finder gives a witness's story. An attorney can impeach a witness by asking about:

• *Bias or prejudice* the witness has toward the issues or parties in the case;

• The *accuracy* of what the witness saw, heard, smelled, etc.;

• *Prior statements* that the witness made which are inconsistent with the witness's testimony in court;

• *Prior criminal convictions* of the witness, but only if they relate directly to truth-telling ability; and

• *Prior acts of misconduct,* but only if they relate directly to the witness's ability to tell the truth. (Such questions may only be asked if the attorney conducting the cross-examination has information showing that the bad conduct actually happened. The attorney may not base the question on some rumor or just ask the question to make the witness look bad.)

If the witness's credibility is attacked on cross-examination, the attorney whose witness has been impeached may ask more questions to try to limit the damage done and restore the wit-

A prosecutor presents his case while another attorney takes notes. (UPI/Bettmann.)

ness's credibility. This is done on **redirect examination** by the lawyer who put the witness on the stand in the first place.

For Discussion

1. Why is eyewitness testimony ("I saw Bill steal the wallet") more trustworthy than something heard secondhand ("Mary told me she saw Bill steal the wallet")? How can the first statement be tested in court? How can the second statement?

2. When are leading questions permitted and prohibited? Why do you think this difference exists?

3. Can you think of examples of relevant testimony that would not be allowed in evidence?

Class Activity: Objection

The trial situations below are based on the Thomas Wade Carter case. Have each student write the letters "a" through "l" down the side of a sheet of paper. Next to each letter write "yes" or "no" to indicate whether an objection should be made in each situation. Give a reason for your answer.

a. Ms. Karen Miller testifies: "I am convinced my little girl was intentionally killed by the Carter boy."

b. Joel Robertson testifies: "A friend of mine said he saw Oscar hit Tom over the head with a beer bottle."

c. The prosecutor asks Gail Duran: "What kind of potato chips did you serve at your party?"

d. Ms. Karen Miller testifies: "I told the police officer that I thought whoever shot Joyce was on drugs."

e. On cross-examination, the attorney asks Gail Duran: "You didn't stop the car when you heard the explosion behind you, did you?"

f. Ms. Karen Miller testifies: "Joyce was shot with a 12-gauge shotgun."

g. Joel Robertson testifies: "Oscar Hanks always parks his truck across the street from his house. It must have been there that day when Joyce Miller was shot."

h. Lt. Tony Jackson of the police department testifies: "We know that Tom Carter had connections with drug dealers in the area."

i. One of the guests from Gail Duran's party testifies: "Tom Carter told me after the fight that he was going to fix Oscar Hanks once and for all."

j. A neighbor of Ms. Miller states that a car with a gun sticking out of the back window drove by at about 15 miles per hour.

k. On direct examination, Carter's attorney asks him: "You never intended to shoot anyone, did you?"

l. Joel Robertson testifies: "If you ask me, a shotgun is effective up to about 20 yards."

Class Activity: Cross Fire

Now that you've had a chance to test your understanding of some basic rules of evidence, take the role of attorneys and prepare to examine witnesses in the case of Thomas Carter.

How to proceed:

1. It is recommended that you invite a lawyer or law student into class to work with the attorney groups and act as judge during the direct and cross-examination of witnesses. (If none is available, the teacher should take the role of judge.)

2. Organize the class into the following groups:
- Six teams of prosecutors (numbered 1-6) consisting of 2-3 students each
- Six teams of defense attorneys (numbered 1-6) consisting of 2-3 students each
- Six witnesses

3. Assignments:

Witnesses

Select one of the six witness descriptions on pages 129-131and study it carefully. For this activity, try to become the character described. Be prepared to answer questions that both the prosecuting and defense attorneys might ask you. When you are on the stand, it will be your job to recall the events leading up to Joyce Miller's killing. Do not add anything to the facts contained in your witness statement.

Attorneys

Teams of attorneys, prosecution and defense, have the following assignments:

Prosecutors:

Team 1—Direct examination of Joel Robertson

Team 2—Direct examination of Gail Duran

Team 3—Direct examination of Lt. Tony Jackson

Team 4—Direct examination of Karen Miller

Team 5—Cross-examination of Thomas Carter

Team 6—Cross-examination of Lillian Sweet

Defense Attorneys:

Team 1—Direct examination of Thomas Carter

Team 2—Direct examination of Lillian Sweet

Team 3—Cross-examination of Joel Robertson

Team 4—Cross-examination of Gail Duran

Team 5—Cross-examination of Lt. Tony Jackson

Team 6—Cross-examination of Karen Miller

To prepare to examine witnesses, carefully review:

(1) "The Rules of Evidence" so that you can raise or counter objections, and

(2) the statement of the witness you are assigned.

Your team should *develop questions* for the witness you are assigned to. Keep in mind the rules of evidence and your team's overall strategy for the case

The prosecution must prove Thomas Carter guilty of murder beyond a reasonable doubt. It must bring up evidence in its favor and anticipate and attempt to dilute the impact of evidence against it. The defense must raise every reasonable doubt it can about Carter's guilt.

In most states, a defendant charged with murder could be found guilty of manslaughter instead. Since Carter has no alibi and doesn't deny being in the car with the shotgun in his hand, the case will boil down to the issue of Carter's *intent* The prosecution will try to prove that Carter knew exactly what he was doing and that he intended to shoot the gun. The defense, on the other hand, will try to show that Carter didn't really mean to hurt anyone and that the gun went off accidentally.

Since you can only cross-examine witnesses about what they testified about in direct examination, cross-examination questions can be difficult to write in advance. But the witnesses' statements should give you an idea of what witnesses are likely to be asked on direct, and you can write cross-examination questions accordingly. You should then be alert during direct examination so you can get rid of any inappropriate cross questions you have developed.

Also, be prepared to object to any statements you believe violate the rules of evidence described on pages 122-127.

4. Examination Procedures:

After all of the teams have developed their questions, role-play the examination of the witnesses. The team assigned to cross-examine a particular witness should be primarily responsible for raising objections to the direct examination, although *all* students on the opposing team may do so. Likewise, a team assigned to direct examination of a particular witness should be primarily responsible for raising objections to the cross-examination of its witness. The visiting attorney or law student should rule on the objections and help debrief the activity.

5. After all witnesses have been examined and cross-examined, discuss:

- Which witnesses were most important to the prosecution and defense? Why?
- Which questions were most effective during the direct examinations? During the cross-examinations?
- Which objections were raised most often? Why do you think this happened?
- What characteristics do you think tend to make a witness seem believable? What characteristics detract from a witness's credibility?
- What qualities would a person need to be a successful trial lawyer? Explain.

Statement of Karen Miller

My name is Karen Miller. I am 25 years old and divorced.

I was home on the evening of July 6. Around 7 p.m., Joyce was playing in the front yard. I asked her to close the front gate and come inside the house, since it was her bath time. As I watched her go to the gate, a black car slowly drove down the block. I think it was a late model Pontiac, but I'm not really sure. Suddenly, the barrel of a rifle or shotgun was pointing from the car window right at Joyce. Before I could say or do anything, there was an explosion, and the car took off quickly.

At that instant, I looked at Joyce and saw her fall to the ground. Horrified, I ran to her and saw blood all over her face and body. She died in my arms before the paramedics arrived.

I can't describe the occupants of the black Pontiac. Still, I think the driver was a young woman.

A red Toyota truck was parked in front of my house that evening. I believe it belonged to a teen-ager named Oscar who lives across the street.

Statement of Joel Robertson

I am Joel Robertson and I am 21 years old. I have known Tom for a few years, but we're not close friends.

On the evening of July 5, I attended a party at Gail Duran's house. I and most of the others at the party drank beer for several hours. Around 3:30 a.m., a fight broke out. I was not involved in the fight, but I saw Tom Carter get hit over the head with a beer bottle. I did not know who did it. I and some of the others at the party took Tom Carter to the hospital for emergency treatment. On the way to the hospital, Carter kept asking who hit him with the bottle. He was really angry. The people in the car suggested several names, including Oscar Hanks.

The next day about 5 p.m., Tom Carter came over to my apartment. Carter was still very angry about what had happened the night before. I know from past experience that Carter is the type of guy to carry a grudge. He's a real hothead. He was always getting into fights with guys at school and in our neighborhood. Carter told me that he thought he knew the guy who split open his scalp. He said he thought the guy was Oscar Hanks. Carter told me, "I'm going to put a scare into that guy that he won't forget."

We watched a video for a while and had a soft drink. Carter was really nervous. A little later, Carter started asking me about my gun collection. I am a hunter and collect rifles and shotguns. Carter was especially interested in one of my shotguns. He asked me to show him how to work it. He also asked me how far a shotgun would shoot. I responded that a shotgun would be effective up to about 20 yards. About 6 p.m., Carter left my apartment.

Statement of Gail Duran

My name is Gail Duran. I am 17. I have been dating Tom Carter for about a year.

On the evening of July 5, I had a party for about 50 of my friends while my parents were on vacation. During the party a lot of people got drunk on beer. Sometime around 3 a.m., a fight broke out among about a dozen guys. Tom was hit on the head with a beer bottle. There was blood all over the place. I asked Joel Robertson and some others to take Tom to the hospital while I tried to get everybody out of the house before the police came.

The next day Tom called me to say he was all right, and would be over to see me later on. Around 6:30 p.m., Tom arrived at my place. He was very upset about getting hit the night before. He said he thought he knew who had hit him with the bottle. He said it was Oscar Hanks. Tom then asked me to go for a ride with him. I agreed to go with him.

Tom asked me to drive his car while he sat in the back. Tom owns a Pontiac Firebird. He told me he wanted to look for Oscar Hanks. He gave me directions to drive to Fourth Street. While driving down Fourth Street Tom said, "Hey, that's his truck. Slow down, Gail." As I slowed down I noticed for the first time that Tom had a shotgun in the back of the car with him.

At this point, I really got scared and began to swerve down the street. I had never seen Tom act this way before. Then there was a loud bang, and Tom yelled to me, "Get us out of here, fast!" I managed to drive out of the neighborhood. I stopped on a quiet street. Tom got into the driver's seat and took me home.

On the way home, Tom told me that the shotgun just went off by itself, but he did not think he had hit anything. I did not actually see the shotgun discharge, but I believe that the swerving motion of the car must have caused Tom to accidentally pull the trigger. Tom would never intentionally shoot anyone. He's always been a sensitive and gentle guy. Sure, he had a few fist fights when we were in high school, but he didn't mean anything by it. He's basically a great guy.

Statement of Thomas Wade Carter

My name is Thomas Wade Carter, age 18. I have recently graduated from high school. I work at an auto parts store.

I was totally shocked when I was arrested for shooting a little girl. I have never been in

serious trouble before. I was suspended from high school once or twice because of problems with other guys, but they always started the fights, not me.

Gail Duran is my girlfriend. She and I have been going together for about a year. I went to her party on July 5, and had a good time drinking beer with my friends until I got in a fight with a dozen other guys around 3 a.m. During the fight, I was struck in the back of the head with a beer bottle. Joel Robertson and some others at the party took me to the hospital. It took five stitches to close the wound on my scalp.

The next day (July 6), I called Gail and told her I was all right and that I would be dropping by later in the day.

I was angry at Oscar and wanted to pay him back some way. So I decided to take my father's shotgun and scare him a little.

After picking up the shotgun, I stopped by Joel Robertson's apartment around 5 p.m. I knew he was a hunter. I got him to tell me how to work a shotgun so I could make Oscar think I was serious. But I never knew the gun was loaded, and I never meant to hurt him. I just wanted to teach him a lesson.

From Joel's place, I went over to see Gail. I asked her to go with me for a drive. I had her drive my car while I sat in the back seat looking for Oscar's house. I knew he lived somewhere on Fourth Street. I also knew he drove a red Toyota truck. Finally, I spotted his truck parked along the street. But the car suddenly lurched, and the next thing I knew, the shotgun went off accidentally. I panicked. I didn't know it was loaded! I told Gail to get out of the neighborhood fast. I did not see anybody in the yard where Joyce Ann Miller was killed and certainly did not aim the shotgun at her. It was an accident.

Statement of Lillian Sweet

My name is Lillian Sweet. I am a retired school principal. I have a Ph.D in educational administration from the University of Illinois. I was a history teacher and a school guidance counselor before I became a principal.

After all the evidence is presented, the defense and prosecution summarize their cases in closing arguments. Although Judge Frump doesn't seem to realize it, the prosecution has the burden of proving its case beyond a reasonable doubt. (Tom Ryan cartoon reprinted with permission.)

I have known Tom Carter since he was a little boy. I've lived down the street from the Carters for almost 20 years and I was the principal of the high school that Tom attended.

I did have to suspend him for brawling with other boys once or twice. But kids will be kids. I think Tom was just following the lead of his friends in those days. As a principal, I was not very seriously concerned about Tom's behavior. I knew he'd grow up to be the fine young man he is today.

Tom has always been a joy to have in the neighborhood. He is kind to old people and children. He helps his mother with grocery shopping. Sometimes he even drives me to my doctor appointments if the weather is bad or he has a free afternoon.

In my opinion, Tom could never have done what he is accused of doing. He's a very stable and responsible young man. He's just not capable of murder.

Statement of Lt. Tony Jackson

NOTE: For Lt. Jackson's statement see the Police Crime Investigation Report on pages 94-95.

Class Activity: The Defense Rests . . .

After the defense's case-in-chief, the opposing counsels make closing arguments. These arguments give the attorneys a chance to summarize their cases, review the testimony of witnesses, and make a last appeal to the judge or jury. For the purpose of this activity the defense makes the first closing argument, followed by the prosecution.

Guidelines for an Effective Closing Statement (Rating Sheet)

An effective closing statement should:

1. Be emotionally charged and strongly appealing (unlike the calm, rational opening statement).

2. Emphasize the facts which support the claims of your side.

3. Note weaknesses or inconsistencies in the opposing side's case.

4. Summarize the favorable testimony.

5. Attempt to reconcile inconsistencies that might hurt your side.

6. Be presented so that notes are barely necessary.

7. Be well-organized (starting and ending with your strongest point helps to structure the presentation and give you a good introduction and conclusion).

8. Focus on reasonable doubt by(*prosecution*) emphasizing that the state has proved the elements of the crime beyond a reasonable doubt; or (*defense*) raising questions which suggest that reasonable doubt exists.

> Proper phrasing includes:
>
> "The evidence has clearly shown that . . ."
>
> "Based on this testimony, there can be no doubt that . . ."
>
> "The prosecution has failed to prove that . . ."
>
> "The defense would have you believe . . ."

9. Conclude with an appeal to convict or acquit the defendant.

In this activity, you will take the role of attorneys developing closing arguments in the case of *People v. Carter.*

How to Proceed

1. Each student should:

- Choose to represent either the prosecution or defense.
- Review the witness statements on pages 129-131 and consider the main points brought out in witnesses' testimony in the previous activity.
- Develop a three-minute closing argument for presentation to the class. (Be sure to follow the above "Guidelines for an Effective Closing Statement.")

2. Select 12 members of the class to act as a jury. They will judge the quality of the presentations. To do this, each must take a blank piece of paper and make a rating sheet as follows:

> Write each presenter's name and role (prosecutor or defense attorney). Under each presenter's name, write the numbers one through nine in a column.
>
> Each of the numbers corresponds to one of the "Guidelines for an Effective Closing Statement." At the close of each presentation, place a check mark next to the item if the presenter's statement met the criterion.

(UPI/Bettmann.)

3. Call on three prosecutors and then three defense attorneys to make closing arguments. After all have presented, poll the jury to find out which prosecutor and defense attorney made the best presentation. Jurors should explain their choices based on the listed criteria.

Case Notes: Instructing the Jury

After closing arguments in a criminal trial, the judge gives the jury instructions it must consider when arriving at a verdict. This process is sometimes called **charging the jury**. The primary purposes of these instructions are to explain the law, point out the elements of a crime that must be proved, and show the relationship of the evidence to the issues on trial. In many states, judges base their instructions on models adopted by the legislature. In other states, judges may develop their own. Still, a judge must be careful. Inaccurate or misleading instructions to the jury are the most common reason for verdicts being overturned on appeal.

Imagine you are in the jury box just as the court clerk in the case of *People v. Carter* rises and announces: "The court will now charge the jury. No one may leave or enter the room during the charge." Judge Coghlan then gives the following instructions:

Ladies and gentlemen of the jury:

It is my duty to instruct you in the law that applies to this case. You must follow the law as I state it to you.

1. Duties of the Judge and Jury

In determining whether the defendant is guilty or not guilty, you—as jurors—must base your decision entirely on the evidence presented during this trial and on the law as explained by me. You must not be governed by mere sympathy, guesswork, emotion, prejudice, or public opinion. You must not be influenced by the mere fact that the defendant has been arrested, charged, and brought to trial.

2. Evidence

If the evidence equally supports two reasonable versions of the truth, one of which points to the defendant's guilt and the other to the defendant's innocence, it is your duty to adopt the version pointing to the defendant's innocence.

3. Credibility of Witnesses

Every person who testifies under oath is a witness. You are the sole judges of the credibility of the witnesses who have testified in this case.

Discrepancies or differences that occur in a witness's testimony, or between one witness and another, do not necessarily mean that a witness is lying. Failure to recollect facts is a common human experience. In addition, two persons witnessing the same incident will often see or hear it differently. You may simply have to decide which version of the facts is more believable.

4. Statements of Counsel and Evidence Stricken from the Record

Any testimony or other evidence rejected or stricken from the record is to be treated as if you had never heard it.

Also, if an objection to a question was sustained, you must disregard the question. This means that you must not speculate about what witnesses might have said if they had been allowed to answer. Neither may you speculate about why an objection was made to a question.

5. Presumption of Innocence—Reasonable Doubt—Burden of Proof

A defendant in a criminal action is presumed to be innocent until proved guilty. This presumption places upon the prosecution the burden of proving the defendant guilty beyond a reasonable doubt. This does not mean no possible doubt must exist, because doubt will always exist. Beyond a reasonable doubt means that after hearing all the evidence, a juror is still convinced to a moral certainty that the defendant is guilty.

6. The Charges in this Case:

Thomas Wade Carter has been charged with two crimes: Second-degree murder and involuntary manslaughter.

Second-Degree Murder

Second-degree murder is the unlawful killing of a human being with malice aforethought.

Malice Aforethought—*Malice* may be either express or implied.

Malice is express when a person intends unlawfully to kill a human being.

Malice is implied when the killing results from an intentional act that

(1) is dangerous to human life, *and*

(2) was deliberately performed with knowledge of the danger and with conscious disregard for human life.

Malice does not necessarily require any ill will or hatred of the person killed.

Aforethought does not imply deliberation or the lapse of considerable time. It only means that the required mental state must come before rather than follow the act.

If you find beyond a reasonable doubt by the evidence presented in this trial that Thomas Wade Carter intended to kill Joyce Ann Miller, then you shall return a verdict of second-degree murder.

OR

If you find beyond a reasonable doubt by the evidence presented in this trial that Thomas Wade Carter intended to fire the shotgun that killed

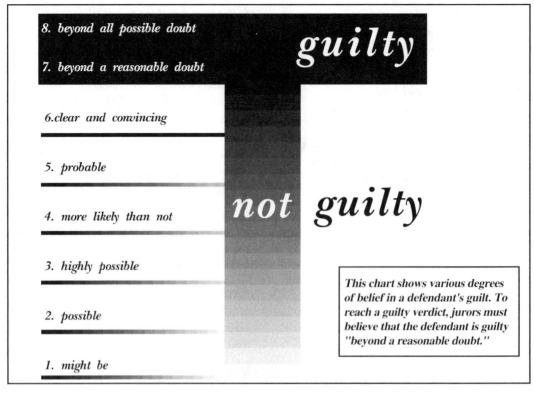

8. beyond all possible doubt

7. beyond a reasonable doubt

guilty

6. clear and convincing

5. probable

not guilty

4. more likely than not

3. highly possible

This chart shows various degrees of belief in a defendant's guilt. To reach a guilty verdict, jurors must believe that the defendant is guilty "beyond a reasonable doubt."

2. possible

1. might be

Joyce Ann Miller, and that the act involved a high degree of probability that death would result, and that it was done with conscious disregard for human life, you shall return a verdict of second-degree murder.

Lesser Charge: Involuntary Manslaughter

Involuntary manslaughter is the unlawful killing of a human being without malice aforethought and without intent to kill. If you are satisfied beyond a reasonable doubt that the killing was unintentional and the direct result of a very dangerous and unlawful act, you shall return a verdict of involuntary manslaughter.

7. Doubt Whether Murder or Manslaughter

If you are satisfied beyond a reasonable doubt that the killing was unlawful, but you have a reasonable doubt whether the crime is murder or manslaughter, you must give the defendant the benefit of this doubt and find it to be manslaughter rather than murder.

8. Unanimous Agreement as to Offense: Second-Degree Murder or Manslaughter

Before you may return a verdict in this case, you must agree unanimously. If you return a verdict of not guilty, it must be agreed on unanimously. If you return a guilty verdict, you must unanimously find him guilty of manslaughter or of murder in the second degree.

9. Each Juror Must Make an Independent Decision

Each of you must decide the case for yourself, but you should also do so only after discussing the evidence and these instructions with the other jurors.

You should not hesitate to change your opinion if you are convinced it is wrong. You should not, however, be influenced one way or the other because the majority of jurors favor a certain verdict.

10. Concluding Instructions

You shall now retire and select one of your number to act as foreman. The foreman will preside over your deliberations. In order to reach a verdict, all jurors must agree to the decision. As soon as all of you have agreed upon a verdict, you shall have it dated and signed by your foreman, and then you shall return to announce it to the court.

For Discussion

1. What things *should* be considered and discussed by the jurors? What things *should not* enter into the jury's deliberations?

2. Review the definition of "beyond a reasonable doubt" in instruction #5. According to this definition, which one of the following statements would be true?

> a. A juror should vote to convict *only* if 100 percent sure that the defendant is guilty.

> b. A juror should vote to acquit if the juror believes there is any possible chance that the defendant is not guilty.

> c. A juror should vote to convict if the juror believes that a very high degree of probability exists that the defendant is guilty.

3. Review the second-degree murder charge against Thomas Wade Carter in instruction #6. According to the prosecution, how was Joyce Ann Miller killed? According to the defense, how was Joyce Ann Miller killed?

Class Activity: We, the Jury

Imagine that you are a juror charged with rendering a final verdict in the case of *People v. Carter*. To complete this activity, follow these procedures:

1. Form two or three juries of 12 students each. (Remaining students may form a smaller jury.)

2. Each jury should appoint a foreman who will help lead discussions, collect signatures on the verdict, date it, and deliver it to the court.

3. You should refer to the judge's instructions on pages 133-135 during your deliberations.

4. During the deliberations, the foreman may wish to take one or more polls to determine if the jury has reached a consensus. Remember your verdict must be unanimous.

5. First determine your verdict on the charge of second-degree murder. If the jury finds Carter not guilty or it deadlocks on this issue, then determine the verdict for involuntary manslaughter.

6. After about 15 minutes, the teacher, acting as judge, will ask if you have reached a verdict.

> • A jury not reaching a unanimous verdict will be considered a hung jury.

> • The foremen of juries reaching a unanimous verdict will deliver it to the court along with the 12 signatures attesting to it.

7. In either case, the judge may poll individual jurors and ask each to explain the reasons for their decisions. (In a real case, a judge polling individual jurors may not ask for the reasons for their decision.)

For Discussion

1. Sometimes juries are unable to reach a verdict and become what is known as hung juries. How is it possible for people who have heard the same evidence to reach different conclusions?

2. How does this jury activity compare to what you know about real jury deliberations? For example, were some students unable to be objective after having taken the role of the defense or prosecution? Did the jurors know too much about the case?

3. Which witnesses did you find most believable? Least credible? What makes a witness credible?

4. Which roles were the most difficult to play? Why?

5. What did you learn about the job of the judge, attorneys, witnesses, and jurors?

Class Activity: Verdict

As a concluding activity, write an essay explaining your personal verdict in the Thomas Wade Carter case.

CORRECTIONS

Jay is 19 years old. Today, he will appear before a judge to be sentenced. He robbed a mini-market at gunpoint. He is about to enter corrections—the part of our criminal justice system that deals with convicted offenders. Jay has a lot to worry about. Will the judge send him to prison? After all, Jay used a gun. Or, will he be given some alternative to prison—probation or some kind of community service?

If you asked Jay's victim, you'd probably hear a demand that he go to prison. If you asked someone familiar with the prison system, however, you might get a different opinion. Some might even argue that Jay should be given a second chance. Many experts believe that contact with hardened criminals only locks someone into a life of crime.

In many parts of the country, Jay could be sentenced to a special program in a group home, where he would work under the supervision of a staff of trained specialists. In that setting, he could receive psychological counseling and job training. Or he could be sent to one of the new boot camp programs that tries to instill self-discipline in young offenders.

This chapter explores how sentencing decisions are made and what the alternatives are—prison, probation, community service, and several innovative programs, which may be promising alternatives to existing programs. We will also explore how prisons developed, the problems they currently face, and some experimental corrections programs that are under way. Finally, you will take a look at what is perhaps the most hotly debated of all corrections issues—the death penalty.

CORRECTIONS AND SOCIETY

The Purpose of Punishment

All societies have maintained the right to punish people who break their rules. But what is the purpose of punishment? What is it supposed to accomplish? This is a difficult question to answer. Experts and lay people alike often disagree. Over the years, different theories have been advanced. Some of these theories involve very different ways of handling wrongdoers—from ducking stools to imprisonment to psychotherapy.

People advocating one approach have often condemned all others as brutal, or unjust, or ineffective. Recently, scholars have tried to bring some order to the debate by developing an inclusive theory of punishment. This theory holds that one approach might work best in one situation while another would be better in a different situation.

The following are brief descriptions of each of the major reasons for punishing a lawbreaker:

Rehabilitation seeks to treat and reform the lawbreaker. Advocates of this theory believe that prison or release programs should try to turn the wrongdoer into a productive member of society. To implement this theory, the prison system has to provide job training, psychological counseling, and educational programs. And these programs should be tailored to the best interests of the individual prisoner. Critics of the rehabilitation theory admit that it may be a noble idea, but they argue that it just doesn't work in practice.

Restitution seeks repayment. The offender repays the victim or community in money or services. Critics say money and services cannot repay for the harm caused by violent crimes.

Incapacitation seeks to isolate a criminal from society to protect ordinary citizens. Confinement in a secure prison makes it impossible for a criminal to commit further crimes in the surrounding society. Critics of this theory point out that most criminals have fixed prison terms, and they will be released sooner or later. If nothing is done to reform them, the protection is only temporary.

Deterrence seeks to prevent further crimes. This can operate in two ways. One way, called *specific deterrence*, targets the criminal in question, hoping that the memory of harsh punishment will deter that criminal from any further crime. *General* deterrence targets other potential criminals. Others will see the harsh punishment and be discouraged from committing the same crime. Critics argue that few criminals expect to be caught, and deterrence is only powerful when criminals fear they will be caught and punished.

Retribution seeks revenge. This is perhaps the oldest theory of punishment, based on the idea that society has to retaliate against a person who commits a crime. This idea dates back to the ancient "eye for an eye" philosophies of Mesopotamian and Judeo-Christian traditions.

Advocates say that by imposing punishment we in some way get even with criminals. Some critics of retribution say it is too cruel for a modern society, and others claim that it does nothing to address serious issues like reforming criminals or protecting the innocent.

Class Activity: The Student Court

In this activity, students will act as members of a student court, assigning penalties to those who break school rules. Wrongdoers may be sentenced to detention, hours of school service, loss of student body privileges, or other penalties your court thinks appropriate.

1. Divide the class into student courts of five students each.

2. In each court:

> a. Appoint a chief judge to lead your discussion and to assign one of the cases below to each student. That student is responsible for taking notes and reporting the penalty in that case to the whole class.

> b. Review the cases below which have come before your court. After discussion, the court should set an appropriate and specific penalty for each wrongdoer.

>> **(1) Chris Hodges** was caught smoking in the restroom. This is his second offense.

>> **(2) Terry Rodriguez** was cited for littering the campus quad area during lunch period.

>> **(3) Kelly Janus** was 20 minutes late to his first period class three days in a row without a legitimate excuse.

>> **(4) Linden Sommerville** started a food fight in the cafeteria by smashing an overripe banana in her friend's hair.

>> **(5) Jan Turner** defaced several library books.

3. Reconvene the whole class. Make headings on the board using the names of the five rule breakers. Have the appropriate member of each court report its recommended penalty and write it under the appropriate heading.

4. For each sentence described, discuss and decide whether it best meets the purposes of: a) rehabilitation; b) restitution; c) incapacitation; d) deterrence; e) retribution; or f) some combination.

Debriefing Questions

1. Which of the sentences recommended by the student courts do you think are fair? Which are not fair? Why?

2. Which of the five theories of punishment comes closest to your idea of what is just? Why?

A Brief History of Punishment in the United States

America has a far higher percentage of its citizens in prison than any country in the world. In the 1980s, the prison population nearly tripled. Well over a million Americans are now in prisons and jails, and at the present rate of increase, we need to build a new 1,000-bed prison every six days.

This huge increase has put the prison system in serious crisis. In some places, five and six prisoners are held in cells built for two. On average, our state prisons are operating at 125 percent of their planned capacity, and some are much worse. The overcrowding is so serious that in almost all states some prisons are under court orders to reduce occupancy or refuse to accept new prisoners.

Some of this increase has resulted from attempts to crack down on drug offenders. The percentage of prisoners convicted of drug offenses has grown from 7 percent to over 30 percent. The main factor in this explosive growth, however, has been the public outcry to do something about crime. Responding to public demand,

An offender stands with his head and hands in a pillory. Beside him, another offender sits with his feet in stocks. Petty offenders often received such public humiliation during Colonial times. (The Bettmann Archive.)

politicians have insisted on more jail time for almost all crimes. In 1975, a convicted felon in California had about a 15 percent chance of serving a prison term. In the 1990s, a felon's chances had increased to 35 percent.

America's attitudes on crime and punishment have changed drastically from the Colonial era, through the 19th century, and even since the beginning of the 20th century. Looking back on this history, we can gain some insight into the problems of prisons today.

Punishment in Colonial America

Before the American Revolution, all the colonies punished even minor offenses very harshly. They would mete out public humiliation for petty offenses. A lawbreaker might have to stand in a public square, hands locked up in a device called a pillory, or sit with feet locked in stocks. In many towns, offenders were tied to ducking stools and dunked into the icy water of a river or pond. Some lawbreakers were forced to wear a symbol of their crime, such as the large red "A" for adultery that was sewn to the dress of the character Hester Prynne in Nathaniel Hawthorne's *The Scarlet Letter*.

More serious lawbreakers might receive

lashings at a public whipping post. Others, particularly runaway slaves in the Southern colonies, might be branded with a hot iron or mutilated by cutting off their toes. In Northern colonies, thieves might have their ears cut off or the letter "T" branded on their necks or faces. This was not only a punishment, but a warning to other thieves. For many serious crimes, the penalty was death by public hanging.

Some colonies had jails to house the accused while they awaited trial. Jailkeepers ran these institutions for profit, and inmates had to pay for their own food and blankets. Some poor inmates starved to death before their trials began. Many inmates were hired out to work as laborers building roads and working farms, and the profits went to the jailkeepers. One observer noted seeing inmates weighed down by "iron collars and chains, to which bombshells were attached, to be dragged along while they performed their degrading service."

Regret and Remorse: The Penitentiary

After the American Revolution, concerned citizens of the new American republic objected to the brutal treatment of criminals. In Pennsylvania, the Quakers, an influential religious group opposed to war and violence, worked for reform. They introduced the idea of locking up criminals behind high thick walls in order to change their behavior. The Quakers hoped that solitary confinement would give criminals the opportunity to think about their deeds and become penitent, or sorry, for what they had done. Early prisons, therefore, came to be called penitentiaries. The Quakers also sponsored other reforms, including separating prisoners by sex, keeping children out of adult jails, and providing food and clothing to inmates at government expense.

This reform movement led to the first prisons as we know them today. In 1790, Philadelphia built a block of cells, each one six by eight feet in size and nine feet high. The Pennsylvania System, as these reforms were called, represented a change in the philosophy of how to deal with criminals. Its purpose was not just to punish, but also to *correct* the behavior of lawbreakers. This new idea of correcting, or reforming, criminal behavior was soon adopted throughout the United States and Europe.

Unfortunately, the system of corrections sponsored by the Quakers seldom accomplished its purpose. Prisoners locked up in solitary confinement frequently became sick, went insane, or died. In 1842, Charles Dickens, the famous English novelist and social reformer, visited the Pennsylvania penitentiaries and reported:

> I believe it, in its effects, to be cruel and wrong. In its intention, I am well convinced that it is kind, humane, and meant for reformation, but I am persuaded that those who devised this system of prison discipline . . . do not know what it is they are doing. I believe that very few men are capable of estimating the immense amount of torture and agony which this dreadful punishment . . . inflicts upon the sufferers . . . . I hold this slow and daily tampering with the mysteries of the brain to be immensely worse than any torture of the body.

Leading a Useful Life: The Work System

The failure of solitary confinement led prison officials to try a new system that emphasized work instead of isolation. Under this system, prisoners were locked up in cells at night. But during the day, they worked together in prison shops and ate in a common dining area. At first, rules banned talking among prisoners. Later reforms allowed conversation.

The work system became widely used, and it still influences prison philosophy today. In many prisons, inmates learned to operate simple machines to manufacture items such as furniture for government offices. In some places, prisoners performed services such as growing food or washing the uniforms of hospital employees.

Treating Criminal Behavior: Rehabilitation

Following the Civil War, a new group of prison reformers questioned the work system. These reformers argued that criminal behavior was like a disease, and the prisons should try to cure the disease with some form of treatment. Prisoners should be **rehabilitated** and ready to take up a normal life in society when they were released.

A rehabilitation program was first tried in 1877 in a youth reformatory at Elmira, New York. Elmira offered its young offenders school classes, vocational training, health care, and counseling. When inmates demonstrated that they were ready for release, they were allowed to leave. Many other youth reformatories soon took up this new system.

(AP/Wide World Photos.)

Adult prisons also adopted parts of the Elmira system. By 1918, doctors, psychologists, and social workers were being brought into the prison to help rehabilitate prisoners. In addition, many states set up separate prison facilities for dangerous prisoners, low-risk prisoners, women, drug addicts, and the criminally insane.

In every era in our history, people have debated how to treat criminals and have tried different methods. In Colonial times, criminals received harsh, sometimes brutal, treatment. After the Revolution, reformers introduced the penitentiary and solitary confinement. When solitary confinement proved too harsh, new reformers pushed for the work system. After the Civil War, another group of reformers fought to introduce rehabilitation. By the 1920s, the rehabilitation model had caught on. But the debate over how to treat criminals didn't stop. Every generation of Americans has carried on this debate. It continues today.

For Discussion

1. Why did prisons develop?

2. Discuss this statement: "The history of corrections has been one of good intentions and bad results." What does it mean? Do you agree with it? Why or why not?

Class Activity

1. Break into small groups and list the advantages and disadvantages of the following kinds of punishment.

    a. Solitary confinement

    b. Hard physical labor

    c. Public humiliation

    d. Physical punishment

    e. Therapy

    f. Fines

2. Discuss the following questions:

    a. Which kind of punishment is still in use today?

    b. Where is it in use?

    c. What types of criminals or crimes might each punishment fit? Why?

    d. What other types of punishment can you think of? What are their advantages and disadvantages?

3. Assign one person in each group to report back to the class on one or two kinds of punishment.

Prisoners in Sing Sing Prison in Ossining, New York, used to wear striped uniforms and march closely together in what was called the "lockstep." (The Bettmann Archive.)

Current Debates about Corrections

For much of the 20th century, the principal purpose of our correctional system has been to rehabilitate criminals. The correctional system was organized to provide counseling and guidance, to get convicted criminals to rethink their attitudes, and to bring them back into society in a positive way. The system tried out many techniques suggested by reformers—psychological testing and therapy, vocational training, and educational programs.

Beginning in the 1970s, however, the idea of rehabilitation came under attack from those who said it just wasn't working. This attack was fed by high **recidivism** rates—the rate of those released from prison who go on to commit further crimes. Approximately 45 percent of all those released from prisons will be arrested again within three years and about 30 percent will be returned to prison.

Some experts now believe that these repeat, or incorrigible, criminals cannot be rehabilitated, and that these hardened criminals should go to prison for as long as possible.

Many polls suggest that the public is fed up with the crime problem and is more than willing to support harsh sentences. Most states have enacted mandatory sentencing laws, which require prison terms for certain crimes. These laws prevent judges from offering lesser sentences such as probation or other alternatives. A few states, such as Texas, even have laws that set a life-without-parole sentence for habitual criminals.

Getting Tough on Criminals

The idea of requiring stiff penalties to deter crime has grown in popularity since the early 1970s. Many states have enacted "use-a-gun, go-to-jail" laws. These laws require a minimum prison term, such as three years, for anyone who uses a gun to commit a crime. Some people feel that stiff mandatory sentences will deter criminals.

Critics of this view argue that few criminals expect to be caught, so penalties are no deterrent. Statistics show that only a small percentage of crime leads to capture and conviction. For example, a burglar has only about a 15 percent chance of being caught for any one burglary. And few criminals have any awareness of current sentencing practices, harsh or otherwise. Deterrence would only be powerful if arrest and conviction were more certain.

The idea of using stiff penalties simply for retribution has also grown in popularity. Many people feel that society has the right and the duty to punish—that criminals have done evil acts and deserve to be treated harshly. Some supporters of retribution even dismiss the idea of deterrence. They don't care whether the punishment deters or not. They simply want criminals punished.

Some advocates of victims' rights have supported this view. They argue that victims who suffer at the hands of criminals need to know that the criminals will suffer too. In 1978, California enacted a law that allowed judges to use victim-impact statements to help determine sentencing. These statements give a detailed account of the effect the crime had on the victim. Almost all states have now passed similar laws to use victim-impact statements to add the victim's pain into the calculation of punishment.

Supporters say these statements are necessary to help victims feel that justice is being done. The victims can then move beyond their own suffering and get on with their lives. Opponents argue that retribution does not really right any wrongs. They feel that overly harsh sentences only brutalize criminals who will eventually be back on the street, ready to create more victims.

Trends and Controversies

One focus of public outrage has been the fact that so much crime seems to be committed by so few. A study by the RAND Corporation, a well-known think tank, found that "most violent predators commit hundreds of serious crimes a year." The RAND study found that the 10 percent of criminals with the highest robbery rates each committed over 135 robberies in a year.

One study of 2,190 repeat offenders estimated that each offender cost the public $430,000 a year in direct losses to victims plus added insurance costs. A long-term study by criminologist Marvin Wolfgang followed the lives of all males born in the years 1945 and 1958 and raised in Philadelphia. A mere 7 percent of this group was responsible for almost all the crime stemming from the group. Those in the 7-percent group had been arrested at least five times each by age 18. They had committed two-thirds of all the violent crime, three-fourths of all rapes, and virtually all the murders.

If this worst 7 percent could be targeted for long terms of maximum-security imprisonment, it might free the resources of the correctional system to try to rehabilitate the less serious offenders.

The RAND study advocated identifying high-rate offenders by adding up a series of factors, based on data from individual criminal records. A high score on the scale would indicate a longer term. A lower score would add up to a shorter sentence. The idea, called selective incapacitation, involves the following questions in identifying offenders:

Has the offender:

1. Been incarcerated more than half of the last two years before the current arrest?

2. A prior conviction for the crime?

3. A juvenile conviction prior to age 16?

4. Ever been committed to a state or federal juvenile facility?

5. Used heroin or barbiturates in the two-year period before the current arrest?

6. Used heroin or barbiturates as a juvenile?

7. Been employed less than half of the two-year period before the current arrest?

A "yes" answer to any of these questions receives one point on the scale. Offenders with 0-1 point are considered low-rate offenders; 2-3 medium; and 4 or more, high-rate offenders.

Such a scale, however, raises many ethical and practical questions. Should you, for example, send someone to prison for crimes not yet committed? And, does the scale discriminate against poor people who have greater difficulty in finding jobs? And more practically, does this scale really predict future criminality?

Another controversial proposal involves setting up a two-tier prison system. The lower tier would be for first-time offenders who have not committed serious crimes. This branch of the system could focus on rehabilitation, education, and job training. The other branch would be reserved for hardened criminals—repeat offenders and those who committed serious crimes. The upper tier would put less effort into rehabilitation. It would be a maximum-security prison system to ensure incapacitation, and it would be strict and harsh to maximize deterrence and retribution.

Supporters of this idea maintain that the two-tier system would address the needs of first-timers, would protect society from those who cannot be rehabilitated, and it would isolate first-timers from hardened criminals. Detractors maintain that the cost of developing two systems would be astronomical. Moreover, the proposal ignores the benefits of alternative programs such as community service, halfway houses, and other supervised release programs.

As our prison system overflows, these far less expensive alternative programs have grown more

"NOW DON'T ACT LIKE ANIMALS!"

(Pett cartoon reprinted with permission.)

attractive. Many experts believe these programs can rehabilitate prisoners, especially non-violent and drug offenders. Some experts predict that in the coming years our corrections system will focus once again on rehabilitation.

For Discussion

1. What are recidivism rates? Why are they important?

2. Why did the corrections system turn away from rehabilitation in the 1980s? Why are some experts predicting the system will return to rehabilitation?

3. Why do some experts advocate long terms for high-rate offenders? What are the advantages of this approach? The disadvantages? Do you think it would be a good idea? Why or why not?

4. What theory of punishment could justify longer sentences for offenders likely to commit more crimes? Which theory or theories would oppose longer sentences for these offenders? Explain.

5. Would you favor the development of a two-tier prison system? Why or why not?

Sentencing

William Smith, a banker, has been convicted of fraud. He secretly altered his bank's computer system to steal one dollar a year from every customer. He has no previous record, and no one was badly hurt by the crime.

Jennie Blaine has been found guilty of manslaughter. She hit and killed an 8-year-old girl while driving drunk. Blaine is the sole support for her own three children and she just lost her job. She has no previous record.

Andy Travers, a heroin addict, has been found guilty of beating an 80-year-old woman to death during a burglary. He has several previous drug convictions.

Should they all go to prison? Would it be better for society if some criminals are given fines, or probation, or mandatory community service, or other alternatives? How would you decide?

Sentencing and the Law

The range of sentences available to a court is defined by federal, state, and local laws. Perhaps the best known limitation on sentencing is the U.S. Constitution's Eighth Amendment, forbidding "cruel and unusual punishment." As interpreted by the courts, the Eighth Amendment forbids barbarous treatment, such as torture or mutilation.

The Eighth Amendment prohibits excessive or inappropriate punishment. For example, a prison sentence of 10 years for stealing a loaf of bread might be thrown out as a violation of the Eighth Amendment. In fact, in 1983 the U.S. Supreme Court ruled that an overly harsh sentence was unconstitutional. A South Dakota court had sentenced a man to life in prison for passing a $100 bad check. The sentence followed a state repeat-offender law that allowed a life sentence for anyone convicted of a fourth felony. A 5-4 majority of the Supreme Court in *Solem v. Helm* (1983) struck down the life sentence. It ruled "as a matter of principle, that a criminal sentence must be proportionate to the crime for which the defendant has been convicted."

The court pointed out three objective factors to decide whether a sentence is proportionate to the crime. These include comparing (1) the seriousness of the crime to the severity of the penalty, (2) the kinds of sentences other criminals were given for the same crime, and (3) the kinds of sentences given in other jurisdictions.

In 1991 in *Harmelin v. Michigan*, however, the Supreme Court seemed to back away from its ruling in *Solem*. Harmelin, an Air Force veteran with no prior record, was convicted of possessing 672 grams of cocaine. Under a Michigan mandatory-sentencing law, he received a sentence of life in prison with no possibility of parole. This is the same sentence that a person convicted of first-degree murder would receive in Michigan. In neighboring Ohio, Harmelin would have received a sentence of from five to 15 years. A 5-4 majority of the court upheld the sentence. Three of the justices in the majority ruled that the sentence was not "grossly disproportionate" to the crime. Two justices, Scalia and Rehnquist, declared that *Solem* was "simply wrong" and that the Eighth Amendment to the Constitution does not require felony sentences to be proportionate to the crime except in death penalty cases.

Aside from the Eighth Amendment, a convicted offender has a number of other rights that affect the sentencing process.

• *Right to Counsel:* The U.S. Supreme Court has ruled that a defendant is entitled to have an attorney participate in any sentencing hearing.

• *Right of Allocution:* In most states, the defendant has the right to make a statement before sentence is passed.

• *No Unreasonable Delay:* Most jurisdictions provide that a sentence must be imposed "without unreasonable delay." Many provide an actual time limit such as 14 or 21 days after conviction.

Fixed vs. Indeterminate Sentences

In the 19th century, most prison sentences were set for a fixed period of time. The judge would impose a specific time of imprisonment, based on the severity of the crime. For example, a robbery might be punished by a year in prison, but an armed robbery would bring a five-year sentence. Prisoners would know at the time of sentencing when their prison terms would end. These sentences were called **fixed**, or **determinate**, sentences.

As prison reformers focused more attention on rehabilitation, the corrections system moved away from determinate sentences. Reformers felt that flexible sentencing could better meet the needs of individual convicts. A criminal who reformed sooner could be released sooner, and one who did not reform, could be kept a longer time. As long as the corrections system stressed rehabilitation, flexible sentences became the norm.

These flexible prison terms became known as **indeterminate** sentences, because there was no pre-determined time to serve. Usually, the sentence was stated as a range of years. For example, forgery might carry a penalty of one to five years in prison; burglary, five to 10 years; manslaughter, five to 20. The judge decided the range of the sentence. How much time the prisoner actually served was left to **parole boards**—groups set up by the state to determine when a prisoner should be released.

In recent years, indeterminate sentencing has come under attack from several directions. Some critics say that flexibility has allowed lenient parole boards to let dangerous criminals out too soon. Other critics claim that indeterminate sentencing produces arbitrary and unjust prison terms. One car thief might serve two years in prison, another five, and another seven. For many prisoners, flexible sentencing made getting out of prison into a game of convincing the parole board that they had been rehabilitated. This created enormous bitterness and frustration, as some prisoners seemed to play the game well and some did not.

Since the 1970s, many states have reintroduced determinate or fixed-term sentencing. In this system, parole boards do not decide when to release prisoners. Instead, judges, using statutory ranges or sentencing formulas, determine the actual length of prison sentences at the time of sentencing. In most parts of the country, there is a trend back to fixed-term sentencing.

A typical Sing Sing Prison cell block, 1915. (The Bettmann Archive.)

Art or Science?

Sentencing a criminal defendant is more of an art than a science.

That statement was made by a prominent criminal court judge in Florida, as he looked back on his years of experience. He knew that a judge has to weigh many factors about a case and about the defendant, trying to predict the effects of different sentencing options. The judge also has to keep in mind society's need to protect itself from dangerous criminals. The judge has to try to be fair, objective, and impartial—all of this while burdened by heavy caseloads and busy schedules.

In some states, the jury recommends a sentence for certain crimes, especially if the death penalty is a possibility. But the responsibility in most cases rests with the judge, and it's a heavy responsibility. Defendants may be losing years of their freedom, even their lives. Every defendant is entitled to careful consideration. And, of course, the judge must consider the innocent citizens in the community. One dangerous criminal turned loose can harm many people.

To begin the sentencing process, the judge must consider the state penal code, which sets out the punishments for crimes. Misdemeanors are generally punished in increments of days or months—up to *one year*—in a county or city jail. Felonies are generally punished in increments of years in state prison.

States with indeterminate sentencing vary on how much discretion they give judges. In some states, the judge decides on both the maximum and the minimum sentences within statutory limits. In other states, the statutes spell out the limits, and the judge has no choice but to apply them. In states with determinate sentencing, judges often have discretion to give alternate sentences to prison. But if they choose to give a prison term, statutes set the term.

In many jurisdictions, statutes allow alternatives to imprisonment for some crimes. These alternatives include suspended sentences, time in a local jail, time served on weekends, community service, working to pay restitution to a victim, time in halfway houses, or being released under the supervision of a probation officer.

Before sentencing, the judge often reviews the life history of the defendant. A pre-sentencing report, usually prepared by the probation department, includes information about the defendant's family background, previous convictions, character, and attitudes. This report helps the judge understand the defendant and decide whether efforts at rehabilitation might be effective. In addition, many jurisdictions require a pre-sentencing court conference with the offender and sometimes a psychological examination.

Factors in Sentencing

After reviewing the record and the defendant's background, the judge imposes sentence. The sentence will depend on many factors. The following are a few factors the judge might consider:

- *The Crime:* Was the harm caused by the crime great or small?

- *The Offender's Actions:* Were the offender's actions brutal, dangerous, and callous, or were they unintentional and restrained?

- *The Victim:* Was the victim an aggressor or was the victim particularly vulnerable due to age or reduced mental or physical capacity?

- *Weapon:* Did the offender use a dangerous weapon or was the offender unarmed?

- *Offender's Participation:* Did the offender plan and promote the crime or simply aid and follow others?

- *Criminal Record:* Has the offender committed previous crimes? How serious were the previous crimes?

- *Psychological State:* Was the offender deliberate and calculating? Or was the offender provoked or under some sort of stress?

- *Age:* Is the offender either very young and inexperienced or old and infirm?

- *Offender's Attitude:* Is the offender hostile and defiant? Or does the offender admit guilt and show remorse?
- *Public Attitude:* How will the public and law enforcement react to the sentence?
- *Other factors might include:* What are the offender's reputation, position in the community, general character, and prior contributions to society?

After weighing these factors, the judge imposes sentence. To imagine what this is like, suppose that you are a judge facing two separate sentencing decisions for two men convicted of burglary.

Max, 43, masterminded a burglary. He has been convicted of burglaries twice before, and he used a gun this time. During the burglary, he terrorized an old couple.

John, 18, never entered the house that was burglarized. He helped his older brother carry off a stereo. He has never been in trouble with the law before, and he says he is very sorry about what he did.

Would you sentence Max differently from John? You can see how sentencing decisions can be influenced by the specific crime and criminal. Of course, many situations are not as clear cut as these. Still, it is the judge's job to weigh many factors in trying to set an appropriate sentence for each crime.

Limits on Judicial Discretion

Judicial discretion in sentencing has been under attack since the 1970s. Critics claim that it leads to inconsistency, even for quite similar crimes, and depends far too much on the inclinations of a particular judge. Different judges can have very different attitudes and values, and these can lead to big differences in their sentencing practices.

Some of these criticisms may come from the public's fear about crime. Judges are sometimes accused of being "too soft" on criminals by giving out lenient sentences. Reacting to public opinion, many states and the federal government have passed laws limiting judicial discretion in sentencing, and in some cases, removing it altogether.

Determinate sentences have removed discretion to some extent. If judges decide to send a convicted defendant to prison, statutes dictate the

---

CRIME BEAT

Imagine you are a crime beat reporter for a local news outlet. Your editor has assigned you to do background research for a series of feature articles on sentencing laws in the United States. Most state sentencing laws are a mix of determinate, indeterminate, and mandatory sentencing laws. Your editor wants you to find out about sentencing laws in your state and what officials think about punishment. Find answers to these questions:

- *Does your state use fixed or indeterminate sentencing?*
- *What sentencing standards are applied by the judges? Where do these come from?*
- *What role, if any, does the jury play in sentencing?*
- *Are there any mandatory sentencing laws in effect? What are they?*
- *Do officials think harsher jail or prison terms are likely to deter criminal behavior? If not, what will?*
- *Do officials think judges should have more discretion in sentencing? Less? Why?*

Submit a one-page summary of your findings.

For ideas on sources for this information, see "Crime Beat" on page 31.

SENTENCING GUIDELINES GRID
Presumptive Sentence Lengths in Months

Italicized numbers within the grid denote the range within which a judge may sentence without the sentence being deemed a departure.

CRIMINAL HISTORY SCORES

SEVERITY LEVEL OF CONVICTION OFFENSE (Common offenses)		0	1	2	3	4	5	6 or more
Vandalism	I	12	12	12	13	15	17	19 18-20
Check Forgery ($200-$2500)	II	12	12	13	15	17	19	21 20-22
Theft Crimes ($2500 or less)	III	12	13	15	17	19 18-20	22 21-23	25 24-26
Theft Crimes (Over $2500)	IV	12	15	18	21	25 24-26	32 30-34	41 37-45
Residential Burglary	V	18	23	27	30 29-31	38 36-40	46 43-49	54 50-58
Kidnapping	VI	21	26	30	34 33-35	44 42-46	54 50-58	65 60-70
Involuntary Manslaughter	VII	48 44-52	58 54-62	68 64-72	78 74-82	88 84-92	98 94-102	108 104-112
Rape	VIII	86 81-91	98 93-103	110 105-115	122 117-127	134 129-139	146 141-151	158 153-163
Murder, 3rd Degree	IX	150 144-156	165 159-171	180 174-186	195 189-201	210 204-216	225 219-231	240 234-246
Murder, 2nd Degree	X	306 299-313	326 319-333	346 339-353	366 359-373	386 379-393	406 399-413	426 419-433

Presumptive stayed sentence; at the discretion of the judge, up to a year in jail and or other non-jail sanctions can be imposed as conditions of probation.

Presumptive commitment to state imprisonment. First-degree murder is excluded from the guidelines by law and has a mandatory life sentence.

Source: adapted from *Minnesota Sentencing Guidelines & Commentary.*

term. But judges can suspend the sentence and put the person on probation.

Mandatory sentencing laws prevent this option. They require judges to sentence offenders to prison terms. Almost every state has passed mandatory sentencing laws for certain situations, such as repeat-offender laws and use-a-gun, go-to-jail laws. Usually, a judge has no option but to impose the mandatory sentence and cannot shorten it, suspend it, or give an alternative sentence. The federal Anti-Drug-Abuse Act of 1986 sets many mandatory minimum sentences for drug offenses. It allows no exceptions for first offenses or other factors.

Sentencing guidelines are a more elaborate attempt to curtail discretion in sentencing. They provide formulas for judges to use in all sentencing decisions. For example, in 1980 Minnesota enacted a grid formula, which reflects two sentencing factors—the crime's severity and the offender's criminal history. The judge does little more than work out where a particular criminal falls on the grid, and the sentence is automatically defined. If the judge wishes to modify the grid sentence, reasons for any variance must be given in writing. Above is a simplified version of Minnesota's grid. Over half the states and the federal government have enacted sentencing guidelines.

Despite the trend toward determinate and mandatory sentences and sentencing guidelines, prisoners rarely serve their full terms. This is because prisoners earn credits, called **good time**, against their full term. They can earn good time by behaving well and participating in special programs. Some jurisdictions allow prisoners to earn as much as one day of good time for every two days served. Prison authorities say they need good-time programs to keep order.

Viewpoints on Limiting Discretion

Some judges support the limits on judicial discretion. They feel that the practice will lead to more consistent sentencing, as well as freeing them from public wrath against judicial leniency. Also some believe that they offer the most effective way of assuring that dangerous criminals are taken off the street.

Other judges have been critical. They feel that a judge is in the best position to weigh all the facts and decide a sentence, and that removing discretion leads to injustices. Appeals-court judges throughout the country have criticized mandatory sentencing, and in 1991 the judges of the Ninth Circuit, the appellate court which covers the seven Western states, issued a statement that mandatory guidelines were "forcing the courts in many instances to impose sentences which are manifestly unjust and harsh."

Several federal trial judges have refused to hear drug cases because of mandatory minimum sentences. They say the mandatory sentences discriminate against minorities. They point to the different mandatory sentences for crack cocaine, a drug used in poor minority communities, versus powder cocaine, a drug used in wealthier communities. Possession of five grams (less than one-fifth of an ounce) of crack results in a mandatory minimum sentence of five years for a first offense. To receive a similar mandatory minimum sentence for powder cocaine, a person must possess 500 grams, over one pound.

Critics also say that mandatory sentencing laws overlook the many offenders who would benefit from community service, drug rehabilitation, or some other alternative sentence. These offenders will simply be swallowed up in prisons and turned into hardened criminals. As a result, they argue, the nation's prisons are filled and cannot keep up with the demand for more cells.

The dispute over discretion in sentencing pits those who believe sentencing is an art against those who want to turn it into a science. The question is: Which will lead to better results?

For Discussion

1. Review the list of sentencing factors on page 147. Which do you think are the most important? Least important? Explain.

2. Are there any additional factors you think judges should consider? What factors should they not consider? Explain.

3. What is the difference between fixed and indeterminate sentencing? What are some arguments for fixed sentences? What are some arguments for indeterminate sentences? Which do you think is more just and why?

4. What are mandatory sentences? What are some arguments for mandatory sentences? What are some arguments for giving judges discretion in sentencing? Which do you think is more just and why?

5. What role do you think each of the following groups should have in sentencing: judges, juries, parole boards, and legislatures? Explain.

6. Do you think good-time programs are more necessary under determinate sentencing or under indeterminate sentencing? Why?

7. Do you agree with the court's ruling in *Solem v. Helm*? Why or why not? What about its ruling in *Harmelin v. Michigan*? Why or why not?

Class Activity: The *Carter* Case: Sentencing

In the last chapter, you considered the criminal case of Thomas Wade Carter. If the jury had found Carter guilty, it could have convicted him of one of two crimes—second-degree murder or involuntary manslaughter. For this activity, half of the groups will assume that Carter was convicted of involuntary manslaughter and the other half, second-degree murder. You will role-play judges imposing an appropriate sentence using the following sentencing statutes:

§575. Determinate-Sentencing Statute

For all determinate sentences, there are three prison terms listed—a lesser term, a standard term, and a greater term. The standard term is the second one listed. It should be imposed unless the judge decides that aggravating factors or mitigating factors dictate the greater or the lesser sentence.

> (a) Involuntary manslaughter is punishable by imprisonment in the state prison for two, three, or four years.

> (b) Second-degree murder is punishable by imprisonment in the state prison for 10, 20, or 30 years.

§606. Indeterminate Sentencing Statute

The court shall impose both a minimum term and a maximum term as follows:

> (a) Minimum term of sentence. The minimum term of an indeterminate sentence shall be at least one year and the term shall be fixed as follows:

>> (1) For involuntary manslaughter, the minimum term shall be fixed by the court and shall not be less than one year nor more than five years.

>> (2) For second-degree murder, the minimum term shall be fixed by the court and shall not be less than 15 years nor more than 25 years.

> (b) Maximum term of sentence. The maximum term of an indeterminate sentence shall be at least three years and the term shall be fixed as follows:

>> (1) For involuntary manslaughter, the term shall be fixed by the court and shall not exceed 15 years.

>> (2) For second-degree murder, the term shall be fixed by the court and shall not exceed 50 years.

§898. Sentencing-Guideline Statute

A. All convicted persons shall be sentenced according to the sentencing guideline grid (on page 149).

A s k
a n

Expert

As a follow-up to the Carter sentencing, write or interview a judge. Explain the details of the case and ask the judge to suggest what kind of sentence might be given in his or her court.

B. If a judge wants to depart from the sentencing guideline, the reason must be compelling and the judge must explain the sentence in writing.

C. Instructions for using the sentencing guideline grid:

> 1. Determine the severity level of the crime.

> 2. Calculate the criminal history score. Juvenile convictions score zero points except for felony convictions which count one point each. Adult convictions score one point for each misdemeanor and two points for each felony.

> 3. Find the box where the severity level of the crime and the criminal history score intersect. This box tells the sentence in months.

>> (a) If the box is shaded, the judge should suspend the sentence and put the offender on probation. At the discretion of the judge, up to a year in jail and other non-jail sanctions can be imposed as conditions of probation.

>> (b) If the box is not shaded, then the judge should impose a sentence within the range given.

Pre-sentencing Report

Below is a pre-sentencing report submitted by the probation department:

Background Report on Thomas Wade Carter

Age: 18

Social background: Thomas Wade Carter is the oldest of five children. As the oldest child, he was pressured to excel in sports and school as his father had done. Around age 12, Carter rebelled against his parents and school. He ran away from home two times. At school, he received failing grades and got into numerous fistfights. He was suspended from junior high once for fighting and from high school once for carrying a knife. His teachers and friends report that Carter had a quick temper and would carry a grudge for a long time. At age 17, Carter was transferred to a continuation high school because of poor attendance and lack of credits at his regular high school. He attended the continuation school and earned enough credits to get a high school diploma. Carter worked for short periods of time as a fast food cook, gas station attendant, and car wash worker.

Prior Record: Carter, Thomas Wade

Age	Arrest Record	Action by Juvenile Authorities
10	Runaway	Counseled and released to parents by police
12	Runaway	Counseled and released to parents by police
13	Curfew	Counseled and released to parents by police
17	Reckless Driving (misdemeanor)	Formal probation (six months)

Age	Arrest Record	Action by Adult Authorities
18	Disturbing the peace (bar fighting) (misdemeanor)	Conviction; $50 fine

Current Background: Carter now lives in his mother's home with his sister and younger cousin. His parents were divorced when he was 16. He contributes $400 per month out of his salary to household expenses. Carter is currently employed as an assistant parts department manager at a local auto dealer. His income is $20,000 per year. His immediate supervisor, Hans Spencer, reports that Carter has performed well in his current position and is effective in dealing with customers. Neighbors report that except for some loud parties and squealing tires, Tom seems to have settled down since high school. A number of his neighbors and friends have offered to vouch for his character.

Police informants indicate that Carter and Oscar Hanks have had a long-standing feud going back to high school. One month before Carter was arrested for the Joyce Ann Miller shooting, he and Oscar Hanks were arrested for disturbing the peace at a local bar. According to some witnesses, Hanks knifed Carter in the leg during the fight at the bar. Carter, however, refused to cooperate with the district attorney in the prosecution of Hanks for assault with a deadly weapon.

Steps for Sentencing Activity

In this sentencing activity, you will assume the role of the judge in the Thomas Wade Carter case. Follow these steps:

1. Break into pairs, each pair acting as judges. Designate each pair either A or B. Assign A pairs a second-degree murder verdict for Carter. Assign B pairs an involuntary-manslaughter verdict.

2. Each statute—determinate, indeterminate, and sentencing guideline—allows judges to choose within a range of sentences. As a pair, review each of the sentencing factors on page 147 and discuss how these factors affect the Carter case.

Refer to information contained in the *Pre-Sentencing Report*. In your pair, discuss the following questions:

- Which circumstances in Carter's situation point to a harsh sentence? Make a list.
- Which circumstances in Carter's situation point to leniency and the probability of his reform? Make a list.

3. As a pair, decide on three sentences, based on the three sentencing statutes:

a. For the determinate statute, specify the exact number of years.

b. For the indeterminate statute, specify both a minimum *and* a maximum number of years.

c. For the sentencing guideline statute, specify the exact number of months. Then figure out the term in years and months for reporting to the class.

4. Assume that your jurisdiction allows you to suspend the sentence under the sentencing statute and to impose an alternative sentence. Discuss and decide whether Carter should serve the statutory prison term or should have his sentence suspended. Prepare a brief written statement justifying your choice. A suspended sentence would take the following form:

> Tom Carter's prison sentence is hereby suspended. Carter will serve one year in a county jail. For a *certain number* of years following county jail, he will be closely supervised by a probation officer and have

to meet *certain probation conditions*. Should Carter violate any terms of probation, he will be returned to prison to serve his prison term.

If you choose to suspend the sentence, decide how long his probation should last and the probation conditions. For a list of possible probation conditions, see page 158.

5. Have a representative from each pair report to the class on the sentences imposed. Write the sentences reported by each pair on the chalkboard.

6. After discussing the sentences submitted, bring the activity to a close by taking a class vote on the choices recorded on the chalkboard.

Debriefing Questions

1. Which group of statutes—determinate, indeterminate, sentencing guideline—had the greatest range of sentences? The smallest range? Why?

2. Which sentences seemed the fairest? The most unfair? Why?

3. Which type of sentencing statute would you support in your state? Why?

4. Would you favor judges having the discretion to give alternative sentences instead of prison terms? Why or why not?

5. In most states, mandatory sentencing laws would force a prison term on Tom Carter because he used a gun. Do you think mandatory sentences are a good idea? Why or why not?

6. There is a great difference in punishment between second-degree murder and involuntary manslaughter. Do you think a jury should be told of the difference before it decides a verdict of guilty or not guilty? Why or why not?

two

ALTERNATIVES TO PRISON

The Need for Alternatives

Average cost to hold someone in prison for a year in the United States: $25,000

Average cost to send someone to a top private university for a year: $22,000

In recent years, the public has grown increasingly impatient with America's crime problem. This has led to an increased demand for strict punishment, tough sentencing, and long prison terms. More and more offenders are imprisoned each year. Prisons and jails have filled and suffer severe overcrowding. Because of the overcrowding, each year federal and state governments spend billions of dollars building and staffing prisons. During the 1980s, space for over 300,000 new prisoners was built. Yet prisons and jails remain overcrowded, and more are slated to be built.

Costs of housing prisoners have become so staggering that many legislators are looking at less costly, but effective, sentencing alternatives. Ironically, many corrections specialists insist that community-based correctional alternatives, which are far cheaper, can be more effective than prison sentences. These alternatives may be better at helping a criminal learn how to function effectively in society. Some common alternatives are fines, probation, community-service programs, and supervision in a halfway house. We will discuss each of these alternatives.

Fines

Imposed in about three-fourths of all cases, fines are the most common punishment inflicted on convicted offenders. They can be imposed along with other punishments, such as probation or prison, or as the sole punishment. If a fine is the only punishment, the offender can continue living at home without supervision and the criminal justice system will get some additional money. As such, fines offer clear cost savings over imprisonment.

But judges seldom impose fines as the sole punishment for serious offenders, because the offenders would remain in the community with no one keeping tabs on them. So usually only low-risk offenses, such as traffic infractions and many misdemeanors, are punished by fines alone.

Fines raise two problems, both involving wealth. The first is purely a practical problem. Since most criminals are poor, does it make sense to punish them with fines? A fine might push an offender into committing new crimes simply to pay for the old one.

The second problem is one of fairness: Fines may let the rich off easy. If two criminals, one rich and the other poor, are fined $500 for the same offense, have they received equal punishment? A $500 fine could create hardship on the poor criminal, but mean little to the rich one.

To balance the equation, some jurisdictions are experimenting with **day fines**, which are calculated on how much a person earns each day. The penalty for drunk driving, for example, might be 30 day fines. This would mean that a person earning $300 per day would pay 30 times $300, or

$9,000. A person earning $20 per day would pay 30 times $20, or $600.

The Supreme Court has rendered one important ruling on the fairness of fines. Judges commonly used to issue alternative sentences, such as 30 days in jail or $300 in fines. In the 1971 case of *Tate v. Short*, a unanimous Supreme Court ruled these alternative sentences unconstitutional. The court stated these sentences violated the equal protection clause of the 14th Amendment, because they forced the poor into jail while permitting the rich to pay their way out.

For Discussion

1. In what circumstances do you think fines are appropriate punishment? When would they be inappropriate? Explain.

2. Do you think fines could substitute for imprisonment in some cases? Why or why not?

3. What are day fines? What problem do they address? Do you think they are a good idea? Why or why not?

4. Do you agree with the Supreme Court's decision in *Tate v. Short*? Why or why not?

Probation

Probation is from the Latin word *to prove*. An offender sentenced to probation is allowed to return to the community, but must regularly prove that he or she meets certain conditions set by the court. The court retains the authority to cancel probation and resentence the offender if the conditions are violated.

Probation was developed in the mid-1800s as a humanitarian measure to keep petty offenders away from the corrupting influence of prisons. By 1925, every state offered probation for juveniles, but it was 1956 before every state offered it for adults.

Probation only works well if it is combined with effective supervision. Offenders must report on a regular basis to a probation officer to make sure they meet all the conditions set by the court. Originally the officer was a judge or a citizen vol-

unteer. Early in the 20th century, however, supervising probation became a career in itself.

Individuals interested in becoming probation officers often take degrees in social work, with special classes in criminology and corrections. Some probation officers also take classes in psychology and therapy in order to help offenders with their emotional problems.

Recent probation theory emphasizes the need to establish strong links between the offender and the community. Family, school, business, and church connections help an offender feel part of a community. These ties make a return to criminal behavior much less likely.

High-Tech House Arrest

In the last few years, courts have begun to experiment with a new version of probation for non-violent criminals. Offenders are required to wear small radio transmitters to monitor their activities and location, usually to make sure they remain at home when they are not at work. So far, this has only been imposed on a voluntary basis, as an alternative to imprisonment.

The offender must wear the transmitter on an ankle or wrist strap. In some systems, the device broadcasts continuously to a second unit on the telephone, and this unit tells the probation department immediately if the offender leaves home. In other systems, the offender is telephoned at random times and must verify being home with a tone from the device.

Electronic house arrest costs less than $10 per day to monitor each device, as opposed to about $100 a day for jail time. In addition, the offender is usually required to pay between $10 and $20 a day. Some advantages for the prisoner are obvious—staying at home, being able to continue in a job, and avoiding the humiliations and dangers of jail. This form of monitoring can also be combined with community service or other forms of community-based corrections. Some experimental programs also use the tracking device to monitor those awaiting trial for minor crimes.

A few critics have objected because electronic monitoring is usually reserved for middle-class

Who Should Be Placed on Probation?

There is general agreement about the criteria that should be used in deciding whether an offender should be placed on probation. The following is a list of factors that might be used by a judge to help identify likely candidates for probation:

a. The defendant did not cause or threaten serious harm.

b. The defendant did not intend to cause or threaten serious harm.

c. The defendant acted under a strong provocation.

d. Some factors tend to excuse or justify the criminal conduct.

e. The victim contributed in some way to the commission of the crime.

f. The defendant has agreed to compensate the victim.

g. The defendant has no history of prior delinquency or criminal activity. Or the defendant's criminal history is far in the past.

h. The criminal conduct was the result of circumstances unlikely to occur again.

i. The defendant's character and attitudes show that he or she is unlikely to commit another crime.

j. The defendant is likely to benefit from probationary treatment.

k. The imprisonment of the defendant would cause excessive hardship to the defendant or his or her dependents.

For Discussion

1. What are some advantages in granting probation to an offender? What are some possible disadvantages?

2. What are some qualities that it would be helpful for a probation officer to have?

3. Do you think high-tech house arrest should be used more commonly? Why or why not? If you

offenders, at least in part because the poor cannot afford to pay the daily charge for the transmitter. Some of the experimental programs address this problem by offering the device for free to those who cannot pay. Most states now have experimental programs of high-tech house arrest for their non-violent criminals. Because it is cheaper than jail time and relieves jail crowding, it seems likely that this practice will become more common in the future.

agree that it should be used, for what crimes is it best suited?

4. Which of the factors for identifying likely candidates for probation do you think are most important? Least important? Why?

Class Activity: Who Gets Probation?

1. Break into small groups. Review the list of factors for identifying likely candidates for probation. Assign two or three of the factors to each person in the small group.

2. Discuss the following cases in your group, one by one. For each case, have each person in the group say whether his or her assigned factors apply to that case. Then discuss whether the factors apply or not.

3. For each case, decide if the offender should be placed on probation.

4. Reassemble the class and report your answers and the reasons for them. Compare your probation decisions with those from other groups.

(A) **Mark Lewis**, while setting off fireworks in a wilderness area, started a fire which burned down a U.S. Forest Service utility shed and destroyed a bulldozer. He has no prior criminal record.

(B) **Barbara Keane** was convicted of pickpocketing. She has one prior conviction for prostitution. She has paid back the money she took and has become actively involved in church charitable work.

(C) **Deanna Doepel** was convicted of the attempted murder of a co-worker. Though she has no prior criminal record, she has been fired from three jobs for assaulting employees. She is currently undergoing therapy.

(D) **Max Perkins** was convicted of embezzling $20,000 from his employer. Twenty years ago, he served one year in prison for forgery. Since that time, he has raised a family and has been active in community-service work.

Revoking Probation

The probation officer is an agent of the court who monitors the activities of **probationers**— offenders on probation. For probation to be effective, probation officers must carefully supervise offenders. Unfortunately, budget constraints often require probation officers to take on heavy caseloads. Officers usually require probationers to report regularly and they sometimes make surprise spot checks of probationers' condition, activities, and whereabouts.

If a probationer violates the terms set by the court, the probation officer has two choices. The officer may issue a warning, or if the violation is serious enough, the officer may order the probationer back to court for a probation revocation hearing.

At a revocation hearing, the judge decides whether to continue probation or revoke it. If probation is revoked, the probationer is usually fined or imprisoned. Sometimes, a judge will continue probation but add new, stricter conditions.

Conditions of Probation

When an offender is convicted and placed on probation, the judge almost always sets a number of conditions of probation. These conditions limit the offender's behavior, and they are often related to the offender's crime or criminal inclinations. On the next page, you will find a list of the kinds of conditions of probation a criminal court judge might set.

NEWSBREAK

Since our prisons are overflowing, the media reports occasionally on alternatives to prison, such as probation, house arrest, community service, halfway houses, and others.

Watch television news broadcasts or search through magazines and newspapers to find out more about a specific alternative. Evaluate its usefulness and present a brief report to the class.

(Asay cartoon reprinted with permission.)

1. Spend a short time in the county jail before probation begins.

2. Pay a specified fine, plus a penalty assessment.

3. Make restitution of a specified amount to the victim through the probation officer.

4. Do not drink alcoholic beverages and stay out of bars.

5. Do not use or possess narcotics or associated paraphernalia, and stay away from places where drug users congregate.

6. Do not associate with persons known by the defendant to be drug users or sellers.

7. Submit to periodic drug testing.

8. Possess no blank checks, write no checks, and have no checking account.

9. Do not gamble, engage in bookmaking, or possess gambling paraphernalia, and do not be present in places where gambling or bookmaking goes on.

10. Do not associate with certain named persons.

11. Cooperate with the probation officer in a defined plan of behavior.

12. Support dependents.

13. Seek and enroll in schooling or job training as approved by the probation officer.

14. Maintain a steady job.

15. Stay at a residence approved by the probation officer.

16. Perform a certain amount of community service each month.

17. Submit to a 10 p.m. curfew.

18. Surrender any driver's license to the court clerk to be returned to the Department of Motor Vehicles.

19. Do not drive a motor vehicle unless lawfully licensed and insured.

20. Do not own, use, or possess any dangerous weapon.

21. Submit to search at any time of day or night by any law enforcement officer with or without a warrant.

22. Obey all laws, orders, rules, and regulations of the Probation Department and of the court.

Class Activity: Probation Revocation Hearing

In this activity, members of the class will role-play a probation revocation hearing. At the conclusion of the role-play, the class will have an opportunity to decide whether probation should be revoked in the case presented.

1. If possible, invite a probation officer, criminal lawyer, or judge to help you conduct and debrief this activity. Ask the guest to compare the procedures in this activity with those followed in your jurisdiction.

2. Divide the class into groups of four. In each group, assign students the following roles: the judge, the probationer who is named Lee Miller, the probation officer, and a public defender. Assign any remaining students as additional probation officers.

3. Read and study the description for your role, and the probation report that follows the role descriptions.

4. When you are ready, conduct the probation revocation hearing with members of your group, using the procedures described below.

> a. The judge opens the hearing and asks if all parties are present and ready.
>
> b. The judge asks the public defender to present the probationer's case.
>
> c. The public defender may cross-examine the probation officer.
>
> d. The public defender may call Lee Miller to testify. If this happens, the judge may also ask questions.
>
> e. The judge may ask the probation officer questions at any time.
>
> f. The public defender should close by summarizing the arguments against revoking Lee Miller's probation.
>
> g. The judge should then ask the probation officer to summarize the arguments in favor of revoking probation. If there is more than one probation officer, both should participate.
>
> h. Finally, the judge decides whether to revoke Lee Miller's probation. Refer to the alternatives listed in the judge's role description in the next section.

5. When you are finished with the simulation, reassemble the entire class and discuss the activity. Judges from each group should announce their decisions and the reasoning behind them. Ask any guests how these simulated decisions compare to the actual decisions handed down in your jurisdiction.

Role Descriptions

Probationer Lee Miller

You feel that circumstances forced you to violate the conditions of your probation. Consequently, you feel your probation should not be revoked. Talk with the public defender who is representing you and discuss the strategy you should follow at your hearing. Decide with the public defender whether you should take the witness stand and testify on your own behalf, but remember that this will subject you to cross-examination by the judge. You have the right to remain silent if you wish.

Public Defender

You will represent Lee Miller at the probation revocation hearing. Discuss with your client the strategy to follow in attempting to convince the judge not to revoke probation. Decide whether to call the probation officer to the witness stand in order to cross-examine the officer's recommendations about revoking probation. Also, decide whether your client should take the witness stand to testify. Your client has the right to remain silent, but if the client does testify, the judge may also ask questions.

Probation Officer

You are Lee Miller's probation officer. You have written the probation report that follows. This will be the focus of this hearing. If you are called to testify, you should defend your recommendation that Miller's probation be revoked and that the one-year suspended jail sentence be imposed.

Judge

You were the trial judge at Lee Miller's trial. After the conviction, you sentenced Miller to a one-year county jail term. Then you suspended the sentence and placed Miller on probation. Today, you must decide what to do in view of the probation violations. Your alternatives are as follows:

1. Continue the probation under the existing conditions.

2. Continue probation with additional conditions that you will impose.

3. Revoke probation and impose the one-year sentence.

Probation Report

Name of Probationer: **Lee Miller**
Age: **38**
Marital Status: **Divorced**
Occupation: **Assembly line worker**
Employer: **United Radio Company**

Current Conviction

1. Probationer Lee Miller was convicted two months ago of manslaughter. Probationer Miller, while driving an automobile under the influence of alcohol, struck and killed a 5-year-old girl.

2. Sentence:

One year in county jail (suspended), $1,000 fine, placed on two-year formal probation.

3. Conditions of probation:

   a. Probationer must pay the fine within six months.
   b. Probationer must not drink any alcoholic beverages and must stay out of places where they are the chief items of sale.
   c. Probationer must cooperate with the probation officer in a plan for commuting without the use of a motor vehicle.
   d. Probationer must provide $200 per month toward the support of the dependent daughter Maria, now residing with the grandmother.
   e. Probationer must maintain employment with United Radio Company.
   f. Probationer must maintain residence at current address, as directed by the probation officer.
   g. Probationer must surrender driver's license to the clerk of the court to be returned to the Department of Motor Vehicles.
   h. Probationer must obey all laws, orders, rules, and regulations of the probation department and of the court.
   i. *Special condition*: Probationer is not to drive any motor vehicle during the period of probation.

Probation Violation Report

1. Two weeks ago at 7:55 a.m., probationer Miller was stopped for speeding and driving erratically by a highway patrol officer. The officer administered several field tests for drunk driving and concluded that probationer Miller may have been driving under the influence of alcohol. Probationer Miller was arrested and taken to a local highway patrol station where a chemical test for alcohol consumption was administered. The result of this test showed no indication of alcohol. Probationer Miller was cited for speeding and driving without a license, then released. Probationer reported the violation and admitted that he had a couple of beers the night before with a friend.

2. Probation Violations:

   a. Probationer Miller drank an alcoholic beverage.
   b. Probationer Miller drove an automobile without a license, and violated the speed law.
   c. *Special condition*: Probationer Miller drove a motor vehicle during the period of probation.

Statement of Probationer

I admit that I drove an automobile and was speeding in violation of my probation. But I reported these violations myself to my probation officer within 24 hours of the incident.

I admit that I had a couple of beers the night before, but only in my own apartment.

(Continued on page 2.)

Page 1

A friend had come over to spend the evening, and brought some beer. But I was asleep by midnight.

I overslept the next morning and had to get to work in half an hour. I have been taking the bus to work, but this takes an hour. I decided to ask a neighbor if I could borrow his car so that I could get to work on time. He said it was okay to take the car.

I already had been late to work two times this month. So I was speeding and moving in and out of lanes to get to work on time. I was afraid that if I lost my job I would not be able to make support payments for my daughter and pay off my fine to the court. Both are conditions of my probation.

As it turned out, I was half a day late for work, but my boss listened to my story and decided to give me one more chance. I believe that I have learned my lesson from this, and promise to strictly follow my conditions of probation in the future.

Recommendations of Probation Officer

Probationer Miller seems to mean well but also appears weak-willed. I recommend that the probation be revoked and the suspended one-year county jail sentence be imposed.

Page 2

Debriefing Questions

1. Did some judges decide differently from others? If so, how do you account for these differences?

2. Assume that there was a great deal of publicity surrounding Lee Miller's original manslaughter trial and that many people in the community were angry because Miller was placed on probation rather than being sent to jail. Do you think the judge's decision should be affected by community feelings of this sort? Why or why not?

3. How is the probation revocation hearing different from a trial? How is it similar?

4. In your opinion, is the probation revocation hearing a fair way to decide whether a probation should be revoked? Why or why not?

Community Service

Probation is only one possible alternative to imprisonment. Another increasingly common alternative is community service. Community service can benefit both the offender and society as a whole, as demonstrated by the following examples.

Chris Lester, 18, was convicted of destruction of public property after he vandalized his school. Because this was his first offense, the judge did not think that a jail sentence was necessary. Instead, the judge fined him $1,000 and required him to clean graffiti off the walls of public buildings.

Albert and Miriam Johnson, a husband and wife, were convicted of criminal child neglect. Because of their religious beliefs, the couple kept their son away from medical care when he was very ill. As a result, the boy nearly died. The judge sentenced the couple to do volunteer work at a nearby state hospital.

The community-service approach to sentencing is generally limited to people who have committed non-violent crimes. These can include traffic offenses, public drunkenness, drug abuse, and white-collar offenses. Often, the assigned work, such as cleaning up graffiti, is directly related to the kind of crime committed.

The Los Angeles County System

Los Angeles County has developed a broad system for referring offenders convicted of misdemeanors to community-service agencies. This system, called the **Court Referral Community Service Program**, involves the cooperation of three groups:

1. *Municipal court judges* who agree to refer some misdemeanor offenders to community service instead of imprisonment or other punishment.

2. *Community agencies* that need volunteer help. These agencies include hospitals, the YMCA and YWCA, the Red Cross, suicide and rape-crisis centers, teen-age hot lines, alcohol and drug-abuse clinics, and many other community-based agencies that depend heavily on volunteers.

3. *Volunteer Action Centers or VACs.* A county-wide system of these centers was in existence before the court referral program. The VACs were set up as clearinghouses for anyone wishing to do volunteer work. They regularly contact community agencies in order to maintain lists of volunteer positions that need to be filled. The courts asked the VACs to begin placing referrals from the court system alongside their regular volunteers. The VACs help find useful jobs in many community agencies for non-violent offenders.

The Case of Cory Baker

Cory Baker, age 40, was speeding in a school zone. He struck and injured a child. Just before the accident, Cory had lost his job as a carpenter on a construction project. In municipal court, Cory was convicted of speeding and reckless driving.

Instead of sentencing Cory to jail, or requiring him to pay a large fine, the judge instructed him to do 40 hours of work for some community-service agency. Cory was referred by the court to a nearby volunteer action center for placement with a community agency.

Within a week, Cory had made an appointment for an interview at a local VAC office. He was asked about his skills and interests, and about his willingness to do volunteer work. Cory said that he was happy to become a court-referral volunteer.

The VAC interviewer then showed Cory a list of volunteer jobs near his home. Cory noticed that several agencies needed skilled workers, including carpenters. He chose the George Henry Home for Boys, a private group home for delinquent boys.

Next, Cory scheduled an interview with the George Henry Home. The director of the home was satisfied with Cory and promptly put him to work.

Cory worked at the George Henry Home for about five hours a week for two months. During this time, he got to know many of the boys, and he showed some of them how to do basic carpentry. The director and staff at the home were impressed with Cory's work. After he had put in his 40 hours of referral volunteer work, Cory was asked to continue at the home as a paid worker. Cory accepted and was hired to set up a carpentry shop for the boys.

Does It Work?

Not all court-referral volunteers are as fortunate as Cory Baker. Nevertheless, most do have a positive experience. As one Los Angeles Municipal Court judge noted:

> Community service . . . can work wonders. That's the beauty of it. Oftentimes, personal stress is the reason the people are here in the first place. If the man gets involved in helping others, he is helping himself as well.

Some critics of this form of sentencing say that it is too soft. They call for stronger punishments such as prison terms. In response to such criticism, a federal judge said, "We have to examine the overall public interest. 'Warehousing' criminals in prison has not been successful. It just spawns more criminals."

For Discussion

1. Do you approve or disapprove of community-service sentencing? Why or why not?

2. Should community-service sentencing be available to convicted adult felons? To juvenile criminal offenders? Why or why not?

3. What might be some problems in expanding community-service sentencing to those convicted of violent crimes?

Community Corrections

Community-service referrals provide one alternative to prison that can help offenders develop roots in their communities rather than pushing them away or locking them out. There are several other programs such as halfway houses and treatment centers that can offer similar benefits. These are often called **community correctional programs**, and they can help offenders such as the following:

Rudy was lonely, bored, and 19. He got talked into something he didn't want to do. At a friend's urging, he helped steal a late-model Mercedes-Benz from a shopping-mall parking lot. Caught only a few blocks away, he is now awaiting sentencing for grand theft auto.

Anna has completed more than two years of a three-year sentence in prison for passing bad checks. This was her second offense. She wants to get out, but she is a little frightened. She wonders what might happen if she can't make it. Without support, will she be tempted to pass bad checks again? She worries whenever she thinks about going out on her own.

Both Rudy and Anna might benefit from a community correctional program. Rudy is not a hardened criminal, and he may only need help learning how to funnel his energies into positive activities. Anna, too, wants to make a go of her life. To make the transition out of prison, she needs to live in a structured environment for a time to give her direction and support.

What is a Community Correctional Program?

Community correctional programs are based in local facilities such as halfway houses, community treatment centers, residential care facilities, and group homes. Local centers offer individualized care and supervision for those who would benefit from such a program. This approach can involve the community more directly in dealing with problems of crime.

Most prisons are run by faraway state and federal agencies. And most jails, though they are locally run, are largely intended to hold people who are awaiting trial or have been given fairly short jail terms for misdemeanors. They offer few opportunities for counseling, rehabilitation, or job training. Advocates of community corrections argue that most of our criminal justice system is already locally based—the police, courts, prosecutors, and public defenders—so there should be local responsibility and control in the correctional system as well.

The community-corrections approach began in the early 1970s. Since then, some states have tried to divert a large percentage of state and county prisoners into correctional programs located closer to their home communities. Community facilities can provide a supervised environment for troubled juveniles, non-violent offenders, and some prison inmates who are ready to start taking steps back into society.

Pre-Release Programs

Some of the first programs developed by the community-corrections movement were halfway houses. These serve as way stations in helping prison inmates back into society. The Federal Bureau of Prisons and most state correctional systems offer pre-release programs. They are mainly for prisoners, like Anna (from our example above), in the last few months of their term who are judged a low risk of returning to crime.

Some pre-release programs operate businesses, providing both income and work experience for the residents. Others simply provide a home and supervision, and the residents are allowed out during work hours to go to jobs in the outside community. As residents demonstrate more responsibility, they are granted more privileges and independence. Gradually, offenders assume complete responsibility for their everyday activities and are ready to re-enter the community.

Beyond Pre-Release Programs

In 1974, Minnesota put into practice a Community Corrections Act. This act extended the state's community corrections beyond pre-release halfway houses. Minnesota's goal was to divert all but the most serious offenders into programs in their home communities. The state set up an extensive community system that accepts many of its offenders into programs *immediately* after sentencing. Those offenders never see the inside of a prison.

Goals of Community-based Corrections

The overriding goal of any community corrections program is to guide ex-offenders back into the community and help them develop positive, law-abiding lifestyles. This process works best under the supervision of professional counselors who can offer support and guidance.

Many offenders may need family, child, and marriage counseling. Others need legal counseling. Ex-alcohol and drug abusers often face severe temptation and require counseling and supervision. Offenders who want to go back to school can discuss their plans with educational counselors. Some may choose job training. Others simply need a therapist or support group to discuss their problems.

Group support can be very important. Many offenders identify best with people who have similar backgrounds and with people who have themselves overcome criminal attitudes and behavior.

The community facilities often look a lot like ordinary neighborhood homes and apartment buildings. They blend in, rather than stand out. Residents have their own bedrooms. Some have roommates. They share cooking and cleaning responsibilities, much like a large family. Residents are encouraged to develop a closeness that offers emotional support, companionship, and shared responsibility.

Obstacles to Community Corrections

There are obstacles facing community-based correctional programs. These obstacles—many deep-rooted in the community itself—keep state, county, and federal correctional administrators from transferring all eligible prisoners into community programs. They include:

• Funding
• Habitual and violent criminals
• Community attitudes

Funding

Operating the nation's prison system now costs from $20 to $30 billion a year, involving tens of thousands of administrators and correc-

---

A s k
a n

Expert

Many communities have ex-convict self-help groups. If there is such a group in your community, ask if it would provide speakers to your class. Questions to ask the visitor might include:

• What are conditions like in prison? What was the hardest part of prison life?

• Did your experiences help you adjust to life after you were released? If so, how? If not, why not?

• What was the hardest aspect about your adjustment to freedom once you were released from prison?

• Do you know about pre-release or halfway house programs? Did you participate in one? If so, what were your experiences?

• Do you think that a community corrections program is helpful to the offender or community? Why or why not?

• How do you feel society should deal with the criminal offender?

tional officers. To divert a large percentage of the nation's prisoners into community correctional programs would require a tremendous restructuring and rechanneling of funds. This would require a fundamental and wrenching reform of a correctional system that is over 100 years old. Many people in the correctional system would resist such sweeping changes.

Habitual and Violent Criminals

Certain types of criminals pose further problems. Halfway houses require a certain minimum level of cooperation and social behavior. Habitual lawbreakers often cannot meet that standard. They have always lived in a criminal culture, and they commonly reject opportunities to explore and develop new community contacts.

In addition, there is a constant fear that offenders with records of violent behavior will not change. They might harm innocent community members while staying in a halfway house. Some programs simply refuse to admit criminals with histories of violence.

Community Attitudes

When an old home or apartment building is converted into a halfway house, nearby residents often fear a wave of crime will sweep their neighborhood or that property values will decline.

Residents predict that homes will be burglarized, women raped, automobiles stolen, and eventually, property values lowered—all because convicts live in the neighborhood and come and go as they please. Fear drastically multiplies if a halfway house resident does in fact commit a crime in the neighborhood. These fears are often reinforced by feelings that halfway houses are soft on criminals and don't punish their residents enough.

These are serious problems. To work properly, community-based corrections need to win the support of the community. And the facilities need to be highly structured, supportive environments with frequent counseling and training and effective supervision. For all their good intentions, community facilities must not endanger their neighborhoods.

For Discussion

1. What are some of the advantages of community-based corrections programs? What are some disadvantages?

2. What types of offenders do you think community-based corrections are appropriate for? Inappropriate for? Why?

3. If a halfway house were proposed for your neighborhood, would you support it? Would your neighbors? Why or why not?

three

PRISONS TODAY

The vilest deeds like poison weeds
Bloom well in prison air:
It is only what is good in man
That wastes and withers there. . . .

 Oscar Wilde, from *The Ballad of Reading*
 Gaol (1898)

Prison in America

If all the Americans who are now in prisons and jails, plus all those on parole and probation, were moved to one place, it would be the second largest city in the United States. America is the world leader in prisoners per 100,000 population. In the 1980s, we nearly tripled our prison population, zooming past South Africa and the former Soviet Union into first place. Some states have seen even faster prison growth. California state prisons went from 22,000 prisoners to over 100,000.

One study has suggested that this vast increase of imprisonment may have kept our streets from getting even more dangerous than they are. Published in *Science* magazine in 1991, the study by the Bureau of Justice Statistics compared population increases to the crime rate. While crime has gone up, it has not gone up as fast as the population has grown. The National Crime Victimization Survey shows that over the last 15 years the numbers of rapes, robberies, assaults, and burglaries per 100,000 of population

have actually gone down. If these crimes had simply kept pace with the population, there would have been 66,000 more rapes per year than actually occurred, 380,000 more assaults, and 3.3 million more burglaries. The study concluded that "if only one -half or even one -fourth of the reductions were the result of rising incarceration rates, that would still leave prisons responsible for sizable reductions in crime."

A more recent study published in *Crime and Delinquency* cast doubt on this conclusion. To examine whether imprisoning more people actually caused the crime rate to go down, the study compared two different states—California and Texas. In 1986, these states had the same incarceration rates. But Texas' rate was leveling off and California's was growing rapidly. California had embarked on an ambitious prison -building program, which quadrupled the number of California's prisoners by 1989. Its incarceration rate grew 192 percent. On the other hand, Texas, confronted with court orders to relieve its overcrowded prisons, decided to release prisoners on parole. Its incarceration rate rose a mere 14 percent during the decade.

During the 1980s, the rate of property crime in California dropped 17 percent while Texas' property crime rate increased 30 percent. This seems to support the *Science* magazine study's conclusion. But the rate of violent crime—assaults, robberies, rapes, and murders—in the two states told a different story. The violent crime rates did not change. California's rate remained higher than Texas'. In other words, putting more people in prison in California and releasing more prisoners in Texas had no effect on the rate of violent crime in the two states.

The *Crime and Delinquency* study even questioned whether California's higher incarceration rate accounted for the difference in property crime rates. The 1980s were a time of great prosperity in California. But in Texas, a recession hit the state in 1985—the same year that the rate of property crime took off. The difference in the two state economies could explain their differing rates of property crime.

Even if extremely high rates of incarceration did reduce crime, critics argue that it is an inefficient, highly expensive way to attack crime. Critics claim we should target dangerous, violent offenders for long-term incarceration and concentrate on alternatives to prison for lesser offenders. These critics warn that we may see a new surge in crime when large numbers of "the prison class of the 1980s" begin to get out. Since prisons have become notorious for creating hardened criminals, they argue that by imprisoning so many people, we may only be postponing our problems and making them worse in the future.

From the history of prisons in America we know that their purpose has evolved over time. Prisons began with an emphasis on enforcing penitence. By the late 1800s this had changed into attempts at rehabilitating offenders. And then, as rehabilitation seemed to be failing in the 1970s, many people came to see the correctional system as little more than a way of keeping criminals off the streets. If we take a close look at life in prison today, we may get a glimpse of what prisons really accomplish.

America's Prison Profile

Today in the United States, there are roughly 1,000 state and federal prisons which hold around 800,000 prisoners. More than 3,000 county and municipal jails hold another 400,000 people. Some prisons may be well-designed, progressive institutions, but far too many are overcrowded, filthy, and brutal. Some have become notorious for extortion, violence, homosexual rape, and vicious racial gangs. In such prisons, the car thief as well as the child molester live out terms that are a virtual hell of fear and savagery.

At their best, our prisons can provide well-planned opportunities for education and vocational training, but at their worst, they offer little more than a few hours a day out of the cell to stand around in a crowded prison yard. More than half of all prison inmates are idle for most of the day. The former head of the Federal Bureau of Prisons has said, "Idleness is the most serious problem in virtually every penal institution."

In some institutions, prisoners who work receive small amounts of pay. In others, they receive nothing. In some prisons, inmates have the freedom to choose their own wardrobe, decorate their cells, and keep personal belongings. In others, spartan cells, drab uniforms, and military-style haircuts are the rule. In short, the prison experience varies, depending on who's in charge and where the prison is located.

The biggest common problem is overcrowding. Almost all state prisons are running between 16 percent and 32 percent above their designed capacities. In some cases as many as 11 prisoners are held in cells designed for four. Overcrowding can lead to discipline problems, unrest, unhealthy conditions, and far too often, violence.

Poor Prison Conditions

The following prison conditions were described in the 1978 Supreme Court decision of *Hutto v. Finney*:

> The ordinary Arkansas convict had to endure . . . "a dark and evil world completely alien to the free world . . . ." Confinement in punitive isolation was for an indeterminate period of time. An average of four, and sometimes as many as 10 or 11, prisoners were crowded into windowless 8' x 10' cells containing no furniture other than a source of water and a toilet that could only be flushed from outside the cell . . . . At night the prisoners were given mattresses to spread on the floor. Although some prisoners suffered from infectious diseases, such as hepatitis and venereal disease, mattresses were removed and jumbled together each morning, then returned to the cells at

random in the evening. Prisoners in isolation received fewer than 1,000 calories a day; their meals consisted primarily of four-inch squares of "grue," a substance created by mashing meat, potatoes, oleo, syrup, vegetables, eggs and seasoning into a paste and baking the mixture in a pan.

Beginning in the late 1970s and continuing into the 1990s, the federal judiciary began ordering states to upgrade their prisons and provide more beds. Cases brought by public-interest lawyers charged that inmates in the most dangerous and overcrowded prisons were being subjected to "cruel and unusual punishment" as forbidden by the Eighth Amendment of the U.S. Constitution.

In several cases, the Supreme Court agreed. It held that the Eighth Amendment prohibits penalties that "transgress today's broad and idealistic concepts of dignity, civilized standards, humanity and decency." (*Estelle v. Gamble,* 1976.)

Some federal courts imposed rigid deadlines to end overcrowding. These deadlines had short-term and long-term effects. In Alabama, for instance, some 200 prisoners were released well before the end of their sentences to satisfy a federal court order. Texas was repeatedly forced to halt new prison admissions to satisfy the courts, and a federal judge threatened the state with fines of $800,000 a day until it alleviated overcrowding. Some Texas legislators even proposed holding prisoners on prison barges, unused oil-drilling rigs, and foreclosed buildings.

In most states, the 1980s saw a surge of new prison construction to try to keep pace with the increasing number of prisoners. Building prisons became a $17 billion a year industry. A new prison could cost as much as $70,000 per cell to build, and annual costs rose to about $25,000 to guard and house each prisoner. Some prison authorities were pleased by the court actions since the judicial orders forced reluctant state legislatures to appropriate funds.

In 1981, the U.S. Supreme Court seemed to back away from further prison reform. The court decided the case of *Rhodes v. Chapman,* which

(The Bettmann Archive.)

had raised the issue of whether confining two prisoners in a cell built for one violated the Eighth Amendment. The court ruled that it did not. Voting 8-1, the justices held that overcrowding does not in itself violate the Eighth Amendment, if overall prison conditions meet contemporary standards of decency. Justice O'Connor wrote for the majority that "harsh conditions" are the price of crime and the Constitution does not require comfortable prisons. The court seemed to be saying it had gone about as far as it would go in ordering reform. Federal courts, however, still can demand changes to prisons where overcrowding causes dangerous, unfit conditions.

Private Prisons

Some states have turned to private industry to help reduce prison overcrowding. Private security firms have gone into the prison business, in some cases contracting to operate existing prisons and jails, and in others, building new prisons for the states. In several cases, private operators have built prisons hoping to get a contract to hold prisoners.

Private prisons exist now in 24 states, and hold about 1 percent of the prison population. Almost all of them are in the South and Southwest. Charles W. Thomas, a criminologist at the University of Florida, estimates that up to 10 percent of all prison beds may eventually be in private hands, mostly in minimum-security institutions.

Private prisons, however, have not yet proven profitable. They have cut costs about 5 percent under state prisons, but none of the large prison corporations has yet shown a profit.

And there are many critics of the idea of privatizing prisons. Ira P. Robbins, a professor at the American University Law School in Washington, D.C., says, "It's privatization run amok." The American Civil Liberties Union has expressed fears that private companies will be less accountable than the state, and may even try to prolong prison sentences to keep earning their per-day fees. Neighbors often wonder if private companies will maintain the same standards for security. Over the long term, there is also a fear that putting a large number of prison beds in private hands will create a permanent lobby in favor of long prison sentences. And the drive to increase profits may well hold back the move to community corrections and alternative sentencing.

Supporters of private prisons dismiss these claims. They argue that private prisons are newer, better managed, and less costly than government-run institutions. As for security, they argue that most private prisons take only minimum-security prisoners anyway. Finally, they maintain that it is unlikely private-prison companies would lobby for longer prison terms because there is such an excess of prisoners already.

For Discussion

1. The United States has the highest rate of incarceration of any country in the world. What are some advantages of locking up so many criminals? What are some disadvantages? Do you think it is a good idea to have so many people locked up? Why or why not?

2. Do you agree with the U.S. Supreme Court decision in *Rhodes v. Chapman*? Why or why not?

3. Do you agree with the idea of privatizing prisons? Why or why not?

Activity: Harsh Sentences

Write a brief essay, either supporting or opposing the following proposition: *Harsh sentences will deter criminals from committing crimes and cause crime rates to drop.*

Prison Revolts

Prison revolts help focus public attention on conditions inside American prisons. In April 1993, for example, the national media reported on the 10-day uprising at the Southern Ohio Correctional Facility in Lucasville, Ohio. The riot left six inmates dead. Several major prison revolts occurred in 1986. But the two most famous revolts took place in 1971 and 1980.

In September 1971, more than 1,200 prisoners at New York's Attica State Prison seized Cell Block D and took 38 guards hostage to protest what they called oppressive prison conditions. Influenced by the political movements of the 1960s, particularly radical African-American organizations, the prisoners immediately organized themselves, setting up a sick bay, clean-up details, an elected negotiating committee, and a security force to guard and protect the hostages. One guard who had been seriously injured was sent out to the hospital and 10 other hostages needing medical aid were released. The prisoners' first statement said, "We are men. We are not beasts, and do not intend to be beaten or driven."

The prisoners met with a mediating team that eventually included the New York director of prisons, lawyers, journalists, and local political leaders. Their demands were mostly for humane treatment: better prison conditions, freedom of religion to allow Muslim worship, meaningful job training, the right to hold political meetings, and an amnesty for the takeover. Most of the demands, except the amnesty, were granted. But this omission became crucial when the injured guard died in the hospital. Still, by the third day, most of the mediators felt they were near a deal if Governor Nelson Rockefeller would come to Attica to give any agreement credibility. Rockefeller thought it would be unwise and stayed away.

On Monday, the fourth day of the revolt, guards and state police assaulted Cell Block D with helicopters and nausea gas. Over 500 men firing rifles and shotguns poured into the yard. Thirty-three inmates and nine hostages were killed by gunfire, and more than 100 other prisoners were seriously wounded. In the aftermath, prisoners were stripped and beaten, and forced to run gantlets of angry guards. Some observers charged that a few of those killed died hours after the prison had been retaken. More than 20 years later, a civil court awarded prisoners millions of dollars in damages for violations of their civil rights after the assault.

Life at Attica

Almost everyone, including the New York head of prisons, agreed that the uprising had been sparked by terrible prison conditions. The following brief summary can only hint at what it must have been like. An inmate entered Attica in shackles and leg-irons. He was issued gray prison clothes and then placed in an isolation cell where he stayed for two full days. After four to eight weeks of lockup for about 20 hours a day, he was assigned a job and transferred to a cell block.

Each prisoner at Attica had a cell about the size of a walk-in closet, six feet by nine feet. The nearest window was across the corridor. He had a bed, a metal stool, a small table, a two-drawer metal cabinet, an open toilet, a cold-water sink, and one 60-watt bulb. For the rest of his imprisonment, he spent 14 to 16 hours a day alone in this cell.

Five hours a day were for work or school, one hour or so for recreation, and about half an hour for each meal. Each man could shower once a week. During weekdays, the daily routine began at 5:50 a.m. and the men were locked in for the night at 6:30 p.m. They could talk between cells until 8 p.m. after which time silence was required. The lights went out at 11 p.m.

Vocational training was mostly work in a huge laundry at 30 cents a day or being assigned with 15 other men to a one -man machine tool in a shop that never dropped below 100 degrees F. There was little education available, the meals were often inedible, and there were hundreds of prison rules. Prison officials read all mail. In addition, more than 75 percent of the prisoners at

---

CRIME BEAT

Imagine you are a crime beat reporter for a local news outlet. Your editor has assigned you to do background research for a series of feature stories on your state corrections system. You will have two assignments:

First, find out the following about the state prison system:

• What is the prison population in your state?

• How many state prisons are there? Of what types?

• How much money does the state spend each year for the maintenance of prisons?

• Are there any private prisons in your state?

• What do officials say are the greatest problems facing prisons and jails today? How can they be solved?

Second, pick a particular jail or prison and find out:

• What is the daily schedule for prisoners?

• What activities outside their cells do they have?

• What personal items can they have in their cells?

• What do they wear?

• Do prisoners receive pay for work they do?

• How often can prisoners have visitors?

• Are the facilities overcrowded?

Submit a one-page summary of your findings. For ideas on sources for this information, see "Crime Beat" on page 31.

Attica were black or Puerto Rican and all 383 guards were white, and charges of racist treatment were common.

The revolt spurred four separate investigations of conditions at Attica and many of the more serious abuses were eventually corrected.

New Mexico State Prison

The revolt at New Mexico State Prison nine years later could hardly have been more different from the one at Attica. In February 1980, prisoners at the New Mexico prison broke into the control room, seized the guards and opened all the cells. The political movements of the 1960s had passed and no one at New Mexico thought of trying to organize or control the revolt. Some prisoners went for the sick bay and started a drug orgy. Others went on a rampage of smashing furniture and setting fires. One group broke into an isolation area where prison informers were held. Thirty-three prisoners were hacked to death or tortured to death with blowtorches. Prison officials tried to negotiate, but they found that there was no one in control.

As the violence died down, most of the prisoners came out one -by-one to surrender peacefully. Those who didn't come out offered no resistance at all when police and National Guardsmen stormed the prison 36 hours later. At Attica, all the deaths except the one guard injured in the takeover had come at the hands of the police. In New Mexico, the inmates themselves had done all the killing.

Despite the differences, post -riot commissions found many of the same abuses in New Mexico. In fact, some conditions were probably worse. In New Mexico, prisoners did not have individual cells, and homosexual rape was widespread. Also, drugs had become much more common by 1980, and many of the prisoners were intoxicated during the riot. The following is one convict's letter, detailing some of his complaints:

> We seldom see any kind of exercise, the heat is turned on high in some of the dorms whether it is a warm day or not, the food is bad, the mail is lost or comes late, the

Smoke billows from the New Mexico State Prison as a National Guard helicopter flies over the scene. During the 1980 prison revolt, over 30 people died. (UPI/Bettmann Newsphotos.)

> lighting in most dorms is bad, and all around we face harassment by the guards.

Attica and New Mexico were by no means the worst prisons in the United States. They were just unlucky enough to have the necessary conditions come together to set off riots. Other prisons have even worse reputations. Louisiana's New Orleans Parish Prison, for example, crams six men into each 7-by-14 cell. Ohio State Prison is a gray and gloomy fortress built in 1834. New York's Sing Sing Prison—its proper name is Ossining Correctional Facility—is almost as old as the Ohio prison and houses prisoners in zoo-like cells stacked five high. And all of these conditions have been made worse by the prison population explosion of the 1980s.

Gangs

Some conditions at Attica and New Mexico have improved since the uprisings, but these prisons are still subject to the overcrowding and other problems that plague most of our maximum -security institutions. Perhaps the biggest new prison problem has been the growth of violent, race -based gangs. Beginning in the 1970s, as dramatized in Edward James Olmos' film *American Me*, these gangs were organized almost exclusively along racial lines. They have spread to almost every American prison. The best known are the Black Guerrilla Family for African-Americans, two competing families of what is popularly called the Mexican Mafia for Hispanics, and the Aryan White Brotherhood.

These groups demand obedience and provide a sense of protection and community for their members. Because of their racial makeup, many of the gangs make heavy use of racist slogans and symbols, and they glory in violent acts against other races. Conflicts among the gangs grew so intense that in the 1980s some institutions such as San Quentin were forced to segregate the bulk of their prisoners by race, putting them into separate prison blocks. Prison authorities were reluctant to give official sanction to racial separation, but they had little choice if they wanted to protect the lives of the prisoners.

For Discussion

1. How did the revolts at Attica and New Mexico prisons differ? Why? Give several reasons.

2. What do you think can be done to prevent future prison revolts? Explain.

3. How might conditions in a maximum-security prison affect a first-time offender?

4. How can the racial divisions that seem to have developed in the prisons be resolved?

Class Activity: Prison in the Classroom

1. Break the class into three or four groups. Select corners of your classroom and, with masking tape, have the students mark off areas nine feet long by six feet wide.

2. In each area, use the tape to mark off an area large enough for a bunk bed, table, two-drawer cabinet, toilet and sink. Put a chair or stool in the open area of this imaginary cell. Assign two students to share this space. Try to imagine spending 14 to 16 hours each day locked up there.

3. Then assign another pair of students to try it. Continue until all the students have had an imaginary prison experience.

4. Now try the same thing with three students in each imaginary cell, then four students. Discuss what overcrowding feels like and how it might cause conflicts.

5. Now, try to remember some event that happened to you about two years ago. Imagine spending all the time since that event in your cell. The average prisoner spends about two years in prison, so you may begin to see what prison life would be like.

Debriefing Questions

1. What do you think would be the most difficult part of prison life?

2. What kinds of conditions should be maintained at prisons? Describe.

3. Should non-violent offenders be locked up with violent offenders? Explain your answer.

Parole

Just as probation comes from the Latin word "to prove," the word *parole* comes from the French for "to speak," or "to give your word." Parole is a process of returning prisoners to society if they have displayed good behavior in prison and if they give their word to avoid further crime. Near the end of their prison terms, prisoners come before a parole board where their behavior and attitudes are examined. Those who are judged rehabilitated or ready for release are granted parole. The parolee is then supervised for a specified time after release to make sure the promise is kept. A parole officer sees to it that the conditions of parole are met and that the parolee makes a successful transition to life on the outside.

Some critics believe that the extensive use of parole is a mistake and too lenient on prisoners. They argue that hardened criminals come to think of tricking the parole board as a game. Others take the view that parole offers a stepping stone back into the real world, and the time of release should be tailored to the individual prisoner.

Today the trend is toward fixed sentences and a reduced role for the parole board. But prisoners serving fixed sentences still can be released on parole by earning good-time credits against their sentences.

In fact, most prisoners are eventually released on parole. The average sentence of all prisoners is now about 76 months, but the average time served is only about 26 months. Nationwide, there are about two-thirds more people on parole at any time than are locked up in prison. Yet the public hears little about this part of corrections.

When the public does hear something about parole, it is usually about one of its failures or mistakes.

Parole has many of the same problems as probation. The number of people to be supervised is growing rapidly while the number of supervisors is staying the same or even shrinking. While county or state officials may oversee probation, a state parole board runs parole in many states. Both systems in most states have suffered badly from budget cutbacks.

The Parole Process

The parole system is generally defined by state statutes, or in the case of federal prisoners, by federal law. Most states have independent parole boards that function as hearing panels to determine whether prison inmates near the end of their term are appropriate candidates for parole. Parole board members are often political appointees who have professional staff members and case workers to advise them.

The case workers compile reports on prisoners eligible for parole. They gather information about an individual's behavior while in prison and what awaits the prisoner in the community. They find out about the prisoner's family, opportunities for employment, access to friends, availability of housing, and the general climate that awaits the parolee in the community. An offer of employment is often key to winning parole board approval. A prisoner's success is much more likely if a stable job is available.

If released on parole, offenders must meet regularly with a parole officer and show that they are living up to the conditions of their release. Most often, these conditions forbid the use of alcohol and controlled substances, possession of firearms, or association with other ex-convicts. Offenders must ask permission to change their residence, to travel from one area to another, to marry, or even to buy a car.

The parole officer tries to develop a positive relationship with the parolees, but at the same time, serves as an officer of the state to watch for any criminal tendencies. If necessary, the parole officer may have the individual jailed pending an

Sirhan Sirhan, who killed U.S. Senator Robert Kennedy in 1968. (UPI/Bettmann.)

investigation of parole violations or new criminal acts.

Ideal caseloads are considered to be roughly 35 per officer, or as few as 20 for serious offenders. In some jurisdictions, however, budget problems have pushed case loads up as high as 200 parolees per case worker. That's only about 12 minutes per week per case, which is rarely adequate to check up on a parolee, let alone offer help or advice.

Notorious Cases

Notorious cases pose special problems. One problem is whether publicity denies some prisoners equal treatment. The case of **Sirhan Bishara Sirhan** illustrates this problem. In June 1968, Sirhan shot and killed U.S. Senator Robert F. Kennedy, who had just won the presidential primary in California. Convicted of murder, Sirhan was sent to the maximum-security Soledad prison in California. A tentative parole date was set for 1982, but a public debate erupted over whether Sirhan should ever be paroled. Many people thought that the killer of a presidential candidate should never walk free. Nearly 4,000 letters flooded the parole board, as well as a petition bearing over 8,000 signatures—all opposing parole.

Sirhan's attorney claimed that his client had a nearly spotless prison record, that his 13 years in prison were already twice as much time behind bars as most murderers served in California, and

that there was no solid evidence that he was any longer a threat to anyone.

The Los Angeles District Attorney presented new evidence that Sirhan was a continuing danger. The D.A. said Sirhan had written two threatening letters in the early 1970s. One corrections department psychiatrist did not feel this was unusual considering the stress that Sirhan had been under. Others were not so sure. The D.A. also cited testimony from fellow prisoners that Sirhan had threatened to kill others. But questions were raised about the accuracy of this testimony.

In its reconsideration of the release date, the board finally denied Sirhan parole. In all subsequent hearings, it has denied him parole. Many people believe the board has based its decisions on the nature of the original crime and worries about Sirhan's continuing danger to others. Some people believe the parole board has yielded to public pressure and will never release Sirhan.

A second problem arises when notorious offenders do get released. Parolees normally must return to the counties they lived in before their conviction. But communities often object to the return of notorious criminals, particularly child molesters and murderers. **Lawrence Singleton** offers an extreme example. In the late 1970s, Singleton picked up a 15-year-old hitchhiker, brutally raped her, chopped off her forearms, and left her in the California desert to die. Somehow she lived. Convicted for the crime, Singleton was sentenced to 12 years in prison. A model prisoner, he earned enough good time to be released in 1987 after only eight years. His crime had aroused so much attention that parole authorities did not know where to place him. They tried convincing other states to take him, but none would. They even talked of housing him on prison grounds. Finally, amid much outcry and media coverage, they placed him in his original community in Northern California. But citizen protests proved so intense that Singleton could not remain. Encountering protests wherever he went, he moved from community to community in Northern California. When his parole ended, he moved to Florida, where he met further citizen protests.

For Discussion

1. How are probation and parole alike? How are they different?

2. What problems do parole officers face?

3. Why do parole boards have less power in states with fixed sentencing laws?

4. What is your opinion in the Sirhan case? Should he have been released? Why or why not?

5. Other infamous convicts, such as Charles Manson and Mark David Chapman, have been repeatedly denied parole. Do you think public opinion or pressure about such cases should influence parole board decisions? Why or why not?

6. Where should notorious offenders be placed if their community does not want them back? Explain your answer.

Staying Out of Prison

Many ex-convicts have difficulty staying out of trouble—and out of prison—once they are released. Ex-convicts have special needs that the parole program alone often cannot address. Several special programs, however, have been developed to help them. One such program, the 7th Step Foundation, uses ex-offenders as counselors to help juveniles, parolees, and those who are soon to be released.

Case Study of an Ex-Offender

The following case study is based on an interview with a 7th Step counselor.

"One of the inmates who had a life sentence without parole organized a group of the most dangerous criminals in the prison. I joined the group. We got together to help keep juvenile delinquents from turning to crime. Every Saturday these kids would be brought into the prison. We would talk to them and show them around. We showed them death row and the electric chair. It really shook them up. That program helped those kids, and it also helped me get turned around.

"When I left prison I felt totally helpless and frightened. I didn't know how to talk to a lady, how to take a lady out, or how to dress. Fitting into society is a real problem. You have a feeling you want to make up for lost time—and it's hard to sit still even for five minutes.

"As far as adjusting to society, I don't know how long it will take. For me, getting in my car and coming to work is a thrill. To go to the icebox and get a drink is a great feeling for me. I've only been out four months. That's a small amount of time compared to 21 years in an institution. The adjustment period is not over, and I don't have any more chances. Next time I'll be sent away for the rest of my life.

"I've been a thief all my life, and I've been a pretty good thief. For me, it is easy to be bad and it's a struggle to be good. I could go out and get money just like that. It's my profession—the only thing I am good at—so far.

"How do you tell someone you've been in prison for 21 years—how do you tell them? How do you tell them you've been arrested for murder? How do you tell them these things and then expect them to give you a job?"

Class Activity: Staying Out

Imagine that you are just paroled and trying to stay out of prison. Write a journal of your experiences in the first few weeks after release. Include the following incidents and give an account about how you dealt with them.

- Finding a place to live.
- Relating to your family and loved ones.
- Searching for a job and going to a job interview.
- Running into an old friend from your criminal days, one you are forbidden to associate with.
- Reflecting on your time in a maximum-security prison.

When everyone finishes, students who want to, should read the journals aloud in class and discuss them.

four

CAPITAL PUNISHMENT

The Death Penalty

Every two months, state maintenance workers enter the strange-looking green room to check it over, whether the room has been used recently or not. They inspect the pipes and vents. Then they lock the doors from the outside and activate the mechanism that drops a sodium cyanide pellet into a bucket of acid. They wait behind glass as lethal gas swirls up around the two chairs bolted to the floor, and they note any adjustments that are necessary. The green room is the gas chamber at San Quentin State Prison in California.

The gas chamber sat unused from 1967 to 1992—through more than 20 years of bitter legal debate over capital punishment—until executions began again in California with the death of the condemned murderer Robert Alton Harris in 1992.

Capital punishment is another expression for the death penalty, or the legal execution of a criminal. The word *capital* comes from the Latin word for head. In ancient times, capital punishment was often carried out by beheading. In America, criminals have been put to death by shooting, hanging, electrocution, poison gas, and lethal injection.

Once a person is sentenced to death in America, most states follow a similar procedure. The sentenced criminal is normally held in a maximum-security prison's special section known as death row. Usually, the prisoners on death row have little contact with other prisoners. Each occupies a small cell alone, and each takes meals and exercises alone. This life may continue for many months and even years during appeals of the sentence. An appeal hearing for a death sentence is automatic in every state except Arkansas.

The most common methods of execution in the United States are, in order, lethal injection, electrocution, and lethal gas. It is argued that these are the most painless and humane methods, although some observers dispute this claim. California uses the gas chamber and lethal injection. In the gas chamber, once the convict is strapped into one of two chairs, a cyanide pellet is released into sulfuric acid and water. As the pellet dissolves, a deadly vapor of cyanide gas escapes and fills the cell. Some criminals have tried to hold their breath, but once they breathe the gas, it takes only about 20 seconds to knock them unconscious. It takes up to 15 minutes for the person to die.

History of the Death Penalty in America

In the American colonies there were legal executions as early as 1630. As in England, the death penalty was imposed for many different crimes, even minor ones such as picking pockets or stealing a loaf of bread. During the 1800s in England, for example, there were 270 different capital offenses, or crimes punishable by death. Gradually, however, England and America reduced the number of capital offenses, until the main focus was on first-degree murder—murders showing deliberation, willfulness, and premeditation.

In the 1800s, many people in America and Europe began to oppose the death penalty altogether. Michigan abolished it in 1845 and Wisconsin entered the Union in 1848 without a death penalty in its statutes. The movement against the death penalty grew stronger after World War II, especially in Europe, where many were weary of so much killing during the war. One by one all the Western European nations and Canada did away with capital punishment, until the United States was the last Western democracy that still executed criminals. Thirteen American states, mostly in the North and Northeast, have also banned the practice, though there is public pressure to reinstate the death penalty in New York and several other states.

Polls showed that public support for capital punishment declined to less than 50 percent in the mid-1960s, but then support started to rise again. By the 1990s, following a decade of widespread impatience with crime and violence, some states such as California were showing almost 80 percent of the population in favor of executing criminals. Other polls showed that 62 percent of the population felt that the death penalty deterred crime, and 51 percent said they would support it even if it did not deter crime.

Recent Legal History of the Death Penalty

Following public protest over capital punishment in the 1950s and 1960s, the number of executions in America gradually declined. In 1967 there were only two, and the following year the Supreme Court struck down death-penalty laws for crimes other than murder—crimes such as kidnapping, rape, and federal bank robbery. That year also saw the beginning of an unofficial moratorium on executions while the Supreme Court studied whether capital punishment was constitutional. No executions took place in the United States from 1968 through 1976.

In the 1972 case of *Furman v. Georgia*, the Supreme Court declared capital punishment unconstitutional as it was then applied. The court said the death penalty was a violation of the Eighth Amendment prohibition against cruel and unusual punishment because there did not seem to be any consistency in who was given a death sentence and who was not. The court suggested that new laws might be acceptable, if they were written more carefully and provided standards for which criminals should be given death sentences.

Between 1972 and 1976, 35 states wrote new capital punishment laws to try to meet the Supreme Court's suggestions. These new laws fell into two broad groups. One group, represented by laws in Georgia, Texas, and Florida, clearly described which capital crimes could be punished by death. These laws set up a weighing system for deciding when the death penalty should be applied. In a separate penalty trial after a conviction for first-degree murder, a jury would consider **mitigating** circumstances that tended to excuse the crime or the criminal's behavior, and **aggravating** circumstances that made the crime seem worse. The court could only sentence someone to death if the aggravating circumstances outweighed any mitigating circumstances.

A second group of laws, represented by statutes from North Carolina and Louisiana, sought to overcome the Supreme Court's objections in another way. These laws simply made the death penalty mandatory for anyone convicted of a capital crime.

In 1976, the Supreme Court in *Gregg v. Georgia* ruled that the first type of law, based on the act of balancing mitigating and aggravating circumstances, was constitutional. This upheld the Georgia, Texas, and Florida death penalties. The court, however, struck down the second type. North Carolina and Louisiana's mandatory death sentences were declared unconstitutional. The court said a mandatory sentence was unduly harsh and rigid, and made no allowance for the particular circumstances of each case.

Executions began again in 1976, though many states still waited for a ruling on one further major issue: whether or not the death penalty was being applied equally. From 1976 through 1985, there were only 50 executions, though almost 2,000 prisoners waited on death rows.

The test case came with the Georgia case of *McCleskey v. Kemp* (1987). In it, lawyers for the condemned man submitted a careful study of how the death penalty had been applied in Georgia during the 1970s.

The study, by University of Iowa Professor David Baldus, showed that blacks who had killed whites had been sentenced to die seven times more often than whites who had killed blacks. Even after accounting for other variables, such as the viciousness of the crime, blacks had been sentenced to die more than four times more often than whites.

In its decision, the U.S. Supreme Court acknowledged that there seemed to be some *statistical* racial discrimination in Georgia's application of the death penalty. But the justices ruled by a 5-4 vote that a mere statistical variation was not enough to invalidate the death penalty. To do that, the defendant would have to show that the state had somehow encouraged the result or that there was actual discrimination in a particular case. Since the defendant had offered no such proof, which would be difficult to acquire, the court upheld the death penalty.

In a series of decisions since *McCleskey*, the court has tended to support the prosecution and make appeal of a death sentence more difficult. The justices have ruled that:

- Death-row inmates have no right to free legal assistance after an initial round of appeals. *Murray v. Giarratano* (1989).

- Inmates may lose their right to appeal if they make procedural errors. *Coleman v. Thompson* (1991).

- Inmates can't take advantage of any rule changes or precedents set *after* they have exhausted their appeals. *Teague v. Lane* (1989) and *Butler v. McKellar* (1990), and *Saffle v. Parks* (1990).

- The death penalty can be applied to mentally retarded criminals. *Penry v. Lynaugh* (1989).

- The prosecution may introduce victim-impact statements in penalty hearings. These statements may detail the pain and suffering of the victim. This

decision overturned several earlier rulings banning such statements because they tend to inflame juries against convicted murderers. *Payne v. Tennessee* (1991).

- Death-row inmates cannot get a federal hearing on new-found evidence proving their innocence unless that evidence overwhelmingly proves their innocence. *Herrera v. Collins* (1993).

Despite all these changes that reinstated and then extended the death penalty, there appears to be a social reluctance to begin executing massive numbers of prisoners. There were fewer than 200 executions between 1976 and the early 1990s, most of those in the South. In fact, five Southern states carried out three-quarters of all executions.

There are more than 2,000 inmates waiting on death rows in prisons across America. Much of this backlog is caused by appeals. Even though recent rulings have made it harder to appeal, it still takes an average of eight years for each prisoner to exhaust the appeals process. And it costs a state from $2 to $3 million to process each case.

For Discussion

1. Why do you think prisons separate those sentenced to death from other prisoners?

2. Why do you think the United States is the only Western democracy that executes criminals?

3. What reason did the Supreme Court give in *Furman* for saying that death penalty statutes were unconstitutional? How did states change their statutes to make them constitutional? Do you agree with the court that these statutes are constitutional? Why or why not?

4. What did the court decide in the *McCleskey* case? Do you agree with its decision? Why or why not?

5. Which of the decisions after *McCleskey* do you agree with? Disagree with? Why?

Class Activity: Taking a Stand on Capital Punishment

When the Supreme Court listened to arguments on both sides of the capital punishment issue, the justices found themselves caught up in one of the most emotional legal battles of the century. The chart on this page summarizes some of the arguments for and against the death penalty.

In this activity, you will take a stand on the death penalty.

Arguments in Favor of the Death Penalty	*Arguments Against the Death Penalty*
1. The existence of capital punishment keeps people from committing serious crimes. It is difficult to find direct evidence of a deterrent effect, but legislatures in many states have studied the problem and decided that it does work.	1. There is no evidence that capital punishment has a deterrent effect. In states that have abolished the death penalty, murder rates have declined or remained the same. Most murderers do not think of the consequences, while many others *want* to be punished. These people will not be deterred.
2. If a person takes a life, that person should pay by giving a life. "An eye for an eye and a tooth for a tooth." This is in accordance with the *punishment* purpose of the criminal justice system.	2. Killing a criminal is an evil on top of an evil. All the Western democracies have abolished it, many religions oppose it, and it is an embarrassment to most civilized people.
3. Capital punishment is simply the strongest punishment in a complete range of punishments. It is reserved for the most serious crimes. And this accords with "due process of law" because jurors are told to consider it very carefully, and there are many steps in the appeals process.	3. It is almost impossible to apply capital punishment fairly. There is evidence to show that African-Americans and other ethnic minorities are sentenced to death far out of proportion to others, especially when a white victim is killed. And there are many other ways that chance and arbitrary decision making can affect the sentence—prosecutorial decisions, plea bargains, the jury's feeling toward the defendant and the crime, and the lawyer's competence. Chance should not be a factor in a life-or-death decision.
4. Some criminals are so dangerous that they cannot be rehabilitated and must never be allowed to live in society. Those who have committed serious crimes should be executed to make sure they never harm anyone again.	4. Life imprisonment without the possibility of parole is punishment enough, and it keeps criminals off the streets just as well as executing them.
5. Capital punishment is specifically allowed by the language of the Bill of Rights. The Fifth Amendment says that no person shall be deprived "of *life*, liberty or property without due process of law."	5. Customs and conditions have changed since the Constitution was written. Just as slavery is no longer acceptable, the death penalty should be considered cruel and unusual punishment.
6. The public wants the death penalty. Polls in some states run as high as 80 percent in favor.	6. Public opinion has gone up and down on the death penalty. No other Western democracy executes criminals. We should join the ranks of these countries.
7. Capital punishment saves the state money. Why should taxpayers pay to support violent criminals for the rest of their lives?	7. Capital punishment is actually more expensive to the state than life imprisonment. At current costs, the appeals and hearings for a single death-penalty case cost the government between $2 and $3 million.

CRIME BEAT

Imagine you are a crime beat reporter for a local news outlet. Your editor has assigned you to do background research for a story on an upcoming execution in another state. Since your outlet may run an accompanying feature on capital punishment in your state, your editor wants you to find out:

• Is there a death penalty in your state? Under what circumstances does it apply?

• Are there any prisoners on death row in your state? If so,

how many?

• What is the method of execution, if any, employed in your state? (If capital punishment is not used in your state, what is the method used in a nearby state?)

Submit a one-page summary of your findings.

For ideas on sources for this information, see "Crime Beat" on page 31.

1. Have the class form a line based on how each person feels about the death penalty. Make one end of the room mark the spot for those who absolutely favor the death penalty. The other end marks the spot for those who are absolutely opposed to capital punishment. The stronger that people feel one way or the other, the closer they should be to the ends of the line. Those unsure of their opinion belong in the middle.

2. Select the first person from each end of the line. These people are advocates—pro and con—for argument number one on the chart. Have them sit together at a table and silently read and think about argument one. **The advocates' job is to present their assigned argument in their own words.**

3. Select the second person from each end of the line. These people are advocates for argument number two. Have them sit together at a different table and read argument two. Continue through the line until you have tables with pro and con advocates for all seven arguments.

4. Assign the remaining students to sit as arbiters at the tables. **The arbiters' job is to evaluate the advocates' arguments.**

5. Give the advocates 30 seconds each to make their arguments to the arbiters at their table.

6. After hearing the arguments, have the arbiters form a new line showing how they now feel about capital punishment. Like before, one end of the line should mark absolute approval and the other end absolute disapproval of the death penalty.

7. After forming a new line, let each pair of advocates make their arguments in turn to the standing arbiters. After each pair has spoken, let the arbiters move on the line if they are swayed by the argument.

Debriefing Questions

1. Which arguments for and against the death penalty do you find most convincing? Least convincing? Why?

2. Can you think of other arguments for or against the death penalty?

3. One of the stated aims of the death penalty is to prevent potential criminals from committing serious crimes due to the fear of being executed. Do you think the death penalty deters murders? Why or why not?

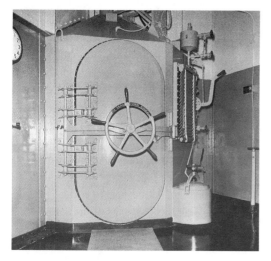
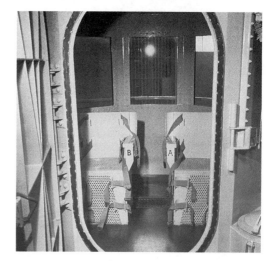

Prisoners executed in California's San Quentin gas chamber face the sealed door. Witnesses view the execution through the opposite wall, which is glass lined. (The Bettmann Archive.)

Class Activity: Life or Death

1. Divide the class into four groups. Each will play the role of the sentencing jury in one of the cases described below. Each jury will be asked to decide its case using the following capital punishment statute:

Statute

After finding a defendant guilty of murder in the first degree, the jury shall look at the circumstances of the crime and at the character of the individual defendant. If it finds the aggravating circumstances of the crime and the defendant outweigh the mitigating circumstances, it shall return a recommendation of the death penalty. Otherwise, it shall recommend life imprisonment.

2. The defendant in each case has already been convicted of first-degree murder. Each jury must determine the penalty. The only two choices available are life imprisonment or death.

3. When jurors apply the statute, they should first make a list of the *mitigating circumstances*, those that seem to call for mercy. Then they should list *aggravating circumstances*, or those that make the crime seem especially violent or repulsive. Jurors should then weigh the *mitigating* and the *aggravating* circumstances against each other. If they feel the case calls for leniency, they should recommend life imprisonment. If they think the case is particularly barbarous or savage, they should recommend death. The recommendation does not have to be unanimous. Only a majority is required for a sentencing recommendation.

4. When each jury is finished, one student in each group should report the mitigating circumstances your group considered in that case, and another student should report the aggravating circumstances. Finally, a third student should report the sentence you chose, and the number of students who voted each way.

Case 1

Name: **Luby Waxton**

Age: **22**

Sex: **Male**

Luby has been in and out of jail ever since he was a teen-ager. He was convicted of shoplifting, burglary, and assault with a deadly weapon. He received a light sentence for each, because he has the mental capacity of an 8 year old.

On June 3 of this year, Waxton began drinking in the morning. He decided to rob a local grocery store to get some money. That afternoon, Waxton bought a small handgun.

When he got to the market, he entered the store, bought some cigarettes, and then announced a holdup.

Waxton went behind the counter and emptied the cash register. He put his gun to the sales clerk's head and pulled the trigger. The clerk, an old woman, died instantly.

Waxton was convicted of armed robbery and murder in the first degree.

Case 2

Name: **James Woodson**

Age: **24**

Sex: **Male**

Woodson has no prior record of being arrested.

Woodson has been active in the anti-abortion movement. He believes that abortion is murder. After taking part in picketing an abortion clinic, Woodson became frustrated that the clinic remained open. He believed that much stronger action was necessary, but knew his fellow picketers would not go along with him.

So late on the night of July 17, he broke into the clinic. He poured gasoline throughout the first floor and put a match to it. The clinic burned to the ground. Unknown to Woodson, two security guards were on the third floor. They died in the fire.

Woodson was convicted of arson and first-degree murder.

Case 3

Name: **Phong Tran**

Age: **18**

Sex: **Male**

Tran has a series of prior juvenile arrests for petty theft and assault. He has been involved in gang activity for the past five years.

His family immigrated to the United States when he was 7 years old. His father abandoned the family shortly afterward, and his mother could not handle three children by herself. Placed in a foster home at age 13, he ran away and took to the streets.

He found a new family in a local gang, headed by Tony Chin, age 35. Chin provided boys

in the gang free housing, meals, movies, and video games. In return, they ran errands, protected Chin's businesses, and helped Chin's criminal enterprises. Tran looked on Chin as his father.

On January 7 of this year, Chin handed Tran a gun and told him that a "customer" needed a new Mercedes. Tran went to a mini-mall and waited in the parking lot. When Sally Kim drove up in a new Mercedes, Tran ran up, pointed a gun at her, and demanded she get out. The car lurched and Tran shot Kim, killing her.

Phong Tran was convicted of first-degree murder.

Case 4

Name: **Sonia Williams**

Age: **27**

Sex: **Female**

Williams has no prior record.

On September 10 of this year, Williams called the police and reported that she had been raped by a man named Gregg. She was taken down to a hospital where a doctor examined her. He said he could find no evidence of rape.

The police investigated her report and told Williams they could not arrest Gregg. It was dark, they said, and so she could have been mistaken about the identity of the attacker. Besides, they said, Gregg had a perfect alibi for the night in question.

Williams decided to take matters into her own hands. She bought a gun and waited around the corner where he allegedly first attacked her. When Gregg and a friend approached, she told Gregg she had been looking for him and was glad to see him. She invited the two men to go somewhere for a drink. They got into her car and drove to a secluded spot, where she shot and killed both men.

Sonia Williams was convicted of first-degree murder.

Debriefing Questions

1. Do you think different juries would weigh the aggravating and mitigating circumstances differently? If so, is this fair? Why or why not?

2. If you were called to jury duty in a capital case, could you vote for the death penalty if circumstances warranted it? Why or why not?

3. Assume for the moment that you approve of the death penalty. What crimes should it apply to? Why?

Class Activity: A Survey on Corrections in America

Most of us have strong opinions on crime and how it should be punished. Our opinions influence the judgments we make about people and events. Sometimes we are not even aware of the values that lie behind our opinions. We may even support an abstract principle, such as strict justice, without ever stopping to see what the principle means when applied to actual events. This activity will ask you to apply your opinions to specific cases and then compare answers across the whole class.

1. On a blank sheet of paper, write the letters "A" through "L" down the left column.

2. Next to each letter, write the number that indicates the degree of your agreement or disagreement with the statements below.

       5—strongly agree

       4—agree

       3—uncertain

       2—disagree

       1—strongly disagree

3. After you have marked your responses, average the answers across the whole class. (Add all the numbers for each statement and then divide by the number of students providing answers.)

4. Discuss the statements that show the strongest agreement and the strongest disagreement. Why do you think the class responded most strongly to these statements?

A. Ex-convicts should be allowed to hold any job for which they are qualified.

B. Those arrested and charged with crimes should be held in jail until guilt or innocence is decided at their trials.

C. Most individuals now in prison should be released on parole. Only the violent or professional criminals should be kept in prison.

D. Tough judges who hand out long sentences to those who break the law will make people think twice before they commit crimes.

E. Inmates should be held in prison until those in charge are sure they won't commit more crimes after release.

F. The reason we have prisons is to punish criminals.

G. Drug addicts and alcoholics should be treated and counseled rather than put in jail.

H. If the public was more willing to help ex-convicts, fewer would get into trouble again.

I. Instead of prison, most criminals should be required to take jobs so they can pay their victims for the crimes they committed or do something to help the community.

J. I wouldn't mind having a halfway house where ex-convicts live located in my neighborhood.

K. Those convicted of white collar crimes should make restitution to the people or institutions that they victimize.

L. Mandatory sentencing has overburdened the prison system and should be eliminated.

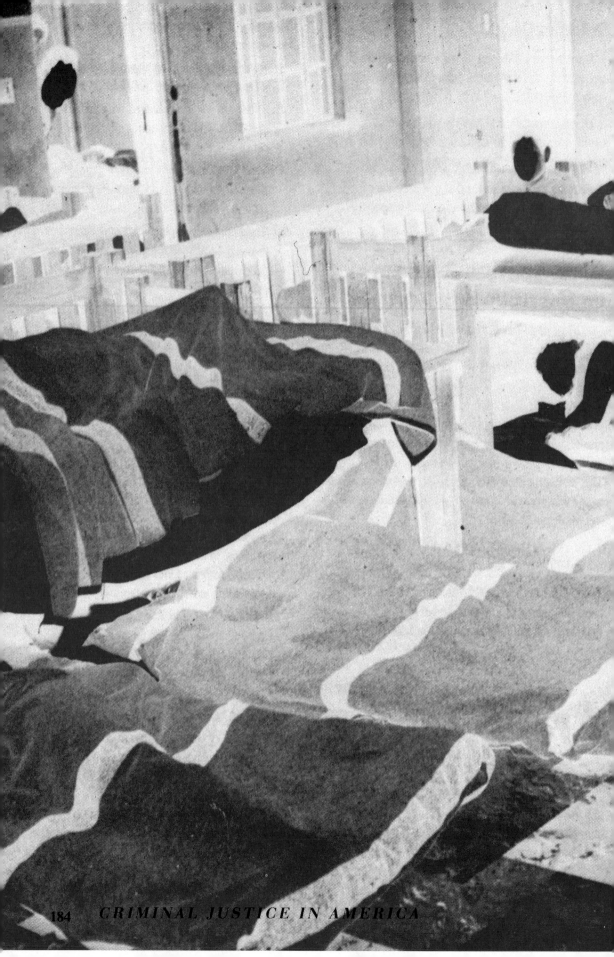

J U V E N I L E
J U S T I C E

In 1716, Elizabeth Hickes of Huntington, England, was accused of witchcraft. Her neighbors reported that Hickes used dolls to cast evil spells. She'd made a number of her enemies very sick. After hearing the evidence, a judge found Hickes guilty as charged, and she was burned alive at the stake. Elizabeth Hickes was born in 1705. She was 11 years old.

What if Elizabeth had been an American born in 1905, 1945, or 1975? In the first place, times have changed and practicing witchcraft is no longer a crime. But what if she were accused of a different crime? What would happen to the 11-year-old Elizabeth Hickes today?

For one thing, she wouldn't get a trial. She'd have a hearing. It would take place in a special juvenile court. Her family history, school records, and other personal information would be closely examined. Even if the juvenile court judge decided something was wrong with Elizabeth, she wouldn't be punished. Instead the court would prescribe a special rehabilitation program designed to help Elizabeth adjust to society.

Why are children treated so differently today? Nineteenth and early 20th century reforms produced two separate systems of justice in America, based on almost opposite philosophies. The adult criminal justice system applies to supposedly mature, responsible persons who have lived, depending on the state, at least 16 or 18 years. All those younger than the specified age fall under the jurisdiction of the juvenile justice system.

Though this dual system is now generally accepted, it does have its critics. Many Americans believe that all persons in trouble with the law, no matter what their age, should have the benefit of the due process protections found in the adult system.

Others argue that some juveniles should be processed according to the rules of the adult system not for their protection, but for society's protection. They feel that the juvenile justice system, with its emphasis on rehabilitation, puts too many young, hard-core criminals back on the streets. The fact that these criminals are only 14 or 15 doesn't prevent them from committing crimes and ruining other people's lives. Others have yet another perspective: Whether or not the theory behind our current juvenile system is correct, it just isn't working. Modifications must be made for the benefit of troubled young people and for the good of society.

After exploring the history and philosophy of the juvenile justice system, this chapter examines issues raised by its critics and supporters. Who ought to be there? What rights should young people have as protection against the system? Should the system focus on rehabilitation or punishment?

Finally, statistics show that people under 18 are responsible for almost 20 percent of American crime. Many criminals start their life of crime as juveniles. To find solutions to our crime problem, we must examine how the law currently treats juveniles and how that treatment can be improved.

FROM CRIMINAL TO DELINQUENT

History: Children and the Law

In the Middle Ages, children took part in adult activities as soon as they could walk and talk. They were working by the age of 5 or 6. Most families needed every available pair of hands to grow enough food or weave enough cloth to survive. Shorter life expectancy also forced people into early adulthood. The average life span was only 40 years. There was no time for a leisurely childhood, much less an adolescence.

Children not only were expected to work hard, they were also expected to obey adult laws. Anyone old enough to commit a crime was thought old enough to be punished for it. Painful forms of trial, like ordeal and combat, and harsh punishments, like being hanged or burned at the stake, were the fate of all criminals, no matter what their ages.

In the 16th and 17th centuries, medieval attitudes began to soften. Though children were still thrust into adulthood at the age of 4 or 5, most of Europe began to think of them as needing adult protection and guidance. In England, the common law reflected this change in attitude. The king or queen became the **parens patriae**—the parent of the country. Representing the monarch, English courts acted as *parens patriae* to manage orphans' estates, protect children's property from wasteful parents, and provide for abandoned young people.

The Age of Reason

About this same time, another important concept worked its way into English common law: the idea of intent. To commit a crime, a person not only had to perform a forbidden action, the person also had to intend to commit that act.

The concept of intent changed how children were treated under English common law. Society now believed that children were naive and innocent. Though they might accidentally cause harm, children did not know enough about right and wrong, or about the effects of their actions, to form criminal intent. Since they couldn't form intent, children couldn't commit crimes.

At what age could they form the intent necessary for committing crimes? The 18th century's answer to this question was based on traditional Christian beliefs which held that 7 was the "age of reason." After age 7, according to the church, children knew the difference between right and wrong and became responsible for their actions and moral decisions.

By the late 18th century, English common law had taken this rationale one step further. English judges usually dismissed cases against defendants under age 7. In recognition of society's changing view about the length of childhood, they also dismissed cases against persons aged 7 to 14 unless the prosecution could prove that the child was capable of forming criminal intent.

The English criminal justice system treated everyone over 14 years old—and everyone

Mulberry Street, New York City, 1897. A group of children hang out on a street corner. Overcrowding in poor neighborhoods often forced children to band together on the streets. (The Bettmann Archive.)

between 7 and 14 proven capable of forming criminal intent—exactly alike. Officially, all were tried in the same courts by the same rules. If convicted, all were locked up in the same jails and subject to the same harsh penalties. In actual practice, however, the system showed children and adolescents some leniency. For example, although English courts sentenced 103 persons age 8 and under to death between 1801 and 1836, not one of these executions actually took place. Even so, the law allowed people of a very young age to be executed or imprisoned.

Colonists transplanted the English common law, complete with the concepts of *parens patriae*, criminal intent, and the age of reason, to North American soil. The religious beliefs of many of these settlers emphasized training children for obedient, religious, and productive adult lives.

Save the Children

By the 19th century, America was rapidly changing. Factories sprang up across the Northeast, and the nation's urban population was growing faster than its rural population. In 1820, 7 percent of America's people lived in cities. That proportion had risen to 15 percent by 1850 and 35 percent by 1890.

Many of the new city residents were immigrants. Others were country people looking for greater opportunity and a path out of the exhausting routines of rural life. Survival in the city, however, was a full-time occupation. Crowded into small rooms with their struggling family, urban children could find life to be very unpleasant. Understandably, they often escaped to the streets. Other children were abandoned by their parents and turned to picking pockets, shoplifting, begging, and looting for survival.

Often, young people banded together. As early as 1791, children's gangs were noted on the streets of Philadelphia scaring horses with firecrackers. During the 19th century, gangs turned from pranks to serious crime. By the Civil War, youth gangs took part in arson and mob violence, and regularly fought battles with the police.

Though citizens' groups in every American city expressed concern about these wayward youngsters, people were unsure of what to do about them. If caught in a crime, children over 7 and under 14 faced prosecution in the adult criminal justice system and often ended up in adult prisons. Many people questioned the wisdom of this result. Through contact with older criminals, children learned to perfect their skills at robbery, mayhem, and murder. Also, then as now, adults in prison regularly abused younger and weaker inmates.

House of Refuge

Early in the 19th century, American cities began to provide alternatives to adult prisons for children. In 1824, using *parens patriae* as its rationale, the New York City government established the New York House of Refuge for abandoned, deprived, and criminal children. Other state and local governments soon followed suit. These institutions, which came to be known as reform schools, opened in almost every large urban center.

The reform schools tried to break youngsters' bad habits by a combination of religion, education, and hard work. Run by private organizations, many schools, however, began to operate not for reform, but for profit. They glossed over moral and practical education. As headmasters pressed for greater productivity, children spent more time in workshops and less in classrooms.

As living conditions deteriorated, many young people rebelled. In 1859, 15-year-old Dan Crean set fire to the Massachusetts Reform School. Two years later, in another part of the state, angry girls burned their school to the ground. Reform schools, like prisons before them, came to be known as "universities of crime."

Stuck in the System

Once in these schools, students could not easily get out. In 1838, for example, a court committed Mary Ann Crouse to the Philadelphia House of Refuge because her mother complained about her behavior. By the time her father found out, Mary Ann was already locked up. When the House of Refuge refused to release her to his custody, Mr. Crouse began a legal battle to get his daughter back.

His battle eventually took him to the Supreme Court of Pennsylvania. He argued that the House of Refuge had violated his daughter's constitutional rights. Mary Ann had been locked up without a jury trial, a right guaranteed to all Americans.

After lengthy deliberation, the court ruled in favor of the House of Refuge. The court stated that the right to a trial by jury did not apply to juveniles taken to the House of Refuge. It only applied to people accused of crimes. Since Mary Ann was not accused of any crime, she had no right to a jury trial.

According to the court, Mary Ann was institutionalized not because of criminal guilt, but because her mother no longer wanted to take responsibility for her upbringing. Citing the doctrine of *parens patriae*, the court declared that the state, in this instance represented by the House of Refuge, had every right to assume the parental role. As the court concluded, Mary Ann "had been snatched from a course which must have ended in confirmed depravity, and not only is the restraint of her person lawful, but it would be an act of cruelty to release her from it." (*Ex Parte Crouse*, 1838.)

For Discussion

1. What is the doctrine of *parens patriae*? Do you think it has validity today? Why or why not?

2. At what age do you think children should be held criminally responsible for their actions?

3. What were the negative effects of placing juveniles in the adult criminal system?

4. What arguments can you think of against keeping Mary Ann in the House of Refuge?

Founded in 1876, New York's Elmira Reformatory attempted to rehabilitate delinquent juveniles behind its gray walls. (UPI/Bettmann.)

From Criminal to Delinquent: A Time for Reform

Americans cities didn't rely entirely on reform schools to cope with young people in trouble. During the latter half of the 19th century, other innovative ideas developed as well.

Since contact between juveniles and adult criminals was seen as a major problem, many states began setting aside special times for juvenile trials, keeping juvenile records separate from adults, and sentencing juveniles to age-segregated prisons.

Massachusetts began experimenting with probation as an alternative to imprisonment. But probation presented problems when applied to young urban criminals. Sending them back to their communities usually meant returning them to an environment which was the root of their problems. If a juvenile's family couldn't provide a good home, the courts sometimes tried to identify a relative or family friend to take responsibility for the child's probation.

This led to the development of another innovation: the foster family. Recognizing that reform schools or problem families could cause more harm than good, government officials compiled lists of trustworthy families and individuals who could provide temporary care for children in trouble. Abandoned or neglected children were also placed in foster homes.

Though each of the experiments in juvenile reform was successful to some degree, by the 1890s, it became obvious that more inventive methods were needed.

The situation in Chicago was especially bad. The Chicago Reform School reeked with vice and crime. Judges preferred to send all but the most hardened juvenile offenders to the adult jail. They felt the jail was a safer environment. The school's reputation was so bad that when it burned in 1871, the government refused to provide money to rebuild it. This left Chicago, one of the nation's largest cities, with no system for handling neglected or criminal young people.

The Chicago Women's Club stepped in to fill the gap. It set up a school for young people serving time in the city's jails. It opened a city police station for women and children arrestees so they wouldn't have to mingle with hardened male criminals.

Working with juveniles made club members come to some radical conclusions. Members felt that treating juveniles in the adult criminal justice system made matters worse. Why not start over and build a separate justice system, just for juveniles, based on principles related to the needs and problems of children?

In the first place, club members believed that no rational adult could hold children responsible for their actions. Wayward, disobedient, and criminal behaviors, they believed, were diseases caused by poverty and neglect, circumstances over which a child had no control. One might as logically blame children for catching the measles as blame them for running away from troubles at home or following bad examples set by friends.

Secondly, the concept of crime—specific prohibited acts—was too limited to help children. Certainly, young persons must be prevented from robbing, raping, and murdering. But they also must be protected from other, less well-defined actions, like associating with immoral people, staying out too late at night, or disobeying authority. These actions greatly damaged young people by encouraging bad habits and leading to more destructive behavior.

Furthermore, it was unfair to label children as criminals. A new word for wrongdoers was needed. The word "delinquent" seemed much more appropriate. The Women's Club also decided that children convicted of crimes should not be punished. Instead, young persons who committed delinquent acts should be re-educated and rehabilitated so they would not repeat their offenses.

Moreover, young persons should not necessarily undergo the same rehabilitation programs. Some children would best benefit from the harsh life of reform school. Others would do better in the gentler care of foster parents. Still others could be returned to their families on probation. Each child should receive **individualized treatment**.

Finally, since no one was being punished, there was no need for the carefully regulated trial process of the adult courtroom. That process

tended to intimidate children and might be more a hindrance than a help, the Women's Club reasoned. To consider each child's best interests and deliver the personalized justice demanded by this new system, a judge needed more freedom than adult procedures permitted. Judges hearing juvenile cases should work in informal rooms, more like counseling offices than courtrooms. Questioning and decision making should also be flexible and informal. Only in such a non-adversarial atmosphere could judges determine appropriate ways to help young people in trouble.

When the Women's Club first raised these ideas in 1892, its own lawyers argued that the system was unconstitutional. Not only did it reverse or suspend the basic principles of American justice, it stripped the accused young persons of their rights. Club members retorted that children needed help, not rights.

In spite of the initial negative response, the Women's Club proposal was widely discussed. In 1898, the Illinois State Board of Charities asked the Chicago Bar Association to draft legislation based on the club's plan. After hearings, the Illinois legislature passed the Juvenile Court Act. The nation's first juvenile court officially opened its doors on July 1, 1899.

Other states responded enthusiastically to this new system. Within 25 years, all but Maine and Wyoming had passed laws based on the Illinois model. Over the years, court decisions and administrative policies have slightly modified the juvenile justice system. But the current juvenile justice systems throughout the United States owe their roots to that first Chicago experiment.

For Discussion

1. Do you agree with the reasoning advanced by reformers in the Chicago Women's Club? Why or why not?

2. Are young people incapable of forming criminal intent? Should they be treated rather than punished when they harm others?

3. Should young people who commit crimes be treated differently from adults?

Class Activity: Same or Different?

Working in small groups, examine each of the four pairs of cases listed below. In each, after considering the individuals' intent and responsibility, decide whether the juvenile and adult should receive the same treatment or punishment. Be prepared to explain the reasons for your decision. After your group decides all the cases, present your findings to the class and compare your decisions with those made by other groups.

Case 1

- Jerry, 27, lives in an adult apartment complex. One of his neighbors regularly holds loud parties which last long into the night. After a frustrating confrontation late one evening, Jerry picks up a rock and throws it through his neighbor's window.

- A neighbor chases Harold, 10, and his friends from her yard and warns them not to play baseball on her property. In retaliation, Harold throws a rock through her window.

Case 2

- Cynthia, 35, finds out that her husband is leaving her. At the height of an argument, she kills him.

- Mike, 8, is furious with his 4-year-old sister for ruining his favorite toy. He picks up his father's shotgun and kills her.

Case 3

- When the store clerk's back is turned, Connie, 23, slides an expensive scarf into her purse and walks out of the store. Apprehended by store detectives on the sidewalk, she complains that she tired of paying exorbitant prices for everything.

- Nancy, 14, steals a digital watch from a department store display. Her only excuse, when she's caught, is that her friends dared her to do it.

Case 4

- Jim, 39, makes obscene phone calls to women in his neighborhood. He enjoys their confused and helpless reaction and likes to give them a good scare.

- Andy, 15, makes an obscene phone call to one of his teachers. He wants to see how she will react.

Debriefing Questions

1. Which cases were the most difficult to decide? Why?

2. Do you think the criminal justice system should treat children differently from adults? If so, at what age should they be treated the same as adults?

Different Worlds

Under current law, the treatment of juveniles differs greatly from that of adults. Though the specifics of treatment vary from state to state, the chart notes many common differences in the juvenile and adult systems.

ADULT SYSTEM:	JUVENILE SYSTEM:
Persons can be legally **arrested** if they are suspected of committing a **crime**.	Juveniles can be **taken into custody** if they are suspected of committing a **delinquent act**.
The state files formal criminal charges in the form of an **indictment** or **information**.	The state files a **petition** with the juvenile court.
Persons may be released on **bail** or **on their own recognizance** or **may be held in jail** until trial.	Juveniles may be released into **custody of their parents**; may be **held in custody** until an official hearing; or may be placed on **probation** without an official hearing.
Decisions are made by **judges** and **juries**.	Decisions are made by **hearing officers, commissioners, juvenile court judges**.
A **trial** determines whether or not an accused person is guilty beyond reasonable doubt of a specific crime.	An **adjudicatory hearing** determines the truth or falsity of the petition beyond a reasonable doubt.
After a **verdict of guilty**, a **sentencing hearing** is held to determine the sentence.	After a **finding of delinquency**, a **dispositional hearing** determines if the juvenile is in need of state supervision or care.
A convicted person may be placed on **probation, fined,** or sentenced to a specified length of confinement in a **jail** or **prison**.	Juveniles judged in need of care are made **wards of the court**. They may be placed on **probation**, removed from their family and placed in a group or individual **foster home**, **fined**, or committed to an unspecified length of confinement in a **reform school, state institution,** or **camp**.
Before the end of a prison term, a prisoner may be released and put on **parole**.	After release from confinement, juveniles may be supervised in a program of **aftercare**.
Proceedings and records are **public**.	Proceedings and records are kept **private**.
The main goal is **punishment**.	The main goal is **rehabilitation**.

For Discussion

1. Which differences seem to be merely words? If some differences are just words, does it make any sense to use different words? Why or why not?

2. What are the major differences between the two systems? Try to explain some of these important differences in light of the early 20th-century reforms. In your opinion are these differences justified? Explain.

THE PROBLEM OF DELINQUENCY

What is Delinquency?

The definition of delinquency varies greatly from state to state. Specific acts and behaviors are often classified as delinquent for two general reasons. Such actions either:

a) would be termed criminal if committed by an adult, or

b) are thought harmful to young people because they might be dangerous or lead to criminal behavior. (These are often called **status offenses** because they only apply to those who have the status of juveniles.)

Status offenses cover a wide variety of behaviors—running away from home, drinking alcohol, skipping school, disobeying parents, violating curfews, etc. Some states classify youth who exhibit these behaviors as "wayward" or "incorrigible." Others term status offenders as CHINS, PINS, or MINS—children, persons, or minors in need of supervision. Other states simply lump all the behaviors together as delinquent.

Since states must define status offenses, the laws can be quite broad and even vague. California's old section 601 of its Welfare and Institutions Code was a good example:

Any person under the age of 18 years who persistently or habitually refuses to obey the reasonable and proper orders or directions of his parents . . . or school authorities, . . . or who is habitually truant . . . *or who . . . is in danger of leading an idle, dissolute, lewd, or immoral life*, is within the jurisdiction of the juvenile court which may adjudge such person to be a ward of the court. (Emphasis added.)

California's code no longer contains the emphasized words.

For Discussion

1. What is delinquency?

2. What are status offenses? Do you think they should be classified as delinquent behavior?

3. Why do you think California removed the words "*who . . . is in danger of leading an idle, dissolute, lewd, or immoral life*" from its code?

Class Activity: Are You Now or Have You Ever Been?

What is delinquency? What kinds of people should be processed through the juvenile justice system? To help clarify your opinions about these issues, complete the following activity.

In many states, the actions described below will justify a finding of delinquency when committed by persons under 18. Form small groups. Read the list carefully. As a group, discuss the items using these questions:

• Which are actually crimes?

- Of the remainder, which do you think are harmful to young people? Why?
- Which of the actions on the list should not, in your opinion, be classified as delinquent?

  a. Taking a car without the owner's permission

  b. Disobeying your parents

  c. Cutting school

  d. Going into a building you aren't supposed to be in

  e. Running away from home

  f. Taking something from a store without paying for it

  g. Driving recklessly

  h. Buying or drinking alcoholic beverages

  i. Using or selling marijuana or drugs

  j. Smoking cigarettes at school or in public

  k. Hitting a teacher

  l. Having sexual relations

  m. Deliberately damaging school property

  n. Getting in a fight

  o. Taking something that does not belong to you

  p. Staying out past midnight

Debriefing Questions

1. Which of these behaviors did most groups think were criminal? Delinquent? Neither?

2. How would you define a juvenile delinquent?

A Tour of the System

Recent statistics indicate that almost 2 percent of all Americans under age 17 pass through the juvenile justice system each year. The statistics overlook the many juveniles who never enter the system, but who are referred to social welfare agencies because of abuse, neglect, or status offenses. Although the system still takes status offenders in extreme cases, it handles at least seven times as many delinquency cases. The chart on page 196 shows what happens to those brought into the system for delinquency.

The chart shows that police bring most juveniles into the system. But 15 percent are brought in by parents, school officials, and social welfare agencies.

Almost one-fifth of those brought in are accused of violent crimes—murder, rape, robbery, or assault. Over half are detained for property crimes—vandalism, theft, and burglary. Another one-fifth are taken into custody for public-order misdemeanors, such as loitering, trespassing, and public intoxication. The remaining juveniles—about 5 percent—are accused of drug offenses.

At the juvenile court, an intake worker, usually a probation officer or a social worker, must decide what to do with these juveniles. The worker typically looks at the offense, the strength of the case, and the juvenile's history and needs. After consulting with a prosecutor, the worker may choose to file a petition against the juvenile. This will lead to a hearing in juvenile court.

But about half of the juveniles are not petitioned. Of these juveniles, most are simply let go. The remainder agree to be informally processed in the system, often with the understanding that if they break the agreement, a petition will be filed. About one-quarter of those not petitioned are put on probation. The remainder pay fines or restitution, or are referred to social agencies.

Those petitioned must appear at initial hearings. At these hearings, juvenile court judges examine the petitions. They decide to hold adjudicatory hearings for about 60 percent of the petitions. Of the cases not heard, a tiny percentage are waived to adult court. These cases represent the most serious offenders. Most juveniles not having adjudicatory hearings, however, are released. The rest are handled informally. About one-quarter are put on probation. And most others are referred to social agencies.

Finally, what happens to those having adjudicatory hearings? A very small percentage are released or referred to social agencies. Most receive probation. Only about one-third are

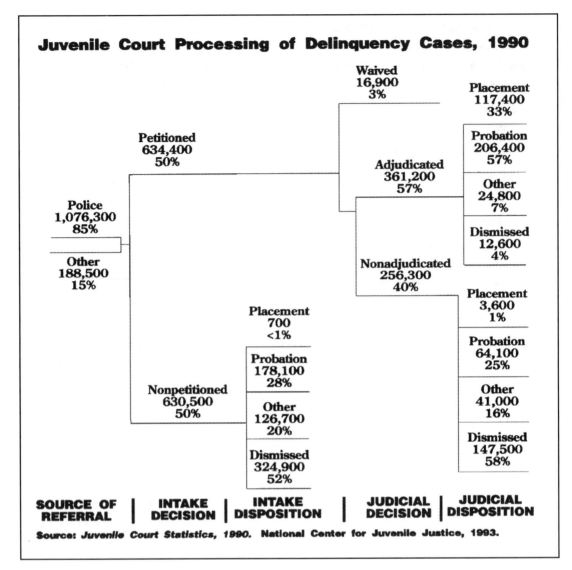

Juvenile Court Processing of Delinquency Cases, 1990

SOURCE OF REFERRAL | **INTAKE DECISION** | **INTAKE DISPOSITION** | **JUDICIAL DECISION** | **JUDICIAL DISPOSITION**

Police 1,076,300 85%

Other 188,500 15%

Petitioned 634,400 50%

Nonpetitioned 630,500 50%

Waived 16,900 3%

Adjudicated 361,200 57%

Nonadjudicated 256,300 40%

Placement 700 <1%

Probation 178,100 28%

Other 126,700 20%

Dismissed 324,900 52%

Placement 117,400 33%

Probation 206,400 57%

Other 24,800 7%

Dismissed 12,600 4%

Placement 3,600 1%

Probation 64,100 25%

Other 41,000 16%

Dismissed 147,500 58%

Source: *Juvenile Court Statistics, 1990.* National Center for Juvenile Justice, 1993.

placed out of their homes into foster homes, group homes, or secure facilities.

As you can see on the chart, many juveniles are put outside the system, or diverted, at each stage. Of the original juveniles taken into custody, fewer than 10 percent wind up placed outside their homes. The juvenile court system relies on decision makers at each stage to act "in the best interests of the child." Each of these decision makers—from the police officer to the intake worker to the juvenile court judge—is given wide discretion in resolving delinquency problems. The system encourages these decision makers to resolve the problems informally, if possible, instead of sending a juvenile deeper into the system.

For Discussion

1. How do you think police officers, intake workers, and juvenile court judges exercise discretion in the juvenile justice system? Give some examples. What are some advantages and disadvantages of this discretion? Explain.

2. Why do you think juvenile justice officials prefer to resolve delinquency problems informally? What are the advantages and disadvantages?

3. Look at the chart. At what stage do juveniles have the best chance of getting their cases dismissed? At what stage do they have the worst chance? How do you account for this?

Class Activity: Who Should Be in the System?

What kind of young people do you think should be processed through the juvenile justice system?

Break into pairs. Write your conclusions on a sheet of paper. Decide which, if any, government agency should be responsible for *juveniles* in the situations described below. (Do *not* answer what agency should deal with the adults in these situations.) Decide whether the juvenile in each situation should be sent to:

- state or local service agencies,
- juvenile courts,
- adult criminal courts, **or**
- no government institution (the matter should be handled privately and not made illegal).

Which, if any, government agency should handle the following juvenile cases?

a. Abuse or neglect. The children are poorly fed or clothed, beaten, sexually molested, or denied vital medical treatment by their parents.

b. Criminal influence. The children are exposed to or taught illegal behavior (e.g. drug abuse, criminal acts) by their parents.

c. Economic hardship. The children have parents who cannot afford to take care of them.

d. Unconventional homes. The children have parents who live according to moral standards different from those of the general community (e.g. unmarried or homosexual parents, those with unusual religious beliefs).

e. Ungovernability. The children cannot be controlled by their parents.

f. Runaways. The children habitually run away from home.

g. Status offenses. The children commit status offenses, such as curfew violations or truancy.

h. Abuse of intoxicating substances. The children use drugs or alcohol.

i. Misdemeanors. The children loiter, joy-ride, make obscene phone calls, etc.

j. Victimless crimes. The children commit victimless crimes such as prostitution.

k. Shoplifting.

l. Major theft or other property crimes.

m. Violent crimes.

Debriefing Questions

Compare your answers with those of other students in your class.

1. Which actions should be handled privately? Why?

2. Which actions deserve court involvement? Why? How do you determine whether juvenile or adult criminal courts should handle the matters?

3. Which actions should be handled by social service agencies? Why?

4. Which situations do most people agree about? Which cause the most disagreement? Why?

Initial Detention of Juveniles

When first taken into custody, juveniles go to a detention center, often called juvenile hall. Unlike adults, juveniles may be held in custody until their hearings without any chance of bail. At the option of a probation officer, they may be released into the custody of their parents before the hearing. If the probation officer decides to keep the juvenile in custody, a judge reviews this decision, usually within 48 hours.

In some jurisdictions, most juveniles spend at least one day in custody. From 1986 to 1990, surveys were taken of pre-hearing detention in three California counties—San Francisco, Los Angeles, and Santa Clara. The surveys revealed that three-fourths of all juveniles were held more than 24 hours regardless of offense.

San Francisco Juvenile Detention Screening Criteria

(Shown: portion of the screening form applied at intake)

NAME OF MINOR _____ PFN _____ ADMIT DATE _____

ADMIT TIME _____

MOST SERIOUS INSTANT OFFENSE _____ ARREST TIME _____

INSTRUCTIONS: Score minor for each factor below and enter the appropriate score in spaces provided in the right hand column.

FACTOR   *SCORE*

1. **MOST SERIOUS INSTANT OFFENSE (Score one charge only)**
    Serious Violent Offenses
    WIC 707(b) offenses 10
    Other listed violent offenses 7
    Narcotics/Weapons Offenses
    Possession of firearms 10
    Sale of narcotics/drugs 7
    Possession of narcotics/drugs for sale 6
    Felony possession of narcotics/drugs 5
    Misdemeanor possession of narcotics/drugs 3
    Property Offenses
    Felonies 5
    Misdemeanors 3
    All Other Crimes or Probation Violations 0   _____

2. **NUMBER OF PRIOR ARRESTS, LAST 12 MONTHS**
    Prior felony arrest within the last 7 days 5
    6 or more total arrests, last 12 months 3
    4 to 5 total arrests, last 12 months 2
    1 to 3 total arrests, last 12 months 1
    No arrests within the last 12 months 0   _____

3. **PROBATION/PETITION STATUS**
    Active cases (select only one score)
    With petition now pending 6
    With last adjudication within 90 days 4
    With last adjudication more than 90 days ago 2
    Not an active case 0   _____

4. **SPECIAL DETENTION CASES (Check whichever applies)**
    Escapee_____ Failed placement_____ Transfer In _____
    Arrest Warr_____ Bench Warr_____ Court Order _____
    Other (describe) _____ 10
    Not Applicable 0   _____

DETAIN RELEASE DECISION SCALE
Score 0-9 = RELEASE Score 10+ = DETAIN   *TOTAL SCORE* _____

Aside from worsening overcrowding, such detention creates several other problems. First of all, it's expensive. San Francisco estimated it cost more than $100 to house one juvenile per night, which amounted to more than $40,000 per year.

Second, it crowds together juveniles who shouldn't be together. In Los Angeles, juvenile hall held those awaiting their hearings along with others who had already had their hearings. These others either were waiting to be placed elsewhere or were serving their time in juvenile hall itself. Serious offenders stayed alongside lesser ones.

Finally, pre-hearing detention creates risks to inmate safety. Not merely do violent offenders present a threat to others, but troubled youth in detention pose a high risk of suicide.

Santa Clara, San Francisco, and Los Angeles counties decided to do something about pre-hearing detention. Obviously, they could not just release all the juveniles. Some posed a threat to the community. Others might not show up for their hearings. The counties had to find a solution that would satisfy the need for public safety. They had to find a way to identify youth in custody who could be safely released.

They came up with a screening checklist for each juvenile. A copy of San Francisco's is on page 198. Probation officers score each juvenile according to this checklist. Those scoring more than 9 points are detained. Those scoring under 10 go home. But the probation officers have the right to override the score. So whether a juvenile scores over or under 10 points, a probation officer still makes the final decision on whether to detain or release the juvenile.

The checklist has thus far proved successful. A 1990 study in San Francisco showed that 94 percent of the juveniles released were not rearrested before their hearings and 100 percent showed up for the hearings. Plus the city reaped savings. In 1989, the juvenile hall averaged 123 juveniles per day. By 1990, the average had dropped to 90.

Class Activity: Detain or Release

Imagine you are juvenile probation officers in charge of intake at a juvenile facility in a large city. It is your job to determine whether juveniles remain in detention or are released to their parents. You use the San Francisco Juvenile Detention Screening Criteria to help you make your decisions. But regardless of the score, you make the final decision to release or detain the juvenile.

Pair up with another student and complete the following steps:

- Working in pairs, review the "Six Sample Cases" below.
- Score each case on a sheet of paper.
- Make a recommendation to release or detain. If your recommendation goes against the Screening Criteria's recommendation, write an explanation for your decision. If the two of you cannot agree on a case, write down both your decisions.

WIC 707(b) Offenses for Screening Criteria

Murder

Arson of an inhabited building

Armed robbery

Rape

Kidnapping

Assault with a deadly weapon

Aggravated assault

Discharging a firearm in an inhabited building

Six Sample Cases

Case #1

Name: **Tom Sugino**

Age: **16**

Charge: **Motor vehicle theft** (felony)

Circumstances: Late one Thursday night, Sugino and a 19-year-old friend hot-wired an expensive sports car parked in the garage of an apartment complex where both worked as maintenance workers. They drove the car 120 miles to an oceanside resort. The theft was discovered approximately 48 hours later when the two young men were arrested for disorderly conduct.

Previous Record: Three recorded detentions by police, all within the last 12 months, two for curfew violations, one for underage drinking. Released on summary probation, without formal adjudication, in all three instances.

Personal Background: Junior in high school—an average student with an average attendance record. Only child, father deceased, lives with mother who works nights as a waitress and his elderly grandmother. Part-time work since age 14, fired from current job because of this incident. One psychologist's report indicates normal profile. Another suggests serious emotional disturbance as a result of father's death.

Case #2

Name: **Linda Dubrensky**

Age: **15**

Charge: **Selling narcotics** (felony)

Circumstances: Dubrensky's arrest came from police undercover work at a local community college where Dubrensky, a high school junior, was not enrolled. After selling small amounts of heroin to police agents posing as students, Dubrensky volunteered to set up a major purchase for agents. In the middle of this $100,000 transaction, both Dubrensky and her 35-year-old supplier were arrested.

Previous Record: Two recorded police contacts (one for curfew violation) in the last year. One prior juvenile adjudication for possession of heroin about eight months ago. Served one month in the County Home for Girls; six months participation in a diversion program for drug abusers.

Personal Background: School records indicate a moderate rate of truancy, a bright student who does not work up to potential. No work record. Medical report indicates that Dubrensky is addicted to heroin. Family of two children, mother, stepfather. Mother works as a tax accountant, stepfather is a currently unemployed aerospace engineer; both are members of Alcoholics Anonymous.

Case #3

Name: **Martin Robinson**

Age: **16**

Charge: **Armed robbery, first-degree murder**
(felonies)

Circumstances: Robinson and three other juveniles, two armed with handguns, robbed a local market. One owner pulled a gun and in the following shootout, the owner, a 66-year-old woman, was killed. Robinson was not armed and did not shoot the woman, but he did most of the talking during the robbery. Robinson and two others, both 14, were apprehended shortly after the incident. The fourth suspect, a 15-year-old, is still at large.

Previous Record: None

Personal Background: School records indicate high rate of truancy. Minimal work record, no steady job at time of arrest. Psychiatric report indicates severe emotional disturbance. Family of three children, mother, grandmother. The mother works as a store clerk.

Case #4

Name: **Patricia Ann Warner**

Age: **15**

Charge: **Breaking and entering, burglary**
(felony)

Circumstances: Warner and her 20-year-old boyfriend broke through the back windows of a local electronics shop after neutralizing the alarm. Police on patrol detected the crime in progress. Warner was apprehended carrying two video cassette recorders to the car. Her boyfriend was picked up several blocks away attempting to escape. In the car, police found a home computer, portable stereo players, and other equipment with an estimated total value of over $7,000.

Previous Record: Two prior detentions for questioning by police. One resulted when Warner and a 32-year-old female companion were picked up for selling dinnerware from the back of a van. Neither female had a bill of sale for the merchandise. Because of her youth, Warner was released without charge. Her companion was cited for peddling without a license, a misdemeanor. One juvenile adjudication for marijuana possession about nine months ago. Spent 10 weeks enrolled in a diversion program.

Personal Background: School records indicate a high rate of truancy; poor scholastic achievement probably caused by a minor learning disability. No work record. Psychological reports indicate emotional instability and suggest the possibility of child abuse in the Warner home. Oldest of four children, both parents presently are employed at blue collar jobs.

Case #5

Name: **Tom Kennedy**

Age: **16**

Charge: **Possession of a concealed weapon**
        (misdemeanor)

Circumstances: Kennedy, not a gang member, has to contend with two rival neighborhood gangs. Although he knows members of both and has been approached to join, he has resisted. Three days ago, a rumor circulated around the school that one gang was out to "smoke" him. Fearing for his life, Tom took his father's unloaded revolver to school the next day. He let word out through his friends that he had a gun and that "nobody had better mess with me." Hearing about Tom's threat, a security guard stopped Tom, frisked him, and called the police.

Previous Record: None.

Personal Background: School records indicate a poor student, but teachers consider him bright. No work record. Family of four children, three younger sisters. Both parents present in home. Father unemployed and has drinking problem. Mother supports family as a cashier in a supermarket.

Case #6

Name: **Roger Duncan**

Age: **16**

Charge: **Arson** (felony)

Circumstances: Roger and a 20-year-old friend set fire to an apartment building under construction in their neighborhood. Roger's mother had been served with an eviction notice earlier in the week. The landlord also owned the burned building. A neighbor saw the two boys fleeing the scene. They were taken into custody the following day.

Previous Record: Three prior detentions in the last year. One month ago was put on probation for shoplifting.

Personal Background: School records indicate a moderate rate of truancy and low scholastic achievement. No work record. Family of five children, two of whom are in jail. Mother present in home. Father's whereabouts unknown.

Debriefing Questions

Go over the cases with the whole class.

1. On which cases did most people agree with the screening criteria recommendation? Were there some cases that most people disagreed with its recommendation? Why?

2. Are there other criteria that you believe should be added? Some that should be changed? Why?

3. What sorts of juveniles, if any, should be held in custody before their hearings? Why?

CHILDREN AND THE CONSTITUTION

The Rights of Juveniles

*P*arens patriae, "individualized treatment," and "the best interests of the child" are the cornerstones of the juvenile justice system. Children are delinquents not criminals; they are not imprisoned; they are detained. This special treatment is often necessary and beneficial. It can also raise serious constitutional questions. What provisions of the Constitution and Bill of Rights apply to juveniles? Which do not? The Supreme Court has faced these problems many times. Consider the following landmark case.

Sorry, Wrong Number

On the evening of June 8, 1964, Mr. and Mrs. Gault of Maricopa County, Arizona, returned from work and couldn't find their 15-year-old son, Gerry. He wasn't at school. He wasn't with any of his friends. After a frantic search, they finally found out police had taken their son to the Children's Detention Home. Gerry had been arrested that afternoon for allegedly making an obscene phone call to a neighbor.

The Gaults rushed to get their son, but the Detention Home would not release him. Instead, the family was told there would be a hearing about Gerry's case the next day. On June 9, an Arizona probation officer filed a petition with the juvenile court. It stated that Gerry was a delinquent minor, but it contained no details about his alleged crime.

Gerry and his parents were not told he could consult an attorney or refuse to answer questions. The offended neighbor wasn't even present at the hearing. After it was over, Gerry was sent back to the Detention Home.

When Gerry was released a few days later, his mother received a notice of another hearing on June 15. Again, the neighbor was absent. Again, no records were kept. When it was over, the juvenile court judge committed Gerald Gault, a juvenile delinquent, to the Arizona State Industrial School until he reached age 21. In other words, Gerry received a six-year sentence. The maximum adult punishment for his alleged crime was a $50 fine and two months in jail.

The Gaults immediately filed a petition of habeas corpus on Gerry's behalf, arguing that their son had been denied his due process rights. The Arizona state courts, however, denied the petition. Because the adult and juvenile systems had different aims, explained the Arizona Supreme Court, they required different definitions of due process. If the state applied strict adult regulations to juvenile cases, it could not provide the individualized justice which was the heart of the juvenile system. Though Gerry's treatment did not meet adult due process requirements, the boy had not been treated differently from other juveniles. Arizona agencies had followed their normal procedures, and the decision to confine the boy was therefore upheld.

Unconvinced, the Gaults appealed to the U.S. Supreme Court. In 1967, the high court responded, shaking the foundation of the American juvenile justice system. A majority of five justices reversed the Arizona ruling and granted the Gaults' habeas corpus petition.

In Re Gault (1967)

Prior to *Gault*, U.S. courts had upheld the idea that young people had a right "not to liberty, but to custody." In other words, their right to protection outweighed their right to independence. In the *Gault* decision, the Supreme Court held that juveniles, just like adults, have a vested interest in not getting locked up. It makes no difference whether the jail is called a reform school, a detention home, or a prison. Any juvenile proceeding which could lead to confinement must follow minimum standards of fairness and due process.

The majority opinion explicitly stated what some of these standards were.

1. *Defendants must be informed of the charges against them.* Notice of the charges is an essential element of a fair trial. Until he found himself in a hearing room, neither Gerry nor his parents knew the charges against him. The official petition, which the Gaults did not see prior to the hearing, said only that Gerry was "in need of protection of this Honorable Court." The Supreme Court was not satisfied with this general charge. Detained juveniles and their parents must be told specifically what conduct is under question and why a hearing is being held. Moreover, this information must be provided well in advance of the hearing so the accused can prepare a response.

2. *All young people subject to confinement have a right to an attorney and must be informed of this right.* The state must provide attorneys for those too poor to afford legal fees. In theory, the hearing and probation officers were supposed to be looking out for the young persons' best interest. But since confinement is so much like punishment, the court decided that young people needed legal counsel. Attorneys would also help young people better understand what was happening to them in the juvenile justice process.

3. *Before questioning at hearings, juvenile court judges must inform young persons of their right to remain silent.* In addition, if a young person refuses to answer questions, that refusal cannot be used as an indication of guilt. Under oath during the habeas corpus proceedings, Gerry's hearing officer testified that at both hearings the boy had confessed to making the offensive phone call. Also under oath, Gerry's mother, who was present at both hearings, denied this claim. She asserted that her son only confessed to dialing the phone, but that another boy had done all the talking. The Supreme Court announced that the conflicting testimony was irrelevant because neither Gerry nor his family had been informed of the boy's right to remain silent. The Constitution protected juveniles as well as adults from self-incrimination.

4. *Juveniles have the right to cross-examine their accusers.* The neighbor who accused Gerry Gault never appeared at a hearing to confirm her accusation or explain why she blamed Gerry for the phone call. The Supreme Court decided that was not fair. Confronting and questioning witnesses is an important part of determining the validity of evidence.

Though it marked the first big step in asserting juveniles' rights, the *Gault* decision was also significant because of the rights it did not guarantee. The court refused to apply its due process requirements to cases where the detained juvenile was sent to a foster home or in other ways "set free." Nor did it insist that juveniles receive all the constitutional protections available to adults. *Gault* left questions about whether other constitutional issues, such as the exclusionary rule, *Miranda* warnings, and the rights to speedy, public, and jury trials, applied to juveniles.

In a series of cases in the 1970s, the Supreme Court ruled on some of these constitutional issues. But in 1984 in *Schall v. Martin*, a more conservative Supreme Court reaffirmed the basic principle of the juvenile justice system—*parens patriae*. In that case, authorities had charged Gregory Martin with robbery, assault, and possession of a weapon. They held him in custody until his adjudicatory hearing under a statute which allowed detaining juveniles who might commit further crimes before their hearing. In upholding this statute, the court recognized that juveniles have an interest in liberty. "But," stated the court, "that interest must be qualified by the recognition that juveniles, unlike adults, are always in some form of custody. . . . They are assumed to be subject to

Does the Fourth Amendment Protect High School Students from Searches by School Officials?

Since its *Gault* decision, the Supreme Court has ruled several times on the rights of juveniles. It has held that the Fourth Amendment applies to juveniles as well as adults. But does it apply to students in school? Does it restrict searches by school officials? Or are these officials merely filling a parental role and, acting as parents, can they conduct searches without restrictions from the Fourth Amendment? In *New Jersey v. T.L.O.* (1985), the court decided how the Fourth Amendment applied to high school students.

In this case, a high school teacher caught T.L.O. smoking in the girl's bathroom. (The court used the student's initials in accordance with New Jersey's practice for juveniles.) When taken to the vice principal, T.L.O. denied smoking. The vice principal took T.L.O.'s purse and searched it. Finding cigarettes and rolling paper, he kept searching. He found marijuana, plastic bags, a roll of dollar bills, and a customer list. So he called the police.

Charged with possession of marijuana with intent to sell, T.L.O. was found delinquent by a juvenile court. T.L.O. appealed the finding, arguing that the search of her purse violated her Fourth Amendment rights. The case ultimately went to the U.S. Supreme Court.

The state of New Jersey argued that the Fourth Amendment only applied to police searches, not to searches by school officials. The Supreme Court rejected this argument. The amendment covered searches by all government officials.

The court similarly rejected New Jersey's claim that because school officials must closely supervise students, students have no reasonable expectation of privacy "in articles of personal property 'unnecessarily' carried into a school." The court stated that students routinely bring legitimate personal items to school—keys, money, pictures, diaries—and there is no reason to deny students an expectation of privacy in these items.

But the court also recognized that schools need to maintain discipline. To determine whether the search was reasonable and constitutional, the court balanced the student's expectation of privacy against the school's need for discipline. In doing so, it made two important decisions about school searches:

- *School officials do not need warrants.* Requiring warrants would disrupt the informal discipline procedures necessary to run a school. All the members of the court agreed with this conclusion.

- *School officials do not need probable cause.* All searches, whether with or without a warrant, traditionally require probable cause. Probable cause means that the facts leading up to the search must be strong enough that an independent, cautious person would have good reason to believe that the person committed a crime (or school infraction). Again, because of the school setting, the court felt school officials needed a lesser standard. The court settled on "reasonableness" as the new standard for school searches. Two justices dissented from the court's decision to abandon the traditional, well-defined probable cause standard.

Since T.L.O. had denied the teacher's accusation of smoking, the court found it reasonable for the vice principal to search her purse for cigarettes. Once he found the rolling paper, the court believed it was reasonable for him to continue searching the purse. So the court found the search constitutional. The dissenters believed that the principal had probable cause to search the purse for cigarettes, but once finding them, had no probable cause to continue rummaging through her purse.

For Discussion

1. Do you think school officials should have probable cause to conduct a search? Or do you think the new reasonableness standard is better suited for schools? Explain.

2. What effects might this decision have on schools and students?

the control of their parents, and if parental control falters, the State must play its part as *parens patriae*." In this role, the state was not punishing Martin by locking him up prior to his hearing, but, according to the court, merely acting to protect him from further wrongdoing.

For Discussion

1. Why do you think Gerry Gault's hearing officer decided that the 15-year-old was delinquent and in need of the state's protection? Do you think Gerry could be defined as delinquent? Why or why not?

2. What rights did the Supreme Court guarantee juveniles in the *Gault* decision? What rights were not guaranteed?

3. It has been said that *In Re Gault* "shook the American juvenile justice system to its foundations." How did it contradict the philosophy behind our juvenile justice system?

4. Do you agree with the court in *Schall* that locking Martin up before his hearing was not meant as punishment? Why or why not?

(CRF Photo.)

Class Activity: The Court Decides

In the years since Gerry Gault's release, the Supreme Court has been asked to answer some of the questions raised by the *Gault* decision. The facts and arguments of four of these important cases are noted below. If you were a Supreme Court justice, what decisions would you reach?

Procedures

1. Form courts consisting of an odd number of students (three or five is preferable).

2. Appoint one member chief justice to lead each court's discussions.

3. Assign each court one of the following cases, making sure that each case is heard by at least one court.

4. Have each court carefully read and discuss the facts and arguments of its case.

5. After the discussion, have each chief justice poll the justices one at a time to express an opinion on the issues of the case (majority wins).

6. Have one representative from each group report its decision and the reason behind it to the class as a whole. If some members of the group disagree with the decision, have a second representative report the minority opinion.

A Standard of Proof

In Re Winship (1970)

Adults can be convicted of crimes only if their guilt is proved beyond a reasonable doubt. In non-criminal cases, the standard of proof is different. To win a civil suit, parties normally only have to have the greater amount of evidence—the "preponderance of evidence," as it is known. Since New York considered juvenile proceedings to be civil, its legislature passed a law stating that delinquency did not have to be proved beyond a reasonable doubt. Juvenile courts could declare a young person delinquent based on a preponderance of the evidence.

Samuel Winship was 12 years old when brought before a New York juvenile court for allegedly stealing $112 from a woman's purse. Based on a preponderance of the evidence, the judge found Samuel delinquent and committed him to a training school until he reached age 18. After state courts upheld the commitment, Samuel appealed his case to the Supreme Court.

On appeal, Samuel's attorneys argued that:

- Winship's commitment was, in effect, punishment for stealing the $112.

- Winship was being punished unfairly because his guilt had not been proved beyond a reasonable doubt.

- The reasonable -doubt standard is an integral part of due process guaranteed by the 14th Amendment.

Attorneys for the state on appeal claimed that:

- Winship's commitment was not punishment. The court made no determination about his guilt. Juvenile courts do not determine guilt because it does not fit the purpose of the juvenile justice system.

- If forced to apply the stricter reasonable - doubt standard, juvenile courts would lose their informality and personalized justice, which are why these courts exist.

- The reasonable -doubt standard comes from English common law. It is not expressly required by the Constitution or the 14th Amendment.

- Each state legislature had the right to determine the standard of proof most appropriate to its own citizens.

Issue for Decision:

Does due process as guaranteed by the Constitution and its 14th Amendment require that juvenile courts apply the reasonable -doubt standard?

Trial By Jury

In Re Burrus (1971)

Barbara Burrus and several of her friends, ranging in age from 11 to 15, strongly disagreed with decisions made by their principal and school board in Hyde County, North Carolina. After organizing a series of demonstrations, they were arrested and turned over to juvenile authorities. If the offenders had been adults, their activities would, at most, have resulted in misdemeanor charges.

Attorneys for the young people requested that:

1) their juvenile hearings be opened to the general public, and

2) they be given jury trials.

The hearing officer denied the request for trial by jury and excluded the general public from the hearings. After the hearings, he declared the young people juvenile delinquents and committed them to an institution until they reached the age of majority. He then suspended all these commitments and placed all the offenders on probation.

An appeal to the North Carolina Supreme Court successfully reversed the commitments, but that court upheld the delinquency findings and ruled that a juvenile was not guaranteed trial by jury under the Constitution. Lawyers for Burrus and her friends appealed the case to the U.S. Supreme Court.

On appeal, Burrus' attorneys argued that:

- The findings of delinquency were, in effect, convictions.

- The Sixth Amendment guarantees Americans a public trial by jury prior to conviction of a criminal offense.

- Barbara and her friends experienced precisely the kind of treatment the Sixth Amendment guarantee of a public jury trial was meant to prohibit. The young people were convicted and sentenced for activities which were at heart political. Had the case been heard in public before a jury, this abuse of the judicial power probably would not have occurred.

(AP/Wide World Photos.)

Opposing attorneys on appeal argued that:

- The findings of delinquency were not convictions and that the young people were never accused of crimes. Such accusations do not fit the spirit of juvenile justice.

- The Sixth Amendment mandates a jury trial only in criminal prosecutions. Trial by jury was not therefore required by the Constitution.

- Requiring that states give juveniles jury trials would turn such proceedings into an adversary process. This would result in delays and formalities which contradict the juvenile system's idealistic goals.

- Privacy in juvenile proceedings protect the reputations of the young people involved.

- The issue of whether to give people public or jury trials should be decided by the individual states.

Issue for Decision:

Under the Sixth Amendment of the Constitution, are juveniles entitled to a public, jury trial in juvenile court?

Trial By Jury

McKeiver v. Pennsylvania (1971)

McKeiver, 15, had never been in trouble before. He joined a group of about 25 young friends as they chased three younger teen-agers down the street. When the group caught up with their victims, they threatened the youngsters and took 25 cents from one boy. McKeiver and a 16-year-old friend were caught and charged with theft and assault. Both boys requested to have their cases tried by a jury and in each instance, the request was denied. At their juvenile hearings, both teen-agers were found to be delinquent. McKeiver was put on probation. His friend was committed to an institution. Ultimately, the case was appealed to the Supreme Court.

On appeal, McKeiver's attorneys claimed that:

- The State of Pennsylvania had interfered with both defendants' rights under the Sixth and 14th amendments by denying them trials by jury.

Imagine you are a crime beat reporter for a local news outlet. Your editor has assigned you to do background research for a series on the rights of juveniles. As a followup to an article on Supreme Court decisions, the second feature will focus on the rights of juveniles in your state. Since states can grant more rights than those provided for in Supreme Court decisions, your editor wants you to find out what rights juveniles have in your state.

Submit a one-page summary of your findings.

For ideas on sources for this information, see "Crime Beat" on page 31.

- Juvenile court proceedings are so similar to criminal trials that defendants' due process rights must be protected.

- Trial by jury is one of the most fundamental of all American due process rights.

- If accused of McKeiver's alleged offense, an adult would have been given a jury trial. It was unfair to discriminate against McKeiver and his friend merely on the basis of their ages.

Attorneys for the state of Pennsylvania on appeal argued that:

- The Constitution only mandates trials by jury in criminal cases.

- No matter how many similar features the two processes share, a juvenile proceeding is not a criminal prosecution. A juvenile hearing differs both in philosophy and in practice from a criminal prosecution.

- A judge or hearing officer is just as competent to determine facts as a jury would be.

- Giving juveniles jury trials would destroy the system's design as a protective mechanism for handling young people in trouble. Government studies have recommended against using jury trials for juveniles.

- Each state should be allowed to decide whether it wishes to extend the right to a jury trial to young people in its own jurisdiction.

Issue for Decision:

Under the Sixth and 14th amendments to the Constitution, are juveniles entitled to a jury trial in juvenile court?

Protection Against Double Jeopardy

Breed v. Jones (1975)

The Fifth Amendment states that no person shall "be subject for the same offense to be twice put in jeopardy . . . ." Simply put, this means that no person can be tried twice for the same crime.

But there are instances where defendants are put on trial twice, which are not considered double jeopardy. Consider the following examples:

- A jury is unable to reach a verdict in George's murder trial. The judge declares a mistrial. George may be tried again.

- George is found guilty of murder. On appeal, an appellate court overturns his conviction because the prosecution introduced illegally obtained evidence at the trial. George may be retried without the illegal evidence.

But the following are clear examples of double jeopardy:

- State X tries George for murder. A jury finds him not guilty. State X may not try George again for the same murder.

- State X tries George for murder. A jury finds him guilty and sentences him to 20 years in prison. State X may not try George again for the same murder when he gets out of prison.

Allen Breed, 17, allegedly committed an armed robbery. Taken to Los Angeles County Juvenile Court, he was detained until a petition against him was heard. At the adjudicatory hearing, two prosecution witnesses testified and Breed testified in his own defense. The juvenile court judge found him delinquent. At the dispositional hearing two weeks later, the juvenile court judge found that Breed did not belong in the juvenile system. The judge ruled that Breed should be tried as an adult. Over objections by Breed's attorney that Breed had already been tried, Breed was transferred for trial. In adult court, he was tried, convicted, and sentenced for armed robbery.

On appeal, Breed's attorneys claimed that:

- Because Breed had already been tried in juvenile court for armed robbery, his trial in adult court violated his right against double jeopardy guaranteed by the Fifth Amendment.

- Juvenile court hearings are essentially criminal hearings. They determine whether the juvenile committed an offense and they may take away the juvenile's liberty.

- Applying double jeopardy protection to juvenile court proceedings will help adjudicatory hearings. Juveniles will be more cooperative if they know what they say will not be held against them in adult court.

- If juveniles are to be transferred to adult court, this must be done before any adjudication in juvenile court.

Attorneys for the state of California on appeal argued that:

- The Constitution only protects against double jeopardy in criminal prosecutions.

- Juvenile court hearings are not criminal proceedings. The juvenile system tries to rehabilitate delinquents. All the court did was determine that Breed did not belong in the juvenile system.

- Even if double jeopardy applies to juvenile proceedings, the adult court proceedings were merely part of the same process as the juvenile court proceedings. Breed was only going to be punished once for his offense. Therefore his trial in adult court did not amount to double jeopardy.

- Juvenile court proceedings are informal and need to be flexible to best treat juveniles' interests.

Issue for Decision:

Under the Fifth and 14th amendments to the Constitution, does an adjudicatory hearing in juvenile court and a subsequent trial in adult court for the same offense amount to double jeopardy?

Debriefing Questions

1. What decision did each student court reach? Compare your decisions with those made by the U.S. Supreme Court, noted in the teacher's guide.

2. What are some of the advantages of applying the reasonable-doubt standard of proof in juvenile cases? What are some of the disadvantages?

3. How might making juvenile hearings public help society? Help accused individuals? Why might this be harmful to society?

4. If you were accused of an unlawful act, would you prefer a jury trial or a delinquency hearing? Why? Would you want proceedings at your trial made public?

5. If juveniles were given jury trials, who should serve on the jury? The juvenile's peers? Adults? A mixture of both groups? Why?

6. Why should double jeopardy protection attach to juvenile hearings? Why should it not?

four

JUVENILE CORRECTIONS

Options for Placing Juvenile Offenders

After finding juveniles delinquent, juvenile court judges must decide what to do with the young offenders. This is called making a disposition. As with adult court judges, they have a number of options. Judges try to choose the option that has the best chance of rehabilitating the particular delinquent youth. Depending on the jurisdiction, judges must choose among:

- **Juvenile detention centers.** These are facilities where juveniles are first brought. Many await their hearing here. Others await placement following disposition. But juveniles may also be confined in these centers, usually for short terms, following a finding of delinquency.

- **Training schools.** Often located in rural settings, these large, state-run institutions typically hold from 100 to 1,000 juveniles. They are meant for the most serious offenders.

- **Small, secure residential facilities.** Holding only 10 to 15 juveniles and an equal number of staff, these facilities confine serious, violent offenders. They may be run by the state, but often small non-profit groups operate them.

- **Camps and ranches.** Located in rural areas, these secure facilities normally accommo-

date about 100 juveniles. They emphasize discipline and school work. Most offer counseling.

- **Boot camps.** Run like Army basic training, these camps subject juveniles to shaven heads, physical training, and strict discipline. Known as shock incarceration, boot camps take juveniles for short terms and try to shock them into changing their behavior.

- **Wilderness programs.** In rigorous outdoor settings, these programs try to build self-esteem and teamwork in troubled youth.

- **Group homes.** Often called halfway houses, these facilities typically house about 20 young people. Juveniles living in these homes often attend school, hold jobs, and move about the community. But they must obey house rules. Most group homes also provide counseling.

- **Substance-abuse treatment centers.** These residences focus on treating drug and alcohol abuse. Like halfway houses, they normally hold about 20 juveniles. But these facilities often limit residents' contact with the community during treatment.

- **Foster homes.** Screened by the state, families take juveniles into their homes. States set standards about food, clothing, and other treatment, and they limit the number of children a foster family may care for. In return, foster families receive a certain amount of money for each child's upkeep.

- **In-home placement.** Under this disposition, juveniles return to their homes.

When judges choose in-home placement or foster homes, they then may have several more options to choose from:

- **Diversion to day treatment programs.** These programs differ greatly. Some are all day, every day. Others meet after school or on weekends. Some replace school. Others teach about the legal system or the effects of substance abuse. Others provide supervised recreational activities. Juveniles diverted to these programs must attend for a specific length of time.

- **Intensive or highly intensive probation.** Working with few juveniles, probation officers meet often with them. In intensive probation, they meet every day. In highly intensive probation, they meet several times a day.

- **Probation.** Juveniles are released under fairly strict conditions. They may, for example, be required to:
  - report regularly to a probation officer;
  - stop associating with certain friends;
  - submit to home or body searches on request; and
  - take a weekly urine test (if they have been detained on a drug charge).

  Juveniles who break the terms of their probation can be returned to court for an alternative disposition.

- **Summary probation.** After assuring the authorities that they will not misbehave, juveniles are released under parental or adult supervision. If they break their promise, the juveniles return to court for stricter treatment and supervision.

Which Options Do Judges Choose?

In most jurisdictions, judges do not have this vast array of choices. Thus they frequently either place juveniles on probation or send them to secure facilities, usually juvenile detention centers or training schools. Community placements and intensive probation are often not available.

Their unavailability is ironic. The juvenile justice system has always encouraged community-based treatments for young people in trouble. Such programs can often more easily adapt to the needs of individual juveniles than institutional programs. But in the late 1970s, a public backlash against community programs arose after juvenile court judges began assigning violent offenders to programs designed for non-violent offenders. Today, many communities have mixed attitudes about both the safety and the effectiveness of rehabilitating delinquents in non-institutional settings.

This backlash arose at the same time that the rate of juvenile arrests started declining. From 1978 to 1988 juvenile arrests for violent crime fell 19 percent. And the relative number of juveniles in society declined during this same period. But starting in 1988, the rate of juvenile arrests for violent crime rose dramatically. It soared from slightly over 300 in 1988 to 430 per 100,000 juveniles in 1990. Since the number of juveniles will increase through the 1990s, the volume of juvenile crime could increase sharply.

States have reacted with different programs to treat juvenile offenders. The urge to get tough on young lawbreakers has taken control in many states. Responding to public demand, legislators have written statutes curbing judges' discretion in sentencing and mandating long periods of detention. They have turned away from the traditional model of rehabilitation to one of punishment. Other states, keeping rehabilitation as a model, have tried to institute more community programs. The states of California and Massachusetts illustrate two diametrically opposed approaches.

Locking Them Up in California

California has 10 percent of the juvenile population in the United States. Yet it houses 35 percent of all the juveniles in custody in the United States. This high percentage reflects California's get-tough-on-crime policy of the 1980s. The state built more prisons, sentenced prisoners to longer sentences, and limited criminal defendants' rights. This policy also resulted in more juveniles in secure facilities for longer periods.

Problems with Locking Up Juveniles

In May 1982, Christopher Peterman, 17, found himself in the juvenile section of the Ada County Jail in Boise, Idaho. He had been picked up because he had failed to pay $73 in traffic tickets. Instead of sending him to the juvenile detention center, authorities sent him to the jail to teach him a lesson. Housed with him were other juveniles sent over from the center because they were too violent or difficult to handle. Five of these juveniles attacked Christopher in his cell. For four-and-one-half hours, they took turns burning, gouging, and kicking him. Christopher died from his injuries.

Christopher's case is a horror story about what can happen when violent and non-violent juveniles are locked up together. Not surprisingly, the results of incarcerating non-violent juveniles with violent adults can be equally as tragic. Rape is a common occurrence. The suicide rate of young people in adult jail is *seven times* greater than those incarcerated with other juveniles. In adult institutions, young people can receive the same rough treatment meted out to adult inmates. Even if the juveniles survive physically, they are likely to carry psychological scars.

In the mid-1970s, almost 500,000 juveniles were locked up in adult jails. In 1974, Congress passed the Juvenile Justice and Delinquency Prevention Act. This law stated that no state could receive federal grants unless it separated adults from juveniles in jails. Congress amended the act in 1980 mandating that adults and juveniles be kept in completely separate facilities. The act also ordered states not to hold status offenders in locked facilities.

Almost all states have removed status offenders from secure facilities. By 1986 the number of juveniles in adult jails had dropped to 60,000. But as many as 20 states had not fully complied with the law. By 1989, the number of states out of compliance had dropped to 15. Because of the law, some federal courts have let juveniles stuck in adult jails sue for damages. These lawsuits will probably force greater compliance by states.

For Discussion

1. What does the 1974 Juvenile Justice and Delinquency Prevention Act compel states to do? How is the act enforced?

2. Do you agree with the purposes of the act? Why or why not?

The California Youth Authority takes charge of the most serious youth offenders in California. It runs 11 large institutions, which average 600 beds each, but which are alarmingly overcrowded. These institutions serve as the places of last resort for serious juvenile offenders. Once locked up by the Youth Authority, offenders serve far more time than adults convicted of similar offenses in California.

The Youth Authority's institutions share the problems of all large training schools. Violence threatens juveniles and officials alike. Gang culture predominates. Drugs somehow make their way in. Suicides occur. The most that can be said

of them is that they keep offenders off the streets. Although almost all training schools make efforts at rehabilitation, these efforts usually fail in such an atmosphere. In fact, 70 percent of the juveniles released from the California Youth Authority are rearrested within one year; 85 percent are rearrested within five years.

Putting Them in the Community in Massachusetts

Jerome Miller became director of Massachusetts' Department of Youth Services in 1970. At first, he tried to reform the large training

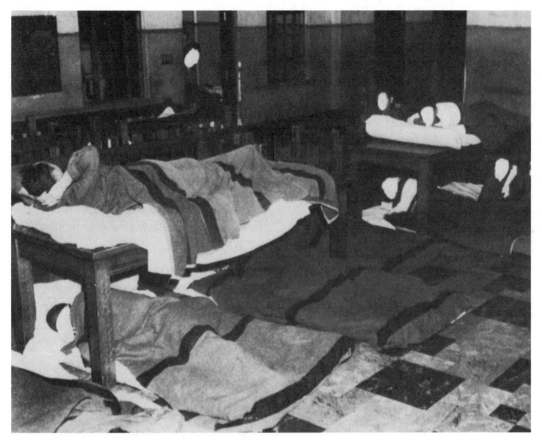

Overcrowding afflicts many juvenile facilities. (UPI/Bettmann.)

schools that held most of Massachusetts' juvenile detainees. He wanted the schools to become centers of rehabilitation. He soon gave up. In 1972, he instituted one of the most radical reforms in the history of juvenile corrections: He closed down all the training schools in the state.

Taking the money saved from closing the expensive-to-run training schools, he invested it in small, secure units for the most dangerous offenders. These sites sheltered no more than 15 juveniles each. While costing even more to run per juvenile than the training schools, they cost less overall because they housed fewer individuals. The remaining juveniles, he sent into community-based programs, run by non-profit agencies.

Today, long after Miller's departure, his department still operates without training schools. It assigns a caseworker for each juvenile put in its care. The caseworker develops a treatment plan for each juvenile and oversees its implementation.

Massachusetts' out-of-home placements consist of:

- 13 small secure units (for the most serious offenders)
- 16 small detention centers (for juveniles awaiting hearings)
- 30 groups homes
- 1 forestry camp
- 7 foster care agencies

The remaining juveniles under the department's supervision are at home. They either attend day treatment centers or are supervised by probation officers. Only the most serious offenders, about 10 percent of the juveniles, remain in the system for long. Placed in secure units for about a year, they move to group homes, and then to highly supervised probation. If they fail at any step, they return to secure units.

Which Works Better?

Differences in geography, size, and populations make it difficult to compare California's and Massachusetts' juvenile corrections. Critics of the California Youth Authority point to its failure to isolate hard-core, violent offenders from mere repeat offenders. They claim these training schools are training grounds for crime, and its students are an overwhelmingly minority population. Critics of Massachusetts' Youth Services claim that the state is releasing dangerous juveniles back into the community where they commit more crimes.

An early study by Harvard's Center for Criminal Justice came to the startling conclusion that Massachusetts had fewer repeat offenders *before* Miller's reforms. It found programs in some parts of the state were not structured to meet the needs of the juveniles. It reported far fewer repeat offenses in other parts of the state where the programs were offering more options to juveniles.

More recent studies by the National Council on Crime and Delinquency found repeat offenses far lower since the reforms. Two studies even tried to compare California's and Massachusetts' rate of repeat offenses. They both found serious offenders passing through Massachusetts' system had a lower rate of repeat offenses than those passing through the California Youth Authority. This was true even though the average length of confinement was far shorter in Massachusetts.

For Discussion

1. What are the benefits and costs of Massachusetts' approach to juvenile offenders? What are the benefits and costs of California's? Which do you think is most effective?

2. Which of the placement options described above sounds least effective for juvenile offenders? Why?

3. Are any of the options better suited to particular problems? Explain.

At Home Plus

Sending juvenile offenders back home has serious risks. The juveniles will likely act as they always have. Why should they change? Nothing in their environment has changed. Many juveniles got in trouble in the first place because of problems with family, friends, or school. Sending them back to these problems risks further problems. Yet sending juveniles back to their homes can help juveniles deal with their problems

Youths fighting vandalism by removing graffiti from walls in their community. (CRF Photo.)

head on. But the young people are going to need help. The following are descriptions of three innovative programs designed for young offenders at home or in foster homes.

Day Treatment Program: Associated Marine Institute

Based in Florida, this privately operated organization runs programs in eight states. The programs focus on improving juveniles' self-esteem and respect for others by building teamwork and academic skills. Attending classes in a marine environment, juveniles learn about boating, scuba diving, and sailing. Each student receives an individual education plan and takes academic classes. Students earn points, which allow them greater privileges and advancement in the programs. Limited to fewer than 50 juveniles at any time, programs last 150 to 170 days. Students return home each night. With one staff

---

CRIME BEAT

Imagine you are a crime beat reporter for a local news outlet. Your editor has assigned you to do background research for a feature article on juvenile corrections in your state. Find out:

- What kind of juvenile offenders are sent to institutions such as juvenile hall, county camps, and state training schools? Why is institutionalization the preferred treatment for these types of offenders? What is the average stay for offenders in these institutions?

- What are local institutions like? What are the living conditions? What provisions are made for recreation? For education? For vocational training or work?

- Approximately what percentage of the juveniles detained in your community are released on probation? What percent are committed to foster care?

- Are there halfway houses or group homes in your community? If so, how many are there? Are there differences between the homes? What criteria are used to determine if a juvenile should be committed to one of these homes?

- What types of diversion programs are offered in your community? Why might a court official send a juvenile to these programs?

- Are there special programs in your community to help juveniles with drug or alcohol problems?

- Which of the available programs offer counseling to juveniles? Which require counseling? Do any offer parental as well as juvenile counseling?

- Do any of the programs provide or emphasize vocational training?

- Which of the available programs most successfully helps status offenders or those accused of misdemeanors or minor thefts? Which works best for juveniles accused of more serious crimes? Are any of the community-based programs used to treat violent offenders?

- Are there high percentages of minorities in any of these programs? If so, do the programs provide role models for these youth?

- What is the average stay for offenders in these different placements?

- Do offenders sometime move from one placement to another? What determines whether they move?

Submit a one-page summary of your findings.
For ideas on sources for this information, see "Crime Beat" on page 31.

One of the most innovative areas of the criminal justice system is juvenile corrections. We have touched on several programs in this book, but many different programs are being tried across the country.

Watch television news broadcasts or search through magazines or newspapers to find out about one of these programs. Evaluate its usefulness and present a brief report to the class.

member for every seven juveniles, staff can give individuals a lot of attention. The juveniles in the programs range in age from 14 to 18and include moderate to serious offenders. Most have eight to 12 offenses. Most students are far below grade level in school on entering the programs. A remarkably low 19 percent of those completing the programs commit offenses again and compared to residential care programs, these programs cost very little.

Highly Intensive Probation: KEY Outreach and Tracking Program

Begun in 1972 after Massachusetts closed its training schools, KEY contracts with the state to provide close supervision of juveniles released to their homes or to foster homes. KEY may serve as the final step in a juvenile's treatment program or it may be the only step. To start a KEY case, the caseworker meets with the juvenile and the juvenile's family, and together they draw up a behavior contract. Each caseworker only has eight juveniles to supervise. So the caseworker meets with each juvenile several times a day. The contacts range from mere checkups to counseling to finding jobs and community services for the juvenile. The program normally lasts 90 days. KEY costs very little compared to secure facilities.

Juvenile Alternative Work Service

At dispositional hearings, Los Angeles County judges sentence juveniles who have broken probation to short juvenile -hall time, normally about 20 days. But this disposition may be put on hold if a juvenile agrees to take part in JAWS, a county-run program. Instead of spending the 20 days in juvenile hall, the juvenile

works for 20 Saturdays or Sundays on JAWS work crews. Los Angeles sends out about 25 of these crews each weekend. With about 10 to 12 members each, the crews do manual, outdoor labor, usually painting and cleaning. If the juvenile forgets to show up or acts up on the job, then the court imposes the original sentence in juvenile hall. But most are happy to take care of their sentences outside juvenile hall. And the county is pleased because it receives money from cities and school districts that contract to have the work done. The money pays for over half the cost of the program, which makes it far cheaper than sending juveniles to juvenile hall.

For Discussion

1. What are the main benefits of all these programs?

2. Which program do you think would be most effective in preventing juveniles from committing another offense? Least effective? Why? Does the program you consider least effective have any value?

Class Activity: Individual Treatment Plan

Meet in groups of three. Imagine you are case workers. You are assigned six cases to provide individual treatment plans. They are the "Six Sample Cases" on page 199. Each case has been found delinquent. Divide the cases equally among members of the group. (If your group has three members, then each member is responsible for two cases.) Using what you have learned about various dispositional options for juveniles, write a treatment plan for each case that you are responsible for. The treatment plan should include various placements, the length of stay in each, and what behavior would allow the juvenile to progress from one placement to another. When you finish, discuss your cases with the other members of your group. Explain the reasoning behind your decisions.

Debriefing Questions

Go over each case and compare the different approaches that members of the class proposed.

1. Which cases were the easiest to decide? The most difficult? Why?

2. Did you choose relatively costly or inexpensive treatment plans?

3. Which of the options you chose are available for juveniles in your area?

The Question of Waiver

- John S., 15, has been charged with murder while attempting to rob a gas station.
- Mary B., 16, has been charged with prostitution, her fifth arrest on this charge. Living by herself on and off since she was 14, she has run away from two foster homes and one halfway house.

What do these two offenders have in common? Both may be subject to waiver—transfer to the adult criminal courts. In certain cases, a motion may be filed in juvenile court asking that it waive its jurisdiction and transfer the matter to a regular adult court. If this motion is granted, the juvenile is then treated just as an adult offender would be. The issue of waiving juvenile jurisdiction with certain types of young offenders has been hotly debated in recent years.

Legal Standards for Waiver

In 1966, a year before *Gault*, the U.S. Supreme Court ruled that, before waiving jurisdiction, juvenile courts must hold a special hearing—often called a fitness hearing (*Kent v. U.S.*). At that hearing, the accused juvenile must be represented by an attorney who has access to all relevant court files. In addition, the hearing officer must state the reasons for the decision in writing so that the decision can be reviewed.

The Supreme Court also issued guidelines for making waiver decisions. Before sending a young person through the adult courts, a hearing officer should consider:

1. How serious was the crime? Does the community need to be protected from the offender?

2. Was the crime committed in a violent or aggressive manner? Was it premeditated?

3. Was it a crime against persons or against property?

4. Will the adult court prosecute the case?

5. Are the co-defendants, if any, adult? If so, should all the defendants be tried together?

6. How sophisticated and mature is the juvenile? (This is to be determined by examining the youth's home life, emotional stability, and lifestyle.)

7. What is the juvenile's prior court record and history of contact with law enforcement?

8. Can the juvenile be rehabilitated through normal juvenile procedures? If so, can the public be protected during the juvenile's treatment?

Almost every state now has a procedure for treating minors as adults in certain cases. Consider some examples.

- In New York, all persons 16 and over, charged with criminal offenses, are processed as adults. In addition, though 14 and 15 year olds are not waived by juvenile courts, all those found guilty of homicide, armed robbery, or rape must be sent to a maximum security facility for at least five years. These commitments allow annual extensions through age 21.
- Forty-eight states have waiver provisions. Vermont law allows waiver at the youngest age—10. Fifteen states and the federal gov-

ernment set no minimum age. Fourteen states set the minimum age at 14.

- In California, prosecutors may request a fitness hearing for all juveniles 16 or older at the time of their alleged crime. All juveniles 16 or older accused of violent crimes are presumed unfit for juvenile court. Their lawyers must prove extenuating circumstances if they are to remain in the juvenile court system.

Many juvenile justice experts doubt that treating more juveniles as adults will reduce the crime problem. "The problem," explains Raymond Vincent, a former juvenile -court judge from California, "is that putting these kids with adults means they may come out with problems that are more serious than the ones they had when they first went in."

A glance at statistics on waivers supports Vincent's fear. Although waivers are supposed to be reserved for the most serious offenders, only 30 percent of the juveniles waived to adult court have committed violent crimes. About half have committed property offenses; 15 percent are drug offenders; and another 6 percent have committed public-order crimes, such as public intoxication. Do non -violent juvenile offenders belong in the adult system?

For Discussion

1. Do you think waiving jurisdiction of some juvenile offenders is a good idea? Why or why not?

2. If you think waiver is a good idea, what offenders should be waived? Explain.

3. Would you add any additional guidelines for determining waiver? Describe them.

Class Activity: A Waiver Hearing

1. You are a juvenile judge in a state which allows a waiver of jurisdiction in cases where the juvenile is over 14 and accused of a felony. Apply the eight general guidelines on page 217 to the "Six Sample Cases" beginning on page 199. Decide which of the young people should be tried as juveniles and which, if any, should be tried as adults. In accordance with the Supreme Court ruling, write a statement of the reasons for your decisions.

2. Meet in groups of three, discuss the six cases, and vote whether each case should be waived.

Debriefing Questions

1. Compare your decisions with those of your classmates. Is there a general agreement about the reasons for these decisions?

2. Based on their alleged crimes, which juveniles represent the clearest threat to the community? Which are least harmful?

3. Based on prior records and personal backgrounds, which juveniles are most potentially harmful?

4. Of these two factors, crime and background, which was most important to your decisions?

5. Which of these juveniles do you think should be punished? Which could be rehabilitated? Which seem most, and least, likely to be rehabilitated by the juvenile justice system?

6. In adult court, these cases will be tried by juries unless the defendants waive their rights to a jury trial. Do you think any of these juveniles would benefit by a jury trial? Why or why not?

7. What do you think should be the youngest age that juveniles should be waived from juvenile court jurisdiction? Why?

8. Are there any circumstances under which juvenile courts should not be allowed to waive jurisdiction?

An electric chair in a state prison. (UPI/Bettmann.)

Wayne Thompson and the Death Penalty

The sixth of eight children, Wayne Thompson grew up in Chickasha, Oklahoma, a small town about 30 miles southwest of Oklahoma City. He also grew up in the shadow of his brother-in-law Charles Keene's violent rages. He saw his sister Vicky beaten by Keene. Sniffing paint, Keene often grew violent and spared no one. He beat Wayne repeatedly. He struck Wayne's mother, other sisters, and even his older brothers. Keene once even carried his infant son on top of his trailer and threatened to drop him off.

When Vicky finally divorced Keene, the family thought their long nightmare was over. But Keene kept returning, threatening and abusing Vicky. Finally, Wayne decided to put a stop to Keene's abuse once and for all. Together with his adult, older brother Tony and two of Tony's adult friends, 15-year-old Wayne Thompson set out to

kill Keene. Before dawn on January 23, 1983, they found Keene at his home in Amber, Oklahoma. They kidnaped him, beat him, cut open his stomach, chest, and throat, and shot him twice. Before heaving his body in a river, they chained it to a cement block.

Twenty-six days later, it surfaced. At the fitness hearing shortly after his arrest, Wayne was certified to stand trial as an adult. Charged with first-degree murder, he was found guilty. During the trial, the prosecution had introduced three color pictures of Keene's body. The prosecution introduced the same pictures at the sentencing hearing. The jury found the murder to have the aggravating circumstance of being "especially heinous, atrocious, or cruel." So it returned a sentence of death for Wayne.

On appeal, Wayne's attorney argued that the pictures should not have been allowed into evidence at trial or at the sentencing hearing. Further, he argued that sentencing a 15-year-old boy to death violated the Eighth Amendment's ban against cruel and unusual punishment.

The Oklahoma Court of Criminal Appeals upheld the conviction. It did agree with the defense on one point: The pictures should not have been allowed in evidence at the trial. But the court said this error was not sufficient to overturn Wayne's conviction because of the overwhelming evidence of his guilt.

Otherwise the court sided with the prosecution. The sentencing judge did not err in admitting the pictures because they helped prove the aggravating circumstance of the murder. The sentence did not violate the Eighth Amendment. Wayne had been certified to be tried as an adult, so he should be sentenced as an adult. Wayne's lawyer appealed to the Supreme Court.

Wayne waited on death row in a cell next to his brother. In separate trials, all three adults had also been found guilty of first-degree murder and sentenced to death. One of the men was killed in a jail-yard fight shortly after his trial. Another's conviction was reversed on appeal because of trial court error, and at his second trial, he was found not guilty.

For Discussion

1. Since the pictures could have proved several relevant facts at Wayne's trial (e.g. that Keene was dead, how he died, etc.), why do you think the appeals court ruled they should not have been allowed in evidence?

2. A trial court's error that is not important enough to overturn a conviction is known as "harmless error." Do you think introducing the pictures at the trial was a harmless error? Do you think the doctrine of harmless error should apply to murder trials? Explain.

3. At the time of Wayne's sentence, 13 states did not allow the death penalty. Of the remaining 37 states, 18 states set the minimum age for execution at 16. The other 19 states had not set a minimum age. Are these statistics relevant in determining whether the death penalty for juveniles under 16 is cruel and unusual punishment? Why or why not? Is it relevant that only a few nations in the world allow such punishment?

4. Do you think that executing juveniles under 16 is cruel and unusual punishment? Explain your answer.

Thompson v. Oklahoma (1988)

In its *Thompson v. Oklahoma* decision, the Supreme Court voted 5 to 3 to throw out Wayne's death sentence. Four of the justices in the majority thought that executing juveniles under 16 violated the Eighth Amendment. But the fifth justice in the majority, Sandra Day O'Connor, did not agree. She stated in a concurring opinion that there probably was a national consensus against executing juveniles under 16. But she voted with the majority only because Oklahoma's death penalty statute had no minimum age. Because Oklahoma may have enacted its death penalty without considering whether juveniles under 16 should be executed, she sided with the majority.

The following year, the Supreme Court considered whether juveniles under 18 could be executed. Two similar cases presented themselves to the court.

One involved a 17 year old (*Stanford v. Kentucky*) and the other a 16 year old (*Wilkins v. Missouri*). Both had brutally murdered victims of their crimes because they wanted to leave no witnesses.

This time the Supreme Court upheld both convictions in 5-to-4 votes. The majority, including Justice O'Connor, argued that the nation had not reached a consensus against executing 16 or 17 year olds. So executing them did not constitute cruel and unusual punishment. In a separate concurring opinion, O'Connor stated this lack of a national consensus made irrelevant the fact that Missouri did not have a minimum age for executions.

The four dissenting justices in an opinion by Justice Brennan made two basic arguments. First, a majority of states and the federal government banned executions of those under 18 and most juries refuse to sentence those under 18 to death. This should add up to a national consensus against executing those under 18. Second, the death penalty is too severe for juveniles—it serves neither retribution nor deterrence.

For Discussion

1. Do you agree with the Supreme Court's decision in Wayne Thompson's case? Why or why not?

2. Do you agree with its decisions in *Wilkins* and *Stanford*? Why or why not?

3. Justice O'Connor cast the crucial swing vote in all three cases. What do you think of her reasoning in these cases?

4. Wayne Thompson was not set free by the Supreme Court's decision. He will now probably serve a life sentence in prison. Many argue that a life sentence is worse than the death penalty. Do you agree? Do you think courts should be allowed to send juveniles to prison for life? Explain.

Class Activity: Should Juveniles Convicted of Murder Be Executed?

1. Have students form a single line in the room according to how they feel about this question:

Should juveniles convicted of murder be executed? Make one end of the room mark the spot for those who believe the death penalty is absolutely right for juveniles convicted of murder. The other end marks the spot for those who believe the death penalty is absolutely wrong for juveniles. The stronger that people feel one way or the other, the closer they should be to the ends of the line. Those unsure of their opinion belong in the middle. In a class of 26 students, for example, the line could look like this:

•absolutely wrong   absolutely right•

ABCDEFGHIJKLMNOPQRSTUVWXYZ

2. While they are standing in line, ask students to pair up with a person next to them in line and share three reasons for their opinions.

3. As indicated by the diagram below, divide the line in half and move students on one half of the line so that they face students in the other half of the line. In this manner, students with strong positions (A B C, X Y Z) should be facing students with moderate positions (K L M, N O P).

A B C D E F G H I J K L M

N O P Q R S T U V W X Y Z

4. With the lines parallel, each student now faces a partner with a vastly different opinion, e.g. A-N.

CRIME BEAT

Imagine you are a crime beat reporter for a local news outlet. Your editor has assigned you to do background research for a feature article on capital punishment for juveniles. Find out if your state has capital punishment. If it does, does it allow juveniles to be executed? Find out the age restrictions on capital punishment.

Submit a one-page summary of your findings.

For ideas on sources for this information, see "Crime Beat" on page 31.

Partners are to exchange opinions with each other. One partner starts speaking. When the first one finishes, the other partner must paraphrase what the speaker said. If the paraphrase is not right, then the speaker should explain again until the partner gets it right. Then the other partner may speak. The partners can go back and forth, but each time they must correctly paraphrase what the other said.

Debriefing Questions

1. Did you find it difficult to paraphrase the other person's opinions? Why or why not?

2. Which reasons did you find most persuasive? Least persuasive? Why?

Current Trends and Controversies

Over the years, reformers have focused on different issues in the juvenile justice system. During the 1960s and early 1970s, advocates pushed for due-process rights for juveniles. The U.S. Supreme Court responded with its *Gault* decision, which declared juveniles did have these rights. Subsequent court decisions and much state legislation further defined juveniles' rights.

Beginning in the early 1970s, reformers turned their focus on detention issues, particularly on restricting who could be in secure lockups. The Juvenile Justice and Delinquency Act of 1974 and its subsequent amendments achieved two major reforms of detention. It outlawed placing status offenders in secure detention, and it mandated separate facilities for adults and juveniles.

The late 1970s and 1980s brought a public demand in many states to get tough on juvenile offenders. Some jurisdictions resisted. Many states, however, started locking up juveniles in record numbers. From 1978 to 1988 the arrest rate for juveniles fell 19 percent, but the incarceration rate of juveniles increased almost 50 percent. In 1989, the violent-crime arrest rate for juveniles shot up. The violent crime wave has prompted some to urge even more harsh sentences on juveniles. Others believe that the crime wave proves that punishment has not worked. They urge a

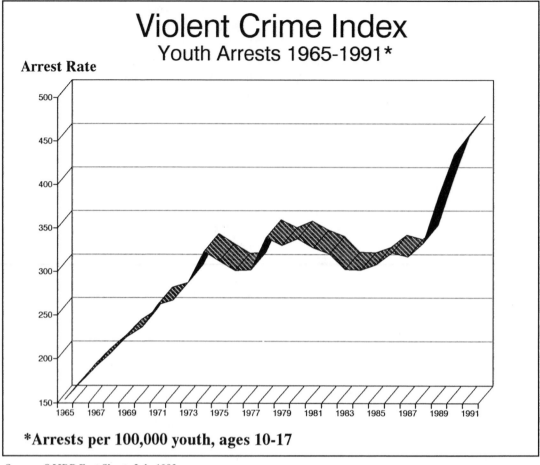

Violent Crime Index
Youth Arrests 1965-1991*

Arrest Rate

500	
450	
400	
350	
300	
250	
200	
150	

1965 1967 1969 1971 1973 1975 1977 1979 1981 1983 1985 1987 1989 1991

*Arrests per 100,000 youth, ages 10-17

Source: OJJDP Fact Sheet, July 1993.

return to the traditional model of rehabilitation for juvenile offenders.

The high detention rates have given rise to another controversy. Today, the overwhelming majority of juveniles in detention are minorities. Although African-Americans make up only 12 percent of the general population, they make up about 44 percent of the juveniles in custody. Only 35 percent of those in custody are white. Blacks do not commit more crimes than whites. The number of whites arrested far surpasses the number of blacks arrested. But as they make their way through the juvenile justice system, blacks tend to stay in the system and end up in custody. Whites tend to get out of the system and not be placed in custody.

So the controversy arises: Does the juvenile justice system unfairly discriminate against minorities, particularly African-American youths?

Many experts believe that racial discrimination does not cause black youth to remain longer in the system. They point to two separate studies which have shown that black judges are more likely than white judges to keep a black juvenile in custody. They believe that social class rather than race explains why blacks stay in the system. Most of the blacks caught in the system come from poor inner-city neighborhoods. Most of the whites come from a middle-class background. If a middle-class white juvenile gets into trouble, the parents may get a lawyer and a psychologist to help. They will come to court with a plan of action. On the other hand, an inner-city juvenile may only have an overworked public defender, who probably will meet the juvenile just before the hearing. This juvenile has limited access to social services, community agencies, or psychologists. And the juvenile's neighborhood may be filled with gangs and drug traffickers. What is the best interest of each child? Given each juveniles' resources, a judge might find it better to let the middle-class juvenile stay at home and better to send the inner-city offender to a detention facility which offers some social services. So social class rather than race may explain the different treatment of whites and blacks.

Other experts disagree. They say that while class may account for some of the disparity, racism also plays a role. The juvenile justice system allows decision makers wide discretion at every stage of the juvenile justice process. Racism, they argue, can easily creep into such a system.

The Office of Juvenile Justice and Delinquency Prevention commissioned a project to examine all the existing research about race in the juvenile justice system. In 1992, the project issued a report concluding that "there is substantial support for the statement that there are race effects in operation within the juvenile justice system, both direct and indirect in nature." By "race effects," the project meant that race explains why blacks remain in the system.

In 1989, Congress amended the Juvenile Justice and Delinquency Act. It required states to examine why so many minorities were in their lockups. States will have to justify any over-representation of minorities at every stage of their juvenile justice systems.

One final controversy should be mentioned. It's one that has plagued the system from its beginning: What should be done with status offenders? Although status offenders have been removed from locked facilities, some still pass through the juvenile justice system along with more serious offenders. Current debate arises over whether status offenders belong in the juvenile justice system at all. Many experts believe status offenders should be treated as cases of abuse or neglect—not as offenders. They argue that the court should turn its control of status offenders over to welfare agencies, private charities, and counseling centers.

For Discussion

1. Do you think the juvenile justice system should focus on rehabilitation or punishment? Why?

2. How do you account for the great number of minority youth in detention? What do you think can be done about it? Explain.

3. Should status offenders be treated as offenders or as cases of abuse and neglect? Why?

Class Activity: What Should Be Done?

Write a brief essay either supporting or opposing the following statement: *Instead of trying to rehabilitate serious offenders, the juvenile justice system should impose longer sentences to keep them off the streets.*

SOLUTIONS

Crime affects all of us. Even if we aren't touched directly, we pay extra for insurance, we worry about the safety of our family and friends, and we worry about where we can walk safely. Americans regularly list crime as one of their top concerns. Billions of dollars are lost every year to criminals, and billions more are spent in the fight against crime.

One major problem in finding solutions to crime comes from basic disagreements over its causes. Sociologists, criminologists, politicians, and ordinary citizens often debate the issue. We begin this unit with an examination of some of the debates about the causes of crime.

We will then turn to an examination of the role government plays in combating crime. You have already seen examples of the direct role played by the police, prosecutors, courts, and correctional systems in dealing with criminals. We will examine our government's crucial role in determining policies to reduce crime. We will take a look at the executive, legislative, and judicial branches throughout our federal system. In our examination, we will discuss the debate over whether our criminal justice system, in its battle against crime, discriminates against minority groups.

Finally, we will address the role ordinary citizens can play in fighting crime. We will explore both negative and positive actions citizens have taken to guard their communities—from vigilante action to neighborhood watch groups. Then you will get a chance to form a citizen task force and make practical proposals for reducing crime.

The problem of crime is complex. Every theory and every proposed solution raises fundamental ethical, political, and economic questions. These questions must be squarely faced if America is to make any progress in its battle against crime.

THE CAUSES OF CRIME

Theories and Approaches

Americans worry about crime, and violent-crime statistics back up these fears. They show that the United States' rate of violent crime far surpasses that of any Western democracy. The city of New York, population 7 million, has more murders each year than the entire nation of Italy, population 58 million. Homicide is the second leading cause of death for Americans age 15 to 30.

Looking at these statistics, doctors at the U.S. Centers for Disease Control have called violent crime an epidemic in the United States. Along with many others, they seek measures to deal with this problem. By examining the causes of crime and violence, they believe individuals, communi-

ties, and the nation can take action to stem the tide of violence in our society.

What then are the causes of crime? There is no easy answer. Some people have argued that all crime comes from inborn traits. Others have insisted that it comes from poverty, discrimination, lack of hope, or the breakdown of family values. Still others have contended that crime comes from personalities warped by drugs, disease, or childhood abuse. The list of possible causes can go on and on.

While few people today would argue crime has but one cause, people still emphasize one factor over another. And they debate whether one factor is a cause or effect of another. The diagram below charts some of the most commonly cited causes of crime. For convenience, we have put them into two groups—(1) social and cultural factors and (2) individual and situational factors. Study the diagram and read the accompanying statements about the various factors.

NUMBER *of* HOMICIDES IN U.S. CITIES AND IN
INTERNATIONAL CITIES *of* COMPARABLE SIZE, *1988*

Population	City	Number of Homicides
		U.S.A/Denmark
470,000	Atlanta	186
	Copenhagen	18
290,000	Tampa	79
	Aarhus	1
235,000	Santa Ana, Calif.	32
	Odensen	3
200,000	Mobile	47
	Aalborg	0
		U.S.A./France
2 million	Houston	408
	Paris	156
800,000	Baltimore	240
	Lyon	66
375,000	Tulsa	40
	Toulouse	10
350,000	Charlotte, N.C.	53
	Nice	21
320,000	Newark, N.J.	113
	Nantes	12
		U.S.A/Great Britain
7 million	New York	1,582
	London	67
863,000	San Antonio	162
	Birmingham	31
730,000	San Francisco	114
	Leeds	22
540,000	Cleveland	124
	Liverpool	14
400,000	Miami	148
	Manchester	16
380,000	Tucson	41
	Bristol	11
282,000	Birmingham	88
	New Castle	8
229,000	Anchorage	17
	Barsley	3
		U.S.A./Japan
7 million	New York	1,582
	Tokyo	111
1 million	Dallas	347
	Hiroshima	14
725,000	San Jose	39
	Chiba	9
500,000	Indianapolis	63
	Amagasaki	11
450,000	Kansas City	116
	Funabashi	5

Source: *The Police Chief*, March 1988, pp. 36-37.

Social and Cultural Factors

Social problems—such as poverty, unemployment, racial discrimination, and child abuse—and cultural influences—such as American values and violence on television—are often mentioned as causes of crime. They do not cause crime in any direct sense. The vast majority of poor people, for example, remain law-abiding all their lives. But these factors may make it more likely that some people turn to crime. In this section, we will examine some of these social and cultural factors.

Poverty and Unemployment

Many people believe that poverty contributes to the crime rate. Statistics do show much higher rates of crime in poor communities. You only have to drive through a high-poverty area and look at the barred windows and security doors to know that the people who live there worry about crime.

In the 1980s, the crime rate started declining. Many criminologists had predicted the decline because the average age of the population was getting older. Since young people commit the bulk of crime, criminologists predicted the crime rate would continue to decline throughout the '80s. But according to the Uniform Crime Reports, in 1984 it started to rise again. Why? Some experts pointed to the increasing rate of poverty. Over the decade, the number of children living below the poverty level went up 21 percent. Many of these children lived in working families, but it was no longer possible to live above the poverty level on minimum wage. The minimum wage, adjusted for inflation, declined 20 percent over the decade.

One of the great causes of poverty, of course, is lack of jobs. Over the 1980s, the unemployment rate went from about 4 percent to about 8 percent. And far worse for poor communities, there were structural changes in the American economy that completely eliminated 2.6 million industrial jobs. In 1970, Los Angeles, for example, was home to industrial plants representing all the major car makers, all the major tire makers, many steel and aluminum companies, and other industries as well. By the early 1990s, they were all gone—either closed or moved to the South or overseas—leaving only aerospace factories. The story is similar in America's "rust belt," the industrial Northeast, where many jobs have also been moved to the South, overseas, or eliminated.

THE PROBLEM: UNEMPLOYED, UNSKILLED, UNEDUCATED, UNMOTIVATED.

THE SOLUTION: BUILD MORE PRISONS.

...BECAUSE SOONER OR LATER, HE'S GOING TO TURN TO DRUGS.

(Kirk Anderson cartoon reprinted with permission.)

Some social scientists have found a direct relationship between joblessness and crime and other social problems. A detailed long-term study by Dr. Harvey Brenner of Johns Hopkins University found that for every 1 percent increase in the unemployment rate, the United States sees:

- 650 extra homicides
- 3,300 extra state prison admissions
- 920 extra suicides
- 500 extra deaths from alcoholism.

Racial Discrimination

What happens to a dream deferred?
Does it dry up
Like a raisin in the sun? . . .
Or does it explode?
    —Langston Hughes

Many people believe America's crime problem stems, in part, from its race problems. Unemployment is highest in minority communities and particularly among young African-Americans and Latinos. One third of all poor children in the country are black, and the poverty rate grew faster for Latinos over the 1980s than for any other group. Almost 45 percent of all black children grow up below the poverty line, compared to 16 percent of white children.

Many criminologists believe that much street crime grows from these high levels of unemployment and poverty. Despair and hopelessness gives rise to crime in these communities. Black males are six times more likely to die from homicide than white males. Crime statistics show that blacks now account for about 60 percent of all robbery arrests.

In fact, statistics show an overrepresentation of African-Americans in all stages of the criminal justice system. Although only 12 percent of the population, African-Americans make up about 30 percent of those arrested for crimes. They make up about 40 percent of those convicted of serious crimes in state courts. And they constitute more than half of all state prisoners. Their rate of incarceration is truly staggering. The United States, which has the world's highest incarceration rate, locks up 455 of every 100,000 people. But it locks up 3,370 of every 100,000 African-Americans.

Child Abuse and Neglect

The family is usually the greatest single influence on a person's life. In a family, we learn how to behave, how to treat other people, and how to view ourselves. Children can be very sensitive to cruelty or lack of affection, which can create anti-social habits or serious mental problems. Some of these problems may not even show up until much later, as the child grows. Many sociologists believe that parents who abuse their children start a cycle of abuse from generation to generation. Abused children often grow up to abuse their children.

In a carefully controlled scientific study reported in *Science* magazine, sociologists found that neglected children were one and one-half more times as likely to commit violent crimes later in life than non-neglected children. Abused children were twice as likely to become violent criminals. Abused children are also six times as likely to abuse their own children. The study concluded that the abusive family was one place where society should try to break the continuing cycle of violence. Neglect and abuse within a family can lay the roots for a life of violent crime.

The number of reported child-abuse cases more than tripled over the 1980s and early 1990s. Some of this increase may have come from renewed attention to the problem and better reporting. But we have now reached the point where more than one American family in 100 has seen some instance of abuse serious enough to be reported to the police. Many cases of abuse undoubtedly never get reported. In New York City alone, more than 100 children die of abuse every year.

Juvenile crime statistics show that teen-age boys who were abused as children are two to three times more likely to turn to crime than other boys of the same age. Some social scientists insist that almost all career criminals, particularly those involved in crimes of violence, were abused as children. Gregory Boyle, a priest who has worked for years in the Los Angeles Latino community, sat down one day to make a random list of the gang kids he knew.

"I didn't stack the deck," he explained. "I just wrote down 67 names sort of stream-of-consciousness." Then he assigned codes to the names to represent an absent father, an abusive father, an alcoholic and abusive father, or an intact family. Only three had intact families. Sixty-four of the 67 gang kids had abusive or absent fathers.

Values That Make Crime More Acceptable

Many people believe that Americans hold certain values or beliefs that may encourage criminal conduct. One such value might be our **love of material goods**. Judging by our mass media, our society seems to place a high value on owning new things. In fact, the cumulative message of most advertising is that happiness only comes from having things. Wealth and material possessions translate into status or position in society. Thus people often want things they cannot afford to buy and some people may steal and rob for this reason.

Another value or belief that some claim affects America's crime rate is the idea that **violence is acceptable** and even admirable. Part of American folklore is the hero who fights criminals. Our movies and television programs often show sheriffs, police officers, and cowboys using guns and violence to combat the violence of criminals. Similarly, such programs may show people committing violent acts. This does not mean that individual Americans favor the use of violence. Rather, it means that Americans may view violence as a normal part of life. Some people believe that this idea may encourage criminal behavior.

Finally, some people have connected our crime problem to the **decline of traditional family values**. They argue that many of our social problems, including crime, stem from the rise of **permissiveness** and the **breakdown of religion**. Permissiveness means being tolerant of a wide range of behavior, especially among children, and of avoiding judgment about the acceptability of others' behavior. Some people believe that permissiveness may encourage toleration of any behavior, even criminal behavior.

Movies and Television

The American Psychological Association says that by the seventh grade, the average American will have watched on television 8,000 murders, plus another 100,000 acts of violence. Does watching this much violence make Americans more prone to violence? In 1972, the U.S. Surgeon General, the highest medical officer in the federal government, announced that "televised violence, indeed, does have an adverse effect on certain members of our society."

In the years that followed, the National Institute of Mental Health, the Department of Justice, the American Academy of Pediatrics, and numerous scientific studies have backed up the words of the Surgeon General. Many social scientists have concluded that televised violence can contribute to antisocial behavior in children. This is particularly true when the children come from violent homes or neighborhoods. It adds to the culture of violence surrounding them. After a five-year study, the American Psychological Association reported in February 1992 that "TV violence can cause aggressive behavior and can cultivate values favoring the use of aggression to resolve conflicts."

The association has set up a Commission on Violence and Youth. Its chairman, Leonard Eron, has claimed that the "single best predictor of how aggressive a young man would be when he was 19 years old was the violence of the television programs he preferred when he was 8 years old."

But defenders of the television industry point to a research study of over 3,000 subjects conducted over a three-year period in the early 1970s. It found no connection between viewing of violence on television and violent behavior. Television programmers contend that television simply reflects the level of violence in society. It does nothing to cause the violence. The causes of violence, they insist, are rooted in various social problems such as increasing poverty and unemployment. Violence in entertainment, as they see it, is being made a scapegoat for society's problems.

Advocacy organizations have been fighting for years to limit violence in the media. Despite the industry's denial of any blame, the major networks agreed in the early 1990s to cut back on the amount of violence shown and to put warnings on violent programs. But the networks are no longer the only players in the TV game. With the growth of cable television, home video, and video games, far more violent material is now available to children.

And the violence seems to be escalating. The 1988 movie "Die Hard," for example, had 18 murders. Its sequel, "Die Hard 2," had 264. Violence also has crept into song lyrics, which often describe murders, suicides, and rapes.

The question of violence in the arts has now become a battleground between those who insist on First Amendment free-speech rights and those who insist the question is really one of corporate responsibility.

For Discussion

1. Which do you think are the most important cultural or social factors that contribute to crime? Which are the least important? Why?

2. Which factors are most difficult to change? Which are the easiest?

3. If all murderers drank milk as children, does this prove drinking milk leads to murder? Explain.

Individual and Situational Factors

Another approach to studying crime is to focus on the individual and on situational factors. Crimes, after all, are committed by particular individuals in particular situations. Are some individuals more likely to commit crimes? Do crimes arise more often in certain situations? Scientists looking at individuals have looked at many possible causes of crime, including such diverse causes as biology and rational choice. Other scientists looking for situational factors in crime have studied guns, alcohol, and drugs. In this section, we will examine some of these individual and situational factors.

Biology

Are some people born criminals?

In the 1800s, several Italian criminologists thought that some people were born criminals and that they could be identified by ears that stuck out, big noses, and crooked faces. At about the same time, criminologists in France tried to build a science called **phrenology**, based on the shapes of peoples' heads. They felt that criminals could be identified by the shapes and positions of bumps on their heads. These theories, identifying criminals by certain physical features, have been completely discredited. In the mid-l960s, however, a similar theory about people with a genetic defect sparked a long-running controversy.

In 1965, researchers at a Scottish prison hospital discovered that an unusual number of inmates had a genetic abnormality. A normal male has an X chromosome and a Y chromosome in each cell in his body. Some of the Scottish prisoners had an extra Y chromosome, so the abnormality was called the **XYY Syndrome**. Individuals with this XYY Syndrome often grew exceptionally tall and developed bad acne in their teen-age years. The researchers developed a theory of a "super-male" with inborn violent tendencies.

A few other prison studies seemed to confirm the theory, though there were still only tiny numbers of XYY individuals involved—nine out of 340 in the original Scottish study. Further studies in the general population, however, have tended to discredit the theory. XYY individuals were observed from birth over a long period of time, and there was very little statistical variance from normal rates of criminal behavior.

Not all criminologists have given up on linking biology and criminal behavior. Some believe that **sociobiology** holds much promise. Sociobiologists do not think there is any "criminal gene." They don't believe that people are born criminals. But they do believe that some people are born with biological traits predisposing them to crime. These people, according to the theory, will not become criminals unless they are brought up under harmful social conditions.

Professors Richard J. Herrnstein and James Q. Wilson, proponents of sociobiology, cite various studies. Studies of twins show that identical twins are much more likely than fraternal twins to have the same criminal records. Unlike fraternal twins, identical twins share the same genetic makeup. So these studies seem to indicate biology plays a role in criminality.

Even more startling are two studies of thousands of adopted boys. The studies compared two groups. In the first group were boys raised by non-criminal adopted parents but whose natural parents were criminals. The second group was exactly the opposite: It had boys raised by criminal adopted parents but whose natural parents were not criminals. Most people would think that the boys in the second group—raised by criminal parents—would be more likely to commit crimes. But the studies found otherwise. The boys in the first group were more likely to have criminal records. In addition, the more criminal convictions that a boy's natural parents had, the more likely a boy raised by non-criminal parents would have a criminal record.

Herrnstein and Wilson point out several biological traits that predispose a person to crime. The first is simply being male. In all known societies, young males account for almost all violent crimes. Experiments have shown male sex hormones increase aggression. Young males often have some trouble adjusting to the hormones. Many engage in rowdy behavior. Some commit crimes.

A second biological trait, according to Herrnstein and Wilson, is intelligence. Studies have shown that criminals generally score low on intelligence tests. It isn't really known why low intelligence and crime are related. One theory is that people with low intelligence may get frustrated with school, grow angry and resentful, and start committing delinquent acts.

Another biological trait, according to Herrnstein and Wilson, is temperament. They point out that high-rate offenders typically are impulsive, rebellious thrill-seekers. To some extent, these characteristics may be inherited.

Sociobiology is very controversial. Critics cast doubt on the twin and adoption studies. They criticize classifying intelligence and temperament as biological traits—these are learned traits. But the critics are far less harsh on Herrnstein and Wilson's prescription for change:

"We know that a very small fraction of all young males commit so large a fraction of serious street crime that we can properly blame these chronic offenders for most such crime. We also know that chronic offenders typically begin their misconduct at an early age. Early family and preschool programs may be far better repositories for the crime-prevention dollar than rehabilitation programs aimed—usually futilely—at the 19-or 20-year-old veteran offender."

Drugs and Alcohol

Thirty-five percent of state prison inmates report they were under the influence of drugs when they committed their crimes. Over 40 percent admit to using drugs every day for the 30 days prior to their convictions. But drugs are not the only substance linked to crime. About half of all persons convicted of violent crimes drank alcohol shortly before committing their crime. Two-thirds of all homicides involve people who have been drinking. And 50 percent of all inmates report drinking at least one ounce of alcohol each day. This compares with 10 percent in the general population.

The connection between crime and alcohol has long been noted. What to do about it is another question. Reformers at the turn of the century managed to pass the 18th Amendment to the Constitution. Effective in January 1920, it banned the sale and distribution of alcohol. But this amendment and laws supporting it were vastly unpopular. People flaunted the law and continued drinking. Gangsters grew rich smuggling and distributing alcohol. In 1933, the 21st Amendment repealed the ill-fated 18th, and alcohol has remained legal in most of the country ever since.

Guns

In the United States each year, handguns are used in about 35 percent of all robberies and in about half of all homicides. Some criminologists tie the easy access to guns, particularly handguns, to America's high rate of violent crime.

(c. 1993, The Washington Post Writers Group. Reprinted with permission.)

Indeed, guns and gun ownership are very common in the United States—far more so than in other democracies, which have stricter gun laws. Social analysts have noted that historically Americans needed guns to survive on the frontier. In more recent years, increases in violent crime, especially in urban areas, have caused millions of Americans to believe that they cannot rely on police protection alone. In national opinion polls, about 40 percent of all households report owning at least one firearm. Experts claim 13,500 of every 100,000 Americans own handguns. As a comparison, the rate per 100,000 in Canada is 3,000, and in Great Britain, under 500. (In Great Britain, which has a very low murder rate, even the police do not normally carry guns.)

The federal government has enacted two major nationwide gun laws. In 1934, it prohibited the possession of machine guns, sawed-off shotguns, and silencers. The Gun Control Act of 1968 limited the importation of cheap handguns, known as Saturday Night Specials, and prohibited the interstate sale of handguns. Otherwise the federal government has basically left the control of guns to states and cities.

The result has been a maze of gun laws varying from jurisdiction to jurisdiction through-out the United States. Most of the laws regulate carrying concealed weapons, transporting firearms, and firing guns within city limits. Others bar gun ownership to convicted felons and the mentally ill. Gun-ownership laws rarely require people to give reasons for purchasing any type of gun. Some cities and states allow nearly unre-stricted purchase and ownership of handguns.

A few states, like New York, have registra-tion and licensing laws that require waiting periods and extensive background checks. Others, like California, have banned the sale of certain kinds of military assault weapons. In 1977, Washington, D.C., in effect banned the sale, pos-session, and manufacture of handguns in the city. There are strong opponents to such laws.

The two main opponents of gun-control laws in the United States are the National Rifle Association and the gun industry. The National Rifle Association represents over 3 million

Guns seized by New York police in a raid of a Bronx social club. (AP/Wide World Photos.)

hunters and gun enthusiasts. The gun industry earns over $2 billion annually. Together they have managed to block much state, local, and national legislation imposing controls on guns.

They cite various reasons for opposing gun control. Their arguments include:

- Gun control impinges on a basic right of all Americans—the right to protect themselves. This right is so important that the Second Amendment to the Constitution guarantees the right to bear arms.

- With our society's high rate of violence and lack of adequate policing, guns offer citizens protection.

- Gun-control laws will only take guns away from law-abiding citizens, because criminals will always find ways of getting guns or other weapons. New York and Washington, D.C.—jurisdictions with strong gun-control laws—have the worst murder rates in the country.

- Instead of penalizing ordinary citizens, the proper way to keep criminals from using guns is to impose harsher penalties on crimi-nals who use them.

Advocates of different gun-control measures might respond as follows:

- The Supreme Court's only significant ruling on the Second Amendment held that the amendment does not give an individual a right to own a gun. It guarantees a state's right to maintain a militia.

- Guns are far more likely to harm members of the owner's household than offer protection against criminals.

- Most of the crimes committed with guns in New York and Washington, D.C., are committed with guns bought in nearby states with lax gun laws.

- We already impose mandatory sentences on criminals using guns. These sentences haven't stopped gun violence. Powerful new handguns, capable of firing many rounds in a minute, are reaching the streets. We must enact national gun laws to control these dangerous weapons.

Both sides cite studies and cases to bolster their arguments. Opponents of gun control, for example, refer to a 1993 study in the *Journal of Quantitative Criminology*. The study found that those who defend themselves with a gun during a robbery attempt are less likely to be injured than those who are unarmed. Some opponents of gun control point to the experience of one small city—Kennesaw, Georgia. In 1982, it took the step of requiring gun ownership of every citizen, except minors, the mentally ill, convicted felons, and conscientious objectors. The city, about 20 miles northwest of Atlanta, has since grown from about 5,000 to over 10,000 inhabitants, but crime in the city has decreased. Many of the city's citizens believe crime has gone down because criminals know their would-be victims have guns.

Advocates of gun control look to the experience of Canada, which has severely restricted handgun ownership. Its national law has required permits to own handguns since 1921. Authorities grant registration certificates only for specific reasons, such as target practice at a shooting range or to protect life. Possessing a handgun without a registration certificate can result in a prison term of up to five years. In November 1978, Canada declared a one-month amnesty for persons to turn in illegally held firearms. Nearly 50,000 guns were surrendered.

In 1988, the *New England Journal of Medicine* published a comparative study of a Canadian city, Vancouver, and an American city, Seattle, which are about 100 miles apart. The risk of being murdered by a handgun was almost five times higher in Seattle. And a person assaulted in Seattle was twice as likely to die as a person assaulted in Vancouver.

The debate over gun control goes on and on. Most researchers agree that guns are a factor in American homicides. But they also agree that more proof is needed to determine whether stricter gun-control laws would reduce the number of homicides.

Rational Choice

Many people believe crime involves rational choice on the part of criminals. This theory takes various forms.

In its simplest form, this theory means that people choose to become criminals. People make some sort of cost-benefit analysis before committing crimes. They calculate the benefits—these could be economic gain, the thrill of committing the crime, or any pleasure they could derive from the crime. They weigh the benefits against the costs. These could be the risk of getting caught, the harshness of punishment, pangs of conscience, or any pain they could receive from the criminal act. If the benefits outweigh the costs, then they will commit the crime.

After making a cost-benefit analysis, certain people would be more likely to choose to commit crimes. Poor people would have more to gain than rich people. **Psychopaths**—people without consciences—would feel freer to commit crimes than most people.

Another form of rational-choice theory does not attempt to explain why people become criminals. It simply notes that criminals act rationally in one sense at least: *Most do not want to get caught.* This means that criminals will most often take the easiest path to commit a crime and may be deterred if something stands in their way. Thus car thieves prefer an unlocked car to a locked car, a car without an alarm to one with an alarm, and an empty car to

THE TWELVE TECHNIQUES OF SITUATIONAL PREVENTION

INCREASING THE EFFORT	INCREASING THE RISKS	REDUCING THE REWARDS
Target Hardening	*Entry/Exit Screening*	*Target Removal*
Steering Locks	Border searches	Removable car radio
Bandits screens	Baggage screening	Exact change fares
Slug rejector device	Automatic ticket gates	Cash reduction
Vandal-proofing	Merchandise tags	Remove coin meters
Toughened glass	Library tags	Phone card
Tamper-proof seals	EPoS	Pay by check
Access Control	*Entry/Exit Screening*	*Identifying Property*
Locket gates	Police patrols	Cattle branding
Fenced yards	Security guards	Property marking
Parking lot barriers	Informant hotlines	Vehicle licensing
Entry phones	burglar alarms	Vehicle parts marking
ID badges	Red light cameras	PIN for car radios
PIN numbers	Curfew decals	LOJACK
Deflecting Offenders	*Surveillance by Employees*	*Removing Inducements*
Bus stop placement		Graffiti cleaning
Tavern location	Bus conductors	Rapid repair
Street closures	Park attendants	Plywood radio signs
Graffiti board	Concierges	Gender-neutral phone lists
Litter bins	Pay phone location	Park Camarro off street
Spittoons	Incentive schemes	
	CCTV systems	
Controlling Facilitators	*Natural Surveillance*	*Rule setting*
Spray-can sales	Pruning hedges	Drug-free school zone
Gun control	"Eye on the street"	Public park regulations
Credit card photo	Lighting bank interiors	customs declaration
Ignition interlock	Street lighting	Income tax returns
Server intervention	Defensible space	Hotel registration
Caller-ID	Neighborhood Watch	Library check-out

(Source: Roland V. Clarke, *Situational Crime Prevention: Succesful Case Studies.*
New York: Harrow and Heston, 1992, p. 13. Reprinted by permission.)

one with a person in it. This logic applies to many crimes. Robbers, for example, seem to prefer lone victims. The risk of being robbed increases tenfold when a person is alone.

According to this theory, the way to cut crime is to make it more difficult, more risky, and less rewarding for the criminal. This can be done in many ways—stronger locks, increased police patrols, fewer people carrying cash, etc. The chart on the opposite page lists quite a few techniques.

The question is: Do these techniques reduce crime or do they merely displace it? What happens, for example, if we make cars difficult to steal by equipping them with anti-theft devices? Will car thieves, frustrated with not being able to break into cars, turn to the violent crime of car-jacking—stealing cars at gunpoint? Or, will they turn to a different kind of stealing, such as committing daytime burglaries? Or, will they stop committing crimes? Researchers have not conclusively answered these questions.

For Discussion

1. Which do you think are the most important individual or situational factors that contribute to crime? Which are the least important? Why?

2. Which factors are most difficult to change? Which are the easiest?

3. Which of all the theories discussed do you think is most important? Which is least important? Why?

4. What additional factors do you think contribute to crime?

5. If scientists were to find that red-haired people commit twice as much crime as other people, what could be done to prevent this crime without violating the constitutional rights of redheads?

6. White-collar crimes are often committed by employed, well-educated people from good family backgrounds. If they don't need money, why would such people commit fraud or embezzlement?

Class Activity: The Causes of Crime

Divide the class into groups of four members each. Each group should:

1. Discuss the various causes of crime and select the one cause it considers most important.

2. Brainstorm solutions to crime, based on the cause it has chosen.

3. Discuss the solutions it comes up with and choose its best solution.

4. Discuss the costs and benefits of this solution.

5. Prepare a brief presentation for the class on the solution.

Reconvene as a class. Have each group make a brief presentation supporting its solution. List the solutions on the board. Hold a class discussion using the following debriefing questions:

- Which causes seemed easier to find solutions for? Why?
- Which solutions would be easiest to put into effect? Why?
- Which solutions do you think would work best? Why?

Take a class vote on which solution it believes is best.

CRIME AND THE GOVERNMENT

The Role of Government

W e Americans often look to government to solve our problems, and the problem of crime is no exception. Politicians, from presidents to mayors, are elected, evaluated, and replaced on the basis of how well they meet our expectations. Political campaigns often center on promises or proposals for reducing crime, yet the problem remains. What *can* government do to help solve America's crime problem?

In this section, we will examine some of the ways government tries to solve the crime problem. First, we take a look at the federal level, with a general overview of the executive, legislative, and judicial branches of government. Then we will focus on a particular federal policy—civil forfeiture. Later in the section, we turn to the state level, take a brief overview of the three branches of state government, and then concentrate on the legislative process of enacting anti-crime laws.

Crime and the Federal Government

The U.S. Constitution divides the power of government into three distinct branches—the executive, legislative, and judicial. The Constitution then lays out the responsibilities and

powers of each branch. All three branches have responsibilities in addressing the crime problem.

The Executive Branch

As head of the executive branch, the president is responsible for enforcing federal laws. Article II, Section 3 of the Constitution holds that the president "shall take care that the laws be faithfully executed." One way that the president exercises this power is by supervising executive agencies and departments, particularly the Department of Justice, headed by the attorney general.

Five main agencies handle most federal investigations:

- The Federal Bureau of Investigation
- The Drug Enforcement Administration
- The Secret Service
- The Postal Inspection Service
- The Bureau of Alcohol, Tobacco, and Firearms.

In addition to the big five, there are many other federal agencies with investigative powers: the Customs Service, the Internal Revenue Service, the Food and Drug Administration, the Immigration and Naturalization Service, and the Securities and Exchange Commission. Most of these agencies can investigate lawbreaking, collect evidence, make arrests, and present cases to federal prosecutors.

Federal cases are prosecuted by the Department of Justice and by its U.S. attorneys throughout the country. U.S. attorneys are appointed by the president.

The Legislative Branch

The Constitution outlines the powers of the U.S. Congress. In the area of criminal justice, Congress makes laws that define federal crimes and set punishments. Some of these laws were made to meet the specific requirements of Section 8 of the Constitution which says that Congress must control America's postal services, mints, revenues, and taxes. To carry out these responsibilities, Congress has passed laws against tampering with the mail, counterfeiting coins, or smuggling. Congress has also passed statutes that outlaw spying and espionage against the United States. And Congress has used its powers over commerce to make laws against carrying stolen goods across state lines or kidnapping. These are all federal crimes.

Congress also makes laws for those parts of the country that do not fall under the jurisdiction of a state government. Some of these are the District of Columbia, federal forests, military bases, post offices, federal courts, and ships at sea or airplanes in the air. In most areas, however, the bulk of the criminal laws are made by state and local legislatures, because the framers of the Constitution did not want all lawmaking power centralized.

Whether a specific act falls under federal or state law depends on the act and on where it is committed. For example, if John Deadly shoots and kills a man on a street in Wichita, he has committed murder and would be tried under the Kansas State Penal Code. On the other hand, if John Deadly kills a letter carrier who is out delivering mail in Wichita, he has not only committed a murder, punishable by the state of Kansas, he has also committed the federal crime of assaulting a federal employee. If he's caught, John can be tried under state law for the murder, and under federal law for the assault.

But the situation is different if John Deadly shoots and kills the letter carrier *inside* the post office. Even though it is in Kansas, the post office is considered federal territory. If John is caught,

he can be tried according to federal murder statutes.

Congress does not merely define crimes. It also passes legislation and creates agencies to study and reduce crime. The Office of Juvenile Justice and Delinquency Prevention (OJJDP) is an example of one such agency. Under congressional mandate to "improve the quality of juvenile justice in the United States," OJJDP allocates federal funds and coordinates programs to reduce juvenile delinquency and exploitation of children.

Activity: TV Quiz

Pretend you are taking part in a TV game show about crime and the U.S. Constitution. Break into teams of two before you begin.

Emcee: Good morning, ladies and gentlemen. We know that the U.S. Constitution is not a collection of criminal laws like your state's penal code, but it does make some general statements about crime. It talks about persons accused of crime and the criminal process. The back of your book on page 275 has sections of the Constitution. You'll use this in our quiz. The quiz has two parts:

Main Questions: Look through each section of the Constitution. For each section, briefly answer in writing: What does this section have to do with crime and criminal justice?

Bonus Questions (in case of a tie): The U.S. Constitution gives a precise definition of only one crime. (1) What crime is it? (2) How is it defined?

Work in your teams to follow the emcee's instructions.

Emcee: You've now all had a chance to work out your answers. Trade your paper with another team and we will mark the ones that are correctly identified. For each one identified, you will get two points. If you are tied, the tie will be broken by referring to the bonus questions. Each bonus counts five points.

The Judicial Branch

The Constitution places the power of the judicial branch in the hands of "one Supreme Court and in such inferior courts the Congress may from time to time ordain and establish." Today, the federal court system consists of three basic levels. On the lowest level are the district courts. These handle trials in the federal system. If a defendant is convicted in a trial court, the defendant may appeal to the next level of courts—the courts of appeals. There are 12 of these courts, each having jurisdiction over a particular part of the United States. On the highest level is the U.S. Supreme Court. It hears appeals from decisions of the courts of appeals. It also can hear appeals of state supreme courts' decisions on issues of U.S. constitutional law.

The U.S. Supreme Court has what is known as **discretionary jurisdiction**. This means that the court does not have to take every appeal. Parties must petition to have their appeals heard by the court. If four justices agree that the court should hear a case, then the court grants what is called a writ of certiorari, and the court will hear the appeal.

In making their decisions, appeals courts and, ultimately, the Supreme Court interpret what the Constitution and other federal laws mean. Decisions can actually overturn laws if they are seen to be in conflict with the Constitution. And decisions can also create new policies by changing the interpretation of what existing law means.

Setting Precedents

It is not just federal courts that interpret laws. Appeals courts at all levels, state and federal, must interpret the meaning of laws. Even trial courts must construe the meaning of statutes. Consider the following criminal statute, passed by the California State Legislature in 1901:

> *Every person who maliciously, forcibly or fraudulently takes or entices away any minor child with intent to detain and conceal such child from its parent, guardian or other person having the lawful charge of*

STATE
COURTS

STATE SUPREME COURT

INTERMEDIATE COURT OF APPEAL

STATE TRIAL COURT

FEDERAL
COURTS

U.S. SUPREME COURT

CIRCUIT COURT OF APPEALS

DISTRICT COURT

The federal judicial system, and most state systems, have three levels of courts.

such child, is punishable by imprisonment in the state prison not exceeding twenty years.

—California State Penal Code, Section 278

Now imagine that a woman takes her 14-year-old niece on a two-week trip to Hawaii against the wishes of the child's parents. The parents are furious and have the woman arrested for violating this law. But the woman argues at her trial that she didn't fraudulently take or entice the child to go.

A California judge must interpret the law. In this case, the judge might decide that the woman did entice the child. Though she didn't drag her niece onto the airplane forcibly, she knew that the idea of the vacation would be too good for the teen-ager to resist and she was taken fraudulently.

The judge's decision does much more than resolve this one case. It sets a **precedent**—or a general rule to follow. The next time someone is charged with child stealing in the same way, the prosecutor can refer to this judgment and ask that the new case be decided according to the precedent. If the precedent is upheld by higher courts, the judge's decisions can alter the law, just as surely as if the legislature had made a new statute to include psychological as well as physical force.

For Discussion

1. For what part of the American criminal legal process is the legislative branch of the federal government responsible? The executive branch? The judicial branch?

2. Describe two crimes that fall under the jurisdiction of federal rather than state law.

3. Explain what discretionary jurisdiction means. Why do you think the U.S. Supreme Court has this type of jurisdiction?

4. How do courts set precedents? How can precedents change the law? Do you think courts should follow precedents? Why or why not?

Federal Policy: Civil Forfeiture

Under state and federal forfeiture statutes, law enforcement officers can seize and confiscate assets used in illegal activity or derived from it. An old procedure adopted from English common law, forfeiture historically played little role in fighting crime in America. But forfeiture grew in importance during the war on drugs in the 1980s. Since drug dealing depends on high profits to survive, forfeiture laws take aim at these profits.

For example, Congress passed the Comprehensive Drug Abuse Prevention and Control Act of 1970. As amended, it now provides for the civil forfeiture of:

(1) illegal drugs;

(2) material and equipment for illegal drug manufacturing;

(3) containers for illegal drugs;

(4) vehicles for transporting illegal drugs;

(5) books and records of illegal drugs;

(6) anything of value exchanged for illegal drugs, including money or anything traceable to the exchange; and

(7) all real property used to facilitate a drug offense.

Law enforcement has increasingly turned to statutes such as this in its fight against crime. From 1985 to 1990, the amount of assets seized under federal statutes grew by over 1,500 percent. In 1990 alone, the federal Drug Enforcement Administration (DEA) seized over $1 billion in assets. The assets included:

• about $364 million in cash.

• almost $346 million in real estate.

• 5,674 vehicles valued at over $60 million.

• 187 vessels worth more than $16 million.

• 51 airplanes worth over $25 million.

More than $427 million worth of these assets was ultimately forfeited to the federal government. The forfeited assets were then either used by the DEA itself or sold and the proceeds turned over to the Department of Justice's Asset Forfeiture Fund. The fund is used for law enforcement purposes.

There are two types of forfeiture laws: criminal and civil. **Criminal forfeiture** laws apply to criminals convicted of crimes. As part of the sentence, the judge confiscates the criminal's assets that were used in the crime or that were derived from it. These laws have caused far less controversy than civil forfeiture laws.

Civil forfeiture laws work differently. If law enforcement officers have probable cause to believe that particular assets have been used in a crime, they can seize them under civil forfeiture laws. The laws are written so that the government is taking action against things, not people. Bizarre case names result: *U.S. v. One 56-Foot Motor Yacht Named Tahuna* (1983) or *U.S. v. One Parcel of Land . . . Commonly Known as 4204 Cedarwood, Matteson, IL* (1985) or *U.S. v. $321,470 in U.S. Currency* (1987).

If no one claims the assets, they are forfeited to the government. If someone does claim them, there will be a civil trial over one issue: Are the assets connected to illegal activity? If so, the property is forfeited to the government. Because the action is supposedly against the property and not against persons, many statutes do not allow claimants to argue that they knew nothing of the illegal activity.

Unlike a criminal trial, in civil forfeiture cases the government does not have to prove its case beyond a reasonable doubt. Instead, the person claiming the property must prove by a preponderance of evidence that the assets are not connected with illegal activity. This means that a defendant could be acquitted of a criminal charge but lose seized property in a civil forfeiture trial. (See *U.S. v. One 1977 Lincoln Mark V*, 1988.)

Forfeiture laws have come under harsh attack. Since law enforcement agencies often get to keep the assets they seize, they have sometimes been accused of acting overzealously. In 1992, for example, Los Angeles County Sheriff deputies shot and killed a Malibu millionaire in a drug raid

Critics claim civil forfeiture laws allow police to violate basic due process rights. (Bob Rogers cartooon reprinted by permission of UFS, Inc.)

on his 200-acre ranch. A federal agent, who had flown over the ranch at 1,000 feet, had thought he observed marijuana plants growing. Deputies obtained a warrant and raided the ranch. A thorough search of the ranch turned up no trace of drugs. The ensuing five-month district attorney investigation concluded that the raid was illegal and that one reason deputies rushed to raid the ranch was because they were anxious to confiscate the high-priced land.

Civil forfeiture laws also raise major Fifth and Eighth Amendment issues. The Eighth Amendment bans the government from imposing "excessive fines." If John smokes a marijuana cigarette at home, can law enforcement confiscate the home? Or would this be an excessive fine? According to the Fifth Amendment, the government cannot take property without due process. If Mary loans her car to Sam, who then uses it in a drug deal, can the government take away Mary's car if she knew nothing about the drug deal? Would this meet due process standards?

In 1993, the Supreme Court responded to the excessive-fines issue in *Austin v. U.S.* In June of 1990, an undercover agent entered Austin's automobile body shop in Sioux Falls, South Dakota, and asked for drugs. Austin agreed to sell him some. Austin left his body shop, went to his mobile home, and came back with two grams of cocaine. Convicted of possession of cocaine with intent to distribute, Austin was sentenced to seven years in state prison. Federal agents seized his body shop and mobile home in a civil forfeiture action. Appealing the forfeiture all the way to the U.S. Supreme Court, Austin argued that this seizure amounted to an excessive fine. The government countered that the Eighth Amendment did not apply to civil actions, only criminal actions. A unanimous Supreme Court held that the Eighth Amendment applies to any fine—civil or criminal—and that the forfeiture amounted to a fine. The court ordered lower courts to decide if Austin's fine was excessive.

The Supreme Court has not yet ruled on the constitutionality of taking assets from property owners who know nothing of any wrongdoing. Many statutes do not allow a so-called "innocent owner" defense, because the civil action is against the assets, not persons. But the court noted in *Austin* that "recent cases have expressly reserved the question whether the fiction could be employed to forfeit the property of a truly innocent owner." If the court does rule that civil forfeiture statutes must allow an innocent-owner defense, it will not affect federal forfeitures much. Most sections, for example, of the Comprehensive Drug Abuse Prevention and Control Act already allow such a defense.

Civil libertarians say that an innocent-owner defense is not enough. They claim that requiring owners to prove their innocence mocks due process. They want Congress or the Supreme Court to ban civil forfeitures. The government, they argue, should have to prove a person guilty beyond a reasonable doubt before forfeiting the person's property. As it stands now, prosecutors do not file criminal charges in many civil forfeiture cases. When they do file charges, prosecutors still most often seek civil forfeitures instead of criminal forfeitures.

The government adamantly supports civil forfeitures. Officials believe the innocent-owner defense offers adequate safeguards. No one even contests forfeitures in eight out of 10 cases. Cary Copeland, director of the Justice Department's Office for Asset Forfeiture, argues that in most cases "the circumstances are so incriminating that nobody wants to challenge us. With all that crime out there we don't have time to run around and take property from innocent people." Advocates of civil forfeiture also point out the long history of civil forfeiture statutes in this country. The first Congress passed a civil forfeiture statute. This is the same Congress that drafted the Bill of Rights.

For Discussion

1. What is the difference between civil and criminal forfeiture?

2. Why do you think prosecutors most often file civil forfeiture actions instead of criminal ones?

3. How are the three branches of government—executive, legislative, and judicial—involved in setting federal civil forfeiture policy?

4. What is an innocent-owner defense? Do you think the Constitution requires such a defense? Why or why not?

5. The Supreme Court ruled in *Austin* that the excessive fines clause applies to civil forfeitures. It then sent the *Austin* case back to lower courts to decide whether the forfeiture was, in fact, excessive. Do you think it was? Why or why not?

6. What are the benefits of civil forfeiture? The costs?

Class Activity: A Debate on Federal Forfeiture

Several members of Congress have proposed eliminating civil forfeiture provisions of the Comprehensive Drug Abuse Prevention and Control Act (except for seizure of the illegal drugs themselves). Forfeitures could still take place, but only after criminal prosecutions. In this activity, you will role-play congressional committee members and supporters and opponents of civil forfeiture. Committee members will first hear from supporters and opponents of civil forfeiture. Then they will meet as a committee, discuss civil forfeiture, and vote on whether it should remain in the federal statute.

1. Divide the class into triads. Assign each student in the triads a role of supporter, opponent, or member of Congress.

2. Regroup the class so they can consult with one another while preparing for the role-play. Supporters of forfeiture should sit on one side of the room, opponents on another side, and members of Congress in front. Supporters and opponents should think up their best arguments, and members of Congress should think of questions to ask each side.

3. Regroup into triads and begin the role-play. Opponents will present their case first. Each side will have two minutes to make its presentation. The member of Congress can interrupt to ask questions.

4. After the presentations, each member of Congress should return to his or her seat at the front of the room. The congressional committee then should discuss and vote on whether civil forfeiture should be eliminated from the statute.

Debriefing Questions

1. What were the strongest arguments for eliminating civil forfeiture? For keeping it? Why?

2. Do you think civil forfeiture violates basic constitutional rights? Why or why not?

3. Would you favor giving up some rights to fight drugs? Why or why not?

4. What do you think could be done to reduce drugs in America? Explain.

An Attack on Crime: The State Level

We must bear in mind that under our federal system of government, the states have primary authority for dealing with most crimes committed within their border, and that includes the vast majority of violent crimes.
> —William French Smith, former U.S. attorney general

Like the federal government, state governments are divided into three branches—executive, legislative, and judicial. State legislatures define crimes and pass other crime bills, which the governor signs into law. State codes define all felony offenses and many lesser offenses, but local governments enact some misdemeanors and local ordinances. In turn, state and local police departments enforce these laws.

People accused of violating state or local crimes appear before state criminal trial courts. Many states have two types of trial courts—called courts of limited and unlimited jurisdiction. Courts of limited jurisdiction try only misdemeanors and lesser offenses. But they may hold pretrial felony hearings also. They are often called municipal, magistrate, or police courts. Courts of unlimited jurisdiction commonly hear felony cases. Depending on the state, these courts are usually called superior, district, circuit, or general-sessions courts.

If convicted, defendants may appeal their cases to appellate courts. Most states have two levels of appeals courts—an intermediate level and the state supreme court. But some states have only a state supreme court. Like the U.S. Supreme

---

CRIME BEAT

Imagine you are a crime beat reporter for a local news outlet. Your editor has assigned you to do background research for a chart that will accompany a story on a convicted murderer who is appealing the conviction. Find out the names of the criminal trial courts and courts of appeal in your state. Make a chart showing your state's court structure.

For ideas on sources for this information, see "Crime Beat" on page 31.

Court, many state supreme courts have discretionary jurisdiction. They choose which cases they will hear by granting writs of certiorari.

If a state supreme court hears an appeal, it has the last word on interpretations of state law and the state constitution. Defendants cannot appeal further unless they charge violations of the U.S. Constitution. Then they may ask the U.S. Supreme Court to hear their cases.

For Discussion

1. What is discretionary jurisdiction? Why do you think many state supreme courts use it?

2. Under what circumstances could the U.S. Supreme Court overrule a state supreme court's interpretation of its state's law? Explain.

3. Why do you think controlling violent crime is primarily the responsibility of the states?

The New Role of State Supreme Courts

As the Supreme Court in recent years has restricted the rights of criminal defendants, defendants have increasingly looked to state supreme courts to protect their rights.

How can a state court offer more protection than the U.S. Supreme Court? The U.S. Supreme Court, after all, makes the final decision on matters of U.S. constitutional law. It decides whether the Constitution guarantees certain rights and what the extent of these rights is. A state supreme court could not, for example, declare that the *U.S.* Constitution gives people a right to privacy in the items they put out for trash collection, because the U.S. Supreme Court in *California v. Greenwood* (1988) has already ruled the U.S. Constitution grants no such right. The U.S. Supreme Court would reverse any contrary decision by a state court.

But a state supreme court could declare that its *state* constitution granted that right. The New Jersey Supreme Court did exactly this in its 1990 *State v. Hempele* decision. It ruled that, under the New Jersey Constitution, residents have a right to privacy in items put in the trash. This right is protected independently by the state constitution. The U.S. Supreme Court cannot overrule this decision, because state supreme courts are the final judges of the meaning of their constitutions.

These constitutions can grant *more* rights than the U.S. Constitution. Thus criminal defendants appealing their convictions often ask state courts to find their rights have been violated under the state constitution. Between 1970 and 1987, state supreme courts ruled in over 350 cases that their constitutions granted more protections than the U.S. Constitution. If the U.S. Supreme Court continues to restrict the rights of criminal defendants, more defendants will look to their state constitutions for protection. But one state, California, has put a stop to this practice. In 1982, the voters of California passed the Victims' Bill of Rights, which limited the rights of criminal defendants under the California Constitution to those granted under the U.S. Constitution.

For Discussion

1. On what basis can state courts grant greater protections for criminal defendants than those guaranteed by the U.S. Constitution?

2. Do you think state courts should do this? Why or why not?

3. Could a state court restrict or deny rights guaranteed by the U.S. Constitution? Explain.

Class Activity: The Fictional State of Columbia

Passing anti-crime legislation is not as simple as learning the facts and holding a debate. In the following section, you will learn some of the ins and outs of state legislation. You will take part in a role-play based on a fictional state's attack on its crime problem. In the role-play, you will serve on a state senate committee discussing an anti-crime bill. First read the background information on the fictional state of Columbia, plus the description of the anti-crime bill, and the description of the state districts.

Columbia is a picturesque mountain and prairie state in the middle of the country far away from the coasts. It has almost 4 million residents, about half of whom live in rural areas on farms or in small towns. Columbia has many dairy farms and egg ranches. It also has a few large agricultural corporations that raise hogs, cattle, corn, and wheat.

Two million Columbians live in cities, almost a million in the biggest city of Athena. Industries in the Athena area mainly make textiles, clothing, and computer hardware. There is one auto assembly plant. A particularly rugged mountain range passes through the western part of the state, and tourists flock to the mountains summer and winter. Tourists also come to see Gold Canyon near the mountains, which is the site of the White Water mining district with many ghost towns and abandoned mines. Many Europeans come to see the mining areas and stay in one of the spas in the foothills. Tourism has become an important addition to a weak economy.

Columbia has a growing crime problem, which got national publicity last year when the daughter of the Danish ambassador was accidentally killed in a mini-market holdup. The crime problem grew serious in Athena when drugs were first imported by a West Coast gang 10 years ago. Since then, the problem has spread to most of the smaller cities in the state.

Senate Bill 1715

State Senator Alan Parsons introduced a bill designed to solve Columbia's crime problem. He incorporated many sweeping changes into his bill, which was assigned the number SB 1715, which stands for Senate Bill 1715. This is the bill.

In the role-play that follows, you will represent one of the following districts in the state of Columbia.

District 1

Most of the district is made up of the richer suburbs of Athena. There are two large modern malls to serve them and the state's only theme park, Prairieland. A lot of the residents are newly wealthy and have moved here to escape the troubles of the inner city. The state capital buildings in Athena are just across the district line, and many of the higher level state administrators live here.

The areas of district 1 nearest the city are often targeted for burglaries and there have been several brutal muggings and rapes on local streets. Recently there has been a number of carjackings, with new models taken from their owners at gunpoint.

The people in district 1 want someone to take action against crime immediately. Many of them, however, are against taxation and they are worried about the budget impact of new anti-crime measures. Also, several important people in district 1 have expressed concerns about the first provision of the bill. They do not want the bill to cover "victimless" crimes, such as drug use or gambling, and they don't want any attention given to white collar crime, such as embezzlement or corporate fraud.

District 2

District 2 is on the opposite side of Athena from district 1, and it includes most of the blue collar suburbs and the industries. It is mostly white, though some African-Americans and Latinos have moved into the edge of the district. A recent recession and the closing of two electronics plants has hit district 2 hard. Almost 12 percent of the work force is unemployed. Even the auto assembly plant has cut production and laid off a quarter of its employees.

In the past, the main problems in the district were juvenile delinquency and fights outside several notorious bars. Now, however, the number of muggings and street robberies is rising. Also, the biggest industries report a number of suspicious fires and acts of sabotage. Gang graffiti has begun to appear on walls everywhere.

People in district 2 are very angry, but they are not sure what to do. Many of them talk about getting tougher on the criminals, and they blame the police. They feel that richer areas like district 1 get much better policing than they do.

Senate Bill 1715

Preamble:

We, the people of Columbia, declare that it is our inalienable right to live in a society free from the fear and threat of criminal attack upon our property and persons. We declare that the men and women who commit crimes are the enemies of our state, our society, and our general welfare. For this reason, we amend the Columbia Constitution and Penal Code to include the following provisions:

Provision 1:

Any person who has been convicted of a felony shall, upon conviction of a second and separate felony, be sentenced to serve five years in addition to whatever sentence the court imposes for the second offense. This penalty is mandatory for all felons upon their second conviction and is to be served without possibility of parole.

Provision 2:

Any citizen who wounds, disables, or apprehends a person committing or attempting to commit a robbery or burglary within the jurisdiction of this state shall be entitled to $2,000 upon the capture and conviction of said felon. In the event of the death of said felon, an award of $2,000 shall be made upon a finding of justifiable homicide by a duly constituted coroner's jury.

Provision 3:

The legislature hereby appropriates $40 million from the general fund for use by county, municipal, or township governments for either of the following purposes:

a. The hiring, training, and maintenance of additional police officers.

b. The renovation of jails or the construction of additional cells in existing jails.

This fund shall be administered and distributed by the state attorney general's office upon application by local governments.

District 3

District 3 is in the northwest part of the state. It includes Gold Canyon and was once the Whitewater Mining district. The minerals were played out long ago, and it is now mainly a picturesque tourist area in the foothills. The district features many resorts and spas. The biggest town is College Park, which contains Columbia State University, and most of the faculty and students live here.

Crime has increased, but not as badly as in other parts of the state. The campus police have the university area under control, and a few extra units of the state police have managed to stop victimization of tourists.

People in the Whitewater area are worried that publicity about crime will scare off tourists. They want a well-publicized anti-crime campaign that will reassure potential tourists. Many other voters in the district, however, are opposed to what they see as repressive legislation like SB 1715.

The people near the university are largely opposed to handguns. They passed a local ordinance to require a long waiting period before purchasing any firearm. They would strongly oppose any state law that would encourage people to buy handguns.

District 4

This district is in the center of the state and largely agricultural. The largest town, Lone Pine, has just over 1,000 people and serves the surrounding farms. There are three very large agricultural corporations that employ hundreds of field hands and some administrators. People in the smaller towns run cafes and gas stations that are dependent on the tourists passing through to the mountains in the west.

A few years ago there was hardly any crime at all in district 4, except an occasional gas station holdup and a rare murder. Recently, gangs from the cities have made raids on the larger farms or on businesses on payroll day. There have even been a few midnight assaults and rapes in the small towns.

Many district residents blame Athena for the crime and they feel no one in the big city takes them seriously. Some are talking about taking the law into their own hands and forming vigilante posses.

District 5

District 5 includes all of the central city of Athena. The residents are mostly poor and many work at service industries in the city core that pay minimum wage. Those who do have jobs in the industries in the suburbs have to commute long distances. African-Americans are about a third of the population, Latinos are another third, and the rest is made up of relatively new Asian immigrants and poor whites.

Crime rates have traditionally been high in district 5, but over the last two years they have actually dropped a little. Many people feel this is because of an active neighborhood-watch program and a well-funded federal jobs program for city youth.

Most urban residents oppose SB 1715. There have been many state cutbacks on welfare programs, and Athenians feel that the extra money proposed in the bill would be better spent combat-

ing poverty. They feel that is the way to fight crime.

Urban residents feel their neighborhood-watch and jobs programs are working, and they would like to see these expanded and reproduced in other population centers in the state. They want more money devoted to social welfare and anti-poverty programs. And they feel the second provision of the bill would just increase the level of violence and encourage dangerous vigilante action.

For Discussion

1. The preamble to SB 1715 declares that criminals are "enemies of the state." Are all criminals enemies of the state? What might be some problems with such an attitude?

2. Reread the provisions of SB 1715 one at a time. Answer the following questions for each:

   • What are some possible consequences if this proposition were enacted into law? Explain.

   • Which of these would have a positive impact on society? Which would have a negative impact? Explain.

Class Activity: A State Senate Committee

In this activity, you will role-play a state senate committee discussing the proposed bill SB 1715.

1. Break the class into committees of five or 10 persons each. Count off in your committee, and either one or two persons in each group will represent one of the five districts described in the previous section. Select a chairperson. Try to arrange your committee so it has an uneven number of members. If that is not possible, chairpersons should be non-voting.

2. Reread your district's description. Before beginning committee deliberations, redivide the class into district caucuses for preliminary discussions. This means all the members representing a particular district, such as district 1, should meet

in one group to discuss the district's reaction toward the three provisions of the bill. Go over which sections the district favors, which it opposes, and discuss changes the district would like in the bill.

3. Return to the senate and meet with your senate committee. In this committee, you will now carefully review all three provisions of SB 1715.

4. *First step.* Committee chairperson or a designated member will read aloud the text of the first provision of SB 1715.

5. *Second step.* Call on members to discuss this provision and how their districts feel about it.

6. *Third step.* Call for amendments. Committee members can propose amendments to the provision. Discuss any amendments and vote on them.

7. *Fourth step.* Now vote on the provision, including any amendments you have added. There are three votes possible:

> *Pass*, which will send the bill to the full senate with a recommendation to pass it;
>
> *Defeat*, which will send the bill to the full senate with a recommendation to defeat it; or
>
> *Table*, which will tie the bill up in committee indefinitely.

8. Repeat the steps for all three provisions of the bill, then write a brief report on the committee's recommendations. Break up the report so that different people on the committee work on different parts of the report.

9. Reconvene the whole class as the full senate, and have each committee read its report. The whole class will then vote on any amendments offered, and will then vote whether to pass or defeat the bill.

Debriefing Questions

1. How does Columbia differ from your state? Which district described is closest to the one you live in? Why?

2. Would the people of your state support such a crime bill? Why or why not?

3. Do you think this exercise was a realistic representation of how your state senate would deal with a crime bill? Why or why not?

The Color of Justice

In Los Angeles, a bystander videotapes police officers beating Rodney King, a black man. People in the African-American community have long complained of cases of police brutality. At long last, they have clear evidence—a videotape. But at the trial in state court, the jury acquits the four officers of using excessive force.

Although two of the officers are subsequently convicted in federal court, many in the African-American and in other minority communities argue that this case shows how difficult it is for people of color to get justice from the criminal justice system. The system, they say, reeks of racial discrimination.

Critics who claim that the system is tainted by racism have cited its treatment of African-American males. For example, statistical studies suggest that more than half of all black males in large cities can expect to be arrested at least once during their lifetime, while only 14 percent of white males are ever arrested. African-Americans make up 12 percent of the U.S. population, but they are 45 percent of all prison inmates and 40 percent of those sentenced to death. Even more startling, a quarter of all African-American males aged 20-29 are right now either locked up, on probation, or on parole.

The question remains whether these statistics are the result of a racist criminal justice system or whether there are other causes. Social scientists and politicians have argued about this question for decades.

In a controversial 1975 article titled, "White Racism, Black Crime, and American Justice," criminologist Robert Staples argued that there was discrimination in the justice system. He said the legal system was made by white men to protect white interests and keep blacks down. Staples charged that the system was characterized by second-rate legal help for black defendants, biased jurors, and judges who discriminate in sentencing.

A dozen years later, sociologist William Wilbanks rejected the discrimination argument. In his book, *The Myth of a Racist Criminal Justice System*, Wilbanks reviewed scores of studies that seemed to show statistical inequalities between whites and blacks in arrest rates, imprisonment, and other areas of criminal justice. He felt the inequalities were due to factors other than racial discrimination, such as poverty and the defendant's prior record.

Other sociologists, too, have suggested that the apparent inequalities have more to do with poverty than race. Street crimes such as robbery and assault, prominent in the statistics, are often committed by people from poor backgrounds. Today, almost 45 percent of all African-American children grow up below the official poverty line, compared to only 16 percent of all white youngsters. These figures grew worse in the 1980s, as job opportunities gradually disappeared from most urban black communities.

The connection between poverty and crime has long been noted. During the 1930s, a much larger part of the white population was poor, and whites committed a greater percentage of street crime. Whites then accounted for nearly 80 percent of those in prison compared to 40 percent today. The question of poverty alone may well account for many of the apparent inequalities in the system.

A RAND Corporation study in 1983, however, unearthed some disturbing data. RAND compared the treatment of whites and blacks at key decision points in the criminal justice system. The researchers found that black defendants seemed to be treated more harshly at key points such as sentencing. But the researchers did not identify a cause for these inequalities. Later studies have provided more insight into this troubling data.

Plea Bargaining

Over 90 percent of all criminal cases never go to trial. The defendant pleads guilty, often after the prosecutor and defense attorney negotiate. The *San Jose Mercury News* conducted a massive study of 700,000 California legal cases over a 10-year period. The paper reported in December 1991 that 33 percent of the white adults who were arrested, but had no prior record, were able to get felony charges against them reduced. Only 25 percent of the African-Americans and Latinos with no priors were as successful in plea bargaining.

The *Mercury News* study did not blame intentional racism for these inequalities. It did, however, suggest that subtle cultural fears and insensitivity contributed to the problem. The study noted that over 80 percent of all California prosecutors and judges are white, while more than 60 percent of those arrested are non-white.

Constance Rice, a lawyer for the NAACP Legal Defense Fund in Los Angeles, explained that when prosecutors and judges use their discretion, "we have always found evidence to support the notion that race plays a role."

Jury Verdicts

In 1985, Cornell law professor Sheri Lynn Johnson reviewed a dozen mock-jury studies. She concluded that the "race of the defendant significantly and directly affects the determination of guilt." In these studies, identical trials were simu-

Police officers handcuff three youths caught up in an anti-gang sweep through south central Los Angeles. (AP/World Wide Photos.)

lated, sometimes with white defendants and sometimes with African-Americans. Professor Johnson discovered that white jurors were more likely to find a black defendant guilty than a white defendant, even though the mock trials were based on the same crime and the same evidence.

And Professor Johnson found that black jurors behaved with the reverse bias. They found white defendants guilty more often than black defendants. Furthermore, the race of the **victim** in the case affected both groups. If the victim was black, white jurors tended to find a white defendant less blameworthy. In the same way, if the victim was white, black jurors found black defendants less blameworthy.

According to these mock-jury experiments, both white and black jurors seem to discriminate. Professor Johnson did not, however, think the juror bias was intentional. "Because the process of attributing guilt on the basis of race appears to be subconscious," Johnson says, "jurors are unlikely either to be aware of or to be able to control that process."

The mock trials did have one encouraging result. When white and black mock jurors met together, as many real juries do, the effect of race tended to disappear. This result seems to indicate that the best way to eliminate racial bias in verdicts is to select racially mixed juries. The U.S. Supreme Court has moved in this direction by prohibiting both prosecutors and defense lawyers from eliminating prospective jurors solely because of race. (See *Batson v. Kentucky*, 1986, and *Georgia v. McCollum*, 1992.)

An earlier study, however, pointed to less clear conclusions. Psychologist J.L. Bernard of Memphis State University examined a jury of six blacks and six whites deadlocked along racial lines over the guilt of a black defendant. According to Bernard, "black jurors as a whole may be more likely to acquit a defendant, regardless of race," because they are more suspicious of police motives and witnesses.

Sentencing

The 1983 RAND Corporation study found that convicted African-Americans were more likely than whites to go to prison. And their sentences were longer. "This disparity," the study concluded, "suggests that probation officers, judges, and parole boards are exercising discretion in sentencing or release decisions in ways that result in de facto discrimination against blacks." **De facto** means the discrimination exists in fact, but without legal authority. It may not be intentional.

Unintended discrimination can occur at many points in the legal process. Probation officers often prepare pre-sentencing reports for a judge. The judge uses the reports to help make sentencing decisions. Reports include information on the criminal's prior record, family background, education, marital status, and employment history. Many African-Americans convicted of crimes come from deprived backgrounds. They may have things in their record—unemployment, trouble in school, family problems—that judges, who largely come from middle-class backgrounds, cannot relate to. This may sway some judges to treat them more harshly in sentencing.

Even when judges have no discretion in sentencing, discrimination can still occur. Some federal mandatory sentences have come under fire recently for discriminating against minorities. Critics point to different sentences mandated for crack cocaine, a drug popular in poor minority communities, and powder cocaine, a drug used in wealthier communities. Under federal law, dealing five grams of crack cocaine gets a first offender a mandatory minimum sentence of five years. To receive a similar mandatory minimum sentence for trafficking in powder cocaine, an offender must possess 500 grams.

In 1991, one state court struck down its similar state laws as unconstitutional. Narcotics laws in Minnesota had mandated a four-year prison term for a first-time conviction for possession of crack cocaine, but probation for possession of powdered cocaine. In striking down the statutes, the Minnesota Supreme Court based its decision on the "correlation between race and the use of cocaine base or powder and the gross disparity in [the] resulting punishment . . . ." (*State v. Russell.*)

Death Penalty

The state of Georgia was the subject of a careful study of 2,000 murder cases prosecuted during the 1970s. The study showed that defendants convicted of killing whites were more than four times more likely to receive the death penalty than those convicted of murdering blacks. The study also revealed that black defendants who murdered whites had by far the greatest chance of being sentenced to death.

A Georgia black man who had been sentenced to death for killing a white police officer used this study in his appeal to the U.S. Supreme Court. He claimed the study proved that Georgia's jurors and judges discriminated against African-American defendants. In a close 5-4 decision, the Supreme Court accepted the results of the study, but ruled that it did not prove the discrimination was intentional. Writing for the majority, Justice Lewis F. Powell concluded that the study failed to "demonstrate a constitutionally significant risk of racial bias affecting the Georgia capital sentencing process." (*McCleskey v. Kemp*, 1987.)

On the whole, most studies confirm that some racial discrimination exists in the American criminal justice system, but that it is not intentional. Legal experts point out that it is often difficult to prove that the outcome of any one case was influenced by unintentional racism. While Supreme Court decisions since 1960 have rooted out many overtly racist practices, such as in police lineups and jury selection, it is more difficult to address unintentional racist factors. Because these factors are rooted in subtle assumptions and fears deeply ingrained in the wider society, only when society changes will they disappear.

Critics of the system, however, insist that inequalities, regardless of their basis, should not be swept under the rug. They maintain that any discrimination is intolerable and must be eliminated.

For Discussion

1. What are the disparities between white and black defendants at each of the following key decision points: plea bargaining, jury verdicts, sentencing, and death penalty.

2. What do you think accounts for these disparities? Explain.

3. According to Andrew Hacker, author of *Two Nations, Black and White, Separate, Hostile, Unequal,* "The feeling persists that a black man who rapes or robs a white person has inflicted more harm than black or white criminals who prey on victims of their own race." Do you agree with this statement? Why or why not?

Class Activity: Toward a Colorblind Justice System

Various proposals have been put forward to prevent discrimination in plea bargaining, jury verdicts, sentencing, and the death penalty. In this activity, you will evaluate a few of these and come up with suggestions of your own. Break into small groups. Assign each group one of the four policy areas below. Each group should read its policy, evaluate it, and report back to the class. To evaluate its policy, each group should answer the following questions:

a. What problem is the policy designed to address? Does it address the problem? Why or why not?

b. Who might support the policy? Who might oppose it? Why?

c. What benefits might come from the policy?

d. What costs might result from the policy?

e. What other policies might address the problem? Are they better? Why?

f. What policy should be adopted? Why?

I. Plea Bargaining

Policy: Plea bargaining should be abolished.

Pros: It will do away with an informal process subject to abuse because the courts do not review it. It will ensure that all defendants have their day in court.

Cons: Doing away with plea bargaining will clog the courts with cases awaiting trial, resulting in increased court costs.

II. Jury Verdicts

Policy: Minority defendants should be allowed to choose at least two jurors who are members of their cultural or ethnic group.

Pros: It will assure that minority viewpoints are represented and that the results of the trial will be accepted by all.

Cons: It amounts to reverse discrimination and may require the seating of biased jurors, making a fair trial impossible.

III. Sentencing

Policy: Federal law should not make first-time drug offenders face mandatory sentences. Judges should be allowed more discretion in sentencing these drug offenders.

Pros: Mandatory minimum sentences cause first-time offenders, mostly minorities, to go into an already overcrowded prison system.

Cons: Mandatory minimum sentences are needed to show we are serious in our war on drugs.

IV. Death Penalty

Policy: Congress should reverse the decision in *McCleskey*. If statistical studies show racial disparities in a state's imposition of the death penalty, then minority defendants should not be sentenced to death in that state.

Pros: Race should play no role in whether or not a person receives the death penalty. The death penalty should be limited to aggravated cases where whites and blacks receive the same treatment.

Cons: Mere discrepancies in statistics should not invalidate the death penalty. A defendant should have to show discrimination in the particular case or that the state intended to discriminate.

Debriefing Questions

1. Which policies garnered the most support? The least support? Why?

2. What other policies did you think of that could prevent racial discrimination in the criminal justice system? Do you think they would work? Why or why not?

3. Why is it important that the criminal justice system not be perceived as racially biased?

three

CRIME AND THE CITIZEN

Getting Involved in Fighting Crime

[I]n Japan, you can walk into a park at midnight and sit on a bench and nothing will happen to you. You're completely safe, day or night. You can go anywhere. You won't be robbed or beaten or killed. You're not always looking behind you, not always worrying. You don't need walls or bodyguards. . . . You're free. It's a wonderful feeling. Here, everybody has to lock themselves up. Lock the door. Lock the car. People who spend their whole lives locked up are in prison.
—Michael Crichton, *Rising Sun*

A mericans fear crime. Almost every year for the last 20 years, a majority of Americans have responded "more" to the Gallup Poll's question, "Is there more crime in your area than there was a year ago, or less?"

The fear of crime has spurred people into taking individual action against crime. They have built walls, bought guns, and installed security systems. A whole new security industry has blossomed. There are now more private security guards than police in the United States.

But today and throughout our history ordinary citizens have banded together to fight crime—sometimes legally and other times illegally. In this section, we will examine some of these crime fighters. We first will take a historical look at **vigilantes**—citizens who responded to crime by

taking the law into their own hands. Then we will look at some actions citizens are taking today to prevent crime.

Vigilantes in American History

Violence and crime have been a major part of American history from the beginning. Vigilantes have been with us almost as long. Repeatedly, groups of citizens have banded together to take the law into their own hands and punish suspected criminals. These groups were usually well organized and had leaders and rules. Before illegally punishing their suspects, they often held some sort of trial. But the accused usually had little chance for a real defense.

Before 1900, vigilantism was relatively common in the United States. Episodes of vigilante justice occurred all over the country. Historians know of well over 300 vigilante movements in American history. Their size varied from small groups of about a dozen people to large organizations including thousands of citizens. Most numbered several hundred. Vigilante groups went by various names, including *regulators*, *slickers*, *stranglers*, *committees of safety*, and *vigilance committees*.

Vigilante organizations were usually formed for some specific purpose. Once the job was done, the vigilantes disbanded. Most operated for less than a year.

In the early years of our country, vigilantes ordinarily whipped, beat, or tarred and feathered those they believed guilty. But by the 1850s, hanging had become widespread. Those not hanged were usually forced to leave the area. Few escaped punishment.

Most vigilante groups were composed of normally law-abiding merchants, ranchers, and other prominent citizens. Their leaders were usually the wealthiest and most important people in the area. Why did these kinds of people resort to an illegal and often violent method of handling criminals? There are several reasons.

The most important reason was that the frontier lacked police, courts, and jails. Until 1900, many people lived in isolated frontier settlements far from established law and order. Faced with doing nothing about rampaging outlaws or taking the law into their own hands, respectable people chose the vigilante solution. Frontier Americans were used to relying on themselves to solve problems.

Another reason for vigilantism had to do with the determination of businessmen and the wealthy to maintain political control over the lower classes. When crime, violence, or political corruption seemed to tip the balance of power in a community toward the lower classes, a vigilante movement, led by merchants, bankers, or large landowners, was often organized.

In some cases, the reason for vigilance committees was simply to keep taxes low. It was much cheaper to take care of criminals by hauling them before a group of vigilantes than paying sheriffs, judges, prosecutors, and jailers to do the job.

Vigilantes Outside the West

The first vigilante movement in America was formed in the South Carolina backwoods in the 1760s. A newly settled frontier area, it had just undergone a costly Indian war with the Cherokees. Orphaned and homeless young people drifted into outlaw bands. These bands stole horses, kidnapped, raped, and robbed.

Since the area had no sheriffs and courts, a group known as the Regulators was organized in 1767. Composed of up to 6,000 normally law-abiding settlers, the Regulators attacked and broke up the outlaw gangs. The lawbreakers were given trials, whipped, driven out of the area, or forced to work on farms. Sixteen were killed.

The Regulators disbanded in 1769 when courts and sheriffs were established. But this group of vigilantes provided a model that many other vigilance movements throughout the country would later copy.

Vigilante movements were set up again and again before the Civil War to deal with horse thieves, counterfeiters, gamblers, and bands of robbers. Vigilantes were particularly active in Alabama, Mississippi, Louisiana, Iowa, Indiana, and Illinois.

In northern Illinois during the 1830s, several gangs of horse thieves and counterfeiters virtually ruled a number of rural counties. The outlaws controlled elections and even burned down a newly built courthouse.

In April 1841, well-to-do settlers formed the Northern Illinois Regulators. On one occasion, two men accused of murder and stealing horses were tried by 120 Regulators before about 500 spectators. The leader of the Regulators served as the judge. One lawyer was appointed to represent the accused, while another lawyer acted for "the people." Witnesses were sworn and testified. Finally, the entire crowd watching the vigilante proceedings voted for the death penalty. Within an hour, the two outlaws were hanged. The Northern Illinois Regulators disbanded after breaking up the gangs of outlaws.

Vigilantes from the West

Vigilante groups were more numerous and generally more deadly in the West. Between 1850 and 1900, about 200 vigilante movements were formed. They executed over 500 accused horse and cattle thieves, murderers, robbers, and others. Texas holds the record for the most vigilante killings with 140. But one Montana vigilante group in 1884 carried out 35 executions. Theodore Roosevelt, working as a cowboy in Montana at this time, wanted to join the vigilantes but never got the chance.

Some historians have attempted to classify vigilante movements as *constructive* and *destructive*. According to this viewpoint, constructive

A mob in Marion, Indiana, in 1930 mills about the lynched bodies of two men. The men had been accused of rape and murder. (UPI/Bettmann.)

vigilante groups got rid of the criminal element quickly, restored order, and then disbanded. These groups usually had widespread public support. Destructive vigilante movements were often divided from within and frequently led to chaos and violence.

A good example of a destructive type of vigilante movement was the Regulator-Moderator War of Shelby County, Texas. In 1840, when Texas was an independent country, a group of Regulators formed to get rid of a corruptring of county officials. The county had attracted a lot of thieves, counterfeiters, and murderers.

The Regulator leader was killed and replaced by a man who took his role so seriously that he wore a military uniform. Soon an opposing group of vigilantes calling themselves the Moderators was formed. But criminals infiltrated both groups. Violence, revenge, and feuds erupted. The original reason for the formation of the vigilante movement was forgotten. An all-out battle broke out between the Regulators and Moderators in 1844 involving hundreds of men. Sam Houston and the Lone Star Republic militia finally stopped the violence.

The Johnson County Invasion is an example of what has been called constructive vigilantism.

Big cattle ranchers, used to grazing their large herds on open range land, took exception when homesteaders began to fence off land. At first, the cattle barons accused the homesteaders of rustling. A few homesteaders were murdered, but no one was ever convicted of the killings. In April 1892, the large cattle ranchers brought in a trainload of heavily armed gunfighters supposedly to go after rustlers. In reality, they were hired to force out the homesteaders. The gunmen quickly went to work and killed two settlers. Enraged, the homesteaders formed a vigilante group, rounded up the invaders, and held them until federal troops arrived. Unfortunately, after being bailed out of jail by the cattle barons, the gunslingers disappeared. So they were never put on trial.

The San Francisco Vigilance Committees

Two of the most famous examples of vigilantism in American history occurred in San Francisco in 1851 and 1856.

In 1851, with the Gold Rush at its peak, San Francisco was wide open, rough, and dangerous. Its police could do little to stop a wave of crimes. A Committee of Vigilance was formed composed of over 500 leading citizens. William T. Coleman, a young merchant, led the committee.

The Committee of Vigilance announced that "no thief, burglar, incendiary, or assassin shall escape punishment, either by the quibbles of the law, the insecurity of prisons, the carelessness or corruption of the police, or a laxity of those who pretend to administer justice." Clearly, these San Francisco vigilantes had a low opinion of those responsible for law and order in the city.

Before the year ended, the committee had whipped one accused criminal, hanged four others, forced 15 to leave the city, and handed over another 15 to legal authorities. After cleaning up the city, the committee disbanded.

But five years later, San Francisco was in worse shape than before. Murders and other crimes were rampant. Even more frightening to San Francisco business leaders was the corrupt political machine that ran the city government.

David C. Broderick, the Democratic Party leader of San Francisco, controlled the city. Kept in power by the votes of Irish-Catholic workers, Broderick stuffed his pockets and those of his friends with public funds. Businessmen resented that their tax dollars financed Broderick and his friends. By 1856, San Francisco was facing bankruptcy. Businessmen in the city who depended on credit from Eastern banks were worried.

James King, editor of the *San Francisco Daily Evening Bulletin*, wrote editorials attacking the crime problem and the corruption of the Broderick political machine. King, who had been a vigilante in 1851, also began to revive talk of vigilante justice. On May 14, 1856, he was shot to death on a San Francisco street.

The following day, William T. Coleman, leader of the vigilantes in 1851, formed a new vigilance committee. Within a few days, the vigilance committee arrested, tried, and hanged one of Broderick's political flunkies for the shooting.

During the next few months, perhaps as many as 8,000 San Franciscans joined the vigilantes. Most were merchants and skilled workers. Few were Irish. Coleman held almost dictatorial powers. With an executive committee of business men, he drew up a list of suspects. People were arrested and tried at vigilante headquarters, which was called Fort Gunnybags because it was protected with sandbags. In all, the committee executed four accused criminals. It put Broderick's henchmen on ships headed for Eastern and foreign ports and told them never to come back to the city. It called Broderick himself before the vigilance committee. When he was released, he left town.

In operation only three months, the vigilance committee disbanded on August 18 with a parade through the city. But the vigilance committee formed a political organization, the People's Party, that controlled San Francisco's city government for the next 10 years.

The San Francisco vigilance committees of 1851 and 1856 were widely publicized and copied throughout the West. Sometimes, however, it was difficult to tell the difference between a vigilance committee and a lynch mob. On July 4, 1851, for example, a bunch of drunken miners smashed into the shack of a Mexican woman in Downieville, California. Thinking she was being attacked, the woman stabbed one of the miners, who later died. The woman was quickly tried by a vigilante jury and sentenced to death. She was hanged from a wooden bridge over the Yuba River.

Was Vigilantism Ever Justified?

There seems to be a vigilante strain that has repeatedly surfaced in American history. Was vigilante justice ever warranted? One former Colorado vigilante thought vigilante justice worked better than legal procedures. "There were no appeals in those days," he said, "no writs of errors, no attorney's fees, no pardon in six months. Punishment was swift, sure, and certain." On the other hand, a New York City newspaper editorial criticizing the San Francisco vigilance

---

Activity: Vigilante Episodes

Read one of the following books, or view one of the following films. Prepare a report to the class on what the book or movie has to say about the vigilante phenomenon in American history.

1. *The Ox-Bow Incident* (novel), by Walter Van Tilburg Clark; *The Ox-Bow Incident* (film), directed by William Wellman.

2. *The Magnificent Seven* (film), directed by John Sturges. (This is a remake of Akira Kurosawa's *Seven Samurai*, but the original is set in Japan and has a slightly different focus.)

3. *To Kill a Mockingbird* (novel), by Harper Lee; *To Kill a Mockingbird* (film), directed by Martin Ritt.

4. *Bad Day at Black Rock* (film), directed by John Sturges.

5. *Quiet Rage: Bernie Goetz in a Time of Madness* (non-fiction book), by Lillian B. Rubin.

committee of 1856 stated: "Better to endure the evil of escape of criminals than to inaugurate a reign of terror which today may punish one guilty head, and tomorrow wreak its mistaken vengeance on many innocent lives."

For Discussion

1. Why did normally law-abiding and well-to-do citizens turn to illegal vigilante methods? Do you think that people today could turn to vigilantism? Explain.

2. How are vigilante groups and lynch mobs different? How are they similar?

3. Do you think vigilantism was ever justified in American history? Do you think it would ever be justified today? Why or why not?

Guardian Angels

In the late 1970s, a high-school dropout named Curtis Sliwa got fed up with the crime rate in New York City and founded a group that some think of as modern vigilantes—The Guardian Angels. Sliwa does not like the name vigilantes. He thinks of his group as an unarmed anti-crime patrol that simply assists the police by patrolling the subways and most dangerous areas of the city.

Sliwa has said, "Our main weapon is our presence."

His followers wear red berets and distinctive T-shirts and often carry two-way radios. Guardian Angels try to break up muggings and street crime, and they have made scores of citizen's arrests. They also phone or radio for help.

The Guardian Angels are largely made up of African-American and Latino youths. They tend to be tough and streetwise. To become a member, a young person must be at least 16 and be recommended by another member. Recruits must take martial arts training and prove themselves out on patrol. In addition, they must either work or go to school. Sliwa and the other wearers of the red berets collect no pay.

In the early 1980s, Sliwa began to expand the Angels to other cities. In 1981, members arrived in Atlanta to help the black community search for a serial killer who was targeting young blacks, and later members went to set up a branch in Los Angeles.

In early 1992, Sliwa was attacked by three men who beat him with baseball bats. Two months later, he was ambushed in a stolen taxicab. A gunman popped up from the front seat and shot him in the chest and legs. Sliwa managed to get away. No one has been caught. Some Guardian Angels speculate that drug dealers may have

Curtis Sliwa (seated) talks to members of his Guardian Angels aboard a New York subway car in 1980. (UPI/Bettmann.)

decided to kill Sliwa, hoping that the Guardian Angels' patrols would collapse.

Police have mixed feelings about Sliwa and the Angels. Some police officers will privately say they approve, but many police departments strongly oppose anything like vigilante groups. They feel the youthful patrollers may get in the way of legitimate police business, may expose undercover police officers by accident, or may make mistakes and hurt innocent citizens. There is also the possibility that if similar vigilante groups become widespread, they could be infiltrated by criminals and become covers for drug smuggling or other illegal activities.

In fact, in 1982 there was a tragic misunderstanding between the police and the Guardian Angels. One of their members, Frank Melvin, was patrolling a housing project in Newark, New Jersey. Melvin tried to open his shirt to show an officer his Guardian Angels T-shirt, but an officer on the rooftop mistakenly thought his partner on the ground was being attacked. The officer opened fire and killed Melvin. The Angels mounted a march to Washington, D.C., to demand an investigation, but the officer was exonerated in court.

Despite some police opposition, many communities welcome the Guardian Angels and similar groups. In the Venice area of Los Angeles, for example, a security company made up of unarmed members of the black religious group the Nation Of Islam has contracted to guard several federal housing projects. Residents report the presence of the Muslim guards in their distinctive uniforms has cut crime, noise, and drug dealing.

For Discussion

1. In what ways are the Guardian Angels similar to vigilantes? How are they different?

2. What might happen if the Guardian Angel group, or similar groups, became more widespread? What problems might arise? What might be some benefits?

3. If you had an opportunity, would you join the Guardian Angels or a similar group? Why or why not?

Crime in the Schools

Crime and violence in the schools have been increasing since the 1950s. A teacher from that decade would be astonished to enter some of our urban schools today and find police in the halls and metal detectors at the doors to keep out guns and knives.

The National School Safety Center at Pepperdine University reports over 3 million crimes a year on school grounds, and almost 200,000 injuries from violence. One study estimates more than 100,000 American students carry guns to class every day. One in 12 students reports being assaulted in school or on the way to school. And 20 percent of teachers report being threatened.

Schools have not always been so hazardous. From the 1950s through the middle 1960s, the main school problems were pranks, some ethnic rivalry, isolated fistfights, and occasional vandalism. For a brief time from about 1968 through the early 1970s, the massive college anti-war movement spilled over into the high schools. There were demonstrations against the war and over local issues, such as integration or local school rules. But by the early 1970s, much more serious problems were being seen. Schools started to experience crimes of violence, drug offenses, rape, even shootings.

Schools and Gangs

Schools, of course, reflect the communities they serve. In the early 1980s, crack cocaine and heavily armed drug-dealing gangs overran many urban communities. Gang members and gang "wanna-bes" adopted symbols such as colored head scarves and football team jackets. In some places, drug dealing and gang rivalries spilled over into the schools. Increased levels of violence in society as a whole affected the schools. Personal feuds over a girlfriend or an insult that would once have ended in a fistfight now turned into a gun battle. In New York City schools during the 1992 school year alone, five teachers, one policeman, two parents, and 16 students were shot.

One response has been to turn schools into prison-like fortresses. Some schools have resorted to metal detectors, steel doors, bright security lights, high walls, and police patrols in the halls. A California school removed all lockers to eliminate hiding places for guns or drugs. Some schools have done away with teachers' bathrooms, so that teachers have to visit the students' bathrooms regularly to discourage illegal activities. Another response, from the National School Safety Center, was to encourage schools to set up student committees to study school safety and even hold court on violators.

One of the casualties of this rise in school crime is quality education. Schools in crisis can no longer educate effectively. Each month thousands of junior and senior high school students are physically attacked. The extra security, the disruption, and the sense of fear, all distract students and teachers from the real job of the schools. As one Washington, D.C., high school student put it, "I want to go to college. I don't want to die."

For Discussion

1. Describe how school conditions differed in each of the following periods: 1950-1968; 1968-1971; 1972-present.

2. Does your school look different from a school of the 1950s? What is different and why?

3. Does your school have a crime problem? If so, what do you think are the primary causes of crime in your school? Explain. What do you think can be done about the problem?

Class Activity: Trouble at Coolidge High

What can be done about violence at school? One approach has been to ask members of the school community to find solutions to the problem. In the activity that follows, imagine that you are part of a School Problems Committee set up to deal with the case study presented below.

A Case Study

Coolidge High School is an old inner-city school which has had trouble with gangs for many years. There are three main rival gangs at school, the Dukes, The Rolling Nineties, and the Vatos. While most gang violence is off campus, at night, and during weekends, the school has suffered extensive vandalism, which appears to be gang-related. Gang names and symbols have been painted on the walls and carved on desks. Threats and challenges appear on the walls of the school entrance. A few fights have broken out, but no one has been seriously hurt yet.

Students are frisked for weapons at the school entrances, and the administration has tried to guard the halls to prevent more graffiti or fighting. Nothing has helped very much, and school morale is very low.

The following steps are being proposed to the School Problems Committee:

1. Teachers should periodically check the classroom furniture and ask students to report any new marks.

2. Felt pens and magic markers should be banned from school.

3. Vandals who are caught should join work teams to clean or repair school property.

4. Parents should be told that they are liable for property destroyed by their children.

5. Teachers and administrators should frequently lecture students about vandalism.

6. The school should set up a school pride campaign.

There is one further proposal, a surprise that came at the last moment. Mr. Martinez is a social studies teacher who has worked well with all three gangs in the school. They respect him. He has given them special tutoring and helped them develop recreation programs. This is his proposal:

Mr. Martinez: "I believe the members of the Dukes, the Rolling Nineties, and the Vatos are now ready to sign a formal truce. Their leaders have told me they realize they have to live together here at Coolidge. They have offered to declare the school a peace zone, to leave their weapons home, and to set up a weekend patrol to guard the school from any outside gangs. In return, they would like a few designated areas on campus to paint their gang graffiti. They promise the graffiti will contain no threats or challenges. And they also want permission to wear their gang caps and jackets at school. I believe this could be an important opportunity, and I decided to bring this offer to you for discussion."

Activity: The School Problems Committee Meets

Divide the class into five groups, each with the following roles:

a. School principal

b. Teacher

c. Student representative, elected by the student body

d. Student body president

e. Parent

Students playing each of these roles will be part of a five-member School Problems Committee. The committee will discuss and decide upon the various proposals to deal with the gang problem, including the proposal from Mr. Martinez. Before forming committees, try to imagine you are the person in your assigned role. How would that person view gangs in the school? What special interest would that person have in the problem?

1. First get together in a group with the other students who play the same role as you. For example, all the students assigned to be the school principal should get together. Discuss how a person in your role would respond to the issue.

2. Now regroup and form School Problems Committees. Each committee should have one principal, one student body president and at least one teacher, parent, and student body representative. The principal should act as the chairperson.

3. Each committee should discuss the Coolidge High problems and the proposals. Before making your recommendations, consider the following questions:

- What are the most serious problems facing Coolidge High?

- Which proposals in the school plan will be effective in dealing with the problems? Which will be ineffective? Why?

- What proposals should be adopted to form the school plan? Why?

4. At the end of the group discussions, the principals should report to the class on each committee's decisions. As a class, discuss the plans that the committees developed. Also discuss whether such school committees can help address the problem of school gangs and crime. You may base your discussion on the following questions:

a. What are the strengths and weaknesses of the various plans? Which one is most likely to be successful?

b. Would you like to see a School Problems Committee formed in your school? Give your reasons.

Activity: What Are Communities Doing about Crime in Schools?

At your school or community library, research about crime in schools. Choose one of the following problem areas: vandalism, burglaries, robberies, assaults on teachers and students, confiscations of weapons, rapes, or murders. Research to find the following:

(a) what schools across the country are doing to attack the problem; and

(b) the latest statistics on this problem in schools.

Report your findings to the class.

c. How should committee members be selected?

d. How much authority should they have?

e. Do students in your school need a place to register complaints?

f. Are there better ways to deal with school crime than through this kind of committee? If so, what are they?

5. Make a list of issues you would take before a committee at your school. In a class discussion, decide which of these issues are the most important.

Burglary Prevention

A **burglary** is an unlawful entry into a building or car with the intent to steal. It is the most common felony in America. There are over 3 million burglaries reported every year, and law enforcement experts believe an amount equal to that go unreported. That works out to more than 16,000 burglaries every day. The reported losses amount to almost $4 billion. To get an idea of how much money that is, imagine earning $1,000 a day. At that rate, it would take you more than 11,000 years to earn $4 billion. Only about 13 percent of these burglaries are ever cleared up by the police.

Burglary is a crime of opportunity. In about a third of all burglaries, force isn't used and nothing is broken. Many people fail to lock their doors or windows, and many others use inadequate locks. This makes the burglar's job easier. In many cases, it's just as easy for a burglar to pick a lock or break it as it is to open a door and walk in.

Perhaps more than anything else, burglars benefit when neighbors do not know each other. A neighbor is literally someone who lives nearby, but the word has come to suggest much more in our culture. Neighbors are supposed to be friendly and helpful. Before this century, neighbors traditionally banded together to help each other build houses and barns, sow and harvest crops, and protect their communities. But in our modern society, such tasks are taken care of by profession-

als, and people move so often that neighborly communities rarely develop. Because of the growing crime problem, many residents are afraid of talking to strangers-including their own neighbors.

These circumstances have made the burglars' task much easier. A stranger can often enter a community without being noticed, and can go right up to a house without the neighbors becoming suspicious.

There have been several local responses to the breakdown of the natural sense of community and the rise of burglaries. Some wealthier communities hire private security companies to patrol their neighborhoods continuously. Other have turned themselves into gated communities, behind high walls and drive-in gates with 24-hour security guards.

One interesting experiment, called the "Broken Windows" plan, was tried out in the 1980s in Virginia. In a high-burglary area, the community carted away trash and abandoned cars, filled in potholes, swept the streets, and painted out graffiti. The burglary rate dropped immediately by 35 percent. The people who ran the experiment argued that broken windows and other signs of urban decay "create fear in citizens and attract predators." They showed that simple attention to the look of an area can dramatically reduce crime.

Another response to the burglary problem has been the development of **neighborhood watch** groups or **block associations**. The police have often encouraged the development of neighborhood watch groups, especially in cities where community-policing programs are being set up. Neighborhood watch groups try to re-establish a sense of community. Members meet to discuss ways to make their area safer. They get to know one another, watch over one another's homes, and sometimes even clean up unsightly areas.

Neighborhood watch programs have proven very successful in reducing crime, according to careful studies conducted in Seattle, San Diego, and Detroit. In one Detroit neighborhood, burglaries were reduced by 62 percent. To see how this can work, we will examine one block association in detail.

The Tierra Bonita Neighborhood Association

Tierra Bonita is an upper-middle-class hillside suburb on the West Coast. Because the houses are set back from the road, isolated by shrubbery and trees, burglars were having a field day there. In particular, burglars were breaking into homes when the residents were away on vacation. The police did what they could to increase patrolling, but there were only three officers available at any one time to cover the whole area. The problem only got worse.

Activity: Organizing a Neighborhood Meeting

As you have learned, neighborhood cooperation is the real key to cutting down on burglaries. If your neighborhood does not already have a neighborhood watch or similar group, you can help organize one. People of all ages who live in the same neighborhood can work together to organize a meeting. You can also use this activity to plan a presentation to your local P.T.A. or a community service club such as the Lions or Rotary. Use the following steps as a guide.

1. Organize yourselves into teams of four or five students. It is helpful if all team members live in the same general vicinity.

2. Find a location for the meeting. This can be someone's home, a clubhouse in a park, a multipurpose room in a library, a banquet room at a local restaurant, or a room at school.

3. Schedule a specific time and date. Evenings or weekend mornings are usually best.

4. Plan a program for the meeting. For helpful hints, review the Tierra Bonita group's meeting. Contact your local police department to see if it can send a burglary expert with a presentation. Some hardware stores and security firms are willing to send someone to demonstrate various locking devices and alarms. Prepare any visual aids you think might be helpful, such as charts of local burglary rates, local maps, or lists of burglary prevention steps. Prepare any handouts, such as maps and phone lists, and prepare name tags for people at the meeting. It can be a nice touch to plan simple refreshments, such as coffee and lemonade.

5. Select a moderator for the meeting. This can be one of your group or a community member who is willing to help.

6. Write a one-page notice announcing the meeting. Be sure to indicate clearly the purpose of the meeting and who is sponsoring it. Include the time, date, and location. A map or careful directions should be part of the notice. Make enough copies for the area and distribute them to residents in the area.

7. Hold the meeting. Be sure to arrive early to move chairs and to set up any displays and refreshments. Greet those arriving and make them feel welcome. For the first meeting, it is often best to wait an extra 15 minutes for latecomers. Don't be discouraged if the turnout is not large. Even a few people can start a program. More will join later. The moderator should open the meeting, explain its purpose, and then introduce the presenters.

Before adjourning, some concrete plan should be made and people should take specific responsibilities. It is a common failing of new groups to decide that certain steps should be taken, but no one takes responsibility for them. At a minimum, you should have a phone list of those present for further contacts.

Remember that one of the main purposes of a neighborhood program like this is to get neighbors better acquainted with one another. This will help them watch out for one another and develop a sense of community. Allow some time at the meeting or after it for socializing.

In desperation, a few energetic residents took the lead and called a meeting. Over 1,600 residents formed the Tierra Bonita Association of Neighborhoods. The association took on many tasks, but its top priority was an anti-burglary program. It formed an anti-burglary committee and they invited the police to a public meeting to discuss the problem.

The police opened the meeting with a video that showed how burglars break in and recommended some simple steps residents could take to safeguard their homes. The residents then set up a neighborhood-watch plan. Each block elected a coordinator, who was to be the primary contact with the police department. Block coordinators collected names and addresses so they knew who lived in their neighborhood. If anything suspicious happened, people could report it to the coordinator. And if someone went away on vacation, the coordinator could arrange to check the house periodically.

The association posted signs at every road leading into the area saying, "Tierra Bonita is a Neighborhood Watch Community." It set up a buddy system, so neighbors could watch one another's homes. Buddies also helped each other

upgrade their locks and window latches. If one family in a buddy group went on vacation, the other could bring in the newspaper, open and close the drapes, and make the house look lived in. Finally, the association agreed to hold regular meetings to keep alive the community spirit they had created and to introduce new residents to the program.

In the first full year of operation, the burglary rate in Tierra Bonita went down by 54 percent.

For Discussion

1. Why do you think it's so difficult for the police to catch burglars without citizen help?

2. What are some easy ways to reduce burglary rates? What can individual homeowners do?

3. How much responsibility should neighbors have for each other? Could neighborhood watches lead to an invasion of people's privacy? How could such problems be avoided?

4. Have you ever seen someone suspicious hanging around a neighbor's house? Did you call the police? Would you if it happened again? Why?

5. Is there a neighborhood-watch plan in your area? How is it working?

Activity: A Home Security Check

Walk through your own home and check how secure it is. While the following precautions will not guarantee protection from burglary, they will help deter it.

- *Door locks.* The best protection for a door is a deadbolt. The bolt should extend at least an inch from the door, and it should have a hardened steel insert. The standard door lock has a beveled tongue only about a half inch long that can be forced open easily by most burglars. Deadbolts with twist handles should not be within easy reach of a glass window.

- *Sliding glass doors.* Burglars often enter houses through one of these doors. They simply lift the door out of its track. To prevent this, bolts or pins should be fitted into holes drilled through the track into the door frame. The bolt or pin can be easily removed from the inside when you want to use the door. A broomstick lying in the track provides some protection, but is much less effective.

- *Sash windows.* For sash windows, a bolt or pin mechanism should secure the two sashes to each other. Some sash locks require a key to open and some require a screwdriver or hexdriver. If windows are never to be opened, a simple screw can be drilled through both sashes into the window frame. If windows are to be opened only a small amount for ventilation, a screw can be fixed firmly in the track, allowing the window to open only two or three inches.

- *Sliding windows.* Sliding windows can be secured in a similar way to sliding glass doors. A pin mechanism can be attached to the sliding window so it slides into a hole in the frame. If you use a simple stop device on the track, make sure it is clamped on firmly. Many of these can be pushed aside with enough force on the window. If you use a stop device or a stick in the track, you should also fit a device on the top of the window to prevent it being lifted out of its track.

- *Louvered windows.* There are no easy ways to make louvered windows completely secure. Burglars can often slide the glass panes right out of their frames. On most louvered windows, the operating lever provides some locking protection if it is closed all the way. Make sure you cannot rotate the panes by hand when the lever is closed.

- *Window bars and grilles.* If the house has window grilles, make sure there is some way to open them from inside in case of fire.

- *Shrubbery and lights outside.* Shrubbery outside the windows should be trimmed so it does not give burglars a place to hide

while they are trying to break in. There should be night lights to help illuminate any dark areas where a burglar might lurk.

- *Valuables.* You should have a list of all the valuable items in the house and their serial numbers. Keep the list in a safe place, so it could be used later to help reclaim any stolen items or to catch a burglar or a dealer in stolen goods. As additional protection, you can engrave your name or social security number on all valuable items and then post a notice prominently in a window that all valuable items in the house are marked. Most police departments will lend an engraving tool to local residents.

- *Alarm system.* If your home has an alarm system, test it to make sure it works. Test the window sensors or motion detectors to make sure they all work.

Class Activity: Fighting Crime in the City of Athena

In this simulation, you will take the role of citizens of Athena, a city plagued by an upsurge in crime. The city has just received special federal funds to help solve its crime problem. A decision must be made about how the funds are to be used. The city council has created a special fund in the mayor's budget, and made the mayor responsible for distribution. Many community members and organizations have a great interest in the decision and some ideas on how it should be made.

A few days ago, Athena's mayor made the following remarks at a meeting of the Chamber of Commerce. The remarks were printed in their entirety in the Athena Daily News. There has been a great deal of discussion about what the mayor said and how the funds should be spent. The text of the mayor's speech follows. Read it and think about recommendations you might make.

The Mayor's Speech

Good afternoon. I'm pleased to report today that Athena is bustling. Our population is growing, our standard of living is increasing, and in the last year alone three major new industries relocated here. These are high-tech corporations, and they brought in new jobs and created business for local suppliers. While I would like to take full credit for these developments, I know many of you have also worked hard to revitalize Athena. All of us here today deserve a warm round of applause for what we have done for our city.

But let's remember that Athena still faces many challenges. One problem in particular stands out. Because of this problem, we have faced deeply personal losses, even deaths of loved ones. Some of us can no longer afford insurance for our businesses or homes. Some of us have given up going out in the evening.

I am speaking, of course, of the upsurge in crime here in Athena. Before I address this issue, I want to make one thing perfectly clear. We do not believe the crime problem has been caused by weak laws, lenient courts, or poor police work.

We have the best criminal justice system in the world. It is not my intention here today to try to fix blame for our problems or find a scapegoat. Our task is to find solutions.

Athena is not alone. Communities throughout the state, indeed, communities across the nation, are experiencing the same increase in crime. The problem is widespread and growing, and the need to find solutions has been noted in the press and in numerous government studies. The federal government has heard the cries for help. It has created a pilot anti-crime program that will make some funds available to the cities. These funds are to be used at our discretion in attacking the crime problem. Under section 108F of the program we are entitled to $200,000 a year. At today's costs, that is not a very large amount, but it is a start and we must use it well.

Because of previous commitments to our Victim's Assistance Program, $80,000 of this money must be earmarked for crime victims. It will be used to cover the medical bills of victims, funeral expenses for their families, and to provide psychological counseling to those left disturbed and frightened. These are the forgotten men, women, and children who have suffered most from the rise in crime. It is altogether fitting that a share of the 108F funds be committed to them.

For the remaining $120,000, the money is to be spent at our discretion, as long as it is targeting crime control. Today I would like to solicit your opinions and suggestions for the use of these 108F funds. How should this money be spent? What programs would you like to see put into effect? To help make these decisions, I am going to appoint a citizens' task force. The task force will be made up of Athenans from all walks of life. It will review suggestions that have already been made by various city departments and citizens' groups, and members of the task force will make their recommendations to me. I remind you that Athenans have solved many problems in the past by working together. If we stick together and share our wisdom with one another, we can take a major stride toward licking this problem, too.

* * *

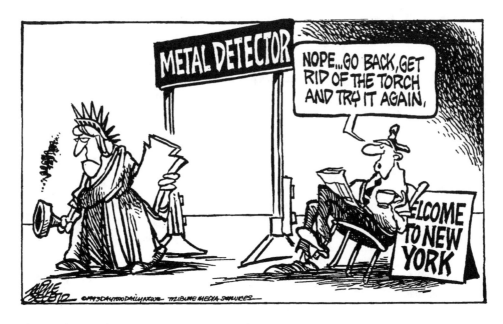

Do solutions to crime have to impinge on liberty? (Peters cartoon reprinted with permission.)

An announcement of the new funds for Athena was made several weeks before the mayor's speech to the Chamber of Commerce. Community groups that thought they had a chance to obtain some of the funds began preparing proposals for programs to be funded by the money. As soon as the mayor let it be known that proposals were requested, several organizations were ready to deliver them. Within a few days, six proposals arrived at the mayor's office.

Not every proposal could be fully funded. Either all would be funded for less than requested or some would not be funded at all. Consequently, representatives of each sponsoring group were eager to influence those who would make the final decision.

This evening, the mayor is holding a reception in honor of the Anti-Crime Task Force. The mayor, staff, and the members of the task force as well as representatives of community organizations will be there.

Those attending the reception understand that this social event is an important opportunity for exchanging views informally, off the record. Both the members of the committee and the representatives of various community organizations know that the decision on who will receive the funds could be influenced by talking to the right people.

For Discussion

1. What is Athena's current problem? Why has the task force been called together?

2. What is the mayor's plan for $80,000 of the 108F funding? Do you agree with this commitment of part of the funds?

Procedures for Activity

In the two-part simulation that follows, members of community organizations will first attend a reception and try to persuade task force members to fund their programs. Then in a public meeting, the task force members will decide how the funds should be allocated.

1. Break into seven groups. The task force should have six to 10 members. The community organizations should have three to five students each. Appoint a chairperson in each group.

Proposals for 108F Grants

Proposal 1: Police Aides
Sponsor: Athena Police Department
Cost: $72,000

This is a six-month program to provide each of the 14 two-officer patrols in the downtown area with one half-time aide. These aides would be students studying police science or public administration. They would take over clerical duties and allow officers to spend more time on patrol. The budget would pay for fourteen aides, at $10 an hour, for 20 hours per week. The program would last six months, providing an additional 7,000 hours of police patrol time.

Proposal 2: Force One Security Patrol

Sponsor: Athena Chamber of Commerce

Cost: $96,720

This six-month program would provide a two-person private security patrol for the downtown area, during non-business hours. The patrol would function from 5 p.m. to 8 a.m. weekdays and round the clock on weekends. The private agency would hire, train, and equip the patrol. The budget covers salaries, expenses, and transportation costs for six months.

Proposal 3: Self-Defense Classes
Sponsor: Urban Youth Association
Cost: $27,000

This year-round program would cover the fees for basic self-defense classes for up to a total of 500 Athenans. The basic course lasts four days a week for three weeks. Columbia Self-Defense normally charges $300 for this course, but by offering it for a large group, they will be charging the city only $54 per person. The Urban Youth Association has agreed to publicize the course and help select participants. Priority will go to low-income and elderly persons.

Proposal 4: Crime Prevention Seminars
Sponsor: Athena Police Department
Cost: $45,000

This is a year-round program that would provide four two-hour discussion seminars a week for one year. The seminars would be taught by police officers and would focus on ways private citizens and neighborhood-watch groups can help prevent crime. The budget would cover officer salaries, publicity expenses, and money for preparing pamphlets and visual aids for the seminars.

Proposal 5: Citizenswatch Patrols
Sponsor: Citizens for Public Safety
Cost: $22,700

This year-round program would help fund Citizenswatch patrols by business people and others. The patrols would cover the downtown and high-income residential areas. The patrol group is already formed and has made 46 citizen's arrests over the last six months. Unfortunately, only half those caught were brought to trial. In many cases, the untrained patrollers collected evidence incorrectly or violated the rights of those they detained. The budget will buy 40 citizen-band car radios and 20 hand-held walkie-talkies to improve communications with the police. Leaders of the group hope getting officers to the scene sooner will improve the conviction rate.

Proposal 6: Crimescope Hotline
Sponsor: Channel 14 Television
Cost: $49,910

This year-round program would provide a 24-hour telephone line, plus $50,000 in reward money to secret witnesses. Channel 14 has offered to raise half the reward money from private sources. Informants would be given code numbers, and their information would be passed on to the police. If the information resulted in a conviction, the informant would be paid a reward.

2. Review the mayor's speech briefly and then read the six proposals for 108F grants.

3. Rank the six proposals in order of which would be the most effective. Which proposal do you think would really help stop Athena's crime problem? Write a list with the most effective on top and the least effective on the bottom.

4. Rank the six proposals again, this time in order of which would be the most effective *for the least amount of money*.

5. Follow your group assignments as follows:

A. Task Force

As a member of this task force, your job is to consider the issues carefully and help the mayor decide on the best way to allocate the 108F funds. The mayor wants the task force to develop a consensus on its views before making its recommendations.

You know that citizen activists will be at the reception and that they will want to talk to you about the funding recommendations you will soon make. So at the reception, be sure to:

- *Give feedback*. Inform citizens of your concerns about their proposals. Ask them to respond to these concerns by giving you arguments to take to the meeting. How they respond can help give you information to make a decision.

- *Speak to people from as many groups as possible*. Those vying for your attention may resent your spending too much time with any one person or group.

- *Remember your political role*. Be polite, listen carefully, but don't make any promises you can't keep. If you back out of a commitment, the committee and the mayor will look foolish.

B. Community Organizations

You want to assure that your organization's proposal is fully understood by as many members of the task force as possible. Your goal at the reception is to convince them that your proposal should be fully funded. When talking with task

force members, review the list of proposals and concentrate on the proposal for your organization.

- Present your best arguments.

- What are the strengths of your organization?

- Why is the proposal a good idea for solving the crime problem in Athena?

- Keep your presentation brief and to the point.

- Ask for a firm commitment in support of your proposal.

- Time at the reception is limited. Before it begins, plan your strategy:

  - Should you concentrate on presenting the reasons why your proposal is best? Or on pointing out weaknesses in the other approaches and proposals? You may want to make use of your rankings of all the proposals.

  - Should everyone in the group talk with as many committee members as they can? Or should each group member focus on a different person? Should you try to convince other groups?

  - Write a slogan for your group.

  - Remember, this is a social occasion. Inappropriate behavior may prejudice members of the committee against you. Avoid arguing or interrupting conversations. See how subtle you can be.

6. Hold the reception.

7. After the reception, the task force should meet in front of the whole class to discuss the proposals and make its recommendation to the mayor. The committee should review and modify, if necessary, its previous rankings. The committee must now decide on how to spend the $120,000.

- Should the committee fund one or two of the programs it feels is most effective?

- Should it partially fund several programs?

- Should it fund the least expensive programs? Will the proposals rated highly serve a broad range of community interests?

- Will the proposals you fund serve more than one segment of the population? This is an open meeting. The entire class will observe your deliberations. Write the following information on the board. Remember the committee cannot spend more than $120,000.

	Request	Award
Police Aides	$ 72,000	
Force One Security Patrol	$ 96,720	
Self-Defense Classes	$ 27,000	
Crime Prevention Seminars	$ 45,000	
Citizenswatch Patrols	$ 22,700	
Crimescope Hotline	$ 49,910	
TOTAL	$313,330	$120,000

8. When the task force has reached a decision on the allocation of the funds, discuss the decision as a class. Use the following questions:

- Which proposals seemed weakest? Which seemed strongest? Why?

- After hearing the task force's discussion, did you change your mind on any of the proposals? Why?

- What seemed to make some groups more successful in persuading the task force?

- What additional proposals can you think of that would help solve Athena's crime problems? Describe and summarize them on the board. What are the strengths of each? What are the weaknesses? Would any of these be better than those proposed to the mayor? Why?

To conclude the discussion, you may wish to conduct a class vote to find out which proposal discussed the class thinks would be the most effective.

Conclusion on Crime

You've gone through chapters on crime, police, the criminal case, corrections, juvenile justice, and solutions. Despite debate over many issues, a few things are clear. America has a significant crime problem. It also has a sophisticated criminal justice system.

Other things aren't quite so clear. Just how serious is America's crime problem? Is America's criminal justice system working and, if so, how well? What should be preserved? What should be changed? Americans—experts and non-experts alike—are divided on the answers to these questions. Differences of opinion on the exclusionary rule, tougher criminal laws, harsher sentencing, the death penalty, handguns, and the causes of crime often reflect and fuel the debate.

Public Perceptions

One thing seems more clear. Scientifically conducted polls indicate that people believe the problem of crime is getting worse. Public attitudes also tend to favor harsher punishment for criminals, less judicial discretion in sentencing, and the death penalty as methods for reducing crime. Apparently, Americans feel that the criminal justice system is just not working.

The news and entertainment media may be contributing to these perceptions. Crime makes a good story. Newspapers and news broadcasts devote significant coverage to crime and criminal-justice issues. Much of the coverage is balanced and factual. Other times it borders on the sensational.

Many movie and television dramas also focus on crimes and criminals for their stories. By the early '90s, television had even developed several "reality shows" that follow real police officers on their patrols. The average viewer sees several murders a week on screen, plus dozens of other acts of violence.

Although the media seems to feed the public's fear of crime, much of that fear is based on reality. Many parts of our cities truly *are* less safe than they were 20 or 30 years ago. Almost everyone has some direct experience of crime—as

(UPI/Bettmann.)

a victim, friend of a victim, or even as someone who just has to pay high insurance rates. Under such conditions, what should be done?

Hardline Answers

Much of the public seems to favor getting tougher on criminals. Responding to this public demand, politicians over the years have made various proposals. Among them are the following:

- Build more prisons.
- Make prison sentences longer.
- Institute and carry out the death penalty for many homicides.
- Get rid of the exclusionary rule.
- Restrict bail for dangerous suspects and for convicted persons waiting on appeals.
- Abolish parole.
- Give judges less discretion in sentencing.
- Make prison sentences mandatory for many crimes.
- Restrict the use of the insanity defense.

- Transfer more juveniles to adult courts.
- Hire more police.

These are just a few proposals for cracking down on criminals. Although many Americans favor getting tougher, there are other views.

Critics of the get-tough approach claim it doesn't work. They argue that we have passed harsher laws, built more prisons, and declared various wars—the war on drugs, the war on crime. This approach has cost the nation a fortune, and it has failed to make our streets safer. According to the critics, it may actually make the streets worse. When the prison class of the 1980s begins to "graduate," we may find our streets dominated by masses of hardened criminals.

When television journalist Richard Threlkeld investigated crime in America for ABC-TV, he said:

> The sense you get, after six months of trekking around our criminal justice system and talking to so many of the cops and criminals and judges and victims who are part of

Following the Los Angeles riots of 1992, a study by RAND Corporation blamed the federal government for ignoring social problems in the nation's cities. (Mark Cullum cartoon reprinted by permission of Copley News Service.)

it, is a sense of surprise. . . . I thought that if we had a lot tougher laws and a lot more cops, we could stop crime. A cop in Chicago put me straight on that. . . . I found that when it comes to stopping crime, getting tough is not the same as getting smart.

Threlkeld went on to quote judges and police officers who attacked mandatory sentencing, moving juveniles into the adult system, and building more prisons. They insisted that these get-tough measures simply don't work. This conclusion was reinforced by a major study released in the early 1990s.

The RAND Study: Urban America

The RAND Corporation is probably America's best-known social policy think tank. It has studied social problems in this country and made policy recommendations on many subjects since 1948. In the wake of the riots in Los Angeles in 1992, RAND prepared a major study on the problems of urban America, including an in-depth focus on crime. This study laid the blame

for most of the problems of the cities directly on the federal government. "The federal government's inadequate response to urban America's tinderbox condition comes as little surprise; for more than a decade, Washington has turned its back on the cities."

The authors of the study discussed how the criminal justice system had been transformed in the 1980s. "Tough-on-crime edicts are not new and have dominated national crime policy since the late 1970s. At that time, the nation shifted its focus away from addressing the 'root causes' of crime and the rehabilitation of criminals toward making crime penalties more swift, certain, and severe."

Focusing on California, the study pointed out that as state spending on criminal justice grew by 70 percent, spending on education grew only 10 percent.

"The impact of tougher sentences (particularly prison sentences) on crime rates is weak at best," the report concluded. "Although prison populations quadrupled in size, the overall per capita crime rate remained essentially unchanged. . . ."

The RAND report cited a statement that was issued by a conference of 450 criminal justice leaders in America. The statement criticized the "lock'em up" approach and urged public officials to be more honest with the public about the failure of prisons to control crime. In signing the statement, Morris L. Thigpen, the Alabama director of corrections, added, "We are on a train that has to be turned around. It just doesn't make sense to pump millions and millions into corrections and have no effect on the crime rate."

The RAND report made three central recommendations about the criminal justice system:

1. We have to begin by acknowledging the limits of a get-tough policy on reducing crime.

2. We have to refocus who we put in prison. We should focus on imprisoning the most likely repeat offenders, and stop sending people to prisons for acts such as simple technical violations of parole.

3. We have to divert some resources to non-penal strategies for crime prevention.

This last statement was the report's central conclusion. "When the public debate focuses so heavily on punishment, it creates a false dichotomy between tough law enforcement and 'soft on crime' social programs. The choice is not one or the other—it must be both. . . . Our expectations of what justice agencies can do should be lowered, and our expectations of what social programs *must* do should rise."

Crime in America, the report concluded, is a broad social problem and it must be attacked with social programs. The RAND authors did not recommend specific programs, such as job training or drug counseling. Instead they encouraged America to begin a national debate on the question. They wanted the country to reconsider its past strictly punitive approach to crime and begin to discuss the sorts of social programs that might make a real difference in attacking urban problems, especially crime.

For Discussion

1. After studying the issues, has your opinion about America's crime problem changed? If so, how?

2. Do you agree with the RAND report that there has been too much emphasis on get-tough policies? Why or why not?

Class Activity: What Should Be Done?

Pretend you are a researcher drafting a study on crime in America. Prepare the concluding section of the report, "Recommendations on the Crime Problem." Use what you have learned from this book, class discussions, outside resources, and your own research. State your own ideas, opinions, and reasons. Prepare a presentation of your conclusion for the class.

APPENDICES

EXCERPTS FROM THE U.S. CONSTITUTION

Selected Sections of the U.S. Constitution, Ratified 1788

Preamble

We, the People of the United States, in Order to form a more perfect Union, establish Justice, insure domestic Tranquility, provide for the common defence, promote the general Welfare, and secure the Blessings of Liberty to ourselves and our Posterity, do ordain and establish this Constitution for the United States of America.

Article I

Section 1. All legislative Powers herein granted shall be vested in a Congress of the United States, which shall consist of a Senate and House of Representatives.

Section 8. The Congress shall have Power . . . To provide for the Punishment of counterfeiting the Securities and Coin of the United States . . . To constitute tribunals inferior to the supreme Court; To define and punish Piracies and Felonies committed on the high Seas, and Offenses against the Law of Nations . . . To make all Laws which shall be necessary and proper for carrying into Execution the foregoing Powers, and all other Powers vested by this Constitution in the Government of the United States . . . .

Section 9. . . .The Privilege of the Writ of Habeas Corpus shall not be suspended, unless when in cases of Rebellion or Invasion the public safety may require it.

No Bill of Attainder or ex post facto Law shall be passed.

Article II

Section 1. The executive Power shall be vested in a President of the United States of America. He shall hold his Office during the Term of four Years, and, together with the Vice President, chosen for the same Term, be elected as follows . . . .

Section 2. The President shall be Commander in Chief of the Army and Navy of the United States, and of the Militia of the several States, when called into the actual Service of the United States; he may require the Opinion, in writing, of the principal Officer in each of the executive Departments, upon any Subject relating to the Duties of their respective Offices, and he shall have Power to grant Reprieves and Pardons for Offences against the United States, except in Cases of Impeachment.

He shall have Power, by and with the Advice and Consent of the Senate to make Treaties, provided two-thirds of the Senators present concur; and he shall nominate and by and with the Advice and Consent of the Senate, shall appoint Ambassadors, other public Ministers and Consuls, Judges of the supreme Court, and all other Officers of the United States, whose Appointments are not herein otherwise provided for, and which shall be established by Law: but the Congress may by Law vest the Appointment of such inferior Officers, as they think proper, in the President alone, in the Courts of Law, or in the Heads of Departments.

Section 3. . . . . He shall take Care that the Laws be faithfully executed . . . .

Section 4. The President, Vice -President and all Civil Officers of the United States, shall be removed from Office on Impeachment for, and Conviction of, Treason, Bribery, or other high Crimes and Misdemeanors.

Article III

Section 1. The judicial Power of the United States, shall be vested in one supreme Court, and in such inferior Courts as the Congress may from time to time ordain and establish. The Judges, both of the supreme and inferior Courts, shall hold their Offices during good Behaviour, and shall, at stated Times, receive for their Services, a Compensation, which shall not be diminished during their Continuance in Office.

Section 2. The judicial Power shall extend to all Cases, in Law and Equity, arising under this Constitution, the Laws of the United States, and Treaties made, or which shall be made under their Authority;—to all Cases affecting Ambassadors, other public Ministers and Consuls;—to all Cases of admiralty and maritime Jurisdiction;—to Controversies to which the United States shall be a Party;—to Controversies between two or more States;—between a State and Citizens of another State;—between Citizens of different States;—between Citizens of the same State claiming Lands under Grants of different States, and between a State, or the Citizens thereof, and foreign States, Citizens or Subjects.

In all Cases affecting Ambassadors, other public Ministers and Consuls, and those in which a State shall be Party; the supreme Court shall have original Jurisdiction. In all the other Cases before mentioned, the supreme Court shall have appellate Jurisdiction, both as to Law and Fact, with such Exceptions, and under such Regulations as the Congress shall make.

The Trial of all Crimes, except in Cases of Impeachment, shall be by Jury; and such Trial shall be held in the State where the said Crimes shall have been committed; but when not committed within any State, the Trial shall be at such Place or Places as the Congress may by Law have directed.

Section 3. Treason against the United States shall consist only in levying War against them, or in adhering to their Enemies, giving them Aid and Comfort. No Person shall be convicted of Treason unless on the Testimony of two Witnesses to the same overt Act, or on Confession in open Court.

The Congress shall have Power to declare the Punishment of Treason, but no Attainder of Treason shall work Corruption of Blood, or Forfeiture except during the Life of the Person attainted.

Article IV

Section 1. Full faith and Credit shall be given in each State to the public Acts, Records, and judicial Proceedings of every other State. And the Congress may by general Laws prescribe the Manner in which such Acts, Records and Proceedings shall be proved, and the Effect thereof.

Section 2. The Citizens of each State shall be entitled to all Privileges and Immunities of Citizens in the several States.

A Person charged in any State with Treason, Felony or other Crime, who shall flee from Justice, and be found in another State, shall, on Demand of the executive Authority of the State from which he fled, be delivered up, to be removed to the State having Jurisdiction of the Crime. . . .

Section 4. The United States shall guarantee to every State in this Union a Republican Form of Government, and shall protect each of them against Invasion; and on Application of the Legislature, or of the Executive (when the Legislature cannot be convened) against domestic Violence.

Article VI

This Constitution, and the Laws of the United States which shall be made in Pursuance thereof; and all Treaties made, or which shall be made, under the Authority of the United States, shall be the supreme Law of the Land; and the Judges in every State shall be bound thereby, any Thing in the Constitution or Laws of any State to the Contrary notwithstanding. . . .

Selected Amendments from the Bill of Rights, Ratified 1791

First Amendment

Congress shall make no law respecting an establishment of religion, or prohibiting the free exercise thereof; or abridging the freedom of speech, or of the press; or the right of the people peaceably to assemble, and to petition the Government for a redress of grievances.

Second Amendment

A well regulated Militia, being necessary to the security of a free State, the right of the people to keep and bear Arms, shall not be infringed.

Fourth Amendment

The right of the people to be secure in their persons, houses, papers, and effects, against unreasonable searches and seizures, shall not be violated, and no Warrants shall issue, but upon probable cause, supported by Oath or affirmation, and particularly describing the place to be searched, and the persons or things to be seized.

Fifth Amendment

No person shall be held to answer for a capital, or otherwise infamous crime, unless on a presentment or indictment of a Grand Jury, except in cases arising in the land or naval forces, or in the Militia, when in actual service in time of War or public danger; nor shall any person be subject of the same offence to be twice put in jeopardy of life or limb; nor shall be compelled in any criminal case to be a witness against himself, nor be deprived of life, liberty, or property, without due process of law; nor shall private property be taken for public use, without just compensation.

Sixth Amendment

In all criminal prosecutions, the accused shall enjoy the right to a speedy and public trial, by an impartial jury of the State and district wherein the crime shall have been committed, which district shall have been previously ascertained by law, and to be informed of the nature and cause of the accusation; to be confronted with the witnesses against him to have compulsory process for obtaining witnesses in his favor, and to have the Assistance of Counsel for his defence.

Seventh Amendment

In Suits at common law, where the value in controversy shall exceed twenty dollars, the right of trial by jury shall be preserved, and no fact tried by a jury, shall be otherwise re -examined in any Court of the United States, than according to the rules of the common law.

Eighth Amendment

Excessive bail shall not be required, nor excessive fines imposed, nor cruel and unusual punishments inflicted.

Ninth Amendment

The enumeration in the Constitution, of certain rights, shall not be construed to deny or disparage others retained by the people.

10th Amendment

The powers not delegated to the United States by the Constitution, nor prohibited by it to the States, are reserved to the States respectively, or to the people.

Selected Later Amendments

13th Amendment, Ratified 1865

Neither slavery nor involuntary servitude, except as a punishment for crime whereof the party shall have been duly convicted, shall exist within the United States, or any place subject to their jurisdiction.

14th Amendment, Ratified 1868

All persons born or naturalized in the United States, and subject to the jurisdiction thereof, are citizens of the United States and of the State wherein they reside. No State shall make or enforce any law which shall abridge the privileges or immunities of citizens of the United States; nor shall any State deprive any person of life, liberty, of property, without due process of the law; nor deny to any person within its jurisdiction the equal protection of the laws.

GLOSSARY

acquit. To find not guilty

affidavit. A written statement made under oath.

affirmative defense. A defense such as insanity, self-defense, and entrapment. If proved by the defendant, it makes the defendant not guilty of the crime even if the prosecution can prove the elements of the crime.

age of majority. The age a person is considered an adult for legal purposes.

aggravated assault. According to the UCR, an unlawful attack by one person upon another for the purpose of inflicting severe or aggravated bodily injury. Normally committed with a weapon.

anthropologists. Scientists who study human customs and cultures.

appellate court. A court that hears appeals; not a trial court.

attorney. A lawyer; legal counsel. A person authorized to practice law.

attorney at law. See **attorney**.

arraignment. A court hearing in which the defendant must enter a plea, such as guilty or not guilty.

arrest. To take a person into custody for the purpose of charging the person with a crime.

arrestee. The person arrested.

arson. According to the UCR, any willful or malicious burning of another's property.

assault. Technically, the immediate threat of attacking someone, but usually it means a physical attack on another person. See **battery**.

assault with a deadly weapon. The crime of attacking someone with a weapon that could cause fatal injuries. See **aggravated assault**.

bail. A pretrial procedure permitting an arrested person to stay out of jail by depositing a set amount of money as security that the person will show up for trial.

bailiff. A police officer assigned to the courtroom to keep order.

battery. The illegal touching of another person, usually an attack. When used in the phrase assault and battery, the assault is the threat of the attack and the battery the physical attack itself.

bench. The judge's desk in the courtroom.

bill of attainder. A legislative enactment that punishes a person in place of a trial. Banned by the U.S. Constitution.

Bill of Rights. The first 10 amendments to the U.S. Constitution, which describe the rights and protections guaranteed to each citizen.

booking. The official process of recording the arrest. A booking officer records the accused's name and address, the charges, and time and place of arrest, and may take fingerprints and photographs of the accused.

bunco. A con game; a swindle.

burden of proof. The responsibility of proving facts in a case. In a criminal trial, the prosecution has the burden of proving its case beyond a reasonable doubt.

burglary. The illegal entry into any building with the intent to commit a crime, such as theft.

capital crime. A crime punishable by death or life imprisonment.

capital punishment. The death penalty.

case in chief. One side's trial evidence. In a criminal trial, the prosecution presents its evidence first. After it rests its case, the defense presents its evidence.

case law. Law made by judges interpreting constitutions, statutes, and other case law; judge -made law.

citizen review boards. An official group, staffed by ordinary citizens, authorized to review complaints of police misconduct.

civil case. A lawsuit between individuals or organizations which normally seeks monetary compensation for damages.

civil court. A court that handles civil cases.

civilian review boards. See **citizen review boards**.

commissioner. An attorney who acts as a judge.

common law. 1. the unwritten law in England that evolved over centuries and is the basis for U.S. law. 2. Case law in the United States as opposed to statutory law.

community policing. A type of policing that stresses community interaction with the police. Also called community-based policing or community-oriented policing.

corrections. The part of the criminal justice system that deals with convicted criminals; it includes jails, prisons, parole, and probation.

crime. An illegal act punishable upon conviction in a court.

crime rate. The amount of crime per so many people in the population.

criminal lawyer. A prosecutor or defense attorney.

criminal negligence. Doing an act with an extreme lack of care for the consequences. It is a state of mind requirement for certain crimes, e.g. involuntary manslaughter.

criminal procedure. The rules for processing someone through the criminal justice system.

criminology. The study of crime.

cross-examination. The questioning of an opponent's witnesses at trial.

deadly force. Force that poses a high risk of death or serious injury to its human target.

defendant. The accused in a criminal trial.

defense attorney. The attorney for the accused.

delinquent act. In most states, this means an act which if done by an adult would be a crime. Some states, however, also include status offenses as delinquent acts.

deterrence. The idea that fear of punishment will prevent crimes. For example, some people might be deterred from robbing banks because they know that bank robbers go to jail.

determinate sentence. A prison sentence for a specific length of time, e.g. five years.

direct examination. An attorney's initial questioning of his or her own witness.

disturbing the peace. The misdemeanor of willfully bothering other people by making a lot of noise.

discretion. The power to choose.

discretionary jurisdiction. The power of some appeals courts, such as the U.S. Supreme Court, to accept or refuse to hear particular appeals. See **writ of certiorari**.

driving under the influence. The crime of operating a motor vehicle while under the influence of drugs or alcohol.

due process. In the Fifth and 14th amendments, the basic requirement that no person can be deprived of life, liberty, or property without a fair trial. This means both fair laws and fair procedures must be used.

embezzlement. The crime of stealing another's property which has been entrusted to you. E.g. a bank teller might embezzle money from the bank.

entrapment. The affirmative defense that the defendant would not have committed the crime if the police had not enticed the defendant.

evidence. The means of determining facts in a trial. Testimony, physical objects, and exhibits are examples of evidence.

exclusionary rule. A judicial rule that prevents the government from introducing illegally obtained evidence at a criminal trial.

extort. To blackmail. To obtain money by threats of harm or of exposure of past deeds.

extortion. Blackmail. See **extort**.

fact finder. The one responsible for deciding the facts of a particular case and coming to a verdict; either a judge or jury.

false imprisonment. The crime of making a false arrest or unlawfully taking someone into custody.

felony. A serious crime usually punished by one or more years of imprisonment in a state or federal penitentiary.

felony murder. Any killing done while a criminal is committing a felony.

fitness hearing. A special hearing in juvenile court to determine whether a juvenile should be tried in adult court.

fixed sentence. See **determinate sentence**.

forfeiture. The confiscation of assets either used in or derived from illegal activity.

forgery. The crime of falsely signing a document with the intent to defraud.

fraud. The crime of obtaining another's property through lies and deceit.

general intent. The voluntary intent to do a prohibited act.

habeas corpus, writ of. A court order requiring authorities to release a prisoner because the court has found that the prisoner is being illegally detained.

hearing. Any court proceeding, such as a trial.

homicide. Literally, human killing. The crimes of homicide range from different degrees of murder to different kinds of manslaughter.

hypothetical. A made-up example.

impanel. To select a jury.

incarceration rate. The number of prisoners per 100,000 population.

incorrigible. Juveniles who cannot be controlled by their parents.

indentured servant. In American history, a person who contracted in return for transportation to America to work for free for a set number of years, usually two to seven.

indeterminate sentence. A prison sentence of an indefinite period of time, for example "one year to 30 years." Under this sentence, prisoners are released when the parole board determines they are rehabilitated.

interrogation. Questioning.

involuntary manslaughter. A killing caused by criminal negligence or an unintended killing that takes place during a misdemeanor offense.

jurisdiction. 1. the geographical area over which particular courts have power; 2. state and federal government.

jurisprudence. The philosophy of law, or the science that studies the principles of law.

larceny. The unlawful taking of another's property with the intention of permanently depriving the owner of its possession and use; theft.

lawyer. see **attorney**.

lynching. A form of mob violence that punishes an accused person without a legal trial. The word comes from the American Revolution and a Colonel Charles Lynch of Virginia, who urged crowds to beat and frighten Tories, supporters of Britain.

magistrate. A court officer who issues warrants; normally a lower-court judge who handles pretrial proceedings or presides over misdemeanor trials.

malice aforethought. A state of mind requirement for murder. It is either an intent to kill or an intent to do an extremely dangerous act with a conscious disregard for the consequences.

marshal. A law-enforcement officer who normally performs duties connected with a court.

mayhem. The crime of mutilating or cutting off a part of someone's body.

mens rea. Guilty mind; the state of mind requirement for crimes.

***Miranda* warning.** A advisory statement about the rights of suspects which police must read to suspects in custody before questioning them. The Supreme Court first required this statement in its *Miranda v. Arizona* decision in 1966.

misdemeanor. A crime less serious than a felony, usually punished by a fine or imprisonment up to one year in a local jail.

mitigate. To make less serious. Mitigating circumstances are circumstances surrounding a crime which tend to make it less serious.

Model Penal Code. A criminal code composed by legal experts at the American Law Institute as a standard that legislatures may want to adopt. Unless sections of it are adopted by jurisdictions, it has no legal authority.

motion. A formal request made to a court.

motion to suppress. A request that the court exclude particular evidence from the trial because it was illegally obtained.

murder. The unlawful killing of another person with malice aforethought.

nolo contendere plea. A plea of no contest. (Latin for "I will not contest it.") It has the same effect as a guilty plea except that the person does not admit guilt. Thus if someone files a lawsuit against the person, the person has not admitted guilt.

notary, or notary public. An official authorized to verify signatures on documents or attest to affidavits.

organized crime. A group that uses a business-like structure, with a boss and subordinates, to carry out crime on an ongoing basis.

pardon. An act by the governor or president that forgives all or part of a prisoner's sentence.

parens patriae. The idea that the state takes the role of parents to protect juveniles.

parole. The conditional release of a prisoner before the end of a prison term.

parole board. A board appointed by the governor which determines when prisoners may be released on parole.

penal. Subject to punishment. A *penal code* is a list of laws defining crimes.

penitentiary. A state or federal maximum-security prison.

plaintiff. The party in a lawsuit who sues the other party.

plea bargain. An agreement struck between a criminal defendant and prosecutor. In exchange for a guilty plea from the defendant, the prosecutor will either (1) drop one of several charges, (2) lower the charge, or (3) recommend a light sentence.

peremptory challenge. During jury selection, an attorney's rejection of a prospective juror that requires no reason be given to the court. Each side has a limited number of these challenges.

perjury. The crime of lying while testifying under oath.

precedent. An issue of law previously decided by a court that other courts follow.

probable cause. Evidence that an independent, cautious person would have good reason to believe.

probation. An alternative to prison. This sentence requires the offender to follow certain conditions, usually under the supervision of a probation officer.

prosecute. To try someone for a crime.

prosecution. The government's side in a criminal case.

prosecutor. The government's attorney who presents the case against a criminal defendant.

prosecutorial discretion. The prosecutor's authority to decide what charges to bring and how to pursue a criminal case.

prostitution. Crime of engaging in a sexual act with another in exchange for money or other compensation.

public defender. An attorney working for a government agency (the public defender's office) which defends criminal suspects who cannot afford their own attorney.

rape. According to the UCR, the carnal knowledge of a female forcibly and against her will.

receiving stolen property. The crime of buying or getting property that the buyer knows is stolen.

recidivism. The committing of further crimes by offenders with previous convictions.

redirect examination. An attorney's requestioning of his or her own witness after cross-examination.

rehabilitation. Helping convicted offenders change their lives so that they can lead productive lives in society.

restitution. Direct payments made from criminal to victim as compensation for a crime.

relevant. Pertinent, appropriate, related to the subject at hand.

robbery. The taking of a person's property by violence or threat of violence; forcible stealing.

search. In *Katz v. United States* (1967), the Supreme Court defined a search as any governmental intrusion into something in which a person has a reasonable expectation of privacy.

seizure. Any taking into possession, custody, or control. Property may be seized, but so may people. An arrest is one form of seizure.

sentence. A punishment for a crime.

sheriff. A county law-enforcement officer.

sodomy. Homosexual or oral copulation.

specific intent. The intent to do a prohibited act on purpose; the intent required for certain crimes, such as theft which requires the specific intent of never returning the property.

status offense. An offense, such as truancy or running away from home, that would not be a crime if committed by an adult.

statute. A written law; a law enacted by the legislature.

statutory law. See **statute**.

sting operation. Undercover police work that sets up a situation to catch criminals in the act.

street crime. A class of crimes usually involving force or violence, such as murder, assault, robbery, or rape.

strict liability. The imposition of criminal responsibility regardless of a person's intent.

testify. To make statements as a witness under oath.

testimony. Statements made by witnesses under oath.

theft. Larceny.

training schools. Large secure facilities which hold juveniles found delinquent.

treason. The crime of a U.S. citizen helping an enemy of the United States.

UCR. Uniform Crime Reporting Program. The nationwide program headed by the FBI that collects police reports of crime.

vandalism. The crime of intentionally defacing or destroying another person's property.

venue. The location of a trial.

verdict. The decision of guilty or not guilty made by the jury or judge.

victimless crimes. Crimes, such as prostitution and possession of illegal drugs, in which everyone involved chooses to be involved.

victimology. The branch of criminology that studies crime victims.

vigilantes. Persons who illegally take the law into their own hands and punish suspected lawbreakers.

voluntary manslaughter. The intentional killing of another person done under extreme provocation and in the heat of anger.

voir dire. During jury selection, the questioning of prospective jurors.

warrant. A court order issued by a judge authorizing a search, an arrest, or a seizure of evidence of a crime.

white-collar crime. A class of property crimes which are usually job-related, such as embezzlement, bribery, and consumer fraud.

writ. A written court order.

writ of certiorari. An order from an appeals court which states the court will hear a case. These writs are granted by appeals courts that have discretionary jurisdiction.

TABLE OF CASES

Michigan v. Harvey, 494 U.S. 344, 110 S.Ct. 1176 (1990)

Miranda v. Arizona, 384 U.S. 436, 86 S.Ct. 1602 (1966)

M'Naghten Case, 8. Eng. Re. 718 (1843)

Murray v. Giarratano, 492 U.S. 1, 109 S.Ct. 2765 (1989)

Murray v. U.S., 487 U.S. 533, 108 S.Ct. 2529 (1988)

New Jersey v. T.L.O., 469 U.S. 325, 105 S.Ct. 733 (1985)

New York v. Quarles, 467 U.S. 649, 104 S.Ct. 2626 (1984)

Nix v. Williams, 467 U.S. 431, 104 S.Ct. 2501 (1984)

Oliver v. U.S., 466 U.S. 170, 104 S.Ct. 1735 (1984)

Oregon v. Mathiason, 429 U.S. 492, 97 S.Ct. 711 (1977)

Palko v. Connecticut, 302 U.S. 319, 58 S.Ct. 149 (1937)

Parker v. Gladden, 385 U.S. 363, 87 S.Ct. 468 (1966)

Parsons v. State, 2 So. 854 (1887)

Payne v. Tennessee, ___ U.S. ___, 111 S.Ct. 2597 (1991)

Penry v. Lynaugh, 492 U.S. 302, 109 S.Ct. 2934 (1989)

People v. Gilmore, 203 Cal. App. 3rd 612, 249 Cal. Rptr. 914 (1988)

Pointer v. Texas, 380 U.S. 400, 85 S.Ct. 1065 (1965)

Powell v. Alabama, 287 U.S. 45, 53 S.Ct. 55 (1932)

Robinson v. California, 370 U.S. 660, 82 S.Ct. 1417 (1962)

Rhode Island v. Innis, 446 U.S. 291, 100 S.Ct. 1682 (1980)

Rhodes v. Chapman, 452 U.S. 337, 101 S.Ct. 2392 (1981)

Saffle v. Parks, 494 U.S. 484, 110 S.Ct. 1257 (1990)

Schall v. Martin, 467 U.S. 253, 104 S.Ct. 2403 (1984)

Segura v. U.S., 468 U.S. 796, 104 S.Ct. 3380 (1984)

Silverthorne Lumber Co. v. U.S., 251 U.S. 385, 40 S.Ct. 182 (1920)

Smith v. Maryland, 422 U.S. 735, 99 S.Ct. 2577 (1979)

Solem v. Helm, 463 U.S. 277, 103 S.Ct. 3001 (1983)

Spano v. New York, 360 U.S. 315, 79 S.Ct. 1202 (1959)

Stanford v. Kentucky, 492 U.S. 397, 109 S.Ct. 2969 (1989)

State v. Hempele, 576 A.2d 793 (1990)

State v. Russell, 481 NW2d 148 (1991)

Tate v. Short, 401 U.S. 395, 91 S.Ct. 688 (1971)

Teague v. Lane, 489 U.S. 288, 109 S.Ct. 1060 (1989)

Tennessee v. Garner, 471 U.S. 1, 105 S.Ct. 1694 (1985)

Terry v. Ohio, 392 U.S. 1, 88 S.Ct. 1868 (1968)

Thompson v. Oklahoma, 487 U.S. 815, 108 S.Ct. 2687 (1988)

U.S. v. Leon, 468 U.S. 897, 104 S.Ct. 3405 (1984)

U.S. v. One 56-Foot Motor Yacht Named Tahuna, 702 F.2d 1276 (9th Cir. 1983)

U.S. v. One 1977 Lincoln Mark V, 453 F. Supp. 1388 (D.C. N.Y. 1978)

U.S. v. One Parcel of Land . . . Commonly Known as 4204 Cedarwood, Matteson, IL, 614 F. Supp. 183 (D.C. Ill.1985)

U.S. v. Ross, 456 U.S. 798, 102 S. Ct. 2157 (1982)

U.S. v. $321,470 in U.S. Currency, 662 F. Supp. 904 (M.D. La. 1987)

Ward v. Texas, 316 U.S. 547, 62 S.Ct. 1139 (1942)

Washington v. Texas, 388 U.S. 14, 87 S.Ct. 1920 (1967)

Wilkins v. Missouri, 492 U.S. 397, 109 S.Ct. 2969 (1989)

Wong Sun v. U.S., 371 U.S. 471, 83 S.Ct. 407 (1963)

REFERENCES

Chapter 1:

Nicole's story. Excerpted from "Women and Violence." Hearings Before the Committee on the Judiciary, U.S. Senate, Part 2, Serial No. J-101-80. Washington, D.C.: U.S. Government Printing Office (1991).

Harry's story. From Harry Karabel. Printed with permission.

Helen's story. From CRF staff member Helen Kwon. Printed with permission.

Rose's story. Excerpted from "Crimes Against the Elderly: Let's Fight Back." Hearing Before the Special Committee on Aging, U.S. Senate, Serial No. 101-26. Washington, D.C.: U.S. Government Printing Office (1991).

Karmen, Andrew *Crime Victims: An Introduction to Victimology* 2nd Edition. Pacific Grove, Calif.: Brooks/Cole Publishing Co. (1990).

Herrington, Lois Haight "Statement of Chairman," *President's Task Force on Victims of Crime*, December, 1982, p. vi.

Magnuson, E. "The Curse of Violent Crime" *Time* March 23, 1981.

Criminal Victimization in The United States, 1991: A National Crime Victimization Survey Report. U.S. Department of Justice, Office of Justice Programs, Bureau of Justice Statistics. December 1992.

Criminal Victimization in The United States, 1973-90 Trends: A National Crime Victimization Survey Report. U.S. Department of Justice, Office of Justice Programs, Bureau of Justice Statistics. December 1992.

Uniform Crime Reports: Crime in the United States 1991 U.S. Department of Justice, Federal Bureau of Investigation. August 1992.

Sourcebook of Criminal Justice Statistics—1991 U.S. Department of Justice, Office of Justice Programs, Bureau of Justice Statistics. 1992.

Victim Rights and Services: A Legislative Directory 1988/1989 prepared by the National Organization for Victim Assistance. U.S. Department of Justice, Office of Justice Programs, 1990.

Adler, Freda, *et. al.*, *Criminology*. New York: McGraw-Hill (1991).

Barlow, Hugh D., *Introduction to Criminology*, Sixth Edition. New York: Harper Collins (1993).

The Victim and Witness Protection Act of 1982 is 18 U.S.C. 1501 *et seq.*

Arthur J. Goldberg's quote from his article "Equality and Government Action" in Volume 39 of *New York University Law Review* (1964).

Silberman, Charles, *Criminal Violence, Criminal Justice*, Random House, New York, 1978.

Thrasher, F., *The Gang*, University of Chicago Press, 1963.

Wizard's story. James Diego Vigil, *Barrio Gangs*, University of Texas Press, Austin, 1988.

B-Dog's story. Leon Bing, *Do or Die*, Harper Collins, New York, 1991.

William Penn trial from How St. Trials 951, 958 (1670).

ALI Model Penal Code Sec. 4.01 (1).

Chapter 2:

Sir Robert Peel quote from Cromwell, P. and Keefer, G., *Police Community Relations*, West Publishing Co. (2nd edition, 1978). Citing, Graham, H., "Community Service." FBI Law Enforcement and Bulletin (October 1975) p. 68.

"I am a policeman because . . ." study cited in Cromwell and Keefer, p. 5.

Study of factors in police use of force cited in *Journal of Police Science and Administration*, Northwestern University School of Law (March 1981).

Baum, Lawrence, *The Supreme Court*. Fourth Edition. Washington, D.C.: CQ Press (1992).

Bouza, Anthony V. *The Police Mystique*. New York: Plenum Press (1990).

Gardner, Thomas J. and Terry M. Anderson *Criminal Law: Principles and Cases*. 5th Edition. St. Paul: West Publishing Co. (1992).

Emanuel, Steven and Steven Knowles, *Criminal Procedure*. Larchmont, New York: Emanuel Law Outlines (12th edition, 1991).

Zalman, Marvin and Larry Siegel *Criminal Procedure: Constitution and Society.* St. Paul: West Publishing Co. (1991).

Packer, Herbert L. "Two Models of the Criminal Process" in *The Limits of the Criminal Sanction* Stanford: Stanford University Press (1968).

Skolnick, Jerome H. and James J. Fyfe *Above the Law: Police and the Excessive Use of Force* Free Press (1993).

Territo, Leonard, James B. Halsted, and Max L. Bromley *Crime and Justice in America.* St. Paul: West Publishing Co. (3rd edition, 1992).

Chapter 3:

Some material in this chapter was adapted with permission from *Fair Trial/Free Press*, Todd Clark and Rebecca J. Novelli, Benziger Bruce & Glencoe, Inc., 1977.

Some of the factors influencing prosecutorial discretion are taken from the "American Bar Association Standards Relating to the Prosecutor Function."

Chapter 4:

Kerr, Peter "The Detoxing of Prisoner 88A0802" *New York Times Magazine* June 27, 1993.

Langan, Patrick A., "America's Soaring Prison Population," *Science* magazine, 29 March 1991.

Ekland-Olson, Sheldon, *et. al.*, "Crime and Incarceration: Some Comparative Findings From the 1980s" *Crime and Delinquency*, Vol. 38 No. 3, July 1992, pp. 392-416.

Flanders, Stephen A., *Capital Punishment: The Facts on File Library in a Book Series* New York: Facts on File (1991).

"Minnesota Sentencing Guidelines and Commentary" St. Paul: Minnesota Sentencing Guideline Commission. August 1992.

The Death Penalty: Opposing Viewpoints Series. Bonnie Szumski, Lynn Hall, and Susan Bursell, editors. St. Paul: Greenhaven Press (1986).

"Jail Inmates, 1991." *Bureau of Justice Statistics Bulletin* U.S. Department of Justice, Office of Justice Programs, Bureau of Justice Statistics. June 1992.

"Capital Punishment, 1991." *Bureau of Justice Statistics Bulletin* U.S. Department of Justice, Office of Justice Programs, Bureau of Justice Statistics. October 1992.

Redefining the Career Criminal: Priority Prosecution of High-rate Dangerous Offenders by Marcia Chaiken and Jan Chaiken. U.S. Department of Justice, Office of Justice Programs, National Institute of Justice *Issues and Practices*. April 1990.

Day Fines in American Courts: The Staten Island and Milwaukee Experiments by Douglas C. McDonald, editor, Judith Greene, and Charles Worzella. U.S. Department of Justice, Office of Justice Programs, National Institute of Justice *Issues and Practices*. December 1992.

"Federal Sentencing in Transition, 1986-90" *Bureau of Justice Statistics Special Report* U.S. Department of Justice, Office of Justice Programs, Bureau of Justice Statistics. June 1992.

"Prisoners in 1992" *Bureau of Justice Statistics Bulletin U.S.* Department of Justice, Office of Justice Programs, Bureau of Justice Statistics. May 1993.

Factors that identify likely candidates for probation. Adapted from: *ALI Model Penal Code*, Sec. 7.01 [2].

Chapter 5:

Mary Ann Crouse case at 4 Warden (PA) 9, 1838. Case and quote cited in Schlossman, Steve L., *Love and the American Delinquent*, University of Chicago, Chicago, Ill., 1977, p.9.

"Unlocking Juvenile Corrections: Evaluating the Massachusetts Department of Youth Services," National Council on Crime and Delinquency, 1991.

"Juvenile Justice: Improving the Quality of Care," National Council on Crime and Delinquency, 1992.

"Juvenile Justice Models for California: New Approaches for Troubled Youth in the Nation's Largest State," National Council on Crime and Delinquency, 1990.

Greenwood, Peter W. "Correctional Programs for Chronic Juvenile Offenders: Characteristics of Three Exemplary Programs." Santa Monica: The RAND Corporation, 1988.

Greenwood, Peter W. and Franklin E. Zimring, *One More Chance: The Pursuit of Promising Intervention Strategies for Chronic Juvenile Offenders.* Prepared under a grant from the U.S. Department of Justice, Office of Justice Programs, Office of Juvenile Justice and Delinquency Prevention. Santa Monica, Calif.: The RAND Corporation, May 1985.

"Arrests of Youth 1990" by Howard N. Snyder. U.S. Department of Justice, Office of Justice Programs,

Office of Juvenile Justice and Delinquency Prevention *Juvenile Justice Bulletin: OJJDP Update on Statistics*. Jan. 1992.

OJJDP Juvenile Court Statistics 1989. Prepared by National Center for Juvenile Justice. Pittsburgh: November 1992.

Office of Juvenile Justice and Delinquency Prevention 1991 Annual Report. U.S. Department of Justice, Office of Justice Programs, Office of Juvenile Justice and Delinquency Prevention.

Miller, Jerome G. *Last One Over the Wall: The Massachusetts Experiment in Closing Reform Schools*. Columbus Ohio: Ohio State University Press (1991).

National Juvenile Custody Trends 1978—1989. U.S. Department of Justice, Office of Justice Programs, Office of Juvenile Justice and Delinquency Prevention. March 1992.

Simonsen, Clifford E. *Juvenile Justice in America* New York: MacMillan Publishing Co. (1990).

Krisberg, Barry and Deborah Neuenfeldt and Audrey Bakke, "Juvenile Intensive Supervision Programs: The State of the Art," *NCCD Focus* (February 1991).

Pierce, Robert and Barbara Yondorf, *Juvenile Justice Reform: State Experiences* National Conference of State Legislatures (1989)

Thompson: Whitford, Ellen "How a Family Tragedy May Lead to a Landmark Court Ruling" in *Scholastic Update* (April 8, 1988).

Pope, Carl E. and William Feyerherm *Minorities and the Juvenile Justice System* U.S. Department of Justice, Office of Justice Programs, Office of Juvenile Justice and Delinquency Prevention *Juvenile Justice Bulletin: OJJDP Update on Statistics* (November 1992).

"Kids in Custody: How the Nation Handles Crimes by Juveniles" by Ron Harris. *Los Angeles Times*, series of four articles running from August 22, 1993 to August 25, 1993.

Zimring, Franklin E. and Gordon Hawkins. *The Citizen's Guide to Gun Control*. New York: Macmillan Publishing Co., 1987.

Pristin, Terry. "Soul-Searching on Violence by the Industry." *Los Angeles Times*. May 18, 1992.

Eron quote on TV violence from Eron, Leonard D., and L. Rowell Huesmann, "The Control of Aggressive Behavior by Changes in Attitudes, Values, and the Conditions of Learning," in *Advances in the Study of Aggression*, edited by Blanchard, Robert J. and D. Caroline, volume 1, Academic Press, Orlando, Fla., 1984.

Wilson, James Q. and Richard J. Herrnstein, *Crime and Human Nature*. New York: Simon and Schuster, 1985.

Celeste Fremon, "G-Dog and the Homeboys," *L.A.Times Magazine*, August 11, 1991.

Dr. Brenner's Study, quoted in the *Deindustrialization of America: Plant Closings, Community Abandonment, and the Dismantling of Basic Industry*, by Barry Bluestone and Bennett Harrison. Basic Books, New York: 1982.

Mauer, Marc "Americans Behind Bars: One Year Later" Washington, DC: The Sentencing Project. 1992.

Vigilantes, *American Violence: A Documentary History,* ed. by Richard Hofstadter and Michael Wallace, Knopf, 1970.

The Broken Windows Plan, "Making Neighborhoods Safe," James Q. Wilson and George Kelling, *Atlantic Monthly*, February 1989.

Richard Threlkeld's conclusions on crime. "World News Report: Crime in America," ABC-TV, February 1983.

RAND study on urban problems, *Urban America: Policy Choices for Los Angeles and the Nation*, RAND, 1992, edited by James B. Steinberg, David W. Lyon, and Mary E. Vaiana.

Chapter 6:

Cathy Spatz Widom, "The Cycle of Violence," *Science*, 14 April 1989.

Sloan, John Henry, *et. al.* "Handgun Regulations, Crime, Assaults, Homicide, A Tale of Two Cities." *The New England Journal of Medicine*. Nov. 10, 1988, pp. 1256-1262.

"Seven Deadly Days." *Time*. July 17, 1989, pp. 30-60.

Photos and Illustrations

AP/Wide World Photos, pages 22, 70, 77, 85, 90, 97, 100, 105, 106, 118, 141, 207, 234, 251.

Anderson, Kirk (Madison, Wisconsin), page 228.

Asay, Chuck (Reprinted by permission of Colorado Springs Gazette Telegraph), pages 69, 158.

Bennett, Clay (Reprinted with permission of the St. Petersburg Times.), page 10

The Bettmann Archive, pages 13, 16, 48, 112, 140, 142, 146, 168, 181, 188.

Callahan (Reprinted with permission of Levin Represents), page 108.

CRF File Photo, pages 205, 214, 264.

Costly, Andrew(CRF), page 103

Cullum, Mark (Reprinted by permisson of Copley News Service), page 242.

Peters, Mike (Reprinted with permission of The Peters Creative Group.), page 267.

Pett, Joel (Reprinted by permission of Lexington Herald Leader), page 144.

Reuters/Bettmann, page 25.

Rogers, Bob (Reprinted by permisson of UFS, Inc.), page 242.

Ryan, Tom K. (Reprinted with special permission of North America Syndicate), page 131.

Summers, Dana (Washington Post Writing Group, © 1993. Reprinted with permission), page 233

Thompson, Mike (Reprinted by permission of Copley News Service), page 21.

UPI/Bettmann Newsphotos, pages 5, 7, 35, 39, 45, 59, 65, 74, 79, 83, 121, 122, 126, 132, 171, 174, 213, 219, 241, 256, 258, 271.

Charts and Graphs

Page 18—Adapted from a chart by the Bureau of Justice Statistics.

Page 149—*Sentencing Guidelines*, Minnesota Sentencing Guidelines and Commentary. Reprinted by permission.

Page 196—*Juvenile Court Statistics, 1990*. National Center for Juvenile Justice, 1993. Reprinted by permission.

Page 198—San Francisco County Juvenile Probation Department. Reprinted by permission.

Page 222—OJJDP *Fact Sheet*, July 1993, Juveniles and Violence: Juvenile Offending and Victimization by Barbara Allen-Hagen and Melissa Sickmund, Ph.D, U.S. Department of Justice, Office of Juvenile Justice and Delinquency Prevention. Reprinted by permission.

Page 227—Reprinted from *The Police Chief*, March 1988, pages 36-37. Copyright held by the International Association of Chiefs of Police, Inc. 515 N. Washington Street, Alexandria, VA 22314. Further reproduction without the express permission from IACP is strictly prohibited. Chart adapted with permission of McGraw Hill, Inc., from p. 233 of *Criminology* by Adler, Mueller, and Laufer, c. 1991

Page 236—Ronald V. Clark, *Situational Crime Prevention: Successful Case Studies*. New York: Harrow and Heston, 1992, p. 13. Reprinted by permission.

Special thanks to:

Ieshia Black, Pamela Evans, Tim Kawahara, Ingrid Sausjord, and Eleanor Song.